THE CONSERVATIVES
IN CRISIS

MANCHESTER
UNIVERSITY PRESS

In memory of Martin Lynch

THE CONSERVATIVES IN CRISIS

The Tories after 1997

edited by Mark Garnett and Philip Lynch

Manchester University Press

Manchester and New York

distributed exclusively in the USA by Palgrave

Copyright © Manchester University Press 2003

While copyright in the volume as a whole is vested in Manchester University Press, copyright in individual chapters belongs to their respective authors, and no chapter may be reproduced wholly or in part without the express permission in writing of both author and publisher.

Published by Manchester University Press
Oxford Road, Manchester M13 9NR, UK
and Room 400, 175 Fifth Avenue, New York, NY 10010, USA
www.manchesteruniversitypress.co.uk

Distributed exclusively in the USA by
Palgrave, 175 Fifth Avenue, New York,
NY 10010, USA

Distributed exclusively in Canada by
UBC Press, University of British Columbia, 2029 West Mall,
Vancouver, BC, Canada V6T 1Z2

British Library Cataloguing-in-Publication Data
A catalogue record for this book is available from the British Library

Library of Congress Cataloging-in-Publication Data applied for

ISBN   0 7190 6330 2 *hardback*
       0 7190 6331 0 *paperback*

First published 2003

11 10 09 08 07 06 05 04 03   10 9 8 7 6 5 4 3 2 1

Typeset in Monotype Bell by
Carnegie Publishing Ltd, Chatsworth Road, Lancaster
Printed in Great Britain
by CPI, Bath

CONTENTS

FIGURES AND TABLES

Figures

Tables

CONTRIBUTORS

Edward Ashbee is co-author of *American Society Today* (2002) and of *US Politics Today* (1999). He has also written a number of articles on contemporary American politics.

Stuart Ball is Reader in History at the University of Leicester. His publications include *Baldwin and the Conservative Party: The Crisis of 1929–1931* (1988), *The Conservative Party and British Politics 1902–1951* (1995), and (as co-editor) *Conservative Century: The Conservative Party since 1900* (1994) and *The Heath Government 1970–1974: A Reappraisal* (1996).

David Broughton is Senior Lecturer in Politics in the School of European Studies at Cardiff University. His publications include *Public Opinion Polling and Politics in Britain* (1995) and he was co-editor of the *British Elections and Parties Yearbook* between 1991 and 1996. He has also written a number of journal articles on Welsh electoral politics.

Philip Cowley is a Lecturer in Politics at the University of Nottingham. His publications include *Revolts and Rebellions: Parliamentary Voting under Blair* (2002) and *Conscience and Parliament* (editor, 1998). He has published numerous articles and chapters on the British Parliament.

Peter Dorey is Senior Lecturer in British Politics in the School of European Studies at Cardiff University. His books include *The Conservative Party and the Trade Unions* (1995), *The Major Premiership* (editor, 1999) and *Wage Politics in Britain: The Rise and Fall of Incomes Policies since 1945* (2001). He has also published numerous articles and chapters on contemporary British Conservatism.

Mark Garnett is a Visiting Fellow in the Department of Politics at the University of Leicester. He is author of *Alport: A Study in Loyalty* (1999) and co-author of *Whatever Happened to the Tories?* (with Ian Gilmour, 1998), *Keith Joseph* (with Andrew Denham, 2001) and *Splendid! Splendid: The Authorised Biography of William Whitelaw* (with Ian Aitken, 2002).

Richard Kelly teaches Politics at Manchester Grammar School. He is author of *Conservative Party Conferences: The Hidden System* (1989), co-author of *British Political Parties Today* (1998) and editor of *Changing Party Policy in Britain* (1999) and *Modern British Statesmen 1867–1945* (1997).

Andrew Lansley CBE MP has been the Conservative Member of Parliament for South Cambridgeshire since 1997. For the 1992 General Election he headed the Conservative Research Department. In June 1999 he was promoted to the Shadow Cabinet as Shadow Minister for the Cabinet Office and led the policy development process for the Conservative Party from 1999 to 2001, including the *Common Sense Revolution* and the 2001 general election campaign.

Peter Lynch is Lecturer in Politics at the University of Stirling. He is author of *Scottish Government and Politics* (2001) and *SNP: A History of the Scottish National Party* (2002). He has also published a number of articles on devolution, nationalism and the political parties in Scotland.

Philip Lynch is Senior Lecturer in Politics at the University of Leicester. He is author of *The Politics of Nationhood: Sovereignty, Britishness and Conservative Politics* (1999) and *Reforming the European Union: From Maastricht to Amsterdam* (co-editor, 2000). He has also written a number of articles and chapters on Conservative politics.

Lord Parkinson of Carnforth was Conservative Party Chairman from 1997 to 1998. As Cecil Parkinson, he served in Margaret Thatcher's Cabinet as Conservative Party Chairman (1981–83), Trade and Industry Secretary (1983), Energy Secretary (1987–89) and Transport Secretary (1989–90).

Mark Stuart is a Research Fellow in the Centre for Legislative Studies at the University of Hull. His publications include *Douglas Hurd: The Public Servant* (1998). He is currently compiling a biography of the late John Smith. He has also written a number of articles on the British Parliament.

Ian Taylor MBE is Conservative MP for Esher and Walton, having entered Parliament in 1987. He was a Parliamentary Private Secretary in the Foreign Office, Health Department and Cabinet Office before becoming Minister for Science and Technology at the Department of Trade and Industry (1994–97). He was Shadow spokesman on Northern Ireland under William Hague until resigning in October 1997. He is now Chairman of the European Movement.

ACKNOWLEDGEMENTS

The editors would like to thank the Bow Group for granting permission to reproduce extracts from Andrew Lansley, *Image, Values and Policy – From Here to the Next Election* (Bow Group Policy Brief, 2002).

ABBREVIATIONS

BBC	British Broadcasting Corporation
CBI	Confederation of British Industry
CCO	Conservative Central Office
CFSP	Common Foreign and Security Policy
COS	Conservative Opportunity Society (US)
CPC	Conservative Political Centre
CRE	Commission for Racial Equality
CSU	Christian Social Union (Germany)
EC	European Community
EIC	Ethics and Integrity Committee
EMU	Economic and Monetary Union
EP	European Parliament
ERM	Exchange Rate Mechanism
EU	European Union
FPTP	first-past-the-post
GDP	Gross Domestic Product
GOP	Grand Old Party (US Republican Party)
GOPAC	GOP Action Committee
IGC	Intergovernmental Conference
JHA	Justice and Home Affairs
LD	Liberal Democrat (Party)
MEP	Member of the European Parliament
MP	Member of Parliament
MSP	Member of the Scottish Parliament
NAFTA	North American Free Trade Agreement
NHS	National Health Service
OMOV	One Member One Vote
PLP	Parliamentary Labour Party
PR	proportional representation
PRSC	Party Reform Steering Committee
QC	Queen's Counsel
QMV	qualified majority voting
RDA	Regional Development Agency
SNP	Scottish National Party
TANF	Temporary Assistance for Needy Families (US)
UKIP	United Kingdom Independence Party

Introduction

Mark Garnett and Philip Lynch

Academic interest in Britain's leading political parties has not always run in parallel with their electoral fortunes. The Labour Party has commanded a fairly consistent level of attention, whether in office or in opposition. But it seems that the Conservatives are fated to be regarded either as unavoidable or irrelevant. For understandable reasons, during the eighteen years of Conservative government after 1979, political scientists and historians did much to redress the balance. But there was always a suspicion that the trend would tail off as soon as the party left office.

It can be argued, though, that since their landslide defeat in the May 1997 general election, the Conservatives have been more interesting even than they were in the late 1980s, when it seemed that their hold on power was unshakeable. Suddenly that ruthless, relentless election-winning machine looked terribly vulnerable, and an organisation that thrives on the exercise of power seemed disorientated. The 1997 election produced the Conservatives' heaviest defeat of the mass democratic era; the party polled almost 6 million votes fewer than at the 1992 general election and at 31.5 per cent its share of the vote was the lowest since 1832. The Conservatives' reputation for party unity, sound economic management and governing competence had been shattered by the travails of the Major government – notably divisions on Europe, sterling's exit from the Exchange Rate Mechanism (ERM) and 'sleaze'. Whereas the Conservatives appeared politically and intellectually exhausted, New Labour was reinvigorated and successfully pitched its appeal at the disillusioned voters of 'Middle England'.

The Conservative Party's survival as a significant political force was now open to serious question for the first time since the crisis over the Corn Laws. John Major resigned as Conservative leader immediately after the election and a number of potential successors lost their seats in the landslide. By electing William Hague as leader, Conservative MPs handed the daunting challenge of restoring the fortunes of a shattered party to the youngest and least experienced of the leadership candidates.

This volume examines the Conservative Party's response to the crisis it faced after the 1997 defeat. It includes chapters on the key challenges facing the party, with contributions from academic experts on the Conservative Party and from three prominent Conservative parliamentarians of the period. The first two chapters are comparative, looking at previous Conservative spells in opposition and at the revival of the US Republican Party for pointers to recovery. The following three chapters then examine the Conservative Party leadership, parliamentary party and voluntary party in the Hague period. Chapters 6–10 focus on Conservative policy and ideology; Chapter 11 examines the party's electoral performance after 1997. Three Commentary pieces by leading Conservatives then draw differing conclusions about the 1997–2001 period, before the editors offer some conclusions.

It is a traditional article of faith for conservatives that the past can provide valuable lessons. In his chapter, Stuart Ball provides a comparative analysis of previous periods when the Conservative Party was in opposition. His discussion leads to an innovative evaluation of each attempt to recover from defeat. The findings lend strong empirical support to the familiar proposition that electoral outcomes depend crucially on government performance; the conduct of the opposition can only reinforce the result, one way or the other. In Ball's rating of each Conservative recovery, that of 1945–51 scores best. This suggests that the party's best hope for long-term revival after 1997 was a radical review of its policies, with the purpose of 'reconnecting' itself to the real concerns of voters. Significantly, though, it implies that only a combination of successful policy renewal with a run of serious misfortunes for the Blair government could have propelled the Tories back into office after one term of opposition; even Winston Churchill's reinvigorated party took two elections to come back.

Ball's analysis suggests that the party leader plays a less important role in Conservative recoveries than a distinctive policy programme and an effective party organisation. This may be somewhat surprising, given the current media obsession with leaders. Immediately after the last three general elections, the defeated leader has resigned, suggesting that the leaders themselves take a more exalted view of their role and responsibilities. But in assessing the record of William Hague between 1997 and his own 'Waterloo' in June 2001, Mark Garnett accepts that he could have made little difference to his party's fortunes. From Hague's own point of view, though, he was right to resign after the 2001 defeat; indeed, his bid for the leadership had been a highly dubious gamble in the first place. If he had delayed his challenge until after what was always likely to be a second depressing result, his chances of reaching Downing Street would have been infinitely better.

While Hague failed to convince much of the electorate of his leadership credentials, at Westminster he was widely admired for his performance at Prime Minister's Question Time. However, at a time when parliament was in low public repute, this proved a doubtful blessing to Hague and his party.

High-profile backbench dissent during the 1992–97 Parliament, particularly on the issue of Europe, ruined the Conservative Party's reputation for unity. By contrast, in 1997–2001 an increasingly apathetic public seemed not to care very much whether the parliamentary party was united or not. Philip Cowley and Mark Stuart examine the Conservative performance at Westminster during these years. There were frequent rebellions against the official party line, but – with the exception of some major revolts on devolution – the dissidents were usually few. Meanwhile, a small number of backbenchers (dubbed 'the awkward squad') who were unhappy about the tactics employed by their leaders, engaged in a parliamentary version of guerrilla warfare, designed to make life uncomfortable for the Blair government. Cowley and Stuart also examine the parliamentary party in the leadership elections of 1997 – the last in which MPs monopolised the selection process – and 2001.

Hague inherited a party organisation which was seething with discontent – not least on the disenfranchisement of ordinary party members in the 1997 leadership election. In his commentary, Hague's first Party Chairman Lord Parkinson recalls the depth of these feelings, and applauds the leader for carrying out the reforms that he had foreshadowed in his campaign speeches. Parkinson argues that without radical changes the party could easily have foundered in the wake of its demoralising general election defeat. From a different perspective Richard Kelly traces the origins of *The Fresh Future* reforms in Chapter 5, providing a detailed critique of the main changes to party organisation. He argues that the 'democratic' nature of these reforms has been overstated. Rather, Hague followed the precedent set by Tony Blair and New Labour, using a process of purported 'democratisation' to reinforce the leader's grip on party management.

Ball argues that while organisational reform is important, past experience shows that at best it has run in parallel with a more general revival of Conservative fortunes. Here, a fundamental problem for the Conservative Party between 1997 and 2001 was that it failed to convince sufficient numbers of voters that it had developed a convincing 'narrative', addressing the negative perceptions of the party which had dogged it ever since 'Black Wednesday' in September 1992. Hague's apparent tactical switch, midway through his leadership, to concentrate his appeal on the party's 'core vote' rather than reaching out to the uncommitted, has been particularly criticised.

In his chapter on Conservative policy, Peter Dorey examines the Conservative position on a series of key issues. He highlights the difficult dilemmas which confronted the party after 1997, notably on economic policy where the urge to promise tax cuts conflicted with voters' demands for public spending on essential services. Here, as elsewhere, party policy makers showed that they had not reached clear conclusions about the reasons for the 1997 landslide. As Dorey shows, New Labour's acceptance of much of the main thrust of Thatcherite economic policy threw the Conservatives off balance; as a result, instead of outbidding New Labour on the ideological right, or returning to a One Nation position which jettisoned the tax-cutting agenda, they tried to face both ways at once.

'Europe', particularly the question of British membership of the single currency, was for many Conservatives the most significant issue facing the party. Hague quickly ruled out British membership of the euro for two parliaments. But as Philip Lynch notes in Chapter 8, the pragmatism of this new position and the 'In Europe, not run by Europe' platform masked a significant move towards Euro-scepticism. This reflected the increase in Euro-sceptic sentiment in the parliamentary party, though pro-Europeans (like Ian Taylor) were persistent and vocal critics. Europe was one of the few areas where the Conservatives were closer to public opinion than Labour, but Hague's 'Keep the Pound' campaign brought little electoral reward.

The 'politics of nationhood' are now a serious problem to the Tories, who had benefited historically from their image as a patriotic party defending the British nation state. In addition to their internal troubles on 'Europe', the 1997 general election left the Conservatives without a single seat in Scotland and rendered their opposition to legislative devolution untenable. Peter Lynch traces how the Scottish Conservative and Unionist Parties adapted to the creation of the Scottish Parliament, exploring the re-organisation of the Scottish party, its electoral fortunes and political prospects in the new Scottish politics. In Chapter 10, Philip Lynch examines issues of identity and nationhood in Conservative politics in the 1997–2001 period, focusing on the 'English Question' and the politics of 'race'. Hague pledged to redress the perceived inequities of New Labour's devolution settlement by introducing the idea of 'English votes for English laws' at Westminster, but he resisted suggestions that the Conservatives should support the creation of an English Parliament. Hague spoke positively of the contributions made to British life by ethnic minority communities, but adopted a populist position on asylum and failed effectively to deal with incidents of racism in his party.

David Broughton's chapter illustrates the predictable results of the Conservatives' failure to develop an attractive, consistent narrative. The tendency of some in the party to see the 1997 result as a mere 'blip' ensured that its opinion poll rating flatlined at around 30 per cent. It was understandable that the leadership should share the outlook of Mr Micawber, and in September 2000 something did 'turn up', in the form of widespread fuel protests. The fact that the ensuing boost in the polls proved short-lived lends extra credence to Ball's suggestion that opposition parties often depend on government failings to improve their popularity. New Labour soon recovered its stride, and the opposition would have lapsed back to its 30 per cent rating even if it had been more credible. In hindsight, the Conservatives were regarded as opportunistic; had the government been more generally distrusted on a range of issues, the surge in Tory support would have lasted much longer. Broughton also shows that the mistake of dwelling on the wrong issues (in order to retain the loyalty of the core vote) continued throughout the election campaign. Hague hoped to force his main campaigning issue, the single currency, to the top of the electorate's agenda. But, despite the Conservatives' focus on Europe, the NHS and education remained the most important issues for voters.

The bald statistics seem to convict the Conservatives under Hague of astonishing perversity – of an electoral deathwish almost unparalleled in the democratic era. During the years of Tory dominance it was argued (notably by the late Jim Bulpitt) that the party had won its position through its mastery of 'statecraft'; that 'Thatcherism' was an election-winning platform, more than an ideological crusade. The 2001 result suggests that this view was mistaken. As Garnett argues in his chapter on ideology, whatever the differences over issues like Europe and personal morality, in 2001 the most serious handicap for Conservatives was the nature of the principles which united them. The One Nation tradition was virtually extinct, even if the parliamentary ginger group of that name continued its meetings. A party wedded to Thatcherism in the key policy area of economic management was incapable of digesting psephological findings, which had indicated even in the 1980s that the ideology was deeply distrusted. Garnett argues that the Conservative Party can now only be understood in the context of liberal ideology; attempts by 'modernisers' to extend this creed to the social sphere might help to overcome the common identification of Conservatives with 'reaction', but even this seems a most unpromising foundation for an electoral comeback.

Hague and his advisers looked towards the United States for potential solutions to problems facing the Conservatives. Edward Ashbee explores the key factors behind the recovery of the Republican Party after the defeat of George Bush (senior) in the 1992 Presidential Election. He examines Republican strategies, from Newt Gingrich's *Contract with America* to the 'compassionate conservatism' which helped to propel Governor George W. Bush into the White House in 2000. Noting Hague's flirtation with 'compassionate conservatism', Ashbee argues that although the Republican revival offered some lessons for the Conservative Party, there are important obstacles to its translation into the very different British context.

In his commentary, Ian Taylor MP warns against the belief that US Republican emphasis on the 'small state' is the model for the Tories to follow. He argues that the party will have to shift its centre of gravity, and dismisses the notion that salvation can be found through a further move to the right. Europe is the main focus of his comments: he is critical of Hague's policy, but welcomes Iain Duncan Smith's pledge to accept the result of a referendum on the euro. Taylor, who made constructive contributions to the debate on public services between 1997 and 2001, also welcomes the signs that the new leadership has woken up to these concerns. However, he deplores the persisting impression that the party is interested in curbing expenditure, rather than making genuine improvements to the public services. But he believes that even a shift of public perception in this respect will not be enough to revive his party, while it remains in thrall to Euro-scepticism. On the basis of Taylor's commentary, it seems safe to suggest that internal Tory politics will continue to be fascinating up to and beyond any referendum on the euro, even if the party continues to languish in the opinion polls.

Andrew Lansley MP led both the Conservative Party's policy development process from 1999 to 2001 and its 2001 general election campaign. In his closing commentary, Lansley defends the Conservative campaign, but recognises that painful lessons still have to be learned. He argues that 'in government, you are judged by what you do. In opposition, you are judged by who you are.' The Conservative Party, he says, now has to renew its image; articulate consistently the values of 'Conservatism' – freedom, community, security, opportunity and respect – that reflect that image; and announce a limited number of policy initiatives to reinforce it.

At the time of writing, it remains an open question whether even the fulfilment of this challenging programme will be sufficient to end the years of Conservative crisis. As the editors note in the Conclusions to this volume, it is an indictment of the 1997–2001 period that the task confronting the present party leadership is essentially the same as it was in 1997 – to learn the lessons of defeat and act on this assessment, as free as possible from rigid ideological presuppositions.

1

The Conservatives in opposition, 1906–79: a comparative analysis

Stuart Ball

The experience of being in opposition for a lengthy period is not one which the modern Conservative Party is used to, and it has tended to find it difficult. Since the 1880s, the Conservatives have grown accustomed to being seen – and to see themselves – as the party of government. They have been in office for so much of the period that exercising power has seemed to be the natural state of affairs, and this adds to Conservative frustration during spells in opposition. The party can feel – even if it does not always articulate this – that their removal has been in some sense unfair or a mistake, and this can hinder an analysis of the situation and the selection of strategies to tackle it. This problem is less apparent in shorter spells out of office, in which the impact of the previous defeat is still strong. However, as time passes, and especially if the prospect of recovery is not becoming apparent, impatience leads to tension and criticism within the party. The Conservatives have generally been better at holding their nerve – and even at staying united – whilst under pressure in government than they have been in the comparatively less-demanding role of opposition. This insecurity, which leads to inconsistencies, rushed decisions, grumbling in the ranks and mutterings about the leadership, has tended to diminish their effectiveness as an opposition party, even though they have often had a vulnerable government as a target. The Conservatives did not make much of their opportunities in 1906–14 or 1929–31, and made a surprisingly limited impact upon troubled Labour governments in 1968–70 and 1976–78. It should perhaps not be a surprise that they made no mark on a much stronger and more successful one in 1997–2001.

During the twentieth century the Conservative Party had seven periods in opposition. This chapter provides a context for the period since 1997 by considering the other six. The first part explores these periods thematically and considers the issues and factors which have determined the effectiveness of the Conservative Party in opposition. In the second part, a new approach is used to make a comparative analysis, from which conclusions and further questions can be drawn.

Themes and issues

Whether in office or in opposition, the fortunes of any party depend upon a combination of internal and external factors. The internal factors are those over which the party or its leaders can exercise some control. These include the choice of priorities, the content of policies, the image projected by statements and propaganda, the campaigning methods, the organisational structures, and the selection of personnel and of the leader. These are affected by the external factors, of which the most important are the performance of the economy (particularly unemployment, industrial relations, prices and incomes); levels of social cohesion, disorder and crime; public confidence in the legitimacy and effectiveness of political institutions; changes in social attitudes and personal mores; and international crises and external threats to national security. In opposition, a party can do little more than respond to the external factors and try to ensure that its position is as coherent and relevant as possible. There is, therefore, a natural tendency to let the government of the day cope with these challenges, and wait for mistakes and opportunities for criticism. However, this can be complicated by the legacies of the previous period in office, either because failures have eroded the party's credibility in a particular area, or because damaging charges of opportunism could be made if previously held positions are abandoned too quickly or drastically.[1] Responses in opposition tend to be cautious and incremental, even when they are presented with a flourish in order to capture public attention. This was the case with three Conservative policy initiatives during periods of opposition which were seen as particularly significant: Arthur Balfour's endorsement of tariffs in his speeches of 1907, Stanley Baldwin's announcement of a 'free hand' policy on food taxes in September 1930, and the publication of the *Industrial Charter* in 1947. In each of these cases there had been several preliminary steps, and although they were presented as bold moves they were actually the minimum needed to maintain party unity and morale.

Although the external factors are the ones most likely to change the political situation and affect public opinion, the opposition can neither predict nor control their timing and effects. For this reason parties in opposition tend to become preoccupied with the internal factors which they can affect, and to give these disproportionate attention. Conservative concerns in opposition have focused on three particular areas. The first of these is leadership, and the issue is straightforward and pragmatic: whether the existing leader still has an adequate range of support. This does not have to be enthusiastic, and may be due to a lack of attractive and credible alternatives and the deterrent effects of the risks involved in a challenge or revolt.[2] However, even if grudging or the product of inertia, leaders need a basic level of acceptance and consent; without this, their authority is undermined and the situation becomes untenable. In the Conservative Party, the leader's position has always depended upon the parliamentary party; the introduction of an election procedure in 1965 merely formalised this. There are always some critics, dissatisfied on political or personal grounds, and the key is rather the attitude of the normally silent mainstream of the backbenchers. At the start of an opposition period their view of the leadership is mainly determined by immediate needs and pressures, and conjectures about the leader's suitability to carry the party to victory at the next election play a smaller part than might be expected.[3] However, their reading of the leader's public standing will always be influential, and Conservative MPs make considerable allowance for the value of a leader who can extend the party's appeal beyond its normal sources of support. This was particularly the case with Baldwin after the 1923 and 1929 defeats, and went far to counterbalance the criticisms of his opposition leadership in 1929–31; in a slightly different way, it was also true of Winston Churchill in 1945–51. Whilst Balfour was considered remote and lacking in popular touch, his position was bolstered with MPs due to his pre-eminent abilities in debate in the Commons. After the stroke which ended Joseph Chamberlain's active career in 1906, Balfour's reputation and prestige overshadowed all of his colleagues in the perception of the press and the public.[4] In addition, his patrician style had some advantages in the more deferential social structure of Edwardian Britain, especially with Conservative supporters. In 1965 the main leadership contenders marked a clear departure from the 'grouse moor' aristocratic image of Harold Macmillan and Alec Douglas-Home; whether Reginald Maudling or Edward Heath was chosen, this would signal a shift of generation and social class, and the elevation of a modern, moderate and meritocratic outlook.

Although going into opposition can involve a change in the Conservative leadership, this has taken place much less often than the myth of leaders falling upon their swords might suggest. John Major was the first Conservative leader to resign his position immediately after losing an election, and his predecessors have generally remained in place. Balfour did so after 1906 through two further elections, Baldwin carried on after each of his defeats, Churchill was a fixture after 1945, and Heath did not contemplate stepping down until his unexpected rejection in the 1975 leadership ballot. The closest previous parallel is Douglas-Home, but his resignation in July 1965 was as much due to his own ambivalence about remaining as leader in opposition as it was to signs of an erosion of confidence.[5] Perhaps of as much significance are the extensive changes in the wider leadership group – the figures of Cabinet rank – which often follow a defeat, especially after a long period in office. This has the effect of removing ministers identified with unsuccessful or unpopular policies and distancing the party from its previous record, although it also means the loss of experience. By 1910, and still more by 1914, the Shadow Cabinet contained almost no one from the 1902–5 Balfour

Cabinet. After 1929 there was open hostility to the continuation of the 'old gang' in the press and from MPs which resulted in extensive changes in the leadership, and this was reflected in the selection of Conservative ministers in the National governments of the 1930s.[6] A group of new faces rose to prominence during 1945–51, and most of these departed after 1964.[7] For slightly different reasons, Margaret Thatcher's Shadow Cabinet of 1979 was notably different in personnel from Heath's in 1974, and few of Major's team remained active after 1997.

Changes of leadership can be problematic, especially as until 1965 the Conservatives had no formal machinery for choosing or removing a leader, and forcing a reluctant leader to quit was likely to be difficult and counter-productive. Before 1965 the Conservatives tended to leave the leadership issue to pressure behind the scenes from senior colleagues, and this was usually aimed at making the leader more active and effective rather than persuading him to quit.[8] Instead, party attention concentrated upon the two other areas of policy and organisation. A reappraisal of policy gave the opportunity to shed negative baggage from the previous period in office, and it was often more important to make clear what the party did not intend to do than to set out its future plans. This was true of the decision to postpone the food tax issue in order to concentrate upon Home Rule in 1913, the dropping of the tariff policy after the 1923 defeat, the acceptance of welfare reforms after 1945, and the rejection of interventionist policies after 1974. There was also a natural search for answers to the problems that had troubled the previous government, although the most ambitious attempt at this, the policy review of 1964–70, was not as helpful as had been hoped when the Conservatives returned to power in 1970. It was not very salient in public awareness and made little impact upon the target groups; in the 1970 election the Conservatives made similar gains in all social categories, and the issue on which the election was won – stability of prices and incomes – was the one where the party had notably failed to develop a policy.[9] Nevertheless, developing new policies – especially if this highlighted new issues – could help to refresh the party's general image and the recovery of confidence in its ranks.

Organisational reform had a similar role, and was an even more obvious sphere of activity. The most serious defeats tended to follow long periods in office, during which the party organisation had declined in efficiency. The complacency and drift which was encouraged by the previous election successes resulted in the organisation being unable to adapt and cope with the period of unpopularity or apathy which came before defeat. Organisa-tional problems were most visible before the three landslide defeats in 1906, 1945 and 1997, but they were also apparent in 1929, 1964 and 1974. This made reorganisation an obvious priority after each defeat, but focusing upon this could also be a means of avoiding less pallatable questions. Only a certain amount can be done to revive an organisation from within, or it becomes an exercise which may look good on paper but lacks substance. Organisational vitality depends upon a motivated membership and the securing of financial resources, and the incentives for these are mainly the result of the external factors in the situation. For this reason, organisational recovery tends to follow from an improvement in a party's popularity, rather than being a first cause of it. After this, the effect can be cyclical, with investment in professional staff and publicity allowing the party to benefit from a return of support. This was the case with the most famous organisational recovery of 1947–51, particularly with Woolton's fund-raising, but even so the outcome of the 1950 and 1951 elections was very close. The changes introduced after 1906, forced by pressure from the National Union, weakened central direction and fragmented the regional level into an ineffectual county localism.[10] The reforms of 1911, which introduced the party chairmanship and a clear departmental structure in the Central Office, improved efficiency but were much less in the public eye; due to the intervention of the war, their fruition was seen in the role played by Central Office in the inter-war era. Lack of funds after the 1929 defeat led to reductions in Central Office staffing, and since the 1960s efforts to improve the organisation have been constrained by the need to economise and cut posts. These pressures could be partly reconciled by structural rationalisation and using new campaigning methods; Edward du Cann was appointed Party Chairman in 1965 because his business experience included modern practices in market research and advertising. After 1964 and 1974, organisational efforts were particularly directed towards groups where the party felt it lacked support, including urban voters, the young and trade unionists.[11] The Community Affairs Department was created at Central Office in 1975 to reach out to newly emerging social networks and groups.[12] Other developments may be of internal significance but have no electoral impact, such as the committee structure introduced in the parliamentary party in 1924.

There is a question as to how much such internal activities matter. They are often held to do so by those who have been involved in them, but this may be a case of busy bees assuming too easily that effort is directly linked to effect.[13] The observation that it is the government which loses an election rather than the opposition winning it has become a cliché, but like most aphorisms it is repeated because it condenses a fundamental truth. If this is so, then there is little more for an opposition to do than wait for the government to run into trouble, and then exploit any opening as thoroughly as possible. This was the basis of Balfour's approach in 1906–9 and of Baldwin's after 1929, and it was certainly Churchill's preference after 1945. However, short-term reactions can cause problems, as in the mismanaged attack on the National Insurance Act in 1911 and too close an identification with the vested interests opposing the National Health Service Bill in 1946, whilst in 1949 Churchill had to disavow a threatened motion of censure on health. The complete decay of the party organisation during the Second World War made organisational recovery a priority, although in choosing Lord Woolton as Party Chairman it is notable that Churchill opted for business rather than political experience. However, Churchill was much more resistant to policy initiatives, fearing that they would be distracting and involve making commitments too soon.[14] Although the unsettled mood of the party after 1945 made some definitions of Conservative principles unavoidable, their significance was more in restoring Conservative self-confidence than in any public effect.[15] This was at best diffuse and long term, and the Conservative recovery in the 1950 and 1951 elections was principally due to the Attlee government's economic problems and austerity measures. However, by the 1960s the belief that the policy reappraisal of 1945–51 had been vital in the revival had become so entrenched that the Conservatives implemented an even grander review. Twenty-three 'policy groups' were established after 1964, and after 1966 this increased to twenty-nine, involving 191 MPs and peers and 190 others.[16] The first fruits of this made little difference in the 1966 election, and the Conservatives lost more ground to a government that still seemed fresh and effective. Having embarked early upon a policy exercise, there was the danger that the positions adopted would become ossified and outdated by the next election but would be difficult to change.[17] The victories in the 1970 and 1979 elections were mainly due to the economic and industrial problems of the Labour governments towards the end of their terms – in particular, the damage done by devaluation in 1968 and the 'winter of discontent' in 1978–79 – than to any Conservative policy statements. If anything, in both cases there were concerns about the radicalism and possible harshness of the Conservative approach. In 1970 the Conservatives fought on a general programme with slogans directed at Labour's record in office, whilst the strategy from the effective 'Labour isn't working' advertising campaign of 1978 to the 1979 election focused upon the government's failures, industrial strife and the need to lower direct taxes. Thatcher gave few definite commitments between 1975 and 1979, and her cautious tactics were designed to keep the options open.[18]

If it is government performance that determines public opinion, the opposition will gain most from a more limited and reactive strategy. It still needs to distance itself from the problems which led to losing office, or it may be unable to reap the benefits from the government's difficulties. This has been a problem for Labour oppositions in the 1930s, 1950s and 1980s, but it has also affected the Conservatives. The clearest examples of being weighed down by the albatross of the past were in 1997–2001 and 1906–14, when the continued currency of the tariff issue deterred urban working-class support. At the same time, the tariff issue monopolised the attention of Conservative MPs and activists, like a black hole into which all else disappeared. Tariff reform enthusiasts wanted no alternatives or distractions; they were convinced that failure in 1906 and 1910 had been due to half-hearted presentation and leadership, and that the answer was to focus everything on this crusade. Other possible initiatives were viewed with suspicion and hostility, especially in the field of social reform.[19] The 1945 defeat was mainly due to condemnation of the record of the 1930s in both foreign and domestic policy, but it was soon apparent that neither Churchill nor the centrist-oriented generation who were rising to prominence amongst the leadership – particularly Anthony Eden, 'Rab' Butler, Harold Macmillan and Oliver Stanley – had any desire to return to pre-war methods. In the 1960s it took some time to shake off the outdated 'grouse moor' image of the later Macmillan years, and Conservative rehabilitation remained in doubt up to the declaration of results in 1970. After 1974, the party's prized reputation for competence in government was badly dented, and there was continuing concern that a Conservative administration would be unable to govern because of inevitable conflict with the trade unions. This was a principal factor in continuing support for Labour and their 'Social Contract', however threadbare it became, and explains the widespread belief that James Callaghan might have won if the election had taken place in autumn 1978. It took the wreck of Labour's industrial credibility in the winter that followed to balance the memories of Heath's conflicts with the miners and the gloom of the 'three day week' of five years before.

As well as shedding the burdens of the past, in opposition a party needs to pull together and avoid factionalism. The latter is likely to give unwelcome reminders of unpopular matters, and undermine the appearance of being a 'government in waiting'. It may be the case that oppositions cannot win elections by their own efforts, but it is certainly true that they can lose them by their mistakes.[20] This can occur in several ways, all of which will deter voters who might otherwise become disillusioned with the government. Visible disunity within a party makes it uncertain which direction it is going to take, and so makes reliance upon it risky. Whilst Labour had this problem in the 1950s and 1980s, the Conservatives have not been immune and it was a particular feature in 1906–14, 1929–31 and after the fall of Heath in 1975; to a lesser extent it was also a factor during the clash beween Heath and Enoch Powell over immigration in 1968–70. Disunity suggests that the opposition will not operate effectively if it is returned to office, and this makes it more likely for the government to be given the benefit of the doubt. Factional disputes also tend to become bitter and obsessive, whilst the finer points of doctrinal dispute are of little interest to the general public.[21] The result can be a party which is preoccupied with its own narrow concerns, and which appears unattractive to potential members or voters. These problems were features of the Conservative oppositions in 1906–14 and 1997–2001, and also in 1929–31 when – despite the impact of the slump and rising unemployment – it was not until Conservative disunity was laid to rest that by-elections began show a significant swing away from the government in late spring and summer 1931.[22] Only one of the three landslide defeats was not followed by continued sniping within the ranks and frequent reminders of the reasons for Conservative discredit, and it is no coincidence that the period after 1945 was by far the most successful of the recoveries.

The public perception of the credibility and image of the opposition is the result of several elements. The first can be termed the 'see-saw' effect, in which the government's poor performance depresses its support and so automatically raises that of the opposition. This can be a powerful and direct force, but it is also unpredictable and capricious. For these reasons, it does not engender as much confidence amongst leaders, party officials and MPs as might be expected, and it produces a brittle and nervous atmosphere. Recovery on this basis can also have negative effects, as the appearance of progress reduces the incentive to tackle difficult issues. The Conservatives particularly experienced this element between 1967 and 1970, first in the opinion poll leads which they enjoyed after devaluation and Labour's difficulties over Europe, industrial relations and prices and incomes, and then in the alarming evaporation of that lead in the spring of 1970.[23] The other elements are the unity and vigour of the opposition, its stance on the most important issues of the day and its general image. The latter is derived from several factors, including party propaganda, but perhaps most influential is the historic identity of the party and the classes and interests with which it is most closely linked. The leadership is another factor in the party's image, but this makes it only part of one amongst several elements which together shape the standing of the opposition – and the latter still remains secondary to the standing of the government.

This raises the question of how much the figure of the party leader matters, and whether Conservatives have over-rated the importance of this. Certainly, there have been recoveries in opposition despite having a little-known or unpopular leader. In May 1968, several months after devaluation, the Conservatives enjoyed a 28 per cent lead over Labour in voting intentions, but only 31 per cent of the sample polled were satisfied with Heath.[24] In 1910 there is little suggestion that Balfour personally was popular, although he had the prestige and visibility of a former Prime Minister. In 1970 and 1979 the Conservative leaders had been selected in opposition and lacked this authority, and they had in different ways a forbidding or strident image and were outshone on television by the more 'human' style of Harold Wilson and James Callaghan, the Labour Prime Ministers. Heath's awkward manner and elitist recreations made it difficult to counter this quasi-Baldwinism, and Thatcher was more vivid and direct in reaching the public; it was in the 1979 campaign that she presented herself in positive contrast as a 'conviction politician'.[25] Even in 1950 and 1951, Churchill may not have been any more attractive than he had been in 1945; it would need to be shown how and why this has occurred, and clearly the Labour newspapers which presented him as a danger to peace were acting on the view that the negative elements were still present. Although this was not strictly a recovery from opposition, it is doubtful if Andrew Bonar Law's personal appeal was a significant factor in the victory gained by the anti-Coalition rebels in the general election of 1922. It is difficult for an opposition leader to compete with the incumbency advantages of prestige and familiarity which a Prime Minister possesses, particularly in media coverage. This suggests that the contribution of the leadership in opposition is less a matter of direct appeal to uncommitted voters, and more of giving the party the cohesion and self-confidence which translate into a sense of purpose. This is then disseminated by the media and has a slow effect upon public perceptions, thus affecting the standing and credibility of the opposition indirectly in what can become a cyclical pattern. Balfour was poorest in this respect (perhaps even more over the Lords in 1910–11 than over tariffs in 1906–10) whilst Baldwin was effective in 1924 but faltered in 1929–30. Heath's personal certainty did not transfer to his followers in 1967–70, but Thatcher was more populist and attuned to the media in 1975–79. On this criteria, the most successful leaders were Churchill in 1945–51, due more to prestige and charisma than to action or substance, and Bonar Law in 1912–14, when his partisan and abrasive methods appealed to the party much more than to the uncommitted.

The Conservatives in opposition tend to mix the desire to act as if still wearing the mantle of government – to appear sober, responsible, consistent and wise – with partisanship and tactical manoeuvre. The temptation to have the best of both worlds is understandable, but sometimes it results in gaining neither. Governments are expected to have answers, but oppositions have to operate without the benefit of civil service advice and support. The Conservatives set out to remedy this in the creation of the Conservative Research Department, which had been under consideration for some time but was founded after the party went into opposition in 1929. This provided evidence to support speeches, policy statements and propaganda, but inevitably it fostered a tone of dryness and caution. The desire to appear 'statesmanlike' encourages the drafting of policies, and the existence of a secretariat means that these can be elaborated in detail. However, these then become commitments and are vulnerable to changing circumstances, whilst they also give the government a target for spoiling attacks – something at which the Conservatives were particularly effective at when in office between 1981 and 1992.

Whilst it may be more productive to concentrate upon parliamentary opposition, this has two limitations. Firstly, although it may be good for morale in the enclosed world of the Palace of Westminster, it is largely invisible to the public and has only a slow and indirect effect upon government popularity. Secondly, troubling the government in the House of

Commons is very difficult if it has a large majority, and it is hard to motivate opposition MPs for repeated efforts that are more likely to result in their own exhaustion. The opportunities in the Commons were therefore limited in 1906–10, 1945–50, 1966–70 and 1997–2001. However, more was achieved in harrying the ministry over Home Rule in 1912–14, in using procedural devices in 1950–51, and in exploiting Labour's lack of a majority in 1975–79. A more cautious strategy was followed in 1923 and 1929–30, as there were benefits from showing that the minority Labour governments had been given 'fair play', and Baldwin was concerned that if an election came too soon it would benefit Labour more than the Conservatives.[26] Until the very end of the century the Conservatives had an overwhelming majority in the House of Lords, but this became the weapon that was too dangerous to be used. After the failure of this tactic in the constitutional crisis of 1909–11, it became clear that using the Lords against important government measures would link the Conservatives with the vested interests of the privileged few. The extension of the franchise in 1918 and the rise of the Labour Party made the position of the Lords even more questionable, and the Conservatives preferred not to draw attention to them. They were sensitive to the charge of 'peers versus people' and of seeming anti-democratic, and the Lords were barely used in 1929–31, 1945–51, and other periods since.[27]

Whatever strategies are adopted in opposition, assessing and addressing the causes of defeat remains the essential first step towards any revival in fortunes. However, whilst this might seem self-evident, it is neither an easy nor an attractive prospect. There is a natural sense of shock in the wake of disaster, and a desire to avoid unwelcome truths. Morale and confidence are already low and may be depressed further, and there is also the danger that an inquest will rake up controversy and make matters worse by widening rifts and adding to factional tensions. For all these reasons, it is easier to let the past lie, and to look forward rather than back. The Conservative Party has rarely liked the idea of wide-ranging enquiries into election defeats, and prefers a pragmatic response of accepting the fact and limiting discussion to technical matters of organisation. The one occasion on which anything more ambitious was officially endorsed was after the 1929 defeat, when critical voices – mainly from 'diehard' MPs unhappy with Baldwin's centrist strategy – persuaded the Executive Committee of the National Union to send a questionnaire to all local associations asking for their analysis of the causes of defeat.[28] Central Office, which administered it, delayed the process and by the time a report was prepared it had lost much of its immediacy and relevance. The critical nature of the replies did not help towards any constructive opposition strategy; the report was quietly shelved, and the experiment has not been repeated. Analysis of the defeats has therefore tended to be informal, individual and mainly conducted in private. This does not necessarily make it more effective: in 1906 Balfour shrugged off his defeat as part of a world-wide trend to socialism that included the 1905 Russian Revolution. Since 1964 defeats have been subjected to more balanced and professional analysis by senior party officials, but their reports have only limited circulation amongst the leadership.

Each defeat has its particular circumstances and causes, but a comparative assessment highlights several common factors in the Conservative defeats during the twentieth century.[29] The most significant of these can be grouped under four headings, of which the first is confusion over what the party stands for on the most important topics of the day. This is more than just difficulty in some areas of policy, and can involve reversals in key areas or promises, failure to present a coherent identity, and loss of certainty and confidence amongst leaders and MPs. It was a marked feature of public perceptions in 1906, 1929, 1945, 1964, 1974 and 1997, and is perhaps the most influential as well as the most common factor. It is linked closely with the second aspect, a sense of failure and powerlessness. This is most often the result of economic problems, as in 1929, 1964, 1974 and 1997, but it was also apparent in the struggle against the Home Rule Bill in 1912–14 and in the troublesome legacy from the inter-war era in 1945. The third factor is a product of long spells in office: the staleness of the ministry and the lack of fresh ideas, often leading to a growing public feeling of 'time for a change'. These three elements can combine to produce a critical climate, particularly from the press, which in turn makes the government rattled and defensive. It then responds poorly to the dissatisfaction of its own supporters, as in 1905–6, 1927–29, 1955–56, 1972–74 and 1993–97. All these factors are more significant than the role of the leader, as they govern the standing of the government as a whole. It certainly will not help if the leader has a negative or weak image, as in 1906, 1964, 1974 and 1997. However, the 1929 and 1945 results show that a popular or respected leader cannot deliver victory if the other currents are flowing against. The final two factors are also consequences of problems in government rather than causes of them. The unity, morale, organisation and finances of the party in office come under strain when its popularity slumps, whilst through the 'see-saw effect' the vigour and strength of the opposition rises. This pattern was particularly apparent in the three most severe Conservative defeats of the century. In each case the opposition party had been troubled and ineffective for several years before Conservative failures transformed the situation, after which the health of their opponents improved to such an extent that they were the stronger and more effective party when the election came in 1906, 1945 and 1997.

A party in opposition can either concentrate upon its core values and express the outlook of its most vigorous and vocal supporters, or it can aim to widen its appeal even if this means changes in outlook and image. The first approach is the easiest, but carries the danger of solidifying in more permanent form the features which had made the party unattractive to voters

and led to the loss of office. This may have been particulary evident in
1997–2001, but it was also a feature of the periods after the defeats of 1906,
1910 and 1929, and was present to a lesser extent after 1964 and 1974. In
practice, it is never a crude choice between the two strategies, and the
common pattern is a mixture of the two. This becomes a matter of balance
and presentation, and managing the inherent conflict.[30] Thus in both the late
1940s and late 1970s there was concern that the combative instincts of the
leader – Churchill and Thatcher respectively – would involve the party in
statements or positions which would deter moderate voters, however well
they might echo the anger or concerns of the party's bedrock. The approach
which Conservative leaders have taken has been shaped by their sense of
where support had been lost, and therefore how it could be regained. There
are two areas to be considered, and their different needs can produce conflict
or uncertainty. The party whilst in office may have disappointed its core
supporters by failing to respond to their needs or adequately protect their
status or economic prosperity. At the same time, defeat would not have
occurred without the loss of ground amongst floating and marginal voters
who had supported the party in its previous victory, but who were not
habitual Conservative supporters or did not think of themselves as such. This
is likely to be due to a poor record in office, especially if there is a sense of
the government having been in office too long and having drifted out of
touch, or if there have been scandals.

Moving back towards the middle ground can be made more difficult by
the changes in the composition of the parliamentary party which also follow
defeat. Safer seats contain a much larger element of the party's core support,
and so do not need to concern themselves as much with the sensitivities of
moderate or floating voters. The competition for the nomination in these
constituencies ensures that they have a range of credible candidates to choose
from, and they are not constrained from selecting the candidate closest to
their own views. Before the Maxwell Fyfe reforms of 1949, the financial
contribution that the candidate would make to the local Association was a
key factor which further tilted selection in favour of the wealthier section of
society. Although this included some MPs of moderate outlook – such as
Anthony Eden, Harold Macmillan and Oliver Stanley – their visibility and
later ministerial careers tends to obscure the fact that most MPs in safe seats
were either in the centre or on the right of Conservative opinion. For this
reason, the loss of marginal seats meant that the proportion of MPs of
moderate outlook (whether by conviction or electoral pragmatism) diminished when the party went into opposition. At the same time, fewer of the
right wing were defeated, and so the centre of gravity in the parliamentary
party shifted in their direction.

This was of crucial importance in 1906, when the landslide reduced the
core of moderates upon whom Balfour had been reliant to less than a quarter

of the parliamentary party, and the tariff reformers now accounted for over a hundred of the 156 MPs in the new House.[31] Balfour could not survive without accepting what he had hitherto avoided, and in the 'Valentine letters' exchanged on 14 February 1906 he accepted that tariff reform 'is, and must remain, the first constructive work of the Unionist Party'. This factor may also help to explain the degree of hostility to the Liberals over Home Rule in 1912–14; even though this was an issue about which Conservatives felt strongly, the tone and methods of the opposition were taken to unprecedented levels.[32] It was also a significant development after the 1929 defeat, when the 'die-hard' wing of MPs had greater prominence and gave strong support to Beaverbrook's campaign for a full tariff policy.[33] However, it was less apparent in 1945 due to the extensive turnover in Conservative candidates in all types of seats; many of the sitting MPs had entered the House between 1918 and 1924, and because there had been no election since 1935 an unusually high number were reaching retirement age and stood down. Their younger successors had mostly fought in the war and so had been exposed to a much wider range of views and experiences, and they were also more aware of the wartime unpopularity of the party. To a lesser extent something similar occurred in the 1960s, with sufficient MPs feeling that the party had an outdated image, to counteract any pull to the right. After 1974, there was tension between the right of the party and the pragmatists and moderates, whose normal claim to competence had been undermined by the failure of the Heath government.[34]

The final factor to affect both Conservative defeats and recoveries was the role of the third party in mainland British politics. Before 1914 this was the Labour Party, and the electoral pact which it had made with the Liberals in 1903 was significant in the elections of 1906 and 1910. Although the pact broke down in some of the by-elections between 1910 and 1914, resulting in Conservative gains, it would have been in both Liberal and Labour self-interest to maintain their 'progressive alliance' if the 1915 general election had taken place. Labour were the most dependent upon the pact, a fact fully realised by their leaders and headquarters, and in December 1910 they had succeeded in imposing better observation of the agreement upon their local parties. If the Lib–Lab pact had operated again, it would have curtailed any further Conservative progress, and almost certainly some of the by-election gains could not have been held against a single 'progressive' opponent and would have reverted to their previous allegiance. From the early 1920s the Liberals were the third-placed party, but their activity had an opposite effect. The presence of a Liberal candidate diverted some of the votes which would have been obtained by the Conservative in a straight fight with Labour, and this was often enough to result in a Labour win. The high proportion of three-cornered contests contributed to the Conservative defeats of 1923 and 1929; in the latter case, the number had doubled since the victory in 1924, and 159 seats were lost.[35] In addition, Liberal revivals were often the product of troughs in Conservative popularity, and this was the case in 1923 (due to the tariff issue) and in 1929, 1964 and 1974 (after Conservative governments had lost direction and encountered stagnant or poor economic conditions). Conversely, the pattern of relative Liberal weakness after periods of Labour government has assisted Conservative recovery. In 1924 Liberal disarray and financial problems resulted in many fewer candidates being nominated, whilst in 1931 the Liberals were allied with the Conservatives in the National government. In many constituencies the Liberals lacked a candidate or stood down, and the result was an effective anti-Labour front from which the Conservatives benefitted the most. One part of the Liberal Party withdrew from the National government before the next election in 1935, but it was only able to run 161 candidates in comparison to the 457 of 1923 and the 513 of 1929; furthermore, the other section, led by Sir John Simon, remained in electoral partnership with the Conservatives. The fall in the number of Liberal candidates from 475 in 1950 to 109 in 1951 was a crucial factor in Churchill's return to power with an overall majority of seventeen seats. Since the Liberal revival in the 1960s the number of candidates has generally remained high, but the Conservatives have benefitted from returns of support. In 1970 the Liberal vote fell by only 1 per cent, but this was enough to cause the loss of six of their twelve seats. The 5.3 per cent fall in the Liberal vote in England and Wales in 1979 contributed significantly to the 8.1 per cent increase in the Conservative share of the vote, and to the recovery of many seats that had been lost to Labour in 1974.

In conclusion, how effective has the Conservative Party been in opposition between 1906 and 1979? The elements which play a part in this are the state of the party in the wake of the defeat which begins the period in opposition, the degree of understanding and acceptance of the causes of that defeat, the cohesion and morale of the parliamentary party, organisational initiatives and their effectiveness, the development of a new programme or image, and most important of all the problems of the government. The Conservatives were in the greatest disarray after the 1906 defeat, and this persisted with factional strife over tariffs up to 1910 and then bitter division over the Parliament Act in 1911. Although unity was restored by the primacy of the Home Rule issue in 1912–14, the party's stance remained entirely negative and there were potential pitfalls in the extreme position adopted in defence of Ulster.[36] In 1923 the first difficult few weeks were followed by a quick recovery of unity, partly because of the advent of the first Labour government. The 1929 defeat was followed by a party crisis which occupied most of the next two years, and little was achieved by the opposition despite the Labour government's minority status and mounting difficulties.[37] The party organisation in the country was at its lowest ebb in 1945, but there was no disunity in the parliamentary party. As well as restoring the organisation and raising substantial funds, the new structures of the Advisory Committee on Policy and the Conservative Political Centre were introduced, improving communications between leaders and followers.[38] Between 1964 and 1970 there were criticisms of Home's leadership and doubts about Heath, but much attention was focused upon the extensive reappraisal of policy. Apart from the leadership contest in 1975 and the glowering presence of Heath, the stresses of the period from 1975 to 1979 were mainly hidden from view.

Analysis and response to the causes of defeat was most effective after 1923, 1945 and 1974, and least after 1906 and 1910. The Conservatives were most united and effective as a parliamentary opposition in 1924 and 1949–51, and fairly effective in 1978–79 and 1912–14. Organisational changes have been adopted after every defeat, but those of 1906–10 made matters worse until the reforms of 1911 introduced new institutions and effective management.[39] The most successful changes were in 1945–51, particularly the Maxwell Fyfe reforms which emphasised a meritocratic approach to candidate selection and helped to refurbish the party's image.[40] The enquiries and initiatives of 1964–70 and 1974–79 were intended to improve efficiency and reach out to areas where party support was weak, but they were hampered by financial stringency.[41] The reappraisal of policy and the development of a fresh, distinctive and relevant programme was carried through to greatest effect in 1923–24 and 1947–51. The latter became the model to follow, but it was less successful in 1964–70 when the visible activity obscured the failure to tackle some crucial issues, and there were problems in conveying the message to the public.[42] The reappraisal of 1975–79 asked more fundamental questions, but at the price of creating divisions and tensions. In 1929–31 resistance to attempts from the 'diehard' and protectionist right to force a change of programme on the leaders caused a serious party crisis, and this was only overcome when the effects of the slump moved public opinion away from free trade and eroded the standing of the government. It is the latter which remains the crucial governing factor. The Conservatives made little impact upon governments which were performing even moderately well, as in 1908–14, 1924, 1929–30, 1945–49, 1964–67 and 1974–78. Their fortunes improved when governments were struggling, whether this was due to political ineptitude, exhaustion or economic depression. It was various combinations of these three elements which acccounted for the brighter Conservative prospects of 1907–8, 1930–31, 1950–51, 1967–69 and 1978–79, but which were absent in 1997–2001.[43]

A comparative analysis

The second section of this chapter uses an experimental approach to compare the different periods in opposition. Any assessment has to consider the fortunes of both the government and the opposition, and needs to reflect the fact that the actions of the government have much greater impact than those of either the governing or opposition parties. A range of factors has been identified and given a numerical ranking as an indication of the extent to which they were present in each of the periods (see Table 1.1). However, to reflect their greater importance, the elements of the government's performance are scored on a scale from 0 (low) to 10 (high), whilst all other factors are scored on a scale of 0–5. The values allocated are of course a personal judgement: they are a method of expressing analysis rather than statements of fact. Nevertheless, whilst there would be differences of view over precise grades, it is likely that this would tend to cancel out and that a reasonable consensus could be arrived at. The exercise of determining a value causes one to reflect and to compare, assessing both the criteria in general and the significance of the factor in each election. This could also be done by using a scale of words or descriptive phrases, but the advantage of using numbers is that it makes possible a cumulative assessment of each period and facillitates comparisons between them. Judging different factors on the same scale is in one sense artificial, as this gives them an equal weighting which they may not have had. However, the aim is to assess the degree to which a factor is present, rather than to determine its precise relative importance.

There are three different aspects to the position of the government, each of which can be separated into a number of factors. First, there is the security of tenure which the government possesses – to put it simply, a government with a large majority in the Commons is much harder to defeat than one which does not have a majority at all. The larger the electoral mountain that the opposition will have to climb, the greater the swing back in public support which will be needed. Being in office gives some benefits of prestige, and this is measured by including the number of years that the government has been in office. The second aspect is the effectiveness of the government's performance, and this is assessed under five headings. Four of these concern the main areas of responsibility: the health of the economy (assessed by factors which most directly affect or concern people, such as unemployment and living standards); social stability and industrial relations; welfare provision; and response to any concerns about the external situation. To these are added a fifth factor, the extent to which the government holds out the promise of an attractive future programme, or whether it seems to be exhausted and simply clinging to office. The third aspect considered for the government is the condition of its supporting party, and this is assessed in terms of the quality of its leadership, its unity and image, and the strength of its party organisation.

Three aspects are also considered for the opposition party, but there are only two factors in each of these and they are scored on the scale of 0–5. The first aspect is the public image of the opposition, and the two factors

Table 1.1 Factors in Conservative recoveries, 1910–79

General election:	1910	1924	1931	1950/51	1970	1979	Total
GOVERNMENT							
Security and inertia							
Years in office (number)	4	1	2	6	6	5	24
Size of majority (0–5)	5	0	0	5	4	1	15
Sub-total	9	1	2	11	10	6	
Performance (0–10)							
Promise for the future	7	6	0	3	2	1	19
Social order, ind. unrest	6	5	4	6	4	1	26
Economy, unemployment	8	5	0	7	6	3	29
Welfare provision	7	5	3	10	5	6	36
External security	5	7	8	8	6	6	40
Sub-total	33	28	15	34	23	17	
Governing party (0–5)							
Leadership	4	4	0	2	3	4	17
Unity and image	4	5	0	3	4	3	19
Organisation	4	4	2	4	3	2	19
Sub-total	12	13	2	9	10	9	
Total	54	42	19	54	43	32	
OPPOSITION							
Image (0–5)							
Appeal of leadership	1	5	4	3	2	2	17
Unity and vigour	2	4	3	4	3	4	20
Sub-total	3	9	7	7	5	6	
Programme (0–5)							
Distinctiveness	4	3	4	4	3	3	21
Attractiveness	1	4	4	4	3	2	18
Sub-total	5	7	8	8	6	5	
Organisation (0–5)							
Effectiveness	2	3	3	5	3	4	20
Resources	2	3	4	5	3	4	21
Sub-total	4	6	7	10	6	8	
Total	12	22	22	25	17	19	

here are the appeal of the leadership and the degree of unity and vigour displayed by the party. The second aspect is the programme which is put forward, and this is assessed for its distinctiveness and its attractiveness – in the latter case, to voters whose support the party lost when it was defeated

and to uncommitted or 'floating' voters. The final aspect is the strength of
the party organisation, assessed in terms of its effectiveness and of the level
of resources which are available to it.

The results of this analysis may contain few surprises, but they highlight
a number of issues. The first of these is that the fate of a government lies in
its own hands. The highest scores for the sub-heading of government
performance are in 1910 and 1950–51, and although four general elections
are involved these are the most limited Conservative recoveries. They show
the lowest increases in the Conservative share of the vote, despite the fact
that they follow a landslide defeat: in January 1910 the Conservative poll
increased by 3.4 per cent over 1906, and in 1950 by only 3.9 per cent over
1945. In January and December 1910 the opposition was unable to displace
the Liberal government, and after a similar experience in 1950 the majority
attained in 1951 was by far the lowest of any Conservative return to office
after a period in opposition. The next highest score under this heading, of
twenty-eight in 1924, saw the Labour Party lose a relatively small number
of seats after its first minority term in office, and the large Conservative
victory was mainly the result of the collapse of the Liberal Party. Although
the overall government score in 1970 is slightly above that in 1924, this is
mainly due to its longer spell in office and the size of the 1966 majority; on
performance it is five points behind 1924, and the image of the governing
party is also poorer. At the other end of the scale, the lowest government
total is, hardly surprisingly, in 1931.

Table 1.2 Conservative electoral recoveries, 1910–79

Date of election	MPs elected		Total votes received		% share of vote	
	No.	Gain	No.	Gain	No.	Gain
January 1910	272	+116	3,104,407	+683,336	46.8	+3.4
29 October 1924	412	+154	7,854,523	+2,339,982	46.8	+8.8
27 October 1931	470	+210	11,905,925	+3,249,700	55.0	+16.9
23 February 1950	298	+88	12,492,404	+2,520,394	43.5	+3.9
25 October 1951	321	+23	13,718,199	+1,225,795	48.0	+4.5
1950–51		*+111*		*+3,746,189*		*+8.4*
18 June 1970	330	+77	13,145,123	+1,726,668	46.4	+5.4
3 May 1979	339	+62	13,697,923	+3,235,358	43.9	+8.1

Note: The figures are comparisons with the previous general election, and the number
of seats gained therefore does not take account of by-election results in the intervening period. The table includes an additional comparison of the combined outcome of
1950 and 1951 with the 1945 result shown in italics.

Within the factors of government performance, the most obvious corre-
lation is between economic performance and a rise in the opposition poll. In

the worst crisis, in 1931 the Conservative share of the votes cast increased by 16.9 per cent, and in 1979 it increased by 8.1 per cent; this is slightly surpassed by the 8.8 per cent increase of 1924, but the latter was assisted by the absence of Liberal candidates from many of the seats which they had fought in 1923. However, in the ranking of factors in the analysis above, the weakest element for the government has not been any part of its record but rather its promise and prospects for the future. This may be due to two reasons: firstly, that governments which have a poor record in office will lack credibility in seeking a further term, and, secondly, that voters need to have confidence in the future programme of a government as well as recognising its achievements. The latter was a factor in 1951, when the employment, welfare and external policies of the Labour government enjoyed widespread approval, but the exhaustion of the government and Cabinet splits over future direction weakened its appeal. A further conclusion which can be drawn is that potential Conservative voters are particularly influenced by threats to the social fabric and by industrial unrest, as this is the second lowest score overall amongst the elements in government performance. Not far after this is the third lowest factor, economic performance, and it must be remembered that recessions affect the self-employed, the shopkeeper, the businessman and the middle class generally as well as the working class. However, the totals above suggest that effectiveness in welfare provision does not save a government if other factors are telling against it, and this is true not only of Labour in 1951 but also of the Conservatives in 1929 and 1974. This factor may also be of less appeal to Conservative supporters, who prize self-reliance and regard dependence on state handouts as a humiliation. Finally, and less surprisingly, it is clear that success in foreign policy cannot outweigh domestic difficulties.

Whilst the scores of the government play the decisive part in these elections, the effectiveness of the opposition is a variable which can either add to or detract from the result. It made a considerable difference in the outcomes of 1910 and 1950–51, despite the very similar scores for the Liberal and Labour ministries: the weakest opposition score is found in 1910, and the highest in 1950–51. In both these periods, the first election sees the recovery of the most surprising losses in the previous landslide defeat, but the outcome of the second is different. A more unexpected feature of opposition performance is that a distinctive programme and effective organisation are more important than the appeal of the leadership. Churchill was at least a mixed blessing in 1951, as his wartime prestige was balanced by vulnerability over his age and the suggestion that his belligerent attitudes would be a danger to peace, and neither Heath in 1970 nor Thatcher in 1979 were considered to be personally appealing figures, especially to moderate opinion. The attractiveness of the Conservative programme – considered in terms of the key issues of the election – was at its highest in 1924, 1931 and 1951, and at its lowest in 1910 and perhaps in 1979, when the sixty-two seats regained is less than might be expected given the difficulties of the government. However, the 1979 opposition performance is helped by strength on the organisational aspects, which is exceeded only by 1951.

As a whole, this analysis underlines the extent to which the fortunes of the opposition depend upon those of the government. However, the opposition can be either hindered or helped in making the best of its opportunities by the effectiveness of the three elements of leadership, image and organisation. A conclusion which can be drawn is that before there can be a Conservative return to power, rather than just a limited ebbing of the tide in the style of 1910, the party will need to find a new message rather than just recycling the old. It will need a distinctive voice, and one which can reach beyond its core support and encourage the return of the members and voters lost since 1992. This is the crucial difference between the periods after the two other major Conservative defeats of this century, and without it the party is likely to repeat the sterility of 1906–14 rather than the recovery of 1945–51.

Notes

1 As was the problem with statements by Portillo and Lilley after 1997.

2 The former was significant in preserving Baldwin's position after the 1923 and 1929 defeats: see Lord Derby's diary entry, 17 December 1923, in R. Churchill, *Lord Derby: King of Lancashire* (London, Heinemann, 1959), pp. 558–9; S. Ball, *Baldwin and the Conservative Party: The Crisis of 1929–1931* (Yale, Yale University Press, 1988), Chs 4–6.

3 The exceptions were after the defeats of 1964 and February 1974, as the outcome meant that another election would not be long delayed.

4 D. Dutton, *His Majesty's Loyal Opposition: The Unionist Party in Opposition 1905–1915* (Liverpool, Liverpool University Press, 1992), pp. 34–5, 37.

5 D. R. Thorpe, *Alec Douglas-Home: The Under-rated Prime Minister* (London, Sinclair-Stevenson, 1996), pp. 378, 387–8.

6 Ball, *Baldwin and the Conservative Party*, pp. 159–61, 189.

7 This was reflected in Thorneycroft's decision not to contest the leadership in 1965, J. Ramsden, *The Winds of Change: Macmillan to Heath, 1957–1975* (London, Longman, 1996), p. 236.

8 Such as the Shadow Cabinet discussion with Baldwin of 25 March 1931, Ball, *Baldwin and the Conservative Party*, p. 150; concerns over Churchill's absenteeism and unpredictability in 1945–47 led to 'half-hearted' hints that he might consider retiring, but no concerted pressure, J. Ramsden, *The Age of Churchill and Eden 1940–1957* (London, Longman, 1995), pp. 178–80.

9 Opinion research summaries, Conservative Party Archive (CPA), Bodleian Library, CCO/180/27/9; L. Johnman, 'The Conservative Party in opposition 1964–1970', in R. Coopey, S. Fielding and N. Tiratsoo (eds), *The Wilson Governments 1964–1970* (London, Pinter, 1993), pp. 202–3.

10 S. Ball, 'The national and regional party structure', in A. Seldon and S. Ball (eds),

   Conservative Century: The Conservative Party Since 1900 (Oxford, Oxford University
   Press, 1994), pp. 206–7; Dutton, *His Majesty's Loyal Opposition*, pp. 128–30.
11 Lord Brooke's Committee of Inquiry into Organisation of the Cities, Minutes and
   Report, 1966–67, CPA CCO/500/1/42. Macleod Report on Young Conservatives,
   and Party Chairman to Heath, 29 October 1965, CPA CCO/20/47/1; *Conservative
   New Groups: The Young Approach* (London, Conservative Central Office, 1968); S. Ball,
   'Local Conservatism and the evolution of the party organisation', in Seldon and Ball
   (eds), *Conservative Century*, pp. 300–1.
12 See the account by its Director, A. Rowe, 'The Community Affairs Department,
   1975–1979: a personal record', in S. Ball and I. Holliday (eds), *Mass Conservatism: The
   Conservatives and the Public since the 1880s* (London, Frank Cass, 2002), pp. 200–17.
13 This assumption colours many personal accounts of 1945–51, in particular Lord
   Butler, *The Art of the Possible* (London, Hamish Hamilton, 1971), pp. 136–7, 143–53.
14 Butler, *Art of the Possible*, p. 135; Ramsden, *Age of Churchill and Eden*, pp. 138, 142.
15 A. Taylor, 'Speaking to democracy: the Conservative Party and mass opinion from
   the 1920s to the 1950s', in Ball and Holliday (eds), *Mass Conservatism*, pp. 85–8.
16 D. Butler and M. Pinto-Duschinsky, *The British General Election of 1970* (London,
   Macmillan, 1971), pp. 66–8; Johnman, 'Conservative Party in opposition 1964–1970',
   p. 187.
17 Johnman, 'Conservative Party in opposition 1964–1970', pp. 189–90.
18 R. Behrens, *The Conservative Party from Heath to Thatcher: Policies and Politics 1974–79*
   (London, Saxon House, 1980), p. 126.
19 Dutton, *His Majesty's Loyal Opposition*, pp. 256–76.
20 S. Ball, 'Failure of an opposition? The Conservative Party in Parliament 1929–1931',
   Parliamentary History, 5 (1986) 94–5.
21 N. Blewett, 'Free-Fooders, Balfourites, and Whole-Hoggers: Factionalism within the
   Unionist Party 1906–10', *Historical Journal*, 11 (1968) 113–19; A. Sykes, 'The Con-
   federacy and the purge of the Unionist Free Traders 1906–1910', *Historical Journal*,
   18 (1975) 349–66.
22 Ball, *Baldwin and the Conservative Party*, pp. 168–71.
23 Johnman, 'Conservative Party in opposition 1964–1970', pp. 198–9, 200–1; Ramsden,
   Winds of Change, pp. 306–7.
24 Butler and Pinto-Duschinsky, *The British General Election of 1970*, pp. 63–5, 174.
25 Behrens, *Conservative Party from Heath to Thatcher*, p. 124.
26 Ball, *Baldwin and the Conservative Party*, pp. 28–9, 56, 75, 77.
27 Ball, 'Failure of an opposition?', pp. 85–6, 94; P. A. Bromhead, *The House of Lords and
   Contemporary Politics 1911–1957* (London, Routledge & Kegan Paul, 1958), pp. 151–9,
   J. D. Hoffman, *The Conservative Party in Opposition 1945–1951* (London, MacGibbon
   & Kee, 1964), pp. 239–40.
28 National Union, Executive Committee, 16 July, 3 and 22 October 1929, 14 January
   1930, CPA NUA/4/1/4; Ball, *Baldwin and the Conservative Party*, pp. 31–3 and Appendix 1.
29 For a fuller analysis, see A. Seldon (ed.), *How Tory Governments Fall: The Tory Party
   in Power since 1783* (London, Fontana, 1996), pp. 453–62, and *passim*.
30 The difficulties of this were acknowledged by Angus Maude before the 1964 defeat,
   in the *Spectator*, 15 March 1963; Johnman, 'Conservative Party in opposition 1964–
   1970', p. 185.
31 Analysis of factional strengths in *The Times*, 30 January 1906; Blewett, 'Free-Fooders,
   Balfourites, and Whole-Hoggers', pp. 96–8.
32 J. Smith, *The Tories and Ireland 1910–1914: Conservative Party Politics and the Home*

Rule Crisis (Irish Academic Press, 2000), Ch. 7; Dutton, *His Majesty's Loyal Opposition*, pp. 226–7.

33 Ball, *Baldwin and the Conservative Party*, pp. 23–4.

34 Behrens, *Conservative Party from Heath to Thatcher*, Chs 2 and 5.

35 S. Ball, '1916–1929', in Seldon (ed.), *How Tory Governments Fall*, p. 264.

36 E. H. H. Green, *The Crisis of Conservatism: The Politics, Economics and Ideology of the British Conservative Party 1880–1914* (London, Routledge, 1995), pp. 297–306.

37 Ball, 'Failure of an opposition?', pp. 90–6.

38 J. Barnes and R. Cockett, 'The making of party policy', in Seldon and Ball (eds), *Conservative Century*, pp. 364–7; P. Norton, 'The role of the Conservative Political Centre, 1945–1998', in Ball and Holliday (eds), *Mass Conservatism*, pp. 183–99.

39 R. B. Jones, 'Balfour's reforms of party organisation', *Bulletin of the Institute of Historical Research*, 38 (1965) 94–101; J. Ramsden, *The Age of Balfour and Baldwin 1902–1940* (London, Longman, 1978), pp. 45–62, 68–9.

40 Hoffman, *Conservative Party in Opposition 1945–1951*, pp. 83–127; Ramsden, *Age of Churchill and Eden*, pp. 109–37.

41 Ball, 'The national and regional party structure', pp. 191–2.

42 Johnman, 'Conservative Party in opposition 1964–1970', pp. 196–7, 202–3.

43 This is not to suggest that the Blair government made no mistakes, but rather that these did not significantly erode its public standing.

2

The US Republicans: lessons for the Conservatives?

Edward Ashbee

Both Labour's victory in the 1997 general election and the US Republicans' loss of the White House in 1992 led to crises of confidence among conservatives. Although there were those in both countries who attributed these defeats to presentational errors or the campaigning skills of their Labour and Democrat opponents, others saw a need for far-reaching policy shifts and a restructuring of conservative politics. This chapter considers the character of US conservatism during the 1990s, the different strands of opinion that emerged in the wake of the 1992 defeat, the factors that shaped the victorious Bush campaign in 2000, and the implications of these events for the Conservative Party in Britain.

George Bush's 1992 defeat was a watershed, bringing twelve years of Republican rule in the White House to a close. Although constrained by Democratic opposition in Congress, the 'Reagan revolution' had, seemingly, ushered in a fundamental shift in the character of US politics. Tax rates had been reduced and there was growing confidence in US economic capabilities. Indeed, Reaganism appropriated a number of the long-term goals that had long been associated with liberalism. In particular, the supply-side policies with which the administration associated itself promised that unfettered market forces would not only increase overall economic growth but also alleviate poverty and address deprivation in the inner-city neighbourhoods. The USA had also, it was said, regained its place in the world through the arms build-up and military intervention in Grenada. There had, furthermore, been shifts in political allegiances. Although there had not been a 'critical' election such as those of 1896 and 1932, some spoke in terms of realignment. In 1980 and 1984, Reagan had attracted a significant proportion of the blue-collar vote, much of which had traditionally been loyal to the Democrats. Indeed, in 1984, he captured 46 per cent of the votes of those living in union households.

How and why was this inheritance squandered in 1992? For Bush himself, the failure to secure a second term was largely inexplicable. His approval ratings had reached 89 per cent during the Gulf War only eighteen months earlier. Furthermore, he faced an opponent who many regarded as morally flawed. As Bush's biographer later asked: 'how in the world could the American people have chosen Bill Clinton over him? He never could understand.' [1] However, conservative journals and organisations did offer answers to the question, all of which laid the basis for different political strategies.

The Gingrich generation and the *Contract with America*

The first of these strategies was tied to the personality and politics of Newt Gingrich. First elected to Congress in 1978, Gingrich played a critical part in forming the Conservative Opportunity Society (COS). It put itself at the forefront of attacks on the Democrats, developed a public policy agenda for the Republicans, and sought to win the levers of power within the party.[2] While some established Washington insiders offered assistance to the grouping, it shared little of the older generation's deference towards Congressional tradition and respect for bipartisan procedures. The COS's efforts were paralleled by initiatives outside of Congress. Gingrich and his associates used a political action committee, GOPAC, to recruit and train Republican candidates

As Ashford notes, Gingrich's thinking defies simple political categorisation.[3] He and those around him in the COS and GOPAC embraced policies that built upon those pursued by the Reagan administration, particularly during its first two years in office. They emphasised the role that could be played by cuts in marginal rates for both personal and corporate taxpayers. Such reductions, it was said, would unlock the supply-side of the economy, unleashing entrepreneurial activity, stimulating growth and, in the long term, generating the income required to balance the federal budget. Alongside supply-side economics, Gingrich and his co-thinkers stressed the need for welfare reform so as to end dependency and bolster self-reliance. They also emphasised the importance of addressing rising crime rates. Law enforcement agencies, it was said, required greater resources.

To an extent, all of this was common ground for conservatives. However, the abrasive tone adopted by Gingrich and the adoption of policies associated with supply-side economics created tensions. Many leading Republicans, particularly those in the Senate such as Bob Dole, who served as chairman of the Senate Finance Committee and then Senate Majority Leader, took a much more traditionalist approach to fiscal policy and regarded the reduction of the federal government budget deficit as a defining priority. The differences between those committed to supply-side economics and the 'deficit hawks' led, at times, to acrimony and bitterness. In a celebrated insult, Newt Gingrich described Dole as the biggest 'tax collector for the welfare state'.[4]

Despite these strains, the COS progressively established its credibility within Republican Party circles. In 1985, it was in the forefront of GOP protests when the Democratic majority in the House of Representatives insisted on seating their party's candidate for the eighth district in Indiana amidst fierce controversy about the outcome of the contest. In May 1989, the COS claimed the scalp of Jim Wright, House Speaker by pressing ethics charges that led to his resignation. However, the turning point lay in events and processes outside of Congress itself. There was a profound shift in the character of the political environment and this created a framework within which Gingrich's politics could become mainstream Republicanism. By the early 1990s frustration with government had become commonplace. At times, stronger emotions were also evident. Whereas in the late 1950s, 73 per cent of those asked had said that they trusted the federal government 'most of the time' or 'just about always', by 1992 and 1994, the figure had fallen to 29 and 21 per cent respectively. Such figures were well below those recorded during the Watergate era.[5] In October 1992, 25 per cent of respondents told interviewers that they were 'angry' with the federal government. A mere 16 per cent were 'satisfied'.[6]

Although fanned by talk radio hosts such as Rush Limbaugh, these sentiments were grounded in the economic and cultural realities of the period. Following the boom of the late 1980s, the USA went into recession. Unemployment rose to 7.5 per cent and there was a dramatic increase in associated indices of social misery. There were also other sources of discontent. There had been a succession of Congressional scandals. The federal government budget deficit represented a visible symbol of government profligacy and led to high levels of debt repayment. At the same time, many felt that the cities were crime-ridden, welfare spending had created an urban underclass, the schools were failing to teach basic literacy skills and, in the eyes of many white men, affirmative action programmes had reduced their employment and promotion prospects.

A number of the Republican state governors – such as Tommy Thompson of Wisconsin who pioneered efforts to reform welfare provision and was later to be appointed as Secretary of Health and Human Services in George W. Bush's administration – had already begun to respond to these sentiments. There was, however, a contrast between initiatives such as these and developments in Washington DC. For many, the Bush administration appeared distant and uninterested in domestic policy concerns. In contrast to the sense of direction seemingly offered at state level and by the Reagan administration, Bush ridiculed the 'vision thing'.[7] He also, as his conservative critics emphasised, backed measures that appeared to expand the scope and powers of government, such as the Clean Air Act and the Americans with Disabilities Act. Furthermore, he had attempted to reach a compromise on gun control by prohibiting the importation of assault weapons.[8] Most significantly of all, despite his celebrated 1988 election pledge, 'read my lips, no new taxes', he agreed – in a 1990 budget compromise with the Democratic majority in Congress – to an increase in marginal tax rates from 28 to 31.5 per cent.[9] In Congress, the measure won backing from only a quarter of Republicans.

For many conservatives, this disoriented voters and fractured the electoral coalition that had served as the basis for Reagan's victories.

Initially, Bill Clinton was the principal beneficiary of these sentiments. However, though the November 1992 election brought him into office, it also brought the sense of popular hostility towards Washington DC 'insiders' out into the open. Standing as an independent candidate, Ross Perot, the Texan billionaire, gained 19 per cent of the vote. These feelings of resentment towards the political 'establishment' continued after the election. Indeed, they were fuelled by the actions of the Clinton administration which enjoyed only the shortest and superficial of political 'honeymoons'. Its uneasy compromise regarding the 'gays in the military' controversy alienated all sides and his proposed health care reforms had to be abandoned in the face of widespread opposition.

All of this laid the basis for Gingrich to establish his pre-eminence among House Republicans and, two years later, for the *Contract with America* to emerge. The Contract was a declaration, incorporating three resolutions and ten bills, signed by almost all Republican House candidates. It was not, however, a manifesto. While the Contract promised that the proposed Congressional reforms would be passed on the first day of the 104th Congress, it was not a pledge to enact legislation. It simply offered an assurance that there would be a vote on the measures included in the Contract during the first hundred days of a Republican-led House. It was not signed by those standing for the Senate. Indeed, some senators were opposed to a number of the proposals, particularly the imposition of term limits. The overall role of the Contract has also been questioned. A survey suggested that only 24 per cent of the electorate were aware of its existence. Just 4 per cent said that it was more likely to make them vote for Republican candidates.[10]

Nonetheless, the Republicans' electoral victories seemed to vindicate Gingrich's strategy in adopting and promoting the Contract. The Republicans gained fifty-two seats in the House giving them a majority for the first time since the 1952 elections. Not a single Republican incumbent was defeated. The newly elected GOP freshmen – who made up almost 32 per cent of the party's ranks – were committed conservatives who rallied around Gingrich. Indeed, at times, their populist sentiments led them to stake out positions with greater rigidity than Gingrich. The Contract also offered a sense of political purpose and direction. During the first hundred days of the 104th Congress, it gained momentum and acquired the moral suasion of a manifesto. Its adoption also shifted the locus of policy initiation from the White House to the House of Representatives and, at the same time, provided a focus for Congressional electioneering which had traditionally been governed by the dictum that 'all politics is local'.

Furthermore, despite the institutional obstacles that the US political system places in the way of legislative reform, twenty-three of the forty items in the Contract were adopted. Most notably of all, the Personal Responsibility and Work Opportunity Reconciliation Act was passed and signed, albeit reluctantly, into law by President Clinton. It ended the system of welfare provision that had been initially established in the 1930s and created in its place the Temporary Assistance for Needy Families (TANF) programme. This imposed time limits on public assistance and introduced work requirements for recipients. At the same time, the Republican victories, and the GOP's legislative offensive, led to a significant change in the character of the Clinton administration. Increasingly, the President appeared to be drawing on a Republican vocabulary. He proclaimed that 'the era of big government is over' and signed the welfare reform bill. He re-emphasised his commitment to the death penalty and school prayer. He also called for the introduction of the V-chip, allowing parents to control their children's television viewing, and signed legislation prohibiting same-sex marriage.[11]

Despite all of this, the Contract did not renew the conservative revolution in the way that its supporters hoped. Some of the most significant legislative proposals that it included were not enacted. More importantly, the Republican strategy of confrontation with the White House failed. It also created tensions and divisions among House Republicans. At the end of 1995, Congress passed a budget that reduced taxes, aimed to balance the budget within a seven-year period, and restructured some federal entitlement programmes. Clinton vetoed the budget reconciliation bill and a number of associated appropriations bills, arguing that the proposed budget threatened the future of education, Medicare and Medicaid. Instead, he offered compromise solutions. As Barbara Sinclair records:

> Republicans were convinced that Clinton would cave in under pressure from the public. When negotiations between them and the White House failed to produce an agreement they considered satisfactory, they several times let appropriations lapse and shut down the government, in one case for twenty-two days over Christmas. Not only did Clinton hold fast, but the public reaction was the opposite of what House Republicans had expected; the public blamed the Republicans, not the president, and Clinton's job-approval ratings went up.[12]

Public opinion – which backed the President by a two-to-one majority – compelled the Republicans to back down. In early January, the Republicans voted to allow federal employees to return to work and the government business continued on the basis of appropriations bills but without an overall budget agreement.

Why did the Republicans lose the battle with the White House? Some attribute the course of events to Clinton's skills as a political strategist, his adoption of a 'triangulation' strategy, and his ability to demonise the Republicans. Clinton was able to frame their proposals, particularly those that concerned the future of Medicare and Medicaid, as extremist, allowing him both to recapture much of the middle ground and set the agenda for his 1996 re-election victory. Others point to Gingrich's volatile personality, and a succession of incidents that attracted negative publicity. However, long-term trends were also in play. The beginnings of an economic and cultural shift were beginning to become evident and the anger that many people felt towards the apparatus of government at the beginning of the 1990s had diminished. Unemployment levels were falling and crime rates had dropped in many of the major cities. Against such a background, there was less of a popular groundswell or enthusiasm for a strategy of all-out confrontation in pursuit of conservative goals.

Although the 1996 elections returned Republican majorities in both houses, the 105th and 106th Congresses (1997–2001) represented a partial return to more traditional forms of Congressional government. There were few policy initiatives. As Owens records:

> On issues like tobacco regulation, health reform and campaign finance, Republicans preferred a wait-and-see strategy, often delaying action, waiting for events to run their course and interest groups to determine the climate of opinion. Issues pursued by Republican leaders were largely of minor political importance, necessitated little political risk and required only small investments of political capital.[13]

Although chastened, Gingrich himself survived as House Speaker until the 1998 mid-term elections. These results represented a further setback for the Republicans. Traditionally, it is the president's party that suffers losses. However, the Republicans not only failed to make gains, but instead lost seats, reducing their majority to eleven. In the aftermath, Gingrich stepped down and the Republican Conference chose Dennis Hastert as House Speaker. While the House Republicans continued to pursue Clinton and impeached him in 1998, Hastert's personality and politics epitomised the renewed sense of pragmatism and caution.

Pragmatism and the 1996 presidential election

Although Gingrich's personality and politics sometimes appear to define the Republican Party during the early and middle years of the decade, other conservative currents were also important, particularly after the 1995–96 budget debacle. Significant numbers of Republicans did not attribute Bush's 1992 defeat to the abandonment of conservative goals but, instead, saw the loss as an inevitable consequence of public weariness after twelve years of Republican rule in the White House. At the same time, they observed, the end of the Cold War had led to a shift in the popular agenda and, against this background, domestic issues came increasingly to the fore. A survey of voters during the 1992 election campaign suggested that foreign policy ranked only eighth in terms of importance. Bush also had to fight on a number of fronts. In the November election, he faced both Clinton, the Democratic contender, and Ross Perot, whose campaign was weighted against the President.

Bush's difficulties were compounded by the actions of some associated with the conservative right. In April 1992, Dan Quayle, the Vice-President, castigated the television sitcom 'Murphy Brown' for its positive portrayal of single parenthood. The speech, critics asserted, confirmed that the Bush campaign was out of touch with the realities of contemporary life. During the Republican primaries and caucuses, Bush was challenged by Pat Buchanan who had served as a speechwriter and publicist in the Nixon and Reagan administrations. Buchanan, sometimes dubbed a paleo-conservative, offered a right-wing populist platform, calling for protectionism, cultural renewal, the outlawing of abortion and opposition to immigration. Although Buchanan's impact diminished in the subsequent primaries, his primetime address to the Republican National Convention commanded widespread attention. While he gave Bush his backing, he called for a cultural war that would 'retake' the USA.

Bush's defeat in the 1992 election therefore led some observers to a very different conclusion to that drawn by Gingrich and his co-thinkers. It showed that subsequent Republican candidates had to distance themselves from the more doctrinaire and radical forms of conservatism. This form of thinking shaped the course of the 1996 presidential election. After some initial hesitation, the party's supporters – who select the presidential candidate through the primaries and caucuses – threw their weight behind Dole. Unlike some of the other contenders, he had substantial name recognition through his role as Senate Majority Leader and his efforts to win the presidential nomination in 1980 and 1988. He was acceptable, as Mayer has noted, to all Republican interests and factions.[14] As has been noted, Dole had a wary and pragmatic approach. Although he selected Jack Kemp – who was closely associated with supply-side economics – as his vice-presidential 'running mate' and adopted a call for a 15 per cent reduction in income taxes, there were profound doubts about the extent to which he was convinced by such a policy. He boasted that he had not read the Republican Party's 1996 platform and could not therefore be bound by it. Instead, for much of the campaign, Dole concentrated his efforts on criticisms of the Clinton administration. He raised the 'character issue' and questioned the scale of the economic recovery since 1993.

Dole was widely seen as more honest and trustworthy than Clinton. However, as the election approached, Clinton led on almost all the critical issues, notably the economy, employment, the future of Medicare, and education. Furthermore, despite Dole's efforts, Clinton's strategists also succeeded in associating the Republican campaign with the 'extremism' of his colleagues in the House of Representatives. Clinton successfully positioned himself as the centrist candidate and reaped the electoral rewards of economic recovery. About eleven million new jobs were created between January 1993, when Clinton had been inaugurated, and November 1996, when he faced re-election. Against this background, the budget deficit, which had dominated political discourse in preceding years, had been substantially reduced. By 1996, some commentators were projecting a surplus for the end of the decade. Against this background, Dole was defeated, gaining only 41.4 per cent of the vote.

The religious right

For much of the 1980s and 1990s, the religious (or Christian) right was an important and integral component of the US conservative movement. Spurred into the political arena by developments such as the shift in women's social and economic roles, the secularisation of education, successive Supreme Court rulings (particularly *Roe* v. *Wade*) and the emergence of the 'gay lobby', evangelical Christians sought the adoption of policies structured around moral traditionalism and family values. In particular, they hoped to outlaw abortion and counter efforts to represent homosexuality and heterosexuality as moral equivalents. However, although the Moral Majority – established in 1979 by the Reverend Jerry Falwell – won adherents, attracted press attention and enjoyed a close relationship with some in the Reagan admin-istration, its overall political impact (if measured in terms of legislative successes) was limited. Furthermore, the organisation was discredited by a succession of scandals involving prominent 'televangelists'.

The Christian Coalition, which was established in the aftermath of the Reverend Pat Robertson's attempts to secure the 1988 Republican presiden-tial nomination, had greater success. By late 1995, it claimed 1.7 million members and supporters who were spread across all fifty states and organised in 1,700 local chapters.[15] The Coalition's understanding of the political process, and the strategy that it developed, were shaped by Ralph Reed, who served as the organisation's executive director from its formation in 1989 until 1997. In Reed's eyes, Bush's 1992 defeat was not a consequence of events such as Buchanan's address to the Republican national convention. Instead, it could be attributed to his failure to associate himself with moral and cultural causes: 'what cost Bush the election was not four days in Houston but the four years preceding the convention'.[16]

The Coalition, and the other groupings associated with the religious right, cited what were regarded as efforts by the Bush administration to court the gay vote and its seeming equivocation when attempts were made to dilute the Republican Party's opposition to abortion.

At the same time, however, Reed drew lessons from the sectarianism that the Christian right had sometimes displayed during the preceding years. In its place, he stressed the importance of coalition building. He acknowledged that born-again evangelical Protestants, the core of the Christian right, represented less than a quarter of the voting age population and did not, furthermore, constitute a homogeneous or disciplined bloc. Indeed, many did not share the Coalition's political priorities. Fewer than a quarter, for example, regarded abortion as a pivotal issue that determined the way in which their votes were cast.[17] Christian conservatives should, therefore, reach out to others.

The process of coalition building took a number of forms. Firstly, limited attempts were made to establish the Coalition's bipartisan credentials by supporting a small number of Democratic candidates. Secondly, Reed encouraged overtures to Roman Catholic voters and, invoking the memory of Martin Luther King, called for racial bridge building. Thirdly, he urged the Christian right to take up 'pocketbook' issues associated with economic conservatism. The strengthening of the family, he asserted, required lower taxation and economic growth. Reed also called upon Christian conservatives to address issues such as health care, crime and education.[18] Fourthly, he backed candidates who were electorally credible, even if they did not subscribe to the Coalition's full agenda. Despite ideological affinities, he withheld support from figures such as Pat Buchanan. Furthermore, in contrast with some of the other groupings associated with the Christian right, he eschewed attempts to tie such candidates to the adoption of specific policies. As he noted in the aftermath of the 1996 election:

> We were not about to dictate terms to Bob Dole. He had won the nomination in his own right, and we had no intention of making harsh demands like those that the labor unions and the radical left had made of presidential nominees in recent years.[19]

However, although Christian conservatives continued to be well represented in the Republican presidential primaries at successive elections, the Christian right lost much of the influence that it had won for itself earlier in the decade. Indeed, in the 2000 elections, there was evidence that some grassroots Christian conservatives were pulling back from the political arena. According to Karl Rove, Bush's chief political advisor, only 15 million of the 19 million religious conservatives who should have voted went to the polls in the 2000 election.[20] Even before this, some reports suggested that the Christian Coalition's earlier membership figures had been overstated and that it had been financially over-committed.

There were two principal reasons why the Christian right lost ground as the 1990s progressed. Despite Reed's strategic planning, the Christian right was undermined by cultural and social shifts. During the 1990s, there was a process of partial 'remoralisation'. After rising dramatically during the years that followed the 1973 *Roe* ruling, which established abortion as a constitutional right, the number of abortions fell from 345 per 1,000 live births in 1990 to 306 in 1997.[21] Similarly, the proportion of divorces fell from 1985 onwards. At the same time, however, gay relationships and premarital sex became more widely accepted. Furthermore, the Lewinsky scandal did little to erode public backing for Clinton. Against the background of these paradoxical trends, the sense of cultural crisis that had contributed to the growth of Christian right organisations lost some of its former potency, while their emphasis upon moral traditionalism seemed outdated and anachronistic to increasing numbers.[22]

'National greatness conservatism'

A further strand within the conservative movement crystallised around the Hudson Institute, the Project for Conservative Reform, and the *Weekly Standard* during the latter half of the 1990s. Although there were few in its ranks, its emergence reflected a shift in mood among some on the right. In 1997, Bill Kristol, the *Weekly Standard* editor and David Brooks, another *Weekly Standard* writer, questioned the libertarian and anti-statist character of contemporary conservatism. They seemed to have Gingrich and those around him in their sights: 'In recent years some conservatives' sensible contempt for the nanny state has at times spilled over into a foolish, and politically suicidal, contempt for the American state.'[23]

In contrast, advocates of 'national greatness conservatism' called for limited but, at the same time, 'energetic' forms of government.[24] Both the domestic and foreign policy implications of this were sometimes uncertain, but a number of policy differences with mainstream conservatism did become evident. 'National greatness conservatives' emphasised civil society and the strengthening of civic life rather than the market. They called on the conservative movement to loosen its ties to commercial interests and corporate lobbyists. They supported campaign finance reform and stressed the importance of environmental protection. They were reluctant to endorse tax reductions that, as they saw it, benefited only the highest income groups.

In foreign policy, those who talked of 'national greatness conservatism' looked back towards Theodore Roosevelt's presidency. He was, according to Brooks, 'unshaking in his courage, balanced in his tactics, and righteous in his cause'.[25] They called for an assertion of US leadership across the globe based upon 'benevolent hegemony'. It would not be based upon business needs, a narrow understanding of the national interest, or the amoral calculus of *realpolitik*. Instead, it was to be informed by moral considerations and a broad understanding of both US needs and the contemporary world order:

> If America refrains from shaping this order, we can be sure that others will shape it in ways that reflect neither our interests nor our values ... The

decision Americans need to make is whether the United States should generally lean forward, as it were, or sit back. A strategy aimed at preserving
American hegemony should embrace the former stance, being more rather
than less inclined to weigh in when crises erupt, and preferably before they
erupt.[26]

This approach led those committed to 'national greatness conservatism'
to argue that the USA should have challenged Chinese ambitions and its
repression of dissidents much more overtly. It should also, they said, have
brought about the downfall of Saddam Hussein and intervened more deci-
sively, and at an earlier stage, in the former Yugoslavia.

This form of thinking drew its proponents towards the candidacy of
Senator John McCain rather than that of George W. Bush during the 2000
Republican presidential primaries.[27] Although there was a significant cultural
gap between the Arizona Senator and Kristol's north-eastern neo-conservat-
ism, there was a degree of political convergence. The liaison continued after
McCain conceded defeat and gave his backing to Bush. Indeed, McCain
sometimes translated the philosophy of 'national greatness conservatism' into
specific policy proposals. He distanced himself from calls for large-scale tax
reductions and instead emphasised the importance of Social Security funding.
Insofar as he backed tax cuts, he argued for mildly redistributive proposals.
In contrast with the Bush plans, McCain's scheme would have given nothing
to the wealthiest 1 per cent of the population and eliminated tax subsidies to
companies

The Republican governors

The governors, some of whom had played a part in shaping the *Contract with
America*, and the 1996 Personal Responsibility and Work Opportunity (or
welfare reform) Act, also played a part in the reshaping of Republican
thinking. Their contribution was partly a matter of political style. Although
a number of the governors, most notably George W. Bush of Texas, embraced
rigorous law and order policies, they also adopted less confrontational and
partisan forms of discourse than many in Congress. However, it was not a
matter of style alone. There were five significant policy differences between
the governors and established Republican politics.

Firstly, the governors' emphasis on the importance of welfare reform and
personal self-reliance was increasingly framed in less punitive terms than
those traditionally employed by Republicans. The references to 'welfare
queens' that had, at times, laced the GOP's rhetoric were displaced by a plea
to assist those who faced systematic forms of disadvantage.

Secondly, as Peter Beinart argued, while many of the governors sought
to end welfare as a long-term entitlement and, at the same time, cut the tax

burden, they also adopted a markedly different approach to other forms of
government provision:

> The nation's Republican governors have embraced a conservatism of easy
> answers. They have cut taxes, slashed benefits for the poor, and cracked
> down on crime. But they haven't taken on the popular spending that feeds
> the middle class: education, roads, sports stadiums, prisons, the environ-
> ment.[28]

Indeed, some of the governors increased spending on education, the
environment and the infrastructure. A report by the libertarian Cato Institute
noted there had been 'an unprecedented acceleration of state spending.
Republican governors who advertise themselves as fiscal conservatives have
been some of the worst offenders.' [29] Despite such warnings, the governors'
strategy worked well during the boom conditions of the late 1990s. However,
it hit difficulties during the economic downturn of 2001–2. Falling revenues
forced the abandonment of proposed tax cuts and led to reductions in
spending programmes.[30]

Thirdly, although the governors distanced themselves from the Congressional revolutionaries who had sought to roll back government across a broad
front, they also recognised the need for the restructuring and modernisation
of government services. In particular, they promoted educational initiatives
and urban renewal programmes. Some, such as Governor Jeb Bush of Florida,
embarked on radical reform. They tied school funding to test results and
endorsed the provision of school vouchers, enabling some parents to select
a school for their children. Jeb Bush also put forward urban renewal proposals
that rested on low-level government activism. These included small business
loans, assistance for faith-based projects, as well as drug and crime prevention
programmes.[31]

Fourthly, the governors distanced themselves from the strident moral
traditionalism of the Christian right. Although their ranks included some in
both the pro-life and pro-choice camps, neither sought to proselytise. Instead,
issues such as gay rights and abortion were downplayed as they sought to
fashion a form of Republicanism that did not prescribe a rigid moral code for
others to follow.

Fifthly, although party identifiers were overwhelmingly white, a number
of Republican governors made systematic attempts to court the minority
vote. George W. Bush, in particular, actively sought to reach out. As Boris
Johnson recorded in February 1999:

> Not only does he sloganise in Spanish. He speaks it … He makes long
> speeches full of the test score of Texan African-Americans; he calls in
> Hispanic adolescents who have learned to read successfully, and uses them
> as props for his orations.[32]

To an extent, this strategy reaped rewards. In the 1998 elections, George W. and Jeb Bush won an estimated 49 per cent and 60 per cent of the Latino vote in Texas and Florida respectively. In Michigan, John Engler attracted 28 per cent of the black vote, almost three times higher than the usual numbers of African-Americans who vote for the GOP in presidential elections across the country.[33]

'Compassionate conservatism'

George W. Bush's campaign for the presidency emerged against this background. It owed much, in terms of the political vocabulary that it employed, to the reforms adopted by the governors. Like both the governors and 'national greatness conservatism', it accepted that government could in some circumstances play an activist role.

Bush's campaign was underpinned by a call for 'compassionate conservatism'. Although the concept defies precise definition, it is closely associated with the work of Marvin Olasky, a professor of journalism at the University of Texas at Austin. He argued that assistance to those in need – through, for example, poverty, drug abuse, mental illness – should be undertaken through faith-based and community organisations rather than government agencies. They could, Olasky asserted, offer more effective and lasting solutions. This was because voluntary organisations would work in a personal and intensive way. Individuals would not simply be regarded as members of a particular category. Furthermore, he argued, there would be a growth in active citizenship. Voluntary initiative would encourage individuals to become more involved in their neighbourhoods and communities.

Olasky's next step was to ask how faith-based and voluntary organisations could be helped. His first answer echoed a familiar conservative tone. Government should, he asserted, pursue a deregulatory policy so as to eliminate the barriers that voluntary and faith-based initiatives often faced. He wanted, as he put it, to see the 'calling off the regulatory dogs'.[34] However, he went beyond this. He asserted the principle of subsidiarity in the provision of assistance. If the family or neighbourhood did not have the resources to help those needing assistance, there was a place for government backing and assistance. The federal government should, however, only become involved if the other tiers of government – at city, county and state level – are unable to respond in an appropriate way. It should work by backing the activities of voluntary organisations rather than directly intervening itself. However, so as to protect the independence of faith-based and community groups, this is most effectively undertaken, Olasky asserted, by establishing tax credits or, failing that, the introduction of voucher systems, enabling the 'consumer' to select a provider. Direct grants by government to voluntary organisations were, he said, the least desirable option.

Although compassionate conservatism was criticised by some commentators for its opaque character, it had three defining characteristics. Firstly, in contrast to some of the notions that underpinned the *Contract with America*, the proponents of compassionate conservatism saw a positive role for government. It was not regarded as simply an economic and political burden. It had a part to play because markets did not clear in all circumstances. According to Steve Goldsmith, a Bush domestic adviser and Mayor of Indianapolis:

> It is the marketplace which creates value, but there are individuals for whom the marketplace isn't working, and there is a role for government in facilitating opportunity inside the marketplace.[35]

In George W. Bush's words, government could play an 'effective and energetic' role. Secondly, compassionate conservatism suggested that the relationship between the apparatus of government and civil society should not be represented as a zero-sum game in which government activity inevitably displaced the actions of private individuals and civic groupings. There could instead be a complementary relationship based upon mutual cooperation. Thirdly, reform was not to be motivated by either punitive or fiscal concerns. Indeed, the delivery of services through voluntary initiative would not necessarily reduce the burden upon the government budget and the taxpayer. As Olasky noted: 'I don't see a likelihood of great reductions in expenditures anytime soon.'[36]

The call for 'compassionate conservatism' was shaped, at least in part, by popular opinion. It corresponded to the concerns of the period. In the mid-1990s, Robert Putnam of Harvard University attracted considerable attention with the publication of the article, 'Bowling Alone', in the *Journal of Democracy*.[37] It charted the decline of traditionally important civic and voluntary organisations. US society had, he argued, become more fragmented and individuals were increasingly isolated. This, he said, was leading to lower levels of social capital and less vibrant forms of democracy. *Bowling Alone* led to calls from across the political spectrum for civic re-engagement. By speaking of active citizenship, compassionate conservatism corresponded with these sentiments.

However, there were also political considerations. Compassionate conservatism not only provided a distinguishing hallmark for Bush that marked him out from other Republican contenders during the primaries and caucuses, but it also had a role in the general election campaign. The phrase 'compassionate conservatism' itself is significant. As David Frum has observed, 'it combines the left's favorite adjective with the right's favorite noun'.[38] It thereby broadened Bush's appeal to moderate voters, a significant proportion of whom had backed Clinton. In particular, it enabled Bush to seek higher levels of support from Roman Catholic voters.

British conservatism

In the aftermath of the British Conservatives' 1997 defeat, the need for a policy rethink was widely accepted. Given the magnitude of their losses, few thought that a swing of the political pendulum would alone bring electoral victory, even after two terms in opposition. Instead, it was argued, the party had to distance itself from the ideological legacy of Thatcherism and seek out policy alternatives.

Against this background, the Bush strategy and the concept of 'compassionate conservatism' held four political attractions. Firstly, the use of the term could enable the Conservatives to recapture a vocabulary that had been, for much of the 1990s, the property of Labour and the left. Secondly, it could be used to address issues such as criminality in terms that supplanted simple calls for punitive measures. It thereby had an appeal that extended beyond the party's core constituencies. Thirdly, 'compassionate conservatism' represented a means by which the party could distance itself from its associations with untrammelled individualism. For many, the spiritual essence of the Thatcher years had been captured in her celebrated claim that there was 'no such thing as society'. In place of this, compassionate conservatism was tied to forms of public policy that sought the restoration of the social fabric. It held out the promise of civic renewal, community regeneration and the strengthening of family networks. Lastly, although compassionate conservatism had some originality as a slogan, it also rested on themes, such as the overweening powers of government, that corresponded closely with the traditional concerns of the party's most loyal supporters.

At times, there were signs that compassionate conservatism was being embraced. By 1999, William Hague seemed to be talking in the same terms as George W. Bush. As Johnson noted:

> Mr Hague extols the 'little platoons', the churches, the charities which he hopes will step in to the areas of care in danger of state monopoly. Mr Bush talks about the 'little armies' ... Mr Hague speaks of social entrepreneurs; Mr Bush speaks of educational entrepreneurs.[39]

Hague's trip to the US in February 1999 was trailed as an attempt to learn from, and understand, compassionate conservatism. His schedule included meetings with Bush, New York City mayor, Rudolph Guiliani, Marvin Olasky and Myron Magnet, author of *The Dream and the Nightmare* which emphasised the close association between individual values and poverty.[40] Sixteen months later, Hague met Olasky again in London and, in October 2000, Hague launched the party's Renewing One Nation team. It promised to 'build relationships with charities, voluntary groups, churches and other faith communities who have frontline experience of rebuilding community life in every corner of our country'.[41] Hague accompanied this with a commitment to 'denationalise compassion'.[42] He also issued a pledge to establish an Office of Civil Society which would be headed by a Cabinet minister.

Nonetheless, these initiatives had only limited significance. Hague returned to Britain talking in terms of 'kitchen table conservatism' rather than 'compassionate conservatism'. The phrase had Canadian rather than US origins. In 1995, the Progressive Conservative Party in Ontario built its election platform on the basis of both formal and informal meetings across the province. Speaking in Toronto, Hague drew conclusions from the Canadian experience:

> In the town halls, living rooms and around the kitchen tables of Ontario Mike Harris [the Progressive Conservative Party leader] went to hear the people of the Province tell him what they thought. This wasn't an electoral gimmick, it was a vital part of putting his Conservatives in touch with the people who support they wanted. We too are determined to be a listening party.[43]

The imprecision of 'listening' was followed by the adoption of populist themes. As the general election came into sight, Conservative frontbenchers talked of lower taxes, individual freedom, smaller government, opposition to the European single currency and a commitment to renegotiate a number of European Union treaties. They also highlighted the case of Tony Martin, the Norfolk farmer who shot an intruder, and emphasised the growing numbers seeking asylum in Britain. In all, as Collings and Seldon have ruefully concluded, 'Hague let policy bob around like a buoy in a choppy sea.'[44]

Why did Hague pull back from compassionate conservatism? His decision to appears to have stemmed from three considerations. Firstly there was a fear, as opinion polls continued to show a large Labour lead, that the party was losing the allegiance of its core constituencies. There was little scope for radical or untried policy initiatives. Secondly, there were doubts about the extent to which Bush's thinking had a relevance to British politics. Nick Kent, a Tory Reform Group vice-chairman and Andrew Marshall, an executive member, argued that compassionate conservatism rested on the minimalist notions of government that formed the basis of US political culture. In countries such as Britain, individuals expected government to play a much more important role in the provision of education, welfare and health care. Such responsibilities could not be handed to charities and faith-based organisations. Much more, they suggested, could be learned from Bush's attempts to win the votes of women and minorities. They pointed to his embrace of 'tolerance' and his efforts to dissociate himself from the unrestrained 'materialism' of earlier years. The Conservative Party could also, they said, make electoral inroads if it asserted its opposition to prejudice much more vigorously and adopted a more visionary approach to issues such as education.[45]

Thirdly, Hague's ability to impose a radical restructuring of the party's goals was constrained by ideological differences within the parliamentary party. Although political circumstances drew many influential Conservatives towards 'post-Thatcherism', there were different priorities and emphases. Indeed, some observers felt that prominent frontbenchers were pursuing their own distinct and personalised agendas (which were tied in some instances to post-election ambitions) and there was a reluctance to rally behind a single banner. In April 1999, Peter Lilley spoke of limits to the efficacy of market mechanisms. While leaving open the possibility of 'internal markets', he ruled out the privatisation of education and health as policy options. Indeed, he committed the party to higher levels of public spending on them.[46] Further-more, it became known that Lilley had originally intended to go further and had planned to suggest that important public services were 'intrinsically unsuited to delivery by the market'.[47] Significant numbers of MPs were antagonised by these assertions which some represented as an accommodation to entrenched interests in the health and education sectors. For his part, Michael Portillo had, from 1997 onwards, talked of adopting a more concil-iatory approach towards groups such as lone mothers, unmarried couples and the trades unions. He was increasingly described as a 'libertarian' and, in some representations, pitted against the 'authoritarian' wing of the party. At the same time, David Willetts spoke of civic conservatism. Conservatives, he asserted, must champion civil society as well as the market. He referred to the importance of community, tradition and neighbourhood.[48] There were also differences about the rate of change that was required. While some advised gradualism, others within Conservative Central Office called for an 'electric shock' comparable with Tony Blair's successful bid to rewrite Clause IV of Labour's Constitution.

However, in the aftermath of the 2001 defeat, there was some evidence that leading Conservatives were again prepared to look across the Atlantic. Iain Duncan Smith visited the US in early December 2001. His engagements included a meeting with George Pataki, governor of New York state. On his return, Duncan Smith commended Pataki's efforts in reforming welfare provision through workfare whereby recipients work in return for public assistance. He also paid tribute to the Republican Party's presidential campaign:

> Yet Bush turned the Clinton–Blair tide and a center right renaissance now crackles through the autumnal air in Washington. He did it by boldly invading territory once seen as the Left's ... Bush took the fight to the enemy and campaigned on issues such as education and welfare reform. It paid off for him; I believe it will pay off for British Conservatives.[49]

Using themes drawn from the Republican governors and the Bush campaign, Duncan Smith argued that the language employed by Conserva-tives had to take a positive form and shift away from the expenditure cuts that welfare reform might generate. In place of this, it should emphasise the provision of greater security and self-esteem for those in poverty. Duncan Smith built upon this in March 2002. Citing conditions in a Glasgow housing estate, he called for the adoption of a strategy directed towards the most 'vulnerable' sections of the population. *The Times* noted that 'it might have been George W. Bush himself addressing the Tory faithful in Harrogate'.[50]

Conclusion

George W. Bush's embrace of 'compassionate conservatism' was a conscious effort to distance himself from the forms of conservatism that had defined Republican thinking earlier in the decade. In particular, Bush sought to distinguish himself from the politics that had underpinned the *Contract with America* and the moralism of the religious right. He drew instead upon themes that had been pursued by the Republican governors, although in contrast with the policies that were adopted at state level, compassionate conservatism did not depict community and faith-based provision for the poor as an opportunity to reduce overall expenditure levels.

This strategy, Al Gore's failings, and the mathematics of the Electoral College, placed Bush in the White House. To what extent can British Conservatives emulate his success? Although there are few specific policy commitments, Duncan Smith has adopted some of the vocabulary associated with Bush and some of the Republican governors. There are, however, formidable obstacles if the party's leadership seeks to embrace 'compassionate conservatism' more fully. Portillo's failure to secure a place in the final round of voting for the leadership bid suggests that many of the party's MPs may be reluctant to make a radical break with the past. More importantly, the character of the contemporary Labour Party should be considered. In Gore, George W. Bush faced an opponent who abandoned some of the political territory that had been taken by Clinton and instead turned to themes associated with the Democratic Party's traditions. At times, the Gore campaign had a populist edge as he turned against corporate interests.

New Labour and 'Blairism' are different. They have not only broken with earlier forms of labourism, they also owe relatively little to the traditions of either social democracy or European Christian Democrats. Instead, there are close parallels between Blair's thinking and that of Bush and a number of the Republican governors. There is, for example, common ground in terms of proposals for welfare reform, the modernisation of education, conceptions of active citizenship and the adoption of a 'tough love' approach to those in need.[51] If the Conservatives choose to follow in Bush's footsteps, they face the problem that, although there is a gap (that may yet widen) between the rhetorical aspirations of Blairism and its achievements, much of the ideological space associated with 'compassionate conservatism' is already occupied.

Notes

1 H. S. Parmet, *George Bush: The Life of a Lone Star Yankee* (New York, Scribner, 1997), p. 508.

2 D. Balz and R. Brownstein, *Storming the Gates: Protest Politics and the Republican Revival* (Boston, Little, Brown & Company, 1996), p. 119.

3 N. Ashford, 'The Contract and beyond: the Republican policy agenda', in A. Grant (ed.), *American Politics: 2000 and Beyond* (Aldershot, Ashgate, 2000), p. 169.

4 CNN. com, *Political races*, http://cgi. cnn. com/ALLPOLITICS/1996/candidates/republican/dole/political. career/

5 National Election Studies, *The NES Guide to Public Opinion and Electoral Behavior: Trust in Federal Government 1958–1998*, www.umich.edu/~nes/nesguide/toptable/tab5a_1.htm.

6 E. C. Ladd and K. H. Bowman, *What's Wrong: A Survey of American Satisfaction and Complaint* (Washington DC, The AEI Press, 1998), p. 95.

7 G. M. Pomper, 'The presidential election', in G. M. Pomper *et al.*, *The Election of 1992* (Chatham, Chatham House, 1993), p. 133.

8 Balz and Brownstein, *Storming the Gates*, p. 178.

9 Parmet, *George Bush*, p. 470.

10 E. Drew, *Showdown: The Struggle between the Gingrich Congress and the Clinton White House* (New York, Simon & Schuster, 1977), p. 33.

11 G. M. Pomper, 'The presidential election', in G. M. Pomper *et al.*, *The Election of 1996: Reports and Interpretations* (Chatham, Chatham House, 1997), p. 187.

12 B. Sinclair, 'The president as legislative leader', in C. Campbell and B. A. Rockman (eds), *The Clinton Legacy* (New York, Chatham House/Seven Bridges Press, 2000), p. 86.

13 J. Owens, 'Congress after the "Revolution": the continuing problems of governance in a partisan era', in Grant (ed.), *American Politics*, p. 51.

14 W. G. Mayer, 'The presidential nominations', in Pomper *et al.*, *The Election of 1996*, p. 52.

15 Balz and Brownstein, *Storming the Gates*, p. 311.

16 R. Reed, *After the Revolution: How the Christian Coalition is Impacting America* (Dallas, Word Publishing, 1996), p. 110.

17 M. Durham, 'The Christian right in American politics', in Grant (ed.), *American Politics*, p. 151.

18 Reed, *After the Revolution*, pp. 226–33.

19 R. Reed, *Active Faith: How Christians are Changing the Soul of American Politics* (New York, The Free Press, 1996), p. 246.

20 D. Milbank, 'Religious right finds its center in Oval Office', *Washington Post*, 24 December 2001.

21 J. W. Wright (ed.), *The New York Times Almanac 2002* (New York, Penguin, 2001), p. 374.

22 E. Ashbee, '"Remoralization": American society and politics in the 1990s', *Political Quarterly*, 71:2 (2000) 192–201.

23 Quoted in B. Kolasky, 'Issue of the week: a whole lot of talking going on', *SpeakOut. com*, 2 October 1997, http://speakout. com/activism/opinions/4834–1. html.

24 W. Kristol and D. Brooks, 'What ails conservatism?', *Wall Street Journal*, 15 September 1997.

25 D. Brooks, 'TR's Greatness: Edmund Morris's return to Teddy Roosevelt', *Weekly Standard*, 7:1, 19 November 2001.

26 W. Kristol and R. Kagan, 'Introduction: national interest and global responsibility',

in R. Kagan and W. Kristol (eds), *Present Dangers: Crisis and Opportunity in American Foreign and Defense Policy* (San Francisco, Encounter Books, 2000), pp. 12–14.

27 F. Foer, 'Great escape: how Bill Kristol ditched conservatism', *New Republic*, 28 May 2001.

28 P. Beinart, 'Republican heartthrobs', *New Republic*, 28 December 1998, p. 28.

29 Beinart, 'Republican heartthrobs', p. 28.

30 B. Maddox, 'Governors running scared', *The Times*, 30 January 2002.

31 C. Rapp, 'Gentle Jeb', *National Review*, 26 October 1998, p. 38.

32 B. Johnson, 'Hague seeks out Texan Bushman for magic formula', *Daily Telegraph*, 13 February 1999.

33 Tony Snow, 'GOP gubernatorial gusto', *Washington Times*, 23 November 1998.

34 M. Olasky, 'What is compassionate conservatism and can it transform America?', Heritage Lectures, 24 July 2000 (Washington DC, The Heritage Foundation), www. heritage.org/Research/PoliticalPhilosophy/loader.cfm?url=/commonspot/security/get file.cfm&PageID=12644 (accessed January 2003).

35 Quoted in N. Ashford, 'George W. Bush and compassionate conservatism: rhetoric or substance', *IPA Review*, 51:3 (1999), 10.

36 M. Olasky, 'What is compassionate conservatism?'.

37 R. D. Putnam, 'Bowling alone: America's declining social capital', *Journal of Democracy*, 6:1 (January 1995), http://muse.jhu.edu/demo/journal_of_democracy/v006/put-nam.html.

38 Quoted in C. R. Kesler, *The Dilemmas of Compassionate Conservatism*, The Claremont Institute, www.claremont.org/publications/kesler991122.cfm.

39 B. Johnson, 'Hague seeks out Texan Bushman for magic formula', *Daily Telegraph*, 13 February 1999.

40 R. Shrimsley, 'Hague to learn from Bush Jnr', *Daily Telegraph*, 24 November 1998; T. Harnden, 'Hague's gamble as he heaps praise on Bush', *Daily Telegraph*, 1 August 2000; and M. Magnet, *The Dream and the Nightmare: The Sixties' Legacy to the Underclass* (San Francisco, Encounter Books, 2000).

41 *Renewing Civil Society: How Conservatives will empower Britain's good neighbours*: www.renewingonenation.com.

42 W. Hague (2000), 'Values for the Twenty-First Century', Speech to the Policy Forum with Britain's Faith Communities, 1 November.

43 W. Hague (1999), *Common Sense Conservatism*, The Albany Club, Toronto.

44 D. Collings and A. Seldon, 'Conservatives in opposition', *Parliamentary Affairs*, 54:4 (2001), 628.

45 N. Kent and A. Marshall (n. d.), *Compassionate Conservatism: Myth or Mirage*, Tory Reform Group, www.trg.org.uk/publications/compassionateconservatism.html.

46 *The Economist*, 22 April 1999.

47 R. Shrimsley, 'Election test for move to shed Thatcher', *Daily Telegraph*, 28 April 1999.

48 'David Willetts reshuffles Toryism', *The Economist*, 4 June 1998.

49 I. Duncan Smith, 'My Manhattan project for a transatlantic conservative revival', *The Times*, 3 December 2001.

50 B. Macintyre, 'Duncan Smith takes a leaf from Bush', *The Times*, 25 March 2002.

51 T. Hames, 'Blair is now more akin to Bush than to Clinton', *The Times*, 28 September 2001.

3

Win or bust: the leadership gamble of William Hague

Mark Garnett

Writing in 1977, Conservative MP Nigel Fisher identified 'two qualifying conditions' for Tory leaders: 'a lengthy spell in Parliament and considerable Cabinet experience'. In combination, he thought these factors 'make it unlikely that in future anyone will become leader of the party at an early age. There will be no more William Pitts'. Fisher's timing could hardly have been more ironic. The 1977 Conservative Party conference saw the emergence of a new oratorical prodigy. As the delegates stood to applaud the sixteen-year-old William Hague, Lord Carrington whispered to his neighbour, 'If he's like that now, what on earth will he be like in 20 years time?'. 'Michael Heseltine?' quipped Norman St John-Stevas.[1]

Twenty years after that exchange Heseltine had finally relinquished his fierce ambition to lead the Conservatives. Hague had only been in Parliament for eight years, and instead of 'considerable Cabinet experience' he had occupied the lowly office of Secretary of State for Wales only since July 1995. But he had been more fortunate than Heseltine – or at least that was how it seemed at the time of the 1997 party conference. At thirty-four he had become the youngest Tory Cabinet minister since Winston Churchill, and now he had been elected Conservative leader, beating Kenneth Clarke on the second ballot of his party's MPs by ninety-two votes to seventy. Admittedly, the Younger Pitt had become Prime Minister at twenty-four, after learning the ropes as Chancellor of the Exchequer for just a year. But the comparison was made, although Hague's unkinder critics put their own spin on this, dubbing him 'William Squitt'.

Fisher's judgement is only one of many ill-fated generalisations about the nature of Tory leadership. The dictum that loyalty to a leader was the Conservative Party's secret weapon was repeated so often that it lapsed into a cliché. But it had never been true. Before the advent of economic liberalism the Tory Party believed in hierarchy, so it was hardly a surprise that its members should place special emphasis on the leadership role. But the same doctrine suggested that when a leader seemed unequal to the exalted task, deposition could be regarded as a duty rather than a crime. Despite the supposed sanctity of the office, almost all of the party's twentieth-century leaders were subjected to serious pressure or plotting. The introduction of leadership elections only formalised this tradition. Almost as soon as the rules were devised, in 1965, Alec Douglas-Home bowed to backbench opinion and resigned. Edward Heath was unceremoniously defenestrated in 1975, and his supplanter, Margaret Thatcher, suffered the same fate in 1990. When John Major submitted himself to re-election in 1995 he was hardly threatening to jump before he was pushed; he had been ushered towards an open window almost continuously since the 1992 general election. Instead of rallying around their figurehead – or even treating his plight with a modicum of sympathy – many Conservatives stepped up their disobedience at the first sight of Major's blood. One of his chief tormenters, Iain Duncan Smith, was rewarded after the 2001 general election, when he seized the crown himself. There was a precedent even for this: in 1922 Austen Chamberlain – the only twentieth-century leader besides Hague who never reached 10 Downing Street – was replaced by Andrew Bonar Law, who had wielded the knife against him.

On the basis of recent experience, at least, Conservative leaders are actually less secure than their Labour (or Liberal Democrat) counterparts, whether they are in opposition or in office. A general decline in deference throughout British society has affected them more than their rivals; in part, at least, this must be a product of the 'sturdy individualism' which so many party members now exhibit in practice and endorse in theory. Although some post-war Labour leaders were worried about faction-fighting to the point of paranoia, none of them left office as a direct result of party pressure. Hugh Gaitskell saw off challenges in 1960 and 1961 with surprising ease, considering that the party had suffered a demoralising election defeat on his watch. In fact, Gaitskell's record is comparable in some ways to that of Hague. After taking over from Clement Attlee in December 1955 he had almost four years to restore his party's fortunes from the position he inherited – an overall Conservative majority of fifty-eight. But after the 1959 general election the deficit between the government and the opposition parties had grown to 100 seats; Labour's tally had actually fallen by nineteen. When other factors are considered this was arguably a worse performance than the Conservatives in 2001. But while Gaitskell soldiered on, Hague hurriedly fell on his sword.

It is perfectly respectable to claim that the result in 2001 would have been the same whatever Hague had done. No one can be sure that the Conservatives would have fared better under a different leader – although it would have been interesting to see how Kenneth Clarke might have exploited the fuel crisis of September 2000. Equally, no one can argue that Hague was an electoral asset to his party. Throughout the Parliament he trailed his party in the opinion polls, sometimes by considerable margins. In April 2001 less than half of Conservative voters thought that their own leader would make the best Prime Minister – the figure for the electorate as a whole was 14 per cent, and later it fell even further.[2] Whatever his impact on the result, seen from his own perspective the period of Hague's leadership was an almost unmitigated disaster. Probably the only silver lining was his marriage in December 1997, although some took a cynical view of this opportune visit from Cupid.

Hague's rivals in the 1997 leadership contest – Clarke, John Redwood, Peter Lilley and Michael Howard – were all at least ten years older than him, and although the vacancy left by Major was not necessarily the last throw of the dice for any of them they would have been foolish to avoid a contest at that time. By contrast, Hague could afford to be a spectator of this race. Given his relative youth, there was no need for him even to campaign on behalf of any of the candidates. Provided that he stood back and made emollient noises about everyone, he could expect a senior Shadow Cabinet post from the winner, whoever this turned out to be. While someone else had a go – and hopefully made a start on the task of taming what sometimes seemed to be an unleadable party – he could quietly build his reputation in advance of a challenge at some convenient moment over the next decade.

Reasons for running

Given the Tory Party's ruthlessness towards failed leaders, Hague's decision to stand in the unpropitious circumstances of 1997 requires some explanation. First, he could be forgiven for underestimating the challenges of the top job within his party, given his untroubled passage through the lower ranks. Even if memories of the 1977 speech had dogged Hague throughout his campaign in the 1989 Richmond by-election, his colleagues in the parliamentary party soon formed a different impression of him. Almost immediately he was recruited by the 'Third Term Group' of MPs which was based on friendship rather than ideology. He seemed as shrewd as he was clubbable. Norman Lamont, then Chief Secretary to the Treasury, picked him as his Parliamentary Private Secretary on the basis of advice from Lord Jopling – an excellent judge – and just one private conversation. Lamont had been warned that Hague was too young for such a responsible job, and for a relative newcomer to the Commons the challenge was redoubled when his boss became Chancellor of the Exchequer. But Hague proved to be competent and wholly reliable from the start. After 'Black Wednesday' there was no question that he would be sent into the wilderness with Lamont; and he excelled as a junior minister at the Department of Social Security from May 1993 to July 1995. As he prepared for his first Cabinet meeting as Secretary of State for Wales he could look back on an ascent which had been swift, but not unduly precipitate. A few years in a more prominent role would complete the uphill work, and also efface the public memory of the 'Tory Boy' speech which was still the only image that allowed the electorate to connect his face with a name.

At Wales, Hague won more admirers, although his predecessor John Redwood sneered that the 'very old baby' compromised too readily with pressure groups and allowed himself to be dominated by his civil servants.[3] In fact by ruffling so many feathers during his own stint – and inviting public ridicule with his incompetent attempt to mime the words of the Welsh national anthem – Redwood had greatly simplified Hague's task. He was not widely blamed when his party failed to win a single seat in Wales in the 1997 general election – another stroke of misleading luck for Hague.

Probably it was this run of good fortune which convinced Hague that he was already too prominent within the party to take on the role of interested bystander in this contest. According to his biographer, he had instantly calculated that he would win if he stood.[4] But in the initial stages it looked as if he would throw in his lot with Howard. He was right to break off this connection almost before it had started; the mistake was to have entertained the unpromising proposal in the first place. Howard had offered him the post of Deputy Leader and the party chairmanship. The first of these was of doubtful advantage, and the second was a positive menace. If the party did well at the next election Howard would have taken most of the credit, leaving him well placed to run for another parliamentary term at least. If it under-performed, Chairman Hague would have made a convenient scapegoat.

Hague's well-founded conviction that the leadership was his for the taking was heavily influenced by the knowledge that two powerful rivals – Heseltine and Michael Portillo – were out of the reckoning. Another key consideration was that he had fewer enemies than any of his potential rivals. Actually his sudden emergence as a promising dark horse in the race should have made him think twice before entering the stalls. He was acceptable to so many of his colleagues because unlike the other candidates he had not alienated either wing of his divided party. This had been the main attraction of Major back in 1990 – hardly an auspicious precedent for Hague. Redwood's supporters underlined the resemblance during the leadership campaign, refer-ring to Hague as 'John Major with A levels'.[5] Whatever their personal qualities, both men only prospered in the middle of the road because they were relatively unexposed; longer service in the top ranks would almost certainly have confronted them with an issue which would have forced them to side openly with one Euro-faction or the other.

Any remaining feeling that Hague was jumping the gun with this early challenge seems to have been dispelled by some excitable friends (a recurrent theme in this story). Given the fate of recent Tory leaders, the decision to run placed Hague among those party members who saw Labour's victory – or at least its unprecedented extent – as something of a freak. Obviously he had confidence in his own abilities, but a respectable Conservative comeback also depended on other factors. Even if New Labour proved as incompetent in office as sanguine Tories expected, Hague was staking everything on a run of adverse publicity for a government whose media machine had won his (undeserved) admiration. And he also needed the 1997 Liberal Democrat surge – fuelled by tactical voting which looked likely to become even more popular – to stop dead. In short, he needed to perform abnormally well, and everyone else to flop badly, if he were even to claw back a sufficient proportion of Labour's lead to make it worthwhile continuing the fight.

Personnel mismanagement

Thus it could be predicted in advance that the circumstances which helped Hague to the top might push him down without a spectacular run of good luck. But he was genuinely unlucky with the Portillo factor. There was always a chance that 'the Future of the Right' (as his admiring biographer had prematurely hailed him[6]) would return to the Commons when a suitable vacancy arose. What Hague could not anticipate was that Alan Clark would die in September 1999 and present Portillo with a seat which was both high profile and ultra-safe, ensuring that his campaign would inspire comparisons between the candidate and the man who had taken the position which had looked to be reserved for him before Stephen Twigg intervened in May 1997.

The real nightmare scenario would have arisen had Portillo won a by-election in a Labour marginal – however unlikely that prospect was for any representative of a party which had failed to gain a seat since 1982. But the contest in Kensington and Chelsea, with all its attendant circumstances, was almost as bad for Hague. After Portillo returned to the Commons the leader and his aides worked themselves up unnecessarily over trivial (and imagined) slights. But it was always going to be difficult to cope with a colleague who had already inspired something of a personality cult within the party, even before he began his personal epiphany after his shock defeat at Enfield, Southgate. And once Portillo was installed as Shadow Chancellor it was always likely that he would use his authority to revise or abandon at least some of the policies he inherited. So Hague had to retreat from pledges with which he was closely identified: on the minimum wage, an independent central bank and the guarantee that taxes would fall as a proportion of national income over the next Parliament.

Despite occasional attempts to appear relaxed in Portillo's company, Hague's resentment was all too obvious. His maladroit handling of the reshuffle which accommodated Portillo in the Shadow Cabinet revealed the extent to which the comeback had caught him off-balance. Hague had managed to offend both Francis Maude, who was moved sideways to shadow Foreign Affairs, and John Maples, who was dropped as a result. This was only one example of Hague's miscalculations over enemies and friends. Perhaps he had no alternative but to sack Viscount Cranborne for insubordination in December 1998. But Cranborne had negotiated an excellent compromise over House of Lords reform – a deal, furthermore, which could have been very embarrassing to Blair – and he had only felt compelled to work behind his leader's back because his position was opposed by Shadow Ministers who had very limited expertise on this issue. His peremptory dismissal of Cranborne – a widely respected figure – presented an interesting contrast to the fate of Jeffrey Archer. Even without the warnings of Sir Timothy Kitson and Michael Crick, Hague should have known that Archer was an impossible candidate for London Mayor – but that if he sought the party's nomination he would win it. Obviously Hague had to say something on Archer's behalf once the selection-process was over; but he made the worst of a bad job by applauding the candidate's 'integrity'. And after messing up over Archer, Hague promptly compounded his crime by antagonising the obvious substitute, Steven Norris.[7]

Hague has even less excuse for his treatment of other senior figures. Like Sir Walter Raleigh in *1066 And All That*, many of his old Cabinet colleagues were despatched for the offence of being left over from the last reign. Talent was not so plentiful on the Tory benches that people like Redwood, Howard, Lilley and Gillian Shephard could safely be evicted in one fell swoop; after all, neither Clarke, Heseltine (nor Major himself) could be recalled to the colours. If the purged politicians were judged guilty by association with failure, Hague himself was not free from the taint. Hague's media supremo Amanda Platell is said to have rated the original frontbenchers 'as dreary second-raters'; but their replacements were either unknown to the public, or all too prominent, like Portillo.[8] Hague seemed an isolated figure by the time of his resignation, and this was at least in part because so many of his best-known colleagues had left the front bench. Before his election Hague had proved himself to be a good team-player, with nothing of the loner in his personal make-up; but his decisions on personnel helped to ensure an excessive and unwelcome concentration on himself during the 2001 election campaign. This would have been a problem anyway, since most commentators expected a comfortable Labour victory and were inevitably tempted to speculate about Hague's own position after the election. But the situation was a sharp contrast to 1970, when Edward Heath had led a well-known supporting cast of Shadow Ministers who could share the spotlight. On that occasion only Enoch Powell of the party's heavyweights had been missing.

The overall impression of Hague's dealings with colleagues of stature is one of insecurity. He seemed happiest with his small coterie of over-protective intimates, notably Platell, his youthful private secretary, George Osborne, and his Chief of Staff, Sebastian Coe. He demonstrated his capacity for unyielding loyalty where they were concerned, as if to compensate for his ruthlessness in discarding weightier colleagues. Although Hague was unlikely to heed Teresa Gorman when she urged him to spend less time with Coe (compared by the maverick MP to 'a parrot on your shoulder'[9]), he must have realised that he would be damaged by the impression that his closest confidants were people who owed their standing in the party entirely to his favour and friendship. Tales of Hague's feats with Coe on the judo mat could only have improved his image if the public respected him already. As it was, they inspired as much ridicule as Hague's naive revelation of preternatural drinking prowess. There was always a feeling that Hague's team was obsessed by his negative poll ratings, and were willing to try anything to change them. But Heath had been less popular than his party for most of the 1966–70 Parliament, and this had not prevented a Conservative victory. If the media had decided that Hague was a loser – exemplified in the *Sun*'s portrayal of him as a dead parrot – the only way to persuade them otherwise was to wait for a suitable opportunity to showcase his 'statesmanlike' qualities.

The Hague entourage performed abysmally over Maude and Portillo. They were old friends, and despite the botched reshuffle nothing had happened to break their existing alliance. But Hague's circle interpreted their continuing amity as a symptom of conspiracy – the itch to copy New Labour was so rampant with them that they talked wildly of secret pacts cemented in high-class restaurants – and the overt hostility was the surest way of making a reality of their fears. Some of Hague's early decisions – the photo-call at the Notting Hill Carnival, his antics in a baseball cap at an amusement park, and his backing for a short-lived campaign to rename Heathrow Airport after Diana, Princess of Wales – were attributed to the urgings of others. At best, this only underlined the impression that Hague had an erratic judgement both of people and of advice. His choice of Cecil Parkinson as his first Party Chairman was one of his few successes; despite his anxiety to emulate Labour's 'modernisers' and make all things new, he had the nous to exploit Parkinson's experience and his popularity at Central Office. But Parkinson was yoked uncomfortably with Archie Norman, whose success in the Asda supermarket chain was far less suitable than he thought for reviving the organisation of a venerable political party. In his obsession with New Labour, Norman outranked even Hague himself.

Since Hague's dealings with his colleagues have been chronicled in undignified detail – including what are purported to be verbatim accounts in Simon Walters' *Tory Wars* – possibly in hindsight his record looks worse than it really was. But at the time it seemed bad enough. Especially after the advent of Portillo, his image always seemed to be projected against a background of bickering. On this front, at least, his leadership gamble had backfired for predictable reasons. He had not earned enough authority over his parliamentary colleagues (let alone the public) to prepare the ground for a successful leadership. Again, the example of John Major should have been instructive here. Perhaps Hague thought that the people who had made Major's period in office so difficult had all defected to the Referendum Party in 1997. In fact they were more likely to have stayed with the Conservatives for another round of blood-letting; despairing moderates were far more likely to leave. Hague himself had shown back in 1977 that the Tories loved a bit of *lese-majeste*. Yet, although his reforms gave ordinary members more of the appearance than the reality of power (see Chapter 5), these gestures to appease grass roots activists were never balanced by a concerted attempt to exert his authority as leader. The overall impression is that of someone for whom events just moved too fast from the moment that he decided to spurn Howard's pact.

Problems with policy

One of the few advantages of opposition is the chance it offers for a renewal of party thinking. But, if anything, Hague's record on policy looks even less impressive than his dealings with colleagues. Despite the internal reforms, policy making was still dominated by the frontbench team, and by the leader in particular. By the time of the 2001 general election Hague's penchant for populist announcements had earned him a new derisive nickname – 'Billy Bandwagon'.

But it had all looked far more promising at the outset. The 1997 party conference was dominated by Hague's decision to exclude the possibility that Britain would join the single currency, at least during the ensuing Parliament. This time Hague was unlucky because everything went misleadingly well in the short term. The policy was rejected by Clarke, Heseltine and other pro-Europeans; Ian Taylor, David Curry and Stephen Dorrell left the Shadow Cabinet in response. But their protests merely drew attention to their lack of support within the party, and that tended to be the story picked up by the media. Hague's decision was nicely calculated to appease the troublesome Euro-sceptics, and maybe to entice some 1997 defectors back to the fold on the (doubtful) assumption that the Referendum Party had cost the Conservatives dearly. An overwhelming vote of support in an unprecedented party ballot consolidated Hague's tactical success. In the early stages of his general election campaign in May 2001 he was confident enough in his policy to risk ridicule by holding up a pound coin, imploring his audience to join him in a last-ditch effort to 'save' a piece of metal which was itself of fairly recent provenance.

The immediate response of Hague's critics was that he was trying to dupe the electorate into thinking that the referendum promised by Labour was a foregone conclusion. This in itself was a wounding argument, which exposed Hague's secret fear that the election would prove to be his own last chance to campaign on the euro. But the problem was even worse than this. Intoxicated by the apparent success of his policy in calming the more hysterical spirits on his right wing, Hague seems to have forgotten that his compromise was vulnerable to logical analysis. Why had he ruled out the euro for just one Parliament? Was he opposed to a single currency in principle, or might he embrace it in certain circumstances? If the latter, he seemed to be saying that these circumstances could not arise in the next five-year period – or that if everything did come right after all, he would deliberately miss the moment. If the former, why on earth did he not rule out the euro forever? In the end the piece of metal was almost irrelevant to the choices of voters in the general election. But Hague's discomfort produced one of the most telling moments of his election campaign, when his position was picked apart by Jeremy Paxman in a BBC *Newsnight* interview. Hague had been badly roughed-up by Paxman in the wake of the Cranborne sacking, and ever since then he had refused to join battle a second time. Since *Newsnight* had featured interviews with all the party leaders, Hague could not refuse forever – and at the first touch of Paxman's scalpel he suddenly looked tired and beaten.

Since his resignation, Hague has been widely criticised for basing his election campaign on the single currency, rather than the public services. Since his party had spent the whole of the previous decade talking about little else, he should not be judged too harshly for this. The mistake, no doubt, was to overrate the Conservative victory in the European Parliament election of June 1999. The turnout for that poll had been miserable; rather than flocking to the Tories disillusioned Labour voters had abstained in what they regarded as an inconsequential contest. But at least the opinion polls favoured the Conservatives on this issue; and if voters had yet to share Hague's own urgency over the euro a barnstorming campaign might shake their complacency (just as Heath's warnings about the economy seem to have registered with a rush just before the 1970 election). In any case, throughout the Parliament the Conservatives had struggled on domestic issues. At the election their disarray was underlined when a Treasury spokesman, Oliver Letwin, divulged his hopes of slashing public spending by £20 billion. The party's official wish list added up to savings of around £8 billion, and Labour was happily attacking even that. Although Tory sums were regarded as irrelevant by the electorate – who knew there was no chance that they would form a government – Letwin's dissent would have been extremely damaging during a normal election. Hague cannot be faulted for refusing to sack Letwin, who mysteriously disappeared for a while after his gaffe. But the incident would have made the party look shambolic even if it had not been faced by an organisation with an iron grip over its candidates; and Hague must take much of the blame for allowing this state of affairs to develop.

Hague's only chance of making headway on the public services had disappeared in April 1999, when Peter Lilley tried to move the party away from its Thatcherite past. Polling had revealed the obvious: the Tories were distrusted on the key areas of health and education. The only way to allay public fears was to moderate the free market rhetoric. But at the time of

Lilley's speech the ideological running within the party was being set by Hague's friend Alan Duncan – an extreme libertarian whose views on a range of subjects would have shocked Lady Thatcher herself. Since he was responsible for policy research Lilley felt that he should clear the ground for new thinking. When he discussed the speech with his leader, Hague raised no objections to what was a moderate and thoughtful text. But hawkish Shadow Cabinet colleagues, including Howard, Duncan Smith and Ann Widdecombe, were alarmed. Unfortunately for Hague and Lilley, functionaries within the party leaked the speech in advance, and spin-doctors grossly exaggerated the extent of Lilley's heresy. Possibly the grass-roots response was over-dramatised, too. The idea that ordinary members were outraged because the speech coincided with a party to celebrate the anniversary of Mrs Thatcher's first general election victory seems preposterous – unless the individuals concerned were Shadow Cabinet members who had spoken to a 'ballistic' Thatcher at the party. But Hague apparently contemplated resignation in the aftermath of Lilley's speech; the policy supremo himself rapidly returned to the backbenches.[10]

In Thatcher's shadow

Hague had good reason to be petrified of Thatcher, who during the leadership campaign had saddled him with what was perhaps the least welcome endorsement in British political history. Although an intervention from her was certain to remind the wider public of the Conservative legacy they had just rejected at the polls, a gently supportive letter in *The Times* might have helped Hague's bid among the leadership electorate – the rump of Tory MPs who had survived the 1997 general election. Unfortunately Thatcher's message was disseminated much further. Stomping around in front of the cameras, she assured the people that Hague would 'follow the kind of government I did'. She kept repeating the name of her little-known champion, giving the impression that she might forget it herself without coaching her memory (in fact, after meeting Hague she had still felt it necessary to ask Redwood the vital question: 'Is he right wing?').[11] Previously she had helped to hamstring Major by styling herself a 'backseat driver' before her successor had the chance to prove himself. This time Hague stood beside his voluble patroness with a fixed smile. Possibly at the time he did not realise that the photo-opportunity had rebounded, but he was well aware of Thatcher's destructive capabilities by the time of her 'The Mummy Returns' speech during the 2001 election campaign. His own weakness at the time of Lilley's speech had left him exposed to that unpleasant resurrection, at any time of Thatcher's choosing.[12]

The spectacular return of 'The Mummy' in person was not strictly necessary; her spirit had been directing from the passenger-seat ever since Lilley's speech. Thatcher remained an icon for 'core' Conservative voters, and an albatross for the leadership. There was no agreed change of strategy after April 1999; party planners still hoped to reach out to uncommitted voters, as well as dragging out the faithful. But in Hague himself there was an unmistakable change of emphasis. Possibly he would have tried to exploit the same issues – the Tony Martin shooting, for example, chimed in with his deep-rooted sense that an Englishman's home is his gun emplacement – but his abrasive, unapologetic tone must have been inspired by a feeling that all this would play very well with the core constituency – the people who still needed to be convinced that he was a fit successor for Thatcher. The Conservative victory in the European election, within two months of Lilley's speech, seemed to confirm that this core vote was at least more reliable than Blair's disparate support; but, as we have seen, there were obvious reasons for treating this result with great caution.

It seems that Hague was now hoping to play to two different audiences – to retain the hearts of the faithful, while wooing the uncommitted – without realising that the first tactic would have nullified the second. To appease the right wing of the party Hague had to do more than simply voice 'populist' concerns; he had to seize on them with the fervour which they associated with their heroine. Thus, while no opposition leader would have spurned the chance to make some capital out of the fuel protests, Hague gave the impression of endorsing actions which endangered emergency services across the country. His 'foreign land' speech of March 2001 was widely interpreted as the culmination of a campaign against 'bogus' asylum seekers. In fact Hague had used the phrase in the context of Europe, but it still seemed that one of his speech-writers had been pillaging the works of Enoch Powell. From the conflicting reports, it seems that Tory 'spin-doctors' were themselves divided as to his real meaning. Some observers had hinted at an element of xenophobia in Hague from the outset; after the leadership election a letter in *The Times* had claimed that 'the Tory Party in Parliament has chosen a rather querulous little Englander'.[13] After the speech it was hardly a surprise that the outgoing Tory MP John Townend should make overtly racist comments – or that Hague's response to that outburst was hesitant (unlike his instant dismissal of Lord Cranborne for being too clever by half).

Possibly Hague's most irresponsible action was his attack on the 'liberal elite' after the Macpherson Report had accused the Metropolitan Police of 'institutional racism'. It was perfectly valid – indeed potentially useful – for him to make sceptical noises. But the cliché 'liberal elite' was a substitute for an argument, rather than a useful tool for a constructive debate. Hague's reaction to the Report was sure to win applause from those who thought that the 'chattering classes' (or the 'politically correct') should be deported along with the blacks. But these voters tended to be concentrated in seats where the Tories were safe anyway. In the London Mayoral election of May 2000 Steve Norris had performed creditably on a platform which acknowledged the very different outlook of urban voters, but, since Norris had distanced himself from the national party, strategists seem to have regarded this precedent as embarrassing rather than instructive. The Conservative defeat at the Romsey by-election on the same night as the Mayoral election should have alerted them to the dangers of their present strategy.

Hague has also been heavily criticised for his opposition to the repeal of Section 28 of the 1988 Local Government Act. The original legislation had proved unworkable: it had only been introduced in the first place as a sop to right-wing opinion. Hague himself had voted to reduce the age of homosexual consent to sixteen, and in one early interview he even refused to disown the idea of gay marriage.[14] But his refusal to change his party's policy on Section 28 was perfectly explicable. He was caught in a double bind. If he had any doubts about the popularity of Section 28 on the right wing of his party, the short-lived cult which sprang up around his combative Home Affairs spokesperson, Ann Widdecombe, will have disabused him. On his other flank, Portillo's confessional speeches, and the passionate advocacy of reform by Norris and others, demanded a cultural transformation of the Conservative Party, even more radical than New Labour's acceptance of market forces.

In the abstract, it might have been possible (and advantageous) for Hague himself to have steered a middle course between these positions. But the depth of feeling among his unrepresentative activists forced him off the fence; and as usual he chose the 'traditionalist' course. He had every reason to admire the institution of the family; after all, by all accounts he seems to have come from a very happy one. But some of his comments – for example, his expression of thanks to religious leaders who opposed Section 28 – were unnecessary genuflections to reactionary opinion. The electoral damage caused by this policy in itself can be exaggerated; whatever Portillo and his admirers might think, the Tories could hardly make a convincing pitch against Labour and the Liberal Democrats for support among minority groups. But there was an immediate cost. The dissenting Tory MP Shaun Woodward was first sacked as a Shadow spokesman, and then defected to Labour, renewing the impression that the party was divided. More damaging was the general impression, that the Conservatives and their leader were determined to look backwards to a mythical time of social conformity. Even a grudging acceptance of diversity would have been better than a rhetorical line which made it less likely that the party could broaden its appeal even in the next Parliament.

Hague's 'political philosophy'

The fact that Woodward was informed of his fate by pager (another telling contrast to the treatment of Townend) suggests that Hague was uneasy with the position he had been forced to take. The power of the right-wing 'core'

constituency – and the ultimate futility of bidding for its lasting affection –
is attested to by the impression that Hague himself seemed to be relatively
free from prejudice. Although he did not add his name to the eight Shadow
Ministers who revealed in October 2000 that they had used soft drugs, some
of his friends since university days had enjoyed the sort of 'experimental'
lifestyles deplored by many Tory activists. In a speech at Bradford just before
the election he sounded sincere when he claimed that: 'It has never mattered
to me whether people are Muslim, Christian, Hindu, Sikh, Jewish, white,
black, or Asian.' But by this time the 'foreign land' speech had been supplemented by Lady Thatcher's attack on multiculturalism. Far from reaching
out to remaining floating voters, Hague's appeal was only likely to confuse
existing Conservative supporters. The same was true of his last-minute
warnings of another Labour landslide.[15]

When Hague resigned the Conservative leadership straight after the
election, he claimed that: 'I believe strongly, passionately, in everything I've
fought for.'[16] Given his various changes – enforced or otherwise – that was
a pardonable exaggeration. But insofar as the remark did convey a general
truth, it underlined Hague's complacency about the status of 'conservatism'
in 2001. His attempts to characterise his own views tended to be unenlightening: 'Supporting those who do the right thing is at the heart of my political
philosophy', he once declared. Jo-Anne Nadler has identified his 'core themes'
as 'freedom, national independence, self reliance, responsibility and enterprise'.[17] The list closely resembles the values of American Republicanism.
Perhaps in the USA Hague's values do resemble those of the 'mainstream
majority'; but the USA remains a 'foreign land' to most of the British, and
in the domestic context much more work was needed to weave these ideas
into a convincing 'narrative'. In particular, Hague seemed quite satisfied that
the electorate shared his own antipathy towards the state. Just conceivably,
a majority could have been brought to agree with this as a general principle.
But as Tony Blair had noted, they would give a different answer in the specific
(and crucial) instances of education and health.

Whether or not Hague's personal creed could ever be fleshed out into a
coherent policy programme remains an open question. At the time of writing,
Duncan Smith is fighting Labour from a similar standpoint, and it is too early
to judge whether his party will ever square its tax-cutting rhetoric with a
reassuring message on public services. Hague himself seems to have laboured
under an additional handicap. From the position he inherited in 1997 it always
made sense to eschew detailed policies as far as possible. The point was to
come up with one or two eye-catching ideas which were invulnerable to
Labour counter-thrusts. Once these attractive policies had been devised they
should have been ring-fenced, and the message hammered home as often as
possible. As we have seen, Hague was forced to abandon some of his key
commitments. But others seem to have been picked up, 'market-tested', then

jettisoned when the Tory poll rating refused to budge from its 'flatline' of around 30 per cent. The inadequacies of management consultancy as an apprenticeship for politics might also be detected in Hague's attitude to slogans. Some of these – 'compassionate' or 'Kitchen Table' Conservatism, the *Common Sense Revolution, Believing in Britain,* and even 'Mainstream Majority' – were worth a sustained trial. But Hague always seemed to be looking around for a winning soundbite, when his priority from the start should have been survival, not victory. The net result was that his sales-pitch to the electorate seemed even less coherent than it really was.

Oddly enough, Hague's most creditable performance in the policy field was his handling of the most intractable problem – the legacy of eighteen years of Tory rule. The opposition was probably right to cease its morale-sapping apologies after the first couple of years. Even so, some of its later attempts to switch the blame to Labour were horribly premature. For example, on the National Health Service one policy document stated that: 'The politicians have moved in and common sense has flown out of the window.' Perhaps so; but the greatest meddlers had been Conservatives (Sir Keith Joseph in the Heath government, and almost every Health Secretary from 1979 to 1997). On this issue the Tory left (in the shape of Clarke) shared the guilt with orthodox Thatcherites, so for once 'sorry' really might have been the hardest word.[18]

Probably Hague will always be remembered best for his performances at Prime Minister's Question Time. His biographer – whose portrait is certainly no hagiography – has claimed that his debating skills 'would have made him a giant in a nineteenth century context'.[19] One still feels that Charles James Fox and Gladstone might have held their own against him. In our very different era Blair was sometimes discomfited, despite his careful preparations and the orchestrated baying from packed Labour benches. But Hague's sallies had little impact outside the House, and for good reason. Prime Minister's Questions continued to fascinate Westminster commentators, but to almost everyone else they merely fostered disrespect for politicians. In any case, if Blair was vulnerable in the sound-bite battle over many issues, the key objective for Hague was to build public confidence in the Tory alternative; and in this he palpably failed.

Conclusion

A negative verdict on the Hague leadership is unavoidable, and while in the immediate aftermath of the 2001 election it would have seemed like kicking an essentially good man when he is down, at the time of writing Hague is well into his rehabilitation, making self-deprecating speeches and researching a book on Pitt the Younger. Any argument advanced by his defenders can be parried by the central fact – that he seized the leadership when a period of tactful silence would have been far more helpful to his burning ambition of one day emulating Pitt. He was never given a fair chance by the media, but his premature bid denied him the chance to live down his unfortunate image, and he could easily have avoided his counter-productive early photo opportunities. The criticism of his sober reaction to the death of Diana, Princess of Wales was grossly unfair; but having sounded the appropriate note Hague should have stuck to it. Instead, he over-reacted, apparently fearing that Blair's ostentatious emoting had caught a public mood which would last long after the funeral. He was far from being the only Conservative to tremble before Labour's supposed mastery of 'spin'; but that merely reinforces the central point, that if he rated his enemies so highly he should have bided his time until their limitations had been exposed.

Lord Parkinson in this volume rightly praises Hague's reorganisation of his party. But this turned out to be the easy part of his challenge. Those who had stayed loyal despite the 1997 meltdown were always likely to be mollified by the impression that their opinions would count for more in future. The real difficulty was to recapture the enthusiasm of the voters who had deserted over the five years since 1992. This would have been a daunting task for any Conservative leader; but the manner of Hague's failure suggests a second fatal misjudgement – an inadequate grasp of the real reasons for the landslide defeat. The new leader seemed blind to the possibility that the voters had turned against the ideas which had fired him since his schooldays – even though there was plenty of objective evidence that the majority had never endorsed them in the first place. This was a monumental error from someone embarking on a gamble: it was as if he was staking everything on a favourite horse, without troubling to glance at its recent form. And even if Hague can be pardoned for exaggerating the attractions of his party's ideology, he even failed to tackle the most obvious of the superficial reasons for the 1997 result. He had good reason to remember Major's problems with disunity; but although he managed the European issue with reasonable success as far as his party was concerned, he relied far too much on inexperienced confidants and caused unnecessary friction among his senior colleagues.

Any judgement of a political leader has to be based on a delicate thought-experiment. One is forced to compare the actual record with two hypothetical scenarios – what an imaginary 'average' leader might have been expected to do, and what the actual leader might have achieved, based on his or her qualities and a realistic assessment of the available options. The resulting yardsticks are unlikely to coincide in every respect, and even the wary commentator can easily slip from one to the other. But in resigning immediately after the 2001 general election, Hague seems to have tacitly accepted that he had let himself down so badly that even the 'average' leader could have done better.

The highest compliment that can be paid to William Hague is that he was right to be so disappointed. Determination, a sense of humour and an impenetrable skin are all essential attributes for a successful Tory leader nowadays; and the fact that Hague's debating skills were no great help to his party should not obscure the intellectual powers which underlay them. Actually his greatest strength was only dimly reflected in those Commons performances. His resilience was truly amazing; and although this undoubtedly helped him at the dispatch box it had advantages across the board. Sometimes he allowed himself to wonder whether he should have delayed his leadership challenge for a few years, but he was capable of banishing such thoughts and plugging on, in the face of opinion polls and media jibes which might have made even Sisyphus stop pushing.

This represents an impressive list of qualities for a political leader. It will never be known whether Hague possessed any of the others – or whether he could have acquired them through a longer apprenticeship, finally putting the 'Tory Boy' image to rest. The other thing we learned about him – the fact that he was a dignified loser – might have earned him respect, but is surplus to the requirements of one-shot gamblers like Hague. For them it is 'win or bust'; posthumous popularity earned by a graceful retirement speech can be no consolation to them. But at least Hague's decision means that he has the advantage of Pitt the Younger in one respect. While the latter found it impossible to abandon the game of politics and died, exhausted, at forty-six, Hague has followed through the logic of his ill-fated gamble, and opted for a prosperous and relaxing retirement.

Notes

1 N. Fisher, *The Tory Leaders: Their Struggle for Power* (London, Weidenfeld & Nicolson, 1977), p. 9; S. Hoggart, *On the House* (London, Robson Books, 1981), p. 112.

2 A. Travis, 'Poll shows Tory voters' faith in Hague is slipping', *Guardian*, 24 April 2001.

3 H. Williams, *Guilty Men: Conservative Decline and Fall 1992–1997* (London, Aurum Press, 1998), p. 189.

4 J.-A. Nadler, *William Hague: In His Own Right* (London, Politico's, 2000), p. 8.

5 Williams, *Guilty Men*, pp. 188 and 125.

6 M. Gove, *Michael Portillo: The Future of the Right* (London, Fourth Estate, 1995).

7 For Hague's handling of the Mayoral election, see M. D'Arcy and R. Maclean, *Nightmare! The Race to Become London's Mayor* (London, Politico's, 2000), Ch. 5.

8 S. Walters, *Tory Wars: Conservatives in Crisis* (London, Politico's, 2001), p. 17.

9 T. Gorman, *No, Prime Minister!* (London, John Blake, 2001), p. 345.

10 Nadler, *William Hague*, pp. 268–9; Walters, *Tory Wars*, p. 117.

11 Williams, *Guilty Men*, p. 198.

12 Nadler, *William Hague*, p. 40.

13 See A. Cooper, 'A party in a foreign land', in E. Vaizey, N. Boles and M. Grove (eds), *A Blue Tomorrow* (London, Politico's, 2001), p. 28, note 20; letter from Mr M. Dunn, *The Times*, 21 June 1997.

14 Cooper, 'A party in a foreign land', p. 19.

15 P. Wintour, 'Millbank gets poll jitters over landslide warning', *Guardian*, 2 June 2001.

16 A. Perkins, 'How secret poll target doomed Hague to the political wilderness', *Guardian*, 9 June 2001.

17 W. Hague, 'The moral case for low taxation', speech to Politeia, London, 14 March 2000; Nadler, *William Hague*, pp. 35–6.

18 *Believing in Britain* (London, Conservative Party, 2000), p. 11.

19 *Believing in Britain* p. 20.

4

The Conservative parliamentary party

Philip Cowley and Mark Stuart[1]

When the Conservative Party gathered for its first party conference since the 1997 general election, they came to bury the parliamentary party, not to praise it. The preceding five years had seen the party lose its (long-enjoyed) reputation for unity, and the blame for this was laid largely at the feet of the party's parliamentarians.[2] As Peter Riddell noted in *The Times*, 'speaker after speaker was loudly cheered whenever they criticised the parliamentary party and its divisions'.[3] It was an argument with which both the outgoing and incoming Prime Ministers were in agreement. Just before the 1997 general election, John Major confessed to his biographer that 'I love my party in the country, but I do not love my parliamentary party'; he was later to claim that 'divided views – expressed without restraint – in the parliamentary party made our position impossible'.[4] And in his first address to the massed ranks of the new parliamentary Labour Party after the election Tony Blair drew attention to the state of the Conservative Party:

> Look at the Tory Party. Pause. Reflect. Then vow never to emulate. Day after day, when in government they had MPs out there, behaving with the indiscipline and thoughtlessness that was reminiscent of us in the early 80s. Where are they now, those great rebels?

His answer was simple: not in Parliament. 'When the walls came crashing down beneath the tidal wave of change, there was no discrimination between those Tory MPs. They were all swept away, rebels and loyalists alike.'[5]

They certainly were. The Conservative parliamentary party elected in 1997 comprised just 165 MPs, lower than at any time since 1906.[6] Moreover, a combination of a higher than usual number of pre-election retirements (seventy-two Conservative MPs had stood down before the election), together with the savage effects of their electoral performance (which accounted, *inter alia*, for a record seven Cabinet ministers), meant that this 165 included few experienced parliamentarians. One defeated Conservative MP, David Sumberg, commented that he did not mind losing his seat 'because he would no longer be able to recognise anyone in the Commons'.[7] A full quarter of the parliamentary party was new; just thirty-six had experience of politics in Opposition.[8] Facing the new Labour government, therefore, was one of the smallest and least-experienced groups of parliamentarians ever to constitute Her Majesty's Official Opposition.

The choice of Hague

Their first main task was to choose John Major's successor. It was the last time the Conservative parliamentary party would be solely responsible for deciding the leadership of the party. It was a power they had gained in 1965 but one of William Hague's first acts as leader was to amend the leadership rules.[9] When his replacement came to be chosen (see below), the party's MPs no longer enjoyed the ultimate power of selection.

But why did the party's MPs choose Hague? Just months before, the then Conservative MP and diarist, Gyles Brandreth, had noted the response in the Members' tea room to the idea of Hague as party leader: *'please,* you cannot be serious!'[10] As well as the absence of other potential candidates, such as Michael Portillo (who had lost his seat in Enfield Southgate, and was thus *de facto,* if not *de jure,* ineligible) and Michael Heseltine (whose attack of angina ruled him out of the race), two other main factors enabled Hague to take the leadership.

First, the right of the party – especially the Euro-sceptic right – shot themselves in the foot. Like many other Conservative leadership contests, there was a clear ideological division between the source of the candidates' support.[11] Kenneth Clarke's support came mainly from pro-European Conservative MPs. Hague's support came mainly from MPs in the centre of the party. But three candidates – John Redwood, Peter Lilley and Michael Howard – drew their support predominantly from the Euro-sceptic right of the party, splitting the sceptic vote into three, and ensuring that they came third, fourth and fifth respectively.[12] But between them they had amassed over seventy votes, enough to have put one of them in first place, at least in the first round of the contest. Had there been just one candidate from the right, therefore, it is entirely plausible that Hague would have ended up in third place in the first round of the contest and been forced to withdraw.

The second main cause of Hague's success was that he was the least unpopular of the candidates. Given the number of candidates standing for election, there were almost bound to be multiple rounds of voting in the contest – in the event there were three – and, as a result, it was crucial for candidates to be able to attract support from MPs whose first choice had dropped out of the race: the winner needed the parliamentary equivalent of sloppy seconds. As Table 4.1 shows, this was exactly what Hague was able to do. After the first round, his vote went up by twenty-one, compared to an increase of fifteen for Clarke, and eleven for Redwood. After the second, his vote went up by thirty, compared to just six for Clarke. At each stage, then, Hague's support went up by the largest amount.

Table 4.1 Changes in support between rounds, 1997

	Round 1	*Round 2*	*Change*	*Round 3*	*Change*
Hague	41	62	(+21)	92	(+30)
Clarke	49	64	(+15)	70	(+6)
Redwood	27	38	(+11)	–	–
Lilley	24	–	–	–	–
Howard	23	–	–	–	–

Hague's inoffensiveness was confirmed by a survey, conducted before the 1997 election, of Conservative MPs and prospective candidates.[13] It asked two key questions. Who would they like to see as party leader? And to whom would they object as party leader? Hague was the only candidate with a respectable level of support who attracted no hostility. Indeed, only one respondent objected to Hague – and that was only because he said that he did not know what Hague stood for.

This enabled Hague to take the leadership, but it also presented him with a problem, because it meant that he enjoyed little enthusiastic support from his parliamentary party. His initial support – those who backed him in the first round of the contest – was limited to a small group of MPs in the centre of the party. Just a quarter of his parliamentary party voted for him as first choice. Indeed, many of that 25 per cent would have preferred Portillo, had he been available. Much of Hague's later support, and even some of his initial support, came to him *faute de mieux*, because there was no one better. As a result, Hague's support was broad – being able to encompass large parts of the parliamentary party – but it was not deep. There was little or no ideological core to his support. There were few people in his parliamentary party who wanted Hague because of what he could deliver.

The party's official stance

Hague's frontbench team during the 1997 Parliament came to be criticised from outsiders for its right-of-centre leanings, a tendency exacerbated when, early on in his leadership, a handful of Europhile MPs resigned from it in protest at the party's shift in stance over the euro. But with such a small parliamentary party, Hague's room for manoeuvre was distinctly limited, and he had to make the most of what he had. Given that the balance of the parliamentary party had over the last few elections been shifting to the (Euro-sceptic) right, it would have been very difficult for him to have appointed anything other than a right-of-centre Shadow Cabinet and frontbench team.[14]

An entirely different criticism came from within the parliamentary party. The Conservative frontbench was criticised by some of its own backbenches for not being adversarial enough towards the government. Yet between 1997 and 2001, the Conservative frontbench opposed 41 per cent of the bills introduced by the government, making it one of the most adversarial oppositions of recent times.[15] Even at the height of adversarial politics between 1979 and 1983, with the gulf between the two parties at its widest since the Second World War, the official opposition, then Labour, voted against just over a third of the Thatcher government's legislation at Second or Third Reading.[16]

To be sure, there was an initial reluctance on the part of the Tory frontbench to oppose most aspects of the government's constitutional reform agenda, especially those bills (involving Scotland, Wales and Northern Ireland) where referendums had been held in the countries concerned. But as the government's agenda moved away from constitutional reform and away from legislation outlined in its election manifesto, so the Conservative frontbench began to oppose a higher proportion of government legislation, reaching a peak of 48 per cent in the second session and 45 per cent in the third. Even on Northern Ireland, traditionally a topic for cross-party agreement, consensus began to break down from June 1998 onwards. Here, despite having supported the Second Reading of the Northern Ireland (Sentences) Bill, the Conservative frontbench opposed the Bill's Third Reading, because they argued that the government had failed to link the issue of prisoner release with the need for the IRA to begin weapons decommissioning. From then on, the Conservatives became more critical of the government's Northern Ireland policy, while remaining broadly supportive of the overall 'peace process'.

But the Conservative parliamentary party did not always act as one. Throughout the Parliament, small groups of Conservative MPs refused to do the bidding of their whips and voted against their party line (usually also voting against the government in the process when the Conservative frontbench advice was to support the government or abstain). In addition to sporadic issue-based rebellions by backbench MPs, there was also a small ginger group of Conservative MPs – dubbed the 'awkward squad' – who set out to cause trouble for the government by throwing as many procedural spanners in the parliamentary works as possible, often against the advice of their own frontbench, and whose activities escalated as the Parliament progressed.

Conservative backbench dissent

The behaviour of Conservative MPs between 1997 and 2001 was almost the mirror image of that of Labour MPs in the same period. Whereas Labour

MPs rebelled infrequently but in quantity, Conservative MPs rebelled more frequently but — with the exception of some very large rebellions at the beginning of the Parliament over devolution — usually in small numbers.[17]

In total, there were 163 occasions when Conservative MPs voted against the advice of their party whips during the Parliament, sixty-seven more than Labour. And although the awkward squad's activities (see below) account for a sizable proportion of that number, there were still 111 rebellions even once we discount their activities. Even without the activities of the awkward squad, therefore, Conservative MPs voted against their party line more times than did Labour MPs. The average size of these rebellions, though, was small (just six MPs), becoming smaller as the Parliament progressed: from eight in the first session to seven in the second, to six in the third, down to five in the final session. And whereas only a minority of Labour MPs broke ranks — albeit a minority that was larger than most people realised — the Conservative backbench rebellions involved some 128 Conservative MPs, just over three-quarters of the parliamentary party, and almost everyone who was a Conservative backbencher at some point in the Parliament.

The largest rebellion came at the beginning of the Parliament. With the Conservative frontbench largely acquiescent over the issue, the majority of Conservative backbench dissent during the first year of the Parliament came from Tory MPs unhappy about the government's proposals for devolution. Five consecutive votes in June 1997 saw an average of thirty-five Conservative backbenchers oppose the Referendums (Scotland and Wales) Bill, establishing the rules of the devolution referendums. The first and largest occurred over the issue of who should be allowed to vote. An amendment by Bill Cash proposed that the Scottish referendum should encompass the whole of the United Kingdom rather than merely those resident in Scotland. Some eighty-two Conservative backbenchers, a full half of the parliamentary party, backed the amendment. Four other rebellions saw twenty, thirty-seven, twenty-two and nine Conservative MPs defy their whips, a total of ninety-four doing so at some point during the Bill's passage.[18]

The other issues to provoke rebellion amongst Conservative MPs ranged widely, but one was largely absent and one was dominant. The absentee was Europe. Despite being the major faultline during the Major leadership, there were remarkably few backbench revolts over Europe (none of them sizeable) under Hague's leadership. The dominant issue was Northern Ireland. It provoked forty separate Conservative rebellions. Again, these tended to be small, averaging just five MPs, but as the parliament progressed, so the number of Conservative MPs prepared to break ranks over the issue grew, and their cumulative impact was considerable, involving fifty-one different MPs, almost a third of the parliamentary party. Backbench unhappiness with the government's policy towards Northern Ireland (and, concomitantly, with their frontbench's stance towards the government) ran deep on the

Conservative benches and may at least help to explain the Tory frontbench shift on the issue in 1998.

The largest rebellion came over the Third Reading of the Northern Ireland Bill (the Anglo-Irish plan to revive the 'peace process'), when sixteen Tory MPs voted against the Bill, in defiance of the frontbench line to abstain; but the most concerted spell of opposition came over the Disqualifications Bill. The Bill dealt with the anomaly created by the Northern Ireland Act 1998 that permitted a member of the Irish Senate to be a member of the Northern Ireland Assembly but not of any other UK legislature. It ended the prohibition against members of the Irish legislature – both the Dail and the Senate – from being a member of any legislature in the United Kingdom, including the House of Commons, the Scottish Parliament, the Welsh Assembly and the Northern Ireland Assembly. The Conservative frontbench stance was to abstain.[19] Many Conservative MPs disagreed. Andrew Hunter spoke for many of his colleagues on the Conservative benches when he described the Bill as 'just the latest obscene landmark in a process that ostensibly began as a peace process, but long ago became, in reality, a sordid, shabby process of appeasement'.[20] The government had hoped to get through the remaining stages of the Bill the following day. But a group of Conservative MPs began a marathon session of filibustering, and the deliberations of the Committee of the Whole House ran from 5.43p.m. on 25 January 2000 to 7.19a.m. the following day. As a result, a full day's business, including Prime Minister's Questions, was lost.[21] Five separate divisions throughout the night and into the following morning saw an average of eleven Conservatives support amendments and block government motions that attempted to hasten the Bill's passage, with a total of thrity-three Conservative MPs voting against their frontbench position at some point.

The most prominent Conservative dissenter on Northern Ireland was Andrew Hunter who cast twenty-six dissenting votes on that issue alone. But because precedence in the debates is given to MPs from Northern Irish parties, even a vociferous opponent of the government's policies like Hunter was restricted to relatively few speeches and interventions, and the Conservative divisions on the issue therefore went largely unnoticed outside of Westminster.

The 'awkward squad'

As well as these *ad hoc* rebellions by Conservative MPs, the Government also faced concerted opposition from a small ginger group of Conservative MPs. Whereas many Labour rebels did not like the labels given them by the media, many members of this group of Conservative MPs, formed around two former ministers, Eric Forth and David Maclean, revelled in their description as 'the awkward squad'. They engaged in a parliamentary form of guerrilla warfare,

with both their behaviour and their *raison d'être* likened by one of the group
to that of the French resistance during the Second World War:

> When France was invaded it was finished. Then two and a half thousand
> out of 40 million joined the *Maquis*. We can't defeat the Government in
> votes, we can't defeat them in argument, since no one ever listens, but we
> can tie them down in the same way that the *Maquis* tied down the Ger-
> mans ... it's only pot shots, but it's a form of opposition.[22]

It would be carrying the military analogy too far to suggest that they
saw their frontbench as quislings or like the leaders of Vichy France, but
many members of the awkward squad certainly thought that their High
Command was too conciliatory and too consensual towards the government
– that Conservative frontbenchers did not have 'the stomach for it'. Singled
out for criticism were the Chief Whip, James Arbuthnot, and the Shadow
Leader of the House for most of the period, Sir George Young, both of whom
many awkward squad members regarded as 'grandees'. 'Some of them learned
their politics with cucumber sandwiches.' These grandees wanted to play by
the rules, accepting the norms of the House and saw anything else as *infra
dig*. Eric Forth and his colleagues, by contrast, saw themselves as parliamentary Clint Eastwoods, playing by their own rules. One described himself as
'a parliamentary yob': 'It's in my nature to play party politics rough.' Collec-
tively, their aim was to cause what one of them called 'buggeration', 'to make
life for the government as miserable as possible'. In some cases, this grew
from a neo-liberal ideological objection to the idea of all but the most minimal
of legislation ('What I want is institutional gridlock. I want it to be nearly
impossible for government to do anything'). But it was just as likely to result
from a belief in the value of confrontational politics, in which the point of
opposition was to oppose, and the role of the backbencher was to hold the
government to account. If the Conservative frontbench would not oppose
the government, then Conservative backbenchers would have to do it.

Despite the label, there was no formal organisation behind the awkward
squad and its membership was both amorphous and variable. The inner core
was essentially just four Conservative MPs. Eric Forth and David Maclean
organised most of the group's various activities, Forth acting as the unofficial
whip, with Gerald Howarth and David Wilshire never far behind. There were
no formal meetings, although the core of the awkward squad were all
members of the Thatcherite 'No Turning Back' Group which met for dinner
once a month, where they would all 'have a good whinge' about the activities
of their own frontbench and 'wish they were opposing things'. Around the
inner core was an outer core, which comprised some twelve MPs, who
were regularly to be found acting in concert with the inner core but who were
less involved in organising their activities. And there was then another group
of MPs, again around twelve in number, who would occasionally join in

(especially once their activities escalated later in the Parliament), but whose involvement was less regular and depended at least in part on the particular issues involved and the tactics being employed. As one said: 'Only the psychotic care enough to stay up all night.'

Initially, Forth and Maclean began by blocking Private Members' Bills, something that the procedures of the Commons makes relatively easy to do.[23] They believed that the government was abusing private members' time by getting backbench MPs to introduce so-called 'handout' bills, government bills in all but name.[24] By blocking Private Members' Bills, therefore, Forth and Maclean aimed to force the bill to be reintroduced later, which would eat up government time.[25] But they also shared an ideological objection to private members' legislation in general, believing that they were badly scrutinised, usually originated with single-issue groups, and nearly always imposed regulations and costs. In their view, it was possible to have 'good' Private Members' Bills, but they had to be totally non-controversial, consisting of just a few clauses. In practice 'precious few' were like this.

As the Parliament progressed, so the awkward squad's activities increased, both in terms of frequency and in terms of the number of MPs involved. The slow start was partly due to the effects of the defeat of 1997 – a process that one MP described as 'getting over the shell shock'. But Conservative MPs also had to adapt to being in opposition, to adjust to the realities of being on the outside, and to discover the more obscure parliamentary procedures with which they could obstruct government business. Once they discovered them, and once they had tasted blood, they realised that causing trouble for the government was 'fun'. It 'gives me a purpose in life', said one, 'gets me up perkier in the morning. It's worth it to see their faces.'

By the third session, the group had begun to object to otherwise non-contentious bills, and to call divisions and filibuster during their passage. At times, the awkward squad's activities were in clear contravention of the Conservative whips. This was especially true of the Disqualifications Bill, where the Conservative frontbench had hoped to embarrass the Prime Minister on his 1000th day in office at Prime Minister's Questions.[26] However, more often than not, the votes occurred late at night when the Conservative whips' line was that their MPs could go home, and very often there was no Conservative line to be rebelling against. The inner core would instead stay around, looking for a fight, forcing divisions, often on otherwise non-contentious statutory instruments. Each division takes between twelve and fifteen minutes, itself wasteful of government MPs' time, but more importantly the prospect of an unexpected division forces the government whips to keep enough MPs in the precincts of the Commons to ensure victory, inconveniencing Labour MPs for hours more than the time taken for the votes themselves. As Austin Mitchell noted in *The House Magazine*'s Commons Diary: 'I'd thought 10p.m. was now a guaranteed P.O.H. (Push Off

Home) time ... Not so. Tonight 200 'volunteers' are kept back until 2.30 to vote down six of Forth's Freedom Fighters.'[27] Even more frustrating for Labour MPs were those occasions when Conservative backbenchers would keep a debate going into the early hours of the morning, only, at some ungodly hour, for the Tories *not* to force a vote.

Perhaps because some of them secretly admired the awkward squad's activities (and perhaps because they could not do much to stop them even if they wanted to), the Conservative whips frequently turned a blind eye, even when the group's activities were in contravention of the party's whip, and no disciplinary action was taken against any of its members. Several members of the awkward squad admitted that if their whips had ever asked them to desist, they probably would have done so. But this attitude did not apply to the inner core. When a Tory whip tried to stop Forth filibustering during the Disqualifications Bill, he was given short shrift: 'Do you really think I've been here for eighteen hours and I've got the chance of losing a day's business and I'm going to give it up now? Piss off.'

By the beginning of the fourth session, the awkward squad's activities had escalated yet further, with them forcing divisions on the principle of a full quarter of the government's legislation, almost as much as the Conservative frontbench objected to. The introduction (as part of the process of 'modernisation' of the Commons) of deferred divisions, something that all Conservative MPs had voted against when they had been proposed (routinely describing them as an 'abomination'), made things even worse. 'Deferred divisions' did exactly what it said on the tin, with some divisions being deferred until the following week, when instead of walking through the division lobbies to record their votes, MPs handed in a ballot sheet between 3.30 and 5p.m., recording their votes on each division. The very first vote using a deferred division – on European Union fish quotas – saw the Conservative Party formally instruct its MPs to spoil their ballot papers by voting twice, an act that provoked a reprimand from the Speaker.[28] And from then on, many deferred divisions saw small 'rebellions' by Conservative MPs. These were as much protests against the system – forcing votes on otherwise uncontroversial issues in order to slow down the process – as revolts over the issues themselves.

If the aim of the awkward squad was to annoy Labour MPs, then they certainly succeeded. Their activities infuriated many Labour backbenchers. Some, especially those first elected in 1997, were annoyed at what they saw as the 'futility of parliamentary games'.[29] As one tired and frustrated MP complained in 2000: 'Here till four the other night, 250 of us, just for 20 Tories.' But Labour annoyance just made the Conservatives more determined. As one Conservative MP said, '[There is] nothing like seeing them rattled to make me want to do it again.' And just as Labour MPs disapproved of the activities of the Conservatives, so the Conservatives disdained the approach of some of the Labour MPs, especially the new ones. Labour MPs, one claimed, disliked 'anything that made their personal life awkward'. Another was more blunt. The New Labour MPs just wanted the rules of the Commons changed 'so that they can go home and change nappies. They think that they are here just to further the project, they see Parliament as an inconvenience, they just want to do what the Master wants.'

Yet amongst some Labour MPs there was grudging admiration for Forth and his colleagues. Some longer-serving Labour MPs, especially the more rebellious, knew that they would have done the same in opposition. During the 1970 Parliament a similar ginger group of Labour backbenchers had been set up by James Wellbeloved, which aimed, amongst other things, to 'knock a bit of stuffing out of the Government backbenchers'.[30] During the early 1980s, when the PLP was falling apart in organisational terms and MPs were beset by reselection battles, two opposition MPs, Dennis Skinner and Bob Cryer, similarly took the fight to the Conservative government by opposing legislation late into the night, prompting one experienced Labour back-bencher to describe Forth as 'Dennis Skinner in drag'. A former Labour Chief Whip ('with a Ph.D. in opposition') confessed that he frequently colluded with the activities of his backbenchers. 'There were many times when I did not have complete control over my backbenchers. There were even more times when I pretended not to have control over them and colluded with them in frustrating the government of the day.'[31] Nor did all Labour MPs object to late nights: 'I worked nights in a steel factory, so if the Tories want to play silly buggers, I'll work nights again.' The sneaking respect for Forth was shown when he was voted 'Opposition Politician of the Year' in the Channel 4 and *The House Magazine* awards in 1999. The opposition to him, though, was equally clear when his name was put up for the House of Commons Commission to succeed Sir Peter Lloyd, and – after a heated debate – he was voted off.[32]

One of the effects of the awkward squad's activities was to increase the pressure on the Labour frontbench to pursue yet further 'modernisation' of the Commons. The resentment their activities caused on the Labour benches was at least partly responsible for the decision to introduce deferred divisions and the programming of almost all government bills in November 2000.[33] One Labour whip, Graham Allen, thought that 'by his antics over the past year or so', Forth had 'done more for the modernisation of this place than serious-minded reformers like myself managed in fourteen years or more'.[34] This compounded Conservative feelings that the government was progress-ively taking away the rights of opposition backbench MPs properly to scrutinise the government, so by the beginning of 2001 what one awkward squad member called a 'destructive cycle' had developed: 'They [the govern-ment] antagonised us, we retaliated by using loopholes, so they closed the loopholes, which antagonised us.'

Near the end of the Parliament one Conservative MP reflected that, for all their effort, the awkward squad seemed to have achieved little. 'No minister has had a heart attack yet', he said ruefully.[35] Another thought that they had achieved 'no immediate tangible result ... all we've done is keep people up late'. But that was all most of them had wanted to do. They had not been aiming to defeat the enemy, just to take 'pot shots' at it and to cause 'buggeration'. And in that, they had been successful.

Plus ça change ...

The general election of 2001 will not be remembered for any dramatic changes in the composition of the Commons.[36] A total of 560 sitting MPs were re-elected. Just twenty-one were defeated. Eighty-five per cent of the House was therefore exactly the same after the election as it had been before – the lowest turnover since 1945.[37] The turnover on the Conservative benches was slightly higher (there were thirty-three new Conservative MPs, although seven of these were 'retreads', former MPs returning to the Commons), but the overall number of Conservatives rose by just one. Indeed, given that one of the Conservative gains was Tatton – a seat held by the Independent MP Martin Bell since 1997, but in which Bell was not standing in 2001 – the net Conservative gain from other political parties was effectively nil.

Just as four years before, their first task was the choosing of a new leader. William Hague's reforms may have ended the parliamentary party's monopoly in leadership selection, but the parliamentarians remained extremely important, far more so than in other British political parties. The new rules involved the party's wider membership in the country (see Chapter 5), but only once the incumbent leader has resigned (that is, they give party members no say over ejecting an incumbent) and the wider membership are merely offered a choice between the two candidates most favoured by the parliamentary party.[38]

Also as in 1997, five candidates stood for the leadership in 2001: Kenneth Clarke, Iain Duncan Smith, Michael Portillo, Michael Ancram and David Davis. A multiple ballot system was used to choose the final two candidates to go through to the ballot of the party membership, with the bottom placed candidate being eliminated after each round.

Unfortunately the first round saw two candidates, Davis and Ancram, share the wooden spoon, leading to the vote being held for a second time. The party's rules were widely criticised for not foreseeing such a possibility ('Can't they get anything right?' asked the *Daily Mail*; 'Chaos', said the *Sun*), with surprisingly little criticism focusing on the two candidates themselves for failing to withdraw from the race in the interests of the party. The re-run contest, two days later, saw both Davis and Ancram lose votes, whilst the front three candidates improved their positions slightly. Ancram was then eliminated from the contest; Davis withdrew (albeit after initially attempting to stay in the running).[39] Both urged their supporters to vote for Duncan Smith.

The second round proper saw Clarke top the poll (fifty-nine votes), followed by Duncan Smith (fifty-four). Portillo – who had been in front in the first two rounds, and who was widely seen as the frontrunner – came third by one vote and was therefore eliminated.

Table 4.2 Changes in support between rounds, 2001

	Round 1	Round 1 (re-run)	Change	Round 2	Change
Clarke	36	39	(+3)	59	(+20)
Duncan Smith	39	42	(+3)	54	(+12)
Portillo	49	50	(+1)	53	(+3)
Davis	21	18	(−3)	–	–
Ancram	21	17	(−4)	–	–

There were clear ideological divisions between the candidates' supporters. 'All five candidates drew their principal support from their natural ideological constituencies.'[40] Clarke's support came predominantly from the party's wets, but also – because he was perceived by some to be an electoral asset – from the party faithful, those MPs who put the party interest ahead of their own ideological preferences.[41] Duncan Smith and Davis were both Thatcherites, and drew most of their support from that ideological group, with Davis attracting the backing of the awkward squad. Ancram, who put himself forward as the compromise candidate, drew his support largely from the party faithful. Portillo's support was perhaps the broadest of all. He drew support from neo-liberals (his own brand of Conservatism), but also from some 'damps' (wet versions of the party's wets) and from some of the party faithful. He also enjoyed the support of the majority of the Shadow Cabinet.

Yet despite this broad support, and despite being widely seen as a shoo-in, he failed to capture enough support to get through to the ballot of the membership. Portillo's problem was easily summed up. Unlike Hague (in 1997), or both Clarke and Duncan Smith (in 2001), Portillo was unable to attract supporters from defeated candidates. As Table 4.2 shows, after the first round his support went up by just one vote (compared to three each for Clarke and Duncan Smith). In the second round – when Clarke's support went up by twenty and Duncan Smith's by twelve – Portillo's support went up by just three, and not enough to keep him in the race. He was almost no MP's second choice. Indeed, there was a sizeable group of Conservative MPs who wanted to stop Portillo at any cost.[42] Portillo himself summed his problem up well: 'I seem to unite people against me in antagonism.'[43]

The sources of this antagonism were various. Portillo suffered from accusations that he (or, more often, his aides, supporters and assorted hangers-on) had been disloyal to Hague (and, prior to 1997, Major). Such accusations appeared repeatedly during the campaign – as with Ann Widdecombe's complaints about 'back-biting' or Amanda Platell's video diary – but these were merely the public manifestations of widespread ill-feeling amongst parts of the parliamentary party.[44] He also suffered both from a sense amongst some MPs that he had shifted his beliefs (apparently abandoning Thatcherism, to the chagrin of those who had kept the faith) and, just as importantly, that there was still no clear sign of exactly what his new beliefs were. As one journalist put it to him when he addressed the parliamentary Press Gallery on the day of the second ballot: 'Are you still on a journey or are you just refuelling?'.[45] In the event, he was going nowhere.

Under the new rules, the Conservative parliamentary party may no longer be kingmakers, but they are still gatekeepers. The gate was closed on Ancram, Davis and Portillo, but allowed Clarke and Duncan Smith through. George Jones in the *Daily Telegraph* claimed that 'the party faces the most fundamental choice over its future since Margaret Thatcher became leader twenty-six years ago'.[46] But that fundamental final choice was no longer the parliamentary party's.

Notes

1 This chapter draws on research funded by the Leverhulme Trust, and reported in Philip Cowley, *Revolts and Rebellions: Parliamentary Voting Under Blair* (London, Politico's, 2002). The authors are very grateful to all the MPs who helped with the research.

2 By 1993 a mere 19 per cent of the electorate considered the Conservatives to be united. This figure fell into single figures for parts of 1996. 'Not since polls asked the question in the early 1970s has the party been so widely regarded as split', wrote Ivor Crewe in 1996. I. Crewe, '1979–1996', in A. Seldon (ed.), *How Tory Governments Fall* (London, Fontana, 1996), p. 432.

3 P. Riddell, 'Tories have yet to face up to their new status', *The Times*, 9 October 1997.

4 A. Seldon, *Major. A Political Life* (London, Weidenfeld & Nicolson, 1997), p. 3; P. Webster, 'Major vents anger at rebels', *The Times*, 8 October 1997.

5 T. Blair, speech to the Parliamentary Labour Party, Church House, London, 7 May 1997.

6 The death of Sir Michael Shersby, MP for Uxbridge, soon after polling day, meant that by the time the Parliament resumed the Conservatives were reduced to just 164 MPs.

7 A. Roth and B. Criddle, *New MPs of 1997 and Retreads* (London, Parliamentary Profiles Services Ltd, 1997), p. i.

8 B. Criddle, 'MPs and Candidates', in D. Butler and D. Kavanagh, *The British General Election of 1997* (London, Macmillan, 1997), p. 202. In the 2001 volume, D. Butler and D. Kavanagh, *The British General Election of 2001* (London, Palgrave, 2002) erroneously claim that the figure was eleven (p. 39). Things may have been bad, but they were not *that* bad.

9 For more details on the changes in the method of selecting the Leader see K. Alderman, 'Revision of leadership election procedures in the Conservative Party', *Parliamentary Affairs* 52:2 (1999) 260–74. More generally, see J. Lees-Marshment and S. Quayle, 'Empowering the members or marketing the party? The Conservative reforms of 1998', *Political Quarterly*, 72:2 (2001) 204–12; R. Kelly 'Democratising the Tory Party', *Talking Politics*, 11:1 (1998) 28–33; and P. Cowley and S. Quayle, 'The Conservatives: running on the spot', in A. Geddes and J. Tonge (eds), *Labour's Second Landslide* (Manchester, Manchester University Press, 2002), pp. 47–64.

10 G. Brandreth, *Breaking the Code* (London, Weidenfeld & Nicolson, 1999), p. 472.

11 See, for example, P. Cowley and M. Bailey, 'Peasants' uprising or religious war: re-examining the 1975 Conservative leadership contest', *British Journal of Political Science*, 30:4 (2000) 599–629; P. Cowley and J. Garry, 'The British Conservative Party and Europe: the choosing of John Major', *British Journal of Political Science*, 28:3 (1998) 473–99.

12 See P. Cowley, 'Just William? A supplementary analysis of the 1997 Conservative leadership contest', *Talking Politics*, 10:2 (1997/98) 91–5, for full details of the analysis.

13 Cowley, 'Just William', pp. 91–2.

14 See, for example, the data in P. Norris, 'Anatomy of a Labour landslide', in P. Norris (ed.), *Britain Votes 1997* (Oxford, Oxford University Press, 1997), Table 7, p. 529.

15 See P. Cowley, *Revolts and Rebellions: Parliamentary Voting Under Blair* (London, Politico's, 2002), Table 10.1.

16 D. Van Mechelen and R. Rose, *Patterns of Parliamentary Legislation* (Aldershot, Gower, 1986). More generally, see R. Rose, *Do Parties Make A Difference?* (London, Macmillan, 1980).

17 Compare Cowley, *Revolts and Rebellions*, Chs 5 and 10.

18 The first session also saw a sizeable rebellion over the Criminal Justice (Terrorism and Conspiracy) Bill. In the second largest Conservative rebellion of the Parliament, forty Conservative MPs joined the sixteen Labour backbenchers who objected to all the Bill's stages being completed in one day.

19 The Conservatives were concerned about the release of paramilitary prisoners in the absence of decommissioning. So, although they abstained on the Bill's Second Reading, they put forward and supported Ulster Unionist amendments during the Bill's Committee stage that insisted that the Bill should not take effect until there had been substantial and verifiable decommissioning.

20 HC Debs, 24 January 2000, col. 66.

21 It was the first time since 14 June 1988 that a sitting of the House had wrecked the next day's sitting. Then MPs sat from 2.30p.m. on Tuesdays until 8.01p.m. on Wednesday as they deliberated the Housing Bill. *The House Magazine*, 31 January 2000.

22 All unattributed quotations in this chapter are drawn from interviews with Conservative (or, occasionally, Labour) MPs in the 1997 Parliament. Simon Hoggart drew a similar comparison: 'They are like guerrillas fighting in the forests and hills, the rag-taggle remains of a defeated army', 'Ragged remains of defeated Tory army fight on', *Guardian*, 20 March 2001.

23 See H. Marsh and D. Marsh, 'Tories in the killing fields', *Journal of Legislative Studies*, forthcoming.

24 They were – but then so has every government in recent years. See D. Marsh and M. Read, *Private Members' Bills* (Cambridge, Cambridge University Press, 1988).

25 As happened with, for example, the Fur Farming Bill, when Forth and Maclean divided the House three times in March and May 1999. As well as talking out many

bills, Forth (and usually Maclean) often divided the House. In the first session, they divided the House on the Fireworks Bill, in the second, the Animal Welfare (Prohibition of Imports) Bill, in the third, the Warm Homes and Energy Conservation Bill, the Age Equality Commission Bill, and, in the fourth, the Outworking Bill, the Christmas Day (Trading) Bill and even the High Hedges Bill!

26 M. White, 'Rebels ruin day 1000 showdown', *Guardian*, 27 January 2000.

27 *The House Magazine*, 15 January 2001. A Labour whip similarly described the awkward squad as the 'provisional wing of the Tory party'. HC Debs, 28 June 2001, col. 833.

28 Even here, though, there were some dissenters. Two MPs voted with the Government, while five voted against the Government.

29 Or, as Quentin Letts put it following Forth's elevation to Shadow Leader of the House following Iain Duncan Smith's election as Conservative leader: '"Go, Forth, and multiply" is what most Labour MPs think of the new Shadow Leader of the House.' Q. Letts, 'HM Opposition: a user's guide', *New Statesman*, 22 October 2001, p. 35.

30 P. Norton, *Dissension in the House of Commons, 1945–74* (London, Macmillan, 1975), p. 389.

31 HC Debs, 28 June 2001, col. 825.

32 HC Debs, 2 February 2000, cols. 1175–6. He was, though, almost immediately put back on to the Commission, only to have to resign his place when he became Shadow Leader of the House after the 2001 Election.

33 See P. Norton, 'Parliament', in A. Seldon (ed.), *The Blair Effect* (London, Little, Brown & Company, 2001), p. 51.

34 HC Debs, 28 June 2001, col. 834. One long-serving Labour MP agreed: 'Forth played into the hands of those, particularly the women, who said: 'If we can't change the hours now, we never will.'

35 This might have been a joke. But perhaps not.

36 For more on the composition of the Commons post-2001, see P. Cowley, 'The Commons: Mr Blair's lapdog?', in P. Norris (ed.), *Britain Votes 2001* (Oxford, Oxford University Press, 2001), pp. 251–64.

37 That is, excluding the two short Parliaments of 1950–51 and February–October 1974.

38 Indeed, there is no compulsion on the parliamentary party to put two candidates forward to the members at the final stage.

39 See, for example, the leader column, 'Down to three please', *Daily Telegraph*, 13 July 2001.

40 P. Norton, 'The Conservative leadership election', *British Politics Group Newsletter*, 106 (2001), p. 12.

41 The various ideological categories are explained in P. Norton, '"The lady's not for turning": but what about the rest? Margaret Thatcher and the Conservative Party', *Parliamentary Affairs*, 43:1 (1990) 41–58. For their continuing viability, see P. Cowley and P. Norton, 'What a ridiculous thing to say! (which is why we didn't say it): a response to Timothy Heppell', *British Journal of Politics and International Relations*, 4:2 (2002) 325–9; and P. Norton 'The Conservative Party: is there anyone out there?', in A. King (ed.), *Britain at the Polls 2001* (Chatham NJ, Chatham House, 2002), pp. 85–8.

42 Indeed, the size of Clarke's final lead – which surprised Clarke himself – was at least partly due to a handful of Duncan Smith supporters who, thinking that Duncan Smith was himself going to top the poll, decided to vote for Clarke in order to block Portillo.

Too clever by half, their actions almost had disastrous consequences for their candidate.

43 Simon Walters, *Tory Wars* (London, Politico's, 2001), p. 207.

44 By far the best single account is Walters, *Tory Wars*.

45 Walters, *Tory Wars*, p. 212. Norton, 'The Conservative leadership election', discusses the extent to which Portillo had (and had not) shifted in his ideological beliefs.

46 G. Jones, 'The choice is Europe or Thatcherism', *Daily Telegraph*, 18 July 2001.

5

Organisational reform
and the extra-parliamentary party

Richard Kelly

As shown by the history of the Labour Party after 1979, electorally defeated parties have a tendency to re-examine their organisation. After all, the main function of political parties is to seek power and the main function of party organisation is to help them achieve it. As such, electoral failure nearly always brings into question a party's internal arrangements – and this was certainly true of the Conservatives after the 1997 general election. As Alan Clark MP noted, 'the Conservative Party is now like a defeated and invaded country, where the old power structures are shattered and the old currency useless'.[1]

The lessons of 1997

After the 1997 defeat, Conservatives were inclined to argue that faulty organisation – particularly in respect of their extra-parliamentary wings – formed a key reason for the dismal showing. This is not to say they discounted their shortcomings in government or the advent of New Labour, but there was a clear sense that the enormity of the defeat could have been avoided had the party been organised differently. To support this thesis, Conservatives pointed to three factors which may have contributed to Labour's landslide.

A LACK OF UNITY

Between 1992 and 1997, the Conservative Party appeared chronically divided and 'at war with itself'.[2] Much of this disunity came from ideological uncertainty, particularly over Europe. Yet the problem was exacerbated by the peculiar nature of the extra-parliamentary party. The great anomaly of the Conservative organisation, dating from its inception after the 1867 Reform Act, was the formal divide between the party's MPs and its volunteers outside Parliament. Far from being a tightly knit party, the Conservatives were a collection of three disparate organisations: the Conservative Party in Parliament, the National Union of Conservative Associations (the voluntary extra-parliamentary party), and Conservative Central Office (the professional or bureaucratic wing of the extra-parliamentary party). As an Inland Revenue report confirmed in 1982, 'the Conservative Party' did not even exist as a legally recognised entity.[3]

After 1992, this organisational fracture had damaging consequences for the party's electability. It meant, for example, that parliamentary leaders had scant power over the reselection of MPs as parliamentary candidates, the National Union's separate status giving constituency members huge autonomy in matters of candidate selection. As a result, Euro-sceptic MPs like Teresa Gorman, having secured the backing of their associations, could be persistently critical of the leadership without seriously endangering their future as MPs.[4] This in turn diverted the loyalty of many Tory MPs; this in turn wounded party unity; this in turn gave an image of ineffectual leadership; this in turn cost votes.

This pitfall reappeared in the run-up to the 1997 general election. Anxious to contain the 'sleaze' factor, the leadership implored the Tatton association not to reselect Neil Hamilton as its candidate. Yet the association could not be compelled to do so, and chose to ignore the leadership's advice. The result was the loss of a safe Tory seat, and grave damage to the Tory cause.[5]

A LACK OF DEMOCRACY

The second vote-losing aspect of Conservative organisation was thought to be a lack of overall democracy. The party's structure was still based upon an arrangement mapped out under Disraeli: one where the extra-parliamentary party would always be subservient to the parliamentary leadership. This arrangement conflicted with the decline of deference among Tory members after 1979.[6] However, there were few concessions to party democracy during the Thatcher and Major governments. The party was supposedly 'reformed' and 'modernised' after 1992 via the twin reports of Sir Norman Fowler and Sir Basil Feldman. Yet the changes wrought were largely cosmetic, producing a 'Board of Management' whose functions were unclear, while confirming the primacy of the parliamentary leadership and the largely unelected nature of Conservative Central Office.[7]

That so little had changed was vividly demonstrated during the 1995 leadership contest. Whereas Labour sent out over 4 million ballot papers to all party members for its leadership contest in 1994, the Tories sent out only 329, the contest still being confined to MPs. To add insult to injury, local parties were 'consulted' by MPs, only for their advice to be frequently ignored. The Hazel Grove association, for example, gave unanimous support to the Prime Minister, yet its MP – Sir Tom Arnold – gave prominent backing to the challenger, John Redwood.[8]

The lack of influence accorded to the extra-parliamentary party, in such a high-profile area as leader selection, did not just foment division, it also strengthened the idea among voters that the party was elitist, insular, old fashioned, arrogant and corrupt – and thus meriting severe punishment in 1997.

A LACK OF MEMBERS

The lack of internal democracy contributed to the third vote-losing aspect of Tory organisation: falling membership. Across the democratic world, declining party membership is an almost inevitable consequence of socio-economic change. Yet, with social deference in decline, it is even harder to recruit members if they are to be denied substantial influence. By 1997, even Tory activists felt that the party was 'still a feudal oligarchy, where power is concentrated in the leader's office'.[9]

Conservative membership looked in poor health and was said to be no higher than 400,000 in 1997.[10] To make matters worse, a huge portion of members were passive and elderly. Holroyd-Doveton's study of the Young Conservatives, traditionally the most energetic wing of the party, claimed that membership had fallen from half a million in the 1950s to about 8,000 by 1995, with Whiteley's team calculating in 1992 that the typical party member was sixty-two and fewer than 150,000 were 'active' in party business.[11]

In an age of voter volatility, a party's electoral prospects are easily harmed by such trends. Psephology showed that, with the demise of nation-wide voting patterns, constituency campaigning was now often decisive, with a link unearthed between a party's vote in key marginal seats and the vigour of its campaign in the constituency concerned.[12] Members also boost a constituency party's revenue, with studies showing that a party performs better in constituencies where it spends an 'above average' amount on local campaigns.[13]

Long before the 1997 campaign started, the party recognised it would struggle with its constituency campaigns, especially in marginal seats where vigorous efforts were needed to counter anti-Tory tactical voting, and where since 1992 there had been a 30 per cent fall in the number of full-time constituency agents (professional organisers, traditionally employed to galvanise local campaigns). This gloomy assessment was later vindicated by the party's own pollsters, ICM, who claimed that 'low intensity' campaigns waged at constituency level led to the loss of up to eighty seats in 1997 – a staggering indictment of the party's membership and organisation.

Organisational reform: a Bennite or Blairite model?

In the aftermath of 1997, the party was apt to recognise that the structures of 1867 were redundant. The 1997 leadership contest (which again disenfranchised the extra-parliamentary membership) strengthened the momentum for change, with all five candidates promising greater unity and intra-party democracy. This consensus, however, merely begged a divisive question – namely, in which order should these two goals be pursued? This may have seemed a bland question, but it was actually crucial to both the distribution of power inside the party and its chances of regaining support.

Had the Conservatives chosen to prioritise party democracy, they might have stumbled on to a path similar to the one Tony Benn charted for the Labour Party between 1979 and 1981 – one which relocated power within the extra-parliamentary ranks, created executive bodies that would be accountable to the extra-parliamentary party, and which sought 'unity' only within the context of member sovereignty; in short, a 'bottom-up' party no longer in thrall to its parliamentary representatives.[14]

However, if the party chose to prioritise 'unity' and managerial cohesion, it would have chosen the path down which Neil Kinnock and then Tony Blair directed Labour after 1983 – one which allowed party leaders and national officials to 'manage' the party more convincingly, which entrusted to those leaders and officials the quest for more members, and which extended party democracy only as a way of serving the leader's strategic goals.[15] In other words, it involved the reinvention of a 'top-down' party that could achieve its aims more expediently and respectably, with the language of party democracy and OMOV ('one member one vote') cloaking the leader's steady accretion of power.

A RADICAL PROPOSAL

In the year leading up to the 1997 election, activists – already sensing defeat – had showed a growing interest in the quasi-Bennite option. Of particular interest was a proposal from the Party Reform Steering Committee (PSRC) – formed by a radical group of association chairmen in 1993 – which involved the abolition of the sprawling National Union, and its replacement by a single, yet pivotal, party committee that resembled Labour's National Executive Committee.

The committee PRSC wanted would have responsibility for all party matters outside Parliament, and would secure greater unity by harnessing senior parliamentarians to senior party activists. Yet it would also secure greater party democracy, and thus galvanise the membership, by ensuring that most committee members were voted in by, and accountable to, the constituency associations (only the leader and the Chairman of the MPs' 1922 Committee being *ex officio*). It was a bold idea with far-reaching implications; but it did not seem implausible given the coded support it received from the National Union Executive Committee, and its chairman Robin Hodgson.

RADICALISM POSTPONED

In the aftermath of the general election, however, the PRSC proposal was forgotten amid John Major's hasty resignation and the spiky leadership

contest. This served to focus the party's mind on just one aspect of organisation – the mechanics of leader selection – while distracting it from deeper
questions about power in the party. This has been corroborated by several
constituency agents, one of whom recalled:

> The leadership contest kept members interested in reform, but from then on
> they were preoccupied with just one area – the selection of party leaders and
> the battles they expected with MPs over who could vote in future.[16]

The membership's failure to see the 'wood for the trees' was to be deftly
exploited by William Hague in the first year of his leadership.

Hague's hijack

On 23 July 1997, Hague effectively hijacked the process of organisational
reform. In a 'declaration' at Central Office, he announced that he would use
the 'mandate' of his leadership victory to 'guide the party towards a fresh
and more modern organisation'.[17] The unilateral nature of this announcement
was telling, as was his failure to make any mention of either the PRSC or
the wider movement for reform inside the party. It suggested that, far from
favouring 'root and branch democracy' (as he hinted days earlier), the new
leader was taking the Kinnock–Blair road to reform, placing superficial unity
above genuine democratic reform.[18]

Hague quickly set up an *ad hoc* committee, charged with producing a
'green paper' of reform proposals in time for the 1997 party conference. Its
composition was instructive. Four of its five members were appointed by the
new leader, with only one – Hodgson – being able to claim some elective
link with the party membership. Surprisingly, there were few grass-root
complaints about this; but the party's Charter Group (set up by Kent activists
in 1981 to lobby for more party democracy) offers a worthy explanation:

> The membership trusted their new young leader to get on with it ... having
> got the ball rolling in 1996, the grass-roots dropped it in 1997. It was then
> picked up by Hague and his henchmen who ran off with it in a completely
> different direction.[19]

To understand why members trusted Hague to 'get on with it', it should
be recalled that Hague had cleverly distanced himself from the status quo by
giving loud support to the OMOV principle for future leadership contests,
an idea supported by most activists since 1992.[20] Yet many Tory MPs like
Archie Hamilton, chairman of the 1922 Committee, opposed it. This enabled
Hague to posture as the grass-roots' champion: a doughty, state-school
educated radical, confronting the parliamentary 'establishment'.

According to one of Hague's supporters, however, what the new leader
really wanted all along was the 'New Labourfication' of the Conservative

organisation, based on Hague's covert admiration for Labour's approach to opposition after 1994.[21] Central to this strategy was new MP Archie Norman, former boss of Asda, a former colleague of Hague's at the McKinsey management consultancy, and one of Hague's most trusted confidantes in the first year of his leadership. According to another Tory MP, Hague envisaged Norman as:

> A Tory Mandelson ... rooting out inefficiency in the party structure and turning it into a Millbank-style, vote-getting unit. The party would be rebuilt according to business management school principles, with the electorate seen as customers and membership as sales staff.[22]

This idea might well have wrought sweeping changes. But a significant extension of party democracy was unlikely to be among them.

Coaxing the members

'BACK ME OR SACK ME'

If, in terms of party management, there were similarities between Norman and Peter Mandelson, in terms of leadership techniques there were also similarities between Hague and Blair. An early illustration came with Hague's decision to organise an all-party ballot on his leadership, thus securing what Blair once called 'a licence from the whole party to drive the whole party'.[23]

To be held in the run-up to the 1997 conference, the ballot asked members to endorse both Hague and his 'six principles' of organisational change: 'unity, decentralisation, democracy, involvement, integrity, openness'. As there were no alternatives on offer, there was only a limited risk factor in Hague's 'back me or sack me' ballot. Nevertheless, among those who voted, almost a fifth rejected their new leader, with an apparent majority failing to vote at all (see Figure 5.1).

BLUEPRINT FOR CHANGE

Insisting that his authority was stiffened, Hague instructed his steering committee to finalise its green paper, *Our Party: Blueprint for Change*, before the close of the conference. Co-authored by Hodgson and new Party Chairman Lord Parkinson, its central suggestion reflected the main theme of the Party Reform Steering Committee, *viz*, the abolition of the National Union, and the creation of a 'single party' overseen by an all-powerful party board. Yet, unlike the PRSC, *Blueprint for Change* was hazy about the content of this committee, and the extent to which it should be elected by party members.

Any idea that the green paper might be assessed at the conference was blighted by the fact that its organisational debate was dominated by the issue of leadership elections – a subject with again drew the wrath of activists (encouraged by a populist speech from Lord Archer). It was accepted,

1 October 1997: Hague's leadership
   Yes: 142,299 (80.7%) No: 34,092 (19.3%)
   Ballot papers returned: 44%

2 February 1998: *The Fresh Future*
   Yes: 110,165 (96.1%) No: 4,425 (3.9%)
   Ballot papers returned: 33%

3 October 1998: Euro policy
   Yes: 175,588 (84.8%) No: 31,392 (15.2%)
   Ballot papers returned: 60%

4 October 2000: Draft manifesto
   Yes: 49,932 (98.8%) No: 576 (1.2%)
   Ballot papers returned: 16%

5 September 2001: Leadership contest
   Kenneth Clarke: 100,864 (39.2%) Iain Duncan Smith: 155,933 (60.7%)
   Ballot papers returned: 79%

Figure 5.1 Conservative all-party ballots, 1997–2001

however, that *Blueprint for Change* would be discussed more thoroughly in the months that followed.

Parkinson organised twenty-six party 'road shows' between October and December 1997, where all interested members could express an opinion about the future shape of the party. Activists were aware that *Blueprint for Change* would form the genesis of a final set of proposals to be voted on – in another all-party ballot – the following spring. If successful, the proposals would then form the basis of a new Conservative Party Constitution.

Over 3,000 members attended the road shows, overseen by Parkinson's team from Central Office. Yet many seemed unhappy with the format. According to one association chairman:

> All we were allowed to do was discuss their proposals and their ideas. They [the Parkinson team] weren't really interested in any initiatives we might have had, and it was made clear that they would be the ones who drew up the final proposals.[24]

THE FRESH FUTURE

The final proposals were indeed drawn up by Parkinson, Hodgson and Hamilton and collated into a 'white paper', entitled *The Fresh Future* and published in February 1998. When comparing *The Fresh Future* with *Blueprint for Change*, there were few signs that membership input made much difference during Parkinson's road shows. This was noticeable in relation to the replacement of the National Union by a new Party Board, the centrepiece of the proposed party constitution (see Appendix p. 103).

One of the most important suggestions of *Blueprint for Change* was that 'about half of the Board should be elected and half appointed by the Leader, including the Party Chairman'. When compared to the PRSC idea, this represented a clear dilution of party democracy; it is perhaps unsurprising that only 50 per cent of respondents expressed agreement, with almost a third disagreeing strongly.[25]

Yet, with breathtaking chutzpah, the authors of *The Fresh Future* went on to dilute even further the Board's democratic content, proposing that only five of its seventeen officers should be elected by the membership. Even these would be elected not by the whole membership, but by the 1,000-odd senior officials on the new National Convention (see Appendix p. 103). Indeed, nine of the Board's members would have no elective connection at all to the constituency membership. Any grass-root dissent, however, was to be quelled by a suspiciously timely development at Westminster.

Just weeks before the ballot was due, it was announced that MPs had relented on the issue of leadership selection, accepting OMOV as opposed to their initial compromise idea of an electoral college. By the time members came to vote on *The Fresh Future* (which would now incorporate the MPs' *volte face*) talk in the party was dominated by what journalists called 'the MPs' surrender' and the 'triumph of the activists' – effectively distracting attention from the Board's undemocratic tendencies.[26] All this made the clear 'yes' vote barely surprising, although the low turnout prompted the Charter Movement to contest the legitimacy of the reforms (see Figure 5.1).

When reflecting on the birth of *The Fresh Future*, the parallels with New Labour party management are almost eerie – particularly in respect of Labour's Clause IV debate of 1994–95. There too was a tightly managed 'consultation' period, with members only allowed to discuss proposals drawn up by the leadership. There too was an all-party ballot to validate change. There too, members could merely ratify or reject the package on offer. And, there too, a new party leader claimed democratic backing for a reform which arguably cheated party democracy.[27]

Fresh Future, fresh oligarchy: the erosion of local autonomy

The associations had very limited control over the new Board's composition. This was a serious, democratic failure given its new and extensive powers over them. Three particular areas of Board jurisdiction suggested that, under the new 'single party' arrangement, the associations had surrendered their former autonomy to the new Party Board, which then granted them responsibility without power. Put simply, members were accountable to this new centralised committee, yet had little influence upon it.

The first of these areas stems from a sub-unit of the Board known as the Ethics and Integrity Committee (EIC), comprising just four people: two QCs appointed by the Party Chairman, the Chairman of the 1922 Committee and the Chairman of the National Convention. It was empowered to act 'whenever the reputation of our party is threatened' by the associations, their chosen candidates or indeed any other party member. According to Article 81 of the new Constitution, the EIC was able to suspend or expel 'any individual who brings the party into disrepute'.[28]

In the mind of most activists, the EIC was set up to prevent any more Tatton-style scenarios, where the party was damaged by a candidate seemingly short of personal integrity. Its work in the Hague era bears out this impression – its most serious task being the investigation, and then suspension, of Lord Archer in February 2000, amid police inquiries into the peer's libel case of 1987. However, 'disrepute' is a loaded term and it might yet be used to debar the reselection of rebellious MPs. If so, the national party bureaucracy has quietly gained more control over both backbenchers and constituency parties: a clear echo of the centralising trends within the Labour Party after 1989.[29]

The second area where associations have been compromised concerns the Board's 'efficiency criteria', a set of standards laid down by the Board which govern the everyday conduct of constituency parties.[30] If these are not met, the Board can step in to reorganise an association, sack its officials and temporarily assume command of its affairs – very similar to what happened in the Labour Party under Kinnock when a string of constituency parties where purged and reformed by national apparatchiks.

The third area concerns the power that national officials may now have to plunder association funds. Although Central Office has been in almost constant debt since 1983, certain associations (like Aylesbury and Hampshire East) are legendarily flush, their surpluses protected by the associations' historic autonomy. However, under the new Constitution, associations are obliged to give the Board annual details of their accounts and, when allied to the 'single party' ethos, this could lead to the Board raiding local party funds in search of central party solvency. As a result, the associations' financial independence, once a vital check upon oligarchic rule within the party, has been discreetly weakened.

The Norman conquest: a reformed Central Office

If the new Board gave constituency members greater responsibility without much extra power, it also gave certain national officials greater power without much extra responsibility. Archie Norman was a prime example of this development. Norman was the new leader's organisational guru – Hague firmly believing that the managerial principles which revived Asda supermarkets could also revitalise the Conservative Party. Norman was appointed to the new position of Chief Executive in July 1998, his brief being to 'overhaul and modernise Conservative Central Office'.[31] It is telling that the appointment was made unilaterally by Hague, clearly unencumbered by the Party Board, the National Convention, or indeed any of the 'democratising' party bodies created by the 1998 reforms.

Norman set about a 'rationalisation' of Central Office (CCO) which involved a £3 million cut in spending, redundancy for 40 per cent of the staff, plus the closure of several regional offices. Those sacked included former campaigns manager Tony Garrett, an official who had worked with the party for twenty-seven years and who had nurtured a large network of useful allies at association level – many of whom were 'outraged' by his departure.[32]

Norman's rationalisation was made more provocative by the management consultant he brought in to assist him: Peter Samuel, someone with impeccable managerial credentials, but also chairman of the Reigate Liberal Democrats and their candidate at the 1997 general election. As one association chairman commented:

> It is bad enough that a man who spends his leisure time fighting our party should be given access to our national office. But it is incredible that he should be paid, out of party funds, to effectively sack loyal servants of the Conservative Party.[33]

The outcome of the Norman–Samuel 'revolution' was what Norman billed a 'World Class Political Centre', unveiled in August 1998 (see Figure 5.2). Plagiarising Labour's Millbank headquarters, it gave CCO a 'war room' format that would grant huge leverage to its Research and Communications Directors, notably Danny Finkelstein and Amanda Platell. Again, such key officials were to be appointed by either Hague or Norman, rather than elected by the membership.

Norman also reshaped two other areas of CCO activity without much regard for party democracy.

FINANCE

The new Income Generation and Marketing Department was to be run, like the old Treasurer's Department, by an appointed party Treasurer – the unelected status of the party's chief fund-raiser being a particular gripe of the Charter Movement and PRSC. It might have been thought that, with the impending Neill report on party funding (limiting national campaign spending and individual donations), the new Department's focus would eschew plutocratic donations for more constituency-based fund-raising.

In fact, the opposite occurred, party fund-raising after 1997 becoming even more synonymous with a handful of wealthy contributors.[34] Tycoon Michael Ashcroft was appointed Treasurer in 1998, largely because his own

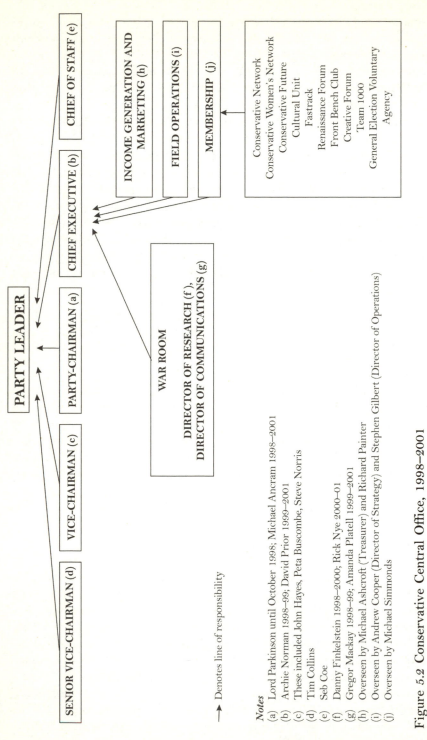

PARTY LEADER

- SENIOR VICE-CHAIRMAN (d)
- VICE-CHAIRMAN (c)
- PARTY-CHAIRMAN (a)
- CHIEF EXECUTIVE (b)
- CHIEF OF STAFF (e)

WAR ROOM

DIRECTOR OF RESEARCH (f),
DIRECTOR OF COMMUNICATIONS (g)

INCOME GENERATION AND MARKETING (h)

FIELD OPERATIONS (i)

MEMBERSHIP (j)

- Conservative Network
- Conservative Women's Network
- Conservative Future
- Cultural Unit
- Fastrack
- Renaissance Forum
- Front Bench Club
- Creative Forum
- Team 1000
- General Election Voluntary Agency

→ Denotes line of responsibility

Notes

(a) Lord Parkinson until October 1998; Michael Ancram 1998–2001
(b) Archie Norman 1998–99; David Prior 1999–2001
(c) These included John Hayes, Peta Buscombe, Steve Norris
(d) Tim Collins
(e) Seb Coe
(f) Danny Finkelstein 1998–2000; Rick Nye 2000–01
(g) Gregor Mackay 1998–99; Amanda Platell 1999–2001
(h) Overseen by Michael Ashcroft (Treasurer) and Richard Painter
(i) Overseen by Andrew Cooper (Director of Strategy) and Stephen Gilbert (Director of Operations)
(j) Overseen by Michael Simmonds

Figure 5.2 Conservative Central Office, 1998–2001

Sources: Archie Norman, MPMO, 14 July 1998; Chris Poole (Secretary, National Convention) letter, 13 June 2001.

donations had 'kept the party going' since 1997.[35] Accounts published in October 2000 showed that Ashcroft was bankrolling the party to the tune of over £1 million a year, making his total contributions since 1997 well over £4 million.[36] Ashcroft's main impact seemed to be in increasing the number of individuals donating over £5,000 – from thirty-three in 1997–98 to 126 in 1999–2000. Donated income increased to £7.2 million (the £5 million promised for the 2001 election by Stuart Wheeler, of the IGIndex spread-betting company, proved especially newsworthy). To Ashcroft's credit, these gifts helped convert a CCO deficit of £8 million in 1997 to a surplus of £4,000 in 2000.

Ashcroft's financial strategy, however, did little to alter the oligarchic nature of power inside the Conservative Party. Having had so little influence over the raising of revenue, activists could do little but complain about dubious expenditure sanctioned by national officials. The 'Listening to Britain' exercise, which ran between July 1998 and July 1999 (see below), cost over £250,000. Yet neither the idea nor its execution was seriously considered by the bulk of party members.[37]

MEMBERSHIP RECRUITMENT

Norman's new Membership and Constituency Services Section was also undemocratically structured and did little to empower constituency members. On becoming leader, Hague had committed himself to expanding the membership to almost a million, with at least half the new members being under thirty-five. However, as with Labour's national membership scheme of the late 1980s, this task was not to be entrusted to existing constituency members. Instead, the task was assigned to a host of unelected – and, to most members, oblique – agencies within CCO's Membership section, all trying to recruit members centrally.

Simply because of their sheer number (see Figure 5.2), it was inevitable that these agencies would overlap and waste party resources in the process. 'Conservative Network', found itself targeting the same 'young professionals' as the new 'Fastrack' outfit, while those running the 'Renaissance Forum' (aimed at 'energetic entrepreneurs') often collided with those from 'Team 1000'.[38]

Despite some slick advertising, these new central bodies had limited impact. The 'Conservative Women's Network', set up to recruit 'high flying professional women', was described in 2001 (by its outgoing chief Peta Buscombe) as a 'depressing failure', with women under forty-five representing just 2 per cent of the membership.[39] It is also striking that the number of ballot papers sent out for the 2001 leadership race (about 318,000) was significantly less than that sent out for the first all-party ballot of 1997 (399,203). This may simply suggest that by 2001 the party had a more realistic view of its membership figures. But it also suggests that, far from rising to the giddy heights predicted by Hague in 1997, membership may have fallen by about a fifth during his leadership.

NORMAN'S LEGACY

Norman's tenure as 'chief executive' ended in the summer of 1999. His claim that the party bureaucracy had been 'streamlined' merits intense scepticism. As Figure 5.2 reveals, it merely produced a labyrinthine structure that lacked any obvious chain of command. The question of who was *primus inter pares* – Party Chairman or Chief Executive – was never resolved; the issue of whether the Senior Vice Chairman (Tim Collins) was primarily responsible to the leader or Party Chairman remained unclear; while the status of Seb Coe (Chief of Staff and one of Hague's most trusted advisors) was problematic for many CCO staffers. By 2001 CCO was in a state of 'internecine confusion', prompting quips that Norman brought about the 'Asdastruction' of party headquarters.[40]

There was little evidence of the 'democratic revolution' promised by Hague in July 1997. The associations' influence upon CCO was unenlarged, while (thanks to the new Board) CCO's influence upon the associations was extended. Although the structures might have been 'fresh', the locus of power was decidedly stale.

Concessions to democracy?

In view of what has been written so far, it is strange to recall Hague's insistence that he had 'democratised' the party. To make sense of this, it must be conceded that, in three corners of the party organisation, there was some evidence of OMOV principles being applied – these being policy formation, candidate selection and leadership selection. Yet the key point about these changes is their origin: most came not from a democratised command structure (which, as we have seen, was not a feature of the 1998 reforms), but from a reformed oligarchy that occasionally trusted the membership. Furthermore, in all three areas, the democratic element was diluted in the interests of centralised party management.

POLICY FORMATION

According to the leadership, the democratisation of policy took two forms. First, Hague's leadership saw the advent of all-party ballots not just on organisational matters but on policy matters too. The first example of this came in the autumn of 1998, when the party was balloted on the leadership's tougher stance on the European single currency (see Figure 5.1).

Although 85 per cent of voters endorsed Hague's policy, far from giving members a rational choice about European policy, the ballot was presented as yet another vote of confidence in the leadership (in which case the 'No's' and abstainers represented an alarming number of anti-Hague members). It was widely recognised within the party that by ordering the ballot, Hague was not simply driven by a desire for party democracy; he also saw it as an effective way of binding the party to his chosen European policy and silencing its critics within the party (again redolent of Blair's Labour Party ballots on Clause IV and the 1997 manifesto).

The second all-party ballot on policy came at the end of 2000, when members were asked to endorse the leadership's draft manifesto, *Believing in Britain*. As with Labour's manifesto ballot of 1996, members were not given the chance to approve or reject specific items; they could either take it or leave it. According to the party's own figures, over four-fifths chose to leave it – the overwhelming 'yes' vote being less important than the fact that so few members took part (see Figure 5.1).

When questioned about the 'take it or leave it' aspect of the manifesto ballot, Central Office officials conceded that the draft had been mainly constructed by the leader's 'A-Team' of senior MPs and advisors: Hague, Lansley, Finkelstein, Michael Portillo, Ann Widdecombe and Francis Maude. Yet it was stressed that that there had been 'an unusually wide' degree of consultation beforehand, particularly during the 'Listening to Britain' exercise of 1998–99.[41]

'Listening to Britain' involved over 1,400 meetings open to the general public and had various offshoots – such as the 200 or so 'Listening to Britain's Churches' meetings that apparently shaped the leader's strong support for marriage. This type of consultation was later complemented by a 'Common Sense Revolution' page on the party's web site: a cybernetic focus group, where browsers were invited to write in two 'common sense suggestions'. Here again, the large number of 'hits' concerning law and order and asylum were said to have affected the details of *Believing in Britain*.[42] Yet the main point about this consultation was that, like New Labour's addiction to focus groups, it short-circuited party members.

In this respect, 'Listening to Britain' represented a vital change in the ethos of the Conservative Party, one which weakened further the autonomy and discretion of its constituency bodies. Even ten years earlier, policy consultation within the party had been quite member-oriented. During the 1980s, and for much of the twentieth century, the Conservative Party's 'conference system' had been a trusted conduit for electorally beneficial advice: the leadership trusting speakers from 'the floor' to transmit voters' opinions, as gleaned by their associations, to those sitting on the platform.[43] This system was judged obsolete by 1997, with 'Listening to Britain' seen as a more direct and effective method of connecting voters to Tory policy makers.

Constituency members were not altogether excluded from this process; but in so far as they were involved, it was simply a case of them carrying out centrally devised procedures (as contained in the *Listening to Britain*

---

1 Conservative Policy Forum General Council commission 'outline documents' from policy specialists

2 Documents sent out to associations

3 Associations form policy forums to discuss documents. Reports sent back to CPF Director

4 Director passes reports to relevant shadow cabinet minister(s)

5 Shadow Cabinet minister or Director replies to associations

6 Associations may debate replies and send subsequent report to Director

7 Shadow cabinet ministers absorb forum reports into speech at main party conference

8 Conference acclaims minister = 'good conference' for party managers.

Figure 5.3 The Policy Forum system

Source: R. Kelly, 'Farewell Conference, Hello Forum', *Political Quarterly*, 72:3 (2001).

Constituency Manual) before passing back the results, verbatim, to Central Office officials. As Andrew Lansley, its Director, commented: 'The rationale was to get in touch with the electorate, to extend our regular contact *beyond members* (italics added) ... and to change the culture of the party.'[44]

There was, however, still some opportunity for members-only contributions to detailed policy development, principally via the 'policy forums' set up under *The Fresh Future* (see Figure 5.3). These forums replicated an idea first outlined in Labour's 1997 *Partnership in Power* document and, as with Labour's own forums, were a response to the supposed failings of the party conference.

After 1997, the establishments of both parties claimed that the party conference did not allow ordinary members to make detailed contributions to policy discussion, and that constituency-based forums were a better mechanism for assimilating grass-root policy ideas. However, it is reasonable to assume that both party hierarchies were also worried about the damaging publicity wrought by stormy conference debates.

From the late 1980s onwards, Tory conferences seemed potentially more explosive than Labour's, as members threw off sycophancy in favour of frank criticism. The 1997 conference showed that this trend had not been abated by opposition; indeed, activists queued up to attack the competence and integrity of the parliamentary party.[45] Consequently, the new leadership was keen to remodel Tory conferences with an eye to those of New Labour: relatively supine affairs, where criticism was often defused by imminent reports from policy forums.

In fairness to the forum system, over 5,000 constituency members were enthused enough to take part between 1999 and 2000, producing over 400 reports on assorted policy issues. In addition, participants often claimed a link between their conclusions and the details of *Believing in Britain*. One example of this came with marriage tax allowance (abolished by Labour in 1999). Hague had initially called for straightforward restoration. Yet, during their discussions of August 2000, forum members showed a surprisingly modern view of marriage and 'lifestyle', with a majority favouring an allowance which only rewards married couples with young children. Three months later, the leadership's own position was softened.[46]

It is interesting that, when explaining its U-turn, the leadership did not acknowledge the membership's influence, claiming instead that the change arose from the Shadow Cabinet's working party. Activists were being gently reminded that, despite their trumpeted role in *The Fresh Future*, the forums could only offer 'advice' on policy, which the leadership was free to disregard. Indeed, the party's U-turn on both the minimum wage and the independence of the Bank of England (accepting both) stemmed not from policy forums, or any consultation with the extra-parliamentary party, but from an inner circle within the Shadow Cabinet; activists being told, *fait accompli*, at the end of 1999.

CANDIDATE SELECTION

In the selection of Conservative candidates for Westminster, European and regional elections, *The Fresh Future* was keen to uphold the OMOV doctrine. Between 1997 and 2001, the Tories were not associated with some of the dubious practises seen in the selection of Labour candidates (the arrival in St Helens South of the Tories' former Communications Director, Shaun Woodward, being the most reported example).

By contrast, the Tories' procedures seemed refreshingly open and inclusive, the selection of Westminster candidates coming from a short-list of three to five candidates at a general association meeting which enfranchised all members. Kensington and Chelsea in 1999, which selected Michael Portillo at a general meeting attended by over 800 members. The principle of selecting at 'open-to-all' general meetings was also observed in the selection of Boris Johnson (Henley) and Paul Goodman (Wycombe).

Party democracy also seemed to have advanced in the selection of European Parliamentary candidates in 1999, competing for the first time under proportional representation (PR). In each of the 'areas' created by the PR system, every party member was entitled to attend a Final Selection Meeting to both choose and grade a list of Tory candidates; in the South East area, this involved over 1,500 turning up at the London Docklands arena which had been hired for the occasion. In the process of selection, it was also clear that (unlike in the Labour Party) prominent individuals were not being 'shoehorned' into safe positions: only four out of 120 interested ex-MPs gained a winnable place, with the rejected including loyalists like Tony Newton and dissidents like Norman Lamont.[47]

The party also emerged with some credit from the selection of candidates for the Scottish Parliament and Welsh and Greater London Assemblies (elected under the Additional Member System of PR), selecting both constituency and regional candidates through meetings open to all members, and again avoiding the charge that senior candidates were guaranteed prime positions, a charge that dogged Labour's Alun Michael in Wales. When selecting the mayoral candidate in Greater London, the party also conducted OMOV postal ballots open to all Greater London members, first selecting Lord Archer over Steve Norris and then, in a 'replay', Norris over Andrew Boff. On both occasions, the postal vote was preceded by a hustings open to all party members, which then voted on the final two candidates.

Although candidate selection afforded a large degree of influence to ordinary members, *The Fresh Future* cemented centrally controlled 'approved lists' of candidates. Apart from those seeking election to local councils, all would-be candidates had to appear on these lists before seeking nomination; and the lists' gatekeepers remained a party vice-chairman appointed by the leader and a clutch of anonymous Central Office officials.

Constituency autonomy was also threatened by the new Ethics and Integrity Committee and its 'efficiency criteria' for the associations, both of which gave national officials a potential veto over local selections. In the years ahead, this potential might well be exploited by a party hierarchy desperate to offer an electable brand of Conservatism, with matching candidates. Here again, New Labour could be an inspiration, Millbank having blocked a series of 'unsound' candidates while in opposition.[48]

LEADERSHIP SELECTION

For many students of party organisation, and for many in the Conservative Party, the 'democratisation' of Tory leadership elections was the defining feature of *The Fresh Future*. Disillusioned by the conduct of Tory MPs during the Major government, and scandalised by their monopoly of the 1997 leadership contest, the associations had demanded a clearer say in choosing party leaders. But the grass-roots' obsession with leadership selection came at a price – an erosion of democracy within the party overall.

Nevertheless, following *The Fresh Future*'s reform of leader elections, Hague claimed a huge advance for grass-root power. There would be no Labour-style electoral college, where some votes carried more weight than others: the new Conservative system would allow its leadership contests to be decided by a pure, OMOV ballot where the vote of an ordinary constituency member was equal to that of a frontbench MP. However, the grass-roots would only get a choice of two candidates – the number having been whittled down by a series of 'quality control' ballots confined to MPs.

The new system was given its first outing following Hague's sudden resignation after the 2001 election. As this was the first Tory leadership contest to enfranchise constituency members, it was always going to be a remarkable contest. Nevertheless, a number of telling points were to emerge about the new system and the state of the party generally.

Firstly, the 'either–or' nature of the final, OMOV ballot was a serious dilution of party democracy, and elicited many complaints from members keen on a wider choice.[49] Indeed, polls suggested that many members, if forced to accept a choice of just two, wanted one involving Iain Duncan Smith and David Davis (the latter being excluded following the second ballot of MPs). These polls also showed considerable anger that one of the two final candidates was Kenneth Clarke, whose views on Europe made him 'an impossible option' for many members unsure about Duncan Smith.[50]

Secondly, following the final MPs-only ballot, party authorities came under pressure (notably from supporters of Portillo) to widen the choice available to members. Only one vote, after all, came between Duncan Smith (who came second) and Portillo (who was eliminated); indeed, only six votes stood between Portillo and Clarke, who topped the final MPs' poll. However, Sir Michael Spicer, chairman of the 1922 Committee, defended the either–or system on the grounds that more candidates might 'diminish the winner's share of the vote', a weak argument given the existence of electoral systems such as that used to elect the Greater London mayor.[51] Had the result of the OMOV ballot been close, the party could have finished with the worst of all worlds – namely, a limited choice for members, which then produced a winner with only the barest of mandates.

Thirdly, despite Clarke's emergence in the final round, there were signs that grass-root opinion influenced the votes of several MPs during the preliminary ballots. Portillo's failure to build up support in the second and third rounds of the parliamentary ballots was apparently affected by the negative vibes many MPs detected about him from their associations.[52] This covert extension of party democracy, however, has to be tempered by the fact that in 476 associations, there was no Tory MP through whom members could transmit their opinions; neither was there any alternative channel provided by the party. As Tories in seatless areas like Liverpool remarked: 'in terms of which two candidates we could choose from, our opinions counted for absolutely nothing'.[53]

A fourth point is that the OMOV ballot was given added importance by the fragmented support of Tory MPs. In the first parliamentary ballot, not one of the five candidates polled even a third of the votes, while in the final ballot no candidate came close to achieving a majority. As such, the membership's choice was unaffected by any clear preference on the part of Tory MPs: the extent to which members could be affected by MPs' preferences thus remains unclear.

Fifthly, thanks to the all-party *finale*, Duncan Smith was able to win the leadership without having won the backing of even a plurality, let alone majority, of his own MPs (Portillo and then Clarke topping the MPs-only elections). Even in the final ballot, barely a third of Tory MPs backed the man who, two months later, became their leader. It remains to be seen how this anomaly will affect Duncan Smith's authority within the parliamentary party. Although he is not the first leader of a major party to be elected by extra-parliamentary members, he is the first to be elected without being the clear favourite among a party's MPs (Kinnock, Smith and Blair all had substantial leads within the MPs' section of Labour's electoral college). Duncan Smith is in uncharted waters as far as modern party leadership is concerned, and it may prove difficult for him to assert discipline over recalcitrant Tory MPs.

Sixthly, the final result, announced on 13 September, suggests that the Conservative Party has even fewer members than previously supposed.[54] CCO had sent out 318,000 ballot papers via the constituency associations (stating that only those who had joined before 28 March could vote). According to CCO, 20 per cent of members 'abstained'. Yet, given that turnout in the four preceding party ballots never exceeded 207,050 (see Figure 5.1), it is reasonable to assume that those who voted in 2001 were practically the whole Conservative membership. *Ergo,* the party may well have fewer than 260,000 members.

The contest also highlighted the mysterious nature of Conservative membership. With the party's national membership scheme being set up in 1998, only about 33,000 members could be identified by party headquarters. Even John Barnes, an academic authority on the party and active constituency member, knew 'next to nothing' about the bulk of members in his own association, claiming that only about 5 per cent were ever seen.[55] Efforts to find out more were hampered by the Data Protection Act and its rigid enforcement by CCO's acting chief executive, David Prior. The two final candidates could not contact members directly, and had to rely on each association distributing their A4-size manifestos to members. As the *Daily Telegraph* remarked this was 'the first election in the history of the world where contenders are unable to know who their electorate is'.[56]

Polls carried out during the contest supported Whiteley *et al.*'s findings, by indicating that about 80 per cent of members were over sixty. But these polls also showed that the membership had become much more exercised by the European issue and more Euro-sceptic as a result – underlined by Clarke's heavy defeat. They also showed that only a third of members accepted the case for 'radical change' within the party: a factor in their hostility to Portillo.[57]

Finally, the OMOV contest highlighted the limited role of the National Convention, billed by *The Fresh Future* as a pivotal body for extra-parliamentary members (see Appendix p. 103). During the contest, it convened only once for a two hour hustings, with attendance circumscribed by its mid-week, afternoon scheduling. Of far more importance were the eight hustings organised across the country during August, which attracted about 5,300 activists.[58]

CHALLENGING THE LEADER

Owing to Hague's voluntary departure, we are yet to gauge fully *The Fresh Future*'s effect upon challenging an incumbent leader. However, both the 1998 rules and the 2001 contest point to a clear limit upon intra-party democracy. The rules state that a vote of confidence can only be sparked by a petition signed by 15 per cent of MPs, that only MPs can vote, that a mere 51 per cent voting 'No' means the leader has lost, and – crucially – that such a leader cannot be a candidate in a subsequent contest. This means that a leader who has won overwhelming support from the grass-roots could still be ousted by a numerically small fraction of party members (just eighty-four MPs according to 2001 figures). Given Duncan Smith's limited support in the MPs-only ballots of 2001, such a scenario is not implausible and was highlighted by the refusal of several prominent MPs (including Clarke, Portillo, Maude, Widdecombe and Norman) to serve in his Shadow Cabinet.

On the other hand, Duncan Smith might be secured by the new and tortuous process of finding a replacement. As we saw in 2001, leadership contests which go beyond Westminster take far longer to complete: whereas it took the Tories less than three weeks to oust and replace Margaret Thatcher, it took them over three months to find a successor to Hague. Subsequently, there may be strong incentives to leave an incumbent alone, as a drawn-out challenge (especially one as acrimonious as the Clarke/Duncan Smith battle) could damage the party even more than the continuation of a lacklustre leader. This calculation that probably saved Kinnock's leadership of the Labour Party between 1990 and 1992, eclipsing the Parliamentary Labour Party's fear that he was an electoral liability.[59] All this suggests that swift and ruthless changes of leadership – a recurrent feature of Tory history – are now less likely thanks to *The Fresh Future*. Far from making future Tory leaders more 'accountable', as Hague suggested, the reform may have simply made them more comfortable.

By the end of 2001, there was a widespread belief inside the party that the 1998 leadership rules would not even survive their first try-out. At the 2001 party conference, the Campaign for Conservative Democracy (led by John Strafford) spearheaded demands for a shorter contest which gave constituency members a wider choice of candidates – an idea supported by several MPs, such as Andrew Tyrie. New Party Chairman, David Davis, accepted the need for 'review and fine-tuning', despite ruling out any 'complete overhaul' of procedures.[60]

Conclusion: new defeat, old lessons

The 1997 defeat undermined Conservatives' faith in their old organisation. Strangely, the party's equally poor showing in 2001 did not ignite similar criticism of their new one. As in 1997, no one seriously argues that the Tories lost because of poor organisation. Yet, when surveying the size of the defeat, and the fact the party made virtually no progress since 1997, we can again argue that flawed organisation was a contributory factor. Although the party looked more cohesive in 2001 than it did in 1997, behind the glossy exterior lay serious organisational problems – problems which were either ignored, or caused, by *The Fresh Future*.

Reflecting on the 2001 defeat, one constituency agent described the Tories' campaign as akin 'to an army which over-relies on heroic officers'.[61] The campaign was heavily centralised, depending to a large extent on the physical stamina of Hague, who covered more miles during a general election campaign than any previous Tory leader. Yet the leader was conspicuously short of foot soldiers in the constituencies he visited.

Most of us who observed the Tories' local campaigns in 2001 would affirm the party's reputation for an ageing, dwindling and inactive membership. Given the importance of constituency campaigning, we might conclude that, as in 1997, the Tories' weak constituency campaigns in 2001 were a crucial reason for the defeat in most target seats. *Inter alia*, this strongly suggests that the reorganisation of 1998 was either irrelevant or ineffective, a new defeat simply highlighting old problems.

As Hague himself argued when he became leader, to get more votes the party needed more members; to get more members it needed more democracy; and to get more democracy it needed to decentralise. Yet, *The Fresh Future* lost sight of this basic thesis and chose instead to ape the centralising trends of the Labour Party – overlooking studies which showed that these trends *retarded* Labour's prospects at the 1987 and 1992 elections, and were only exonerated in 1997 after a disastrous period of Tory government.[62]

It is true that the language of OMOV was heard inside the Tory Party after 1997, and that this sometimes led (as with candidate selection) to greater empowerment of ordinary members. But, as with New Labour, the leadership's use of OMOV was less a sign of thoroughbred democracy than of short-term party management, helping to stifle the leader's critics within the parliamentary party while making the party look more 'modern' and 'inclusive'.[63]

The axis of the 1998 reform was not OMOV, but an overarching Party Board with only limited democratic input. Its existence was to nourish the party's top–down mentality, stifle grass-root initiatives, sanction the unaccountable power of people like Archie Norman, dupe senior MPs into thinking that, by dealing with this Board and its various committees, they were dealing with 'the party', and stall a reform process which, in terms of exalting (and thus attracting) constituency members, still had a long way to go by 1998.

Consequently, by 2001 the party was still languid outside its central headquarters. The party's Area Campaign Directors were left to cover thirty to forty seats each, instead of the ten to twenty which most of them see as conducive to efficiency; the Area Research Departments had all but vanished, leaving many candidates unsure about the constituencies they were contesting; and party organisation was almost non-existent in major cities other than London – partly accounting for the Tories' failure to come even second in any Manchester or Liverpool constituency.

The result of this regional atrophy, and the loss of members that went with it, was obvious during the 2001 campaign: an impossible burden placed upon the leader and his elite corps. As his resignation showed, this burden took a heavy toll upon Hague. But it was one his own reforms invited.

Appendix: *Fresh Future*, fresh structures

THE BOARD

The Board meets once a month and has ultimate responsibility for all aspects of party management outside Parliament. In September 2001, its composition was as follows:

David Davis (Party Chairman)+
John Taylor (Chairman of National Convention)*
David Prior (Deputy Party Chairman and CCO Chief Executive)+
Lord Ashcroft (Chairman, Board of Treasurers)+
Jean Searle (President, National Convention)*
Richard Stephenson (Vice-President, National Convention)*
Don Porter (President, National Convention)*
Caroline Abel-Smith (Vice-President, National Convention)*
Sir Michael Spicer (Chairman of 1922 Committee)+
Lord Hanningfield (Chairman, Conservative Councillors' Association)
Lord Strathclyde (Party leader in House of Lords)+
Bill Walker (Deputy Chairman, Scottish Party)
Henri Lloyd-Davies (Chairman, Welsh Party)
Stephen Gilbert (Director, Field Operations CCO)+
Edward Macmillan-Scott (Leader of Conservative MEPs)+
Lord Trefgarne (Chairman, Association of Conservative Peers)+
Chris Poole (Secretary to the Board – but no vote)+

THE NATIONAL CONVENTION

This is the representative body of the voluntary party and is the successor to the National Union. Comprising about 1000 officials, it meets twice a year: once at its Spring Conference, where its officers and representative on the

Party Board are elected, and again at the main party conference. It is supported by a network of 11 regional councils and 42 area councils. Its membership comprises:

The Chairman of every constituency association

Its Chairman, 2 Presidents, and 2 Vice-Presidents
(who also serve as its representatives on the Board)

Members of Area Management Executives

Regional Co-ordinating Chairmen and their deputies

Representatives of party's youth, women and other recognised
organisations

Its 3 immediate past Presidents

Its 2 immediate past Chairmen

The immediate past Area Chairmen

The immediate past Regional Co-ordinating Chairmen

THE NATIONAL CONVENTION EXECUTIVE

Replacing the National Union Executive Committee, the NCE meets more often than the Convention and prepares reports for its inspection. It includes the Convention's six senior officers and its elected members of the Board.

Notes: * Elected by constituency members via National Convention
+ No elective connection to membership
Source: *The Fresh Future*, Conservative Party 1998; *Conference Guide*, BBC News Research Department, 2001

Notes

1 Quoted in B. Anderson, 'New leader, new voting?', *The Spectator*, 17 May 1997.

2 D. Finkelstein, 'Why the Conservatives lost', in I. Crewe, B. Gosschalk and B. Bartle (eds), *Political Communications* (London, Frank Cass, 1998), pp. 12–15.

3 *Charter News*, April 1989.

4 R. Kelly, 'The whip hand Tory rebels could hold', *Parliamentary Brief*, February 1995.

5 P. Whiteley, 'The Conservative campaign', *Parliamentary Affairs*, 50:4 (1997) 542–54.

6 R. Kelly, *Conservative Party Conferences: The Hidden System* (Manchester, Manchester University Press, 1989).

7 B. Feldman, *Report on the Review of the National Union of Conservative and Unionist Associations* (London, Conservative Central Office, 1993); N. Fowler, *One Party: Reforming The Conservative Party Organisation* (London, Conservative Central Office, 1993).

8 R. Kelly, 'Choosing Tory leaders: time to trust the party?', *Politics Review*, 6:1 (1996) 8–11.

9 *Charter News*, October 1997.

10 P. Webb and D. Farrell, 'Party members and ideological change', in G. Evans and P. Norris (eds), *Critical Elections* (London, Sage, 1999), p. 48.

11 J. Holroyd-Doveton, *Young Conservatives* (Durham, Pentland Press, 1996); P. White-ley, P. Seyd and J. Richardson, *True Blues* (Oxford, Oxford University Press, 1994), p. 202.

12 D. Denver and G. Hands, 'Constituency campaigning', *Parliamentary Affairs*, 45:4 (1992) 528–44.

13 Whiteley *et al.*, *True Blues*, p. 207.

14 E. Shaw, *The Labour Party since 1979* (London, Routledge, 1994), pp. 4–29.

15 P. Gould, *The Unfinished Revolution* (London, Little Brown, 1998), pp. 104–87.

16 Conversation with the author, Manchester, 18 May 1998.

17 W. Hague, *A Fresh Future for the Conservative Party* (London: Conservative Party, 1997).

18 D. Wastell, 'Hague to ballot Tories on reforms', *Daily Telegraph*, 20 July 1997.

19 *Charter News*, October 1998.

20 Whiteley *et al.*, *True Blues*, p. 171.

21 Author's conversation with 'Progress Trust' MPs, Westminster, 15 December 1998.

22 Comments at 'Progress Trust' meeting.

23 S. Driver and L. Martell, *New Labour* (Oxford, Polity Press, 1998), p. 9.

24 Conversation with the author, Manchester, 27 September 2000.

25 *The Fresh Future* (London, Conservative Central Office, 1998), p. 32.

26 See P. Kellner, 'Democratic change that has turned Hague into a dictator', *London Evening Standard*, 17 February 1998.

27 Gould, *The Unfinished Revolution*, pp. 215–22.

28 *The Fresh Future*, p. 30.

29 R. Heffernan and M. Marqusee, *Defeat from the Jaws of Victory* (London, Verso, 1992), pp. 261–301.

30 *The Fresh Future*, p. 31.

31 A. Norman, 'Power to party members', *The House Magazine* (1998).

32 R. Shrimsley, 'Tory chief forced out over £3 million cutback', *Daily Telegraph*, 17 July 1998.

33 Conversation with the author, Manchester, 4 December 1998.

34 C. Challen, *The Price of Power. The Secret Funding of the Tory Party* (London, Vision, 1998).

35 *Charter News*, March 1999.

36 *Conference Guide 2001* (London, BBC News Analysis and Research, 2001), p. 86.

37 J. Lees-Marshment, *The Political Marketing of British Political Parties* (Manchester, Manchester University Press, 2001), p. 213.

38 *Charter News*, March 2000.

39 P. Buscombe, 'Sometimes it's hard to be a Tory woman', *The Spectator*, 1 September 2001.

40 S. Walters, *Tory Wars. Conservatives in Crisis* (London, Politico's, 2001).

41 Author's conversation with James Walsh, Director, Conservative Policy Forum, 2 July 2000.

42 *Listening to Britain: A Report* (London, Conservative Party, 1999), pp. 2 and 12; *The Common Sense Revolution* (London, Conservative Party, 1999); conversation with James Walsh.

43 R. Kelly, 'The party conference', in A. Seldon and S. Ball (eds), *Conservative Century* (Oxford, Oxford University Press, 1994), pp. 221–60.

44 Lees-Marshment, *The Political Marketing of British Political Parties*.

45 G. Jones, 'MPs face the fury of Tory faithful', *Daily Telegraph*, 9 October 1997.

46 R. Kelly, 'Farewell conference, hello forum', *Political Quarterly*, 72:3 (2001) 329–34.

47 R. Kelly, 'Selecting party candidates', *Talking Politics*, 12:1 (1999).

48 P. Norris and J. Lovenduski, *Political Recruitment* (Cambridge, Cambridge University Press, 1995), pp. 65–69.

49 See *Daily Telegraph* letters page, 12 July 2001.

50 B. Brogan, 'Confused Tories dislike Clarke but expect him to win', *Daily Telegraph*, 23 July 2001.

51 N. Watt, 'A sleepwalk into unmitigated disaster', *Guardian*, 20 July 2001.

52 G. Jones, 'Portillo's dream shattered', *Daily Telegraph*, 18 July 2001.

53 Author's interviews, Liverpool, 15 July 2001.

54 Whiteley *et al.*, *True Blues*, p. 25, put membership at about 750,000.

55 M. Bentham, 'So just who are these people?', *Sunday Telegraph*, 19 August 2001.

56 'Undemocratic Tories', *Daily Telegraph* leader column, 1 August 2001.

57 D. Cracknell, 'Poll shows Europe is the main issue for Conservatives', *Sunday Telegraph*, 26 August 2001.

58 Letter to author from Stephen Phillips, CCO Director of Operations and Conferences, 18 October 2001.

59 R. Punnett, *Selecting the Party Leader* (Hemel Hempstead, Harvester Wheatsheaf, 1992), pp. 117–22.

60 A. Grice, 'Activists demand sweeping changes to rules on electing party leader', *Independent*, 9 October 2001.

61 Conversation with the author, London, 9 June 2001.

62 P. Seyd and P. Whiteley, *Labour's Grass Roots* (Oxford, Clarendon Press, 1992), p. 188; P. Seyd and P. Whiteley, 'Why Blair needs his grass roots', *New Statesman*, 6 December 1999.

63 J. Lees-Marshment and S. Quayle, 'Empowering the members or marketing the party? The Conservative reforms of 1998', *Political Quarterly*, 72:2 (2001) 204–12.

6

A question of definition? Ideology and the Conservative Party, 1997–2001

Mark Garnett

In the wake of election defeats in 1970, 1974 and 1979 both the Labour Party and the Conservatives held prolonged inquests into the reasons for their apparent failures in office. These debates – which were often extremely bitter – focused on the underlying principles which had informed the performance of each party. In each case critics claimed that governments had been guilty of ideological betrayal. In 1970 and 1979 Labour's leaders were accused of not being socialist enough; after the fall of the Heath government in 1974 the ex-Prime Minister was attacked for the opposite reason. The 1975 Conservative leadership contest, in which Edward Heath was defeated by Margaret Thatcher, took place against a background of fierce ideological conflict between what came to be known as economic 'wets' and 'dries'.

The 1997 general election produced a more decisive defeat for the Conservatives than any of the three most recent reversals of fortune for either party; and economic policy, the traditional fulcrum of ideological debate, was a key factor for the voters who turned out the Tories after eighteen years of power. Yet after the landslide, under William Hague internal party disagreements about economic policy were confined to skirmishes over the details, notably the extent and timing of tax cuts. Observers of Conservative conferences could be forgiven for thinking that membership of the European single currency had very little to do with economics; but in any case Hague's compromise policy on this issue held up well enough to keep remaining misgivings under control (see Chapter 3). In short, compared to the experience of previous parties after their eviction from office, the post-1997 Conservatives were remarkably united in their approach to economic questions. Those searching for divisions within the party on fundamental principles, concerning human nature and the proper role of government, have to look elsewhere.

It might be argued that commentators on ideology have placed excessive emphasis on economic ideas in the past, and that issues such as law and order and personal morality have always given a more reliable indication of ideological commitment. From a slightly different angle it might be suggested that Conservative infighting under Hague merely reflected a more general decline of 'traditional' ideological debate throughout the Western world. These points have an important bearing on the argument of the present chapter, but limited space prevents the extended discussion that they deserve. Briefly, the first seems to be answered by the potency of economic arguments in recent elections in Britain and elsewhere (for example, Bill Clinton's 'It's the economy, stupid'). After 1997 the economy remained a vital issue in Britain, and under Hague the Conservatives did try to make electoral capital on familiar ideological grounds, denouncing Labour as a socialist party wedded to 'tax and spend' (a peculiar phrase – is there any contemporary government anywhere in the world which eschews these things?). The fact that the old ideological name-calling failed to convince many voters is not a sign that debate over fundamentals is dead; and it is still impossible to evaluate the principles of any major party without reference to economic ideas. The years 1997 to 2001 were merely part of a period in which there was widespread agreement on these matters, so that governments were judged on their competence more than their convictions.

What is 'conservatism?'

The nature of British conservatism has been vigorously contested for much of the post-war period, and after the electoral meltdown of 1997 it was reasonable to expect a flurry of impassioned speeches and pamphlets setting out rival interpretations. Michael Oakeshott, whose name is invoked with respect by almost everyone who addresses this subject, wrote in 1956 that the conservative disposition 'asserts itself characteristically when there is much to be enjoyed'. In hindsight some Conservative politicians have eulogised the 1950s, when their party was in power for all but twenty-two months. But far from thinking that he was fortunate to be living in a golden age, Oakeshott wrote at the time that the conservative disposition was in danger of becoming 'irrelevant, outmanoeuvred, not on account of any intrinsic demerit but merely by the flow of circumstance'. The election of a Labour government in 1997 – with the largest majority in its history and a Prime Minister seemingly set on a mission to destroy the opposition as a meaningful political force – suggested that British conservatism was more threatened than at any time since the French Revolution. Yet even if Oakeshott was right in thinking that conservatism has never thrived at times of crisis, its greatest champions have usually emerged when all seemed lost. After 1997 the stage was set for a new Edmund Burke, to provide conservatives with an eloquent exposition of their faith; anyone who had missed the clarion call at the time of the election can hardly have done so after Blair attacked the 'forces of conservatism' in 1999.[1]

But no one seized Burke's golden trumpet. In fact, the most interesting contribution on the subject suggests that conservatism is dead, or at least irrelevant to contemporary political discourse. According to John Gray, Conservative governments between 1979 and 1997 were anything but 'conservative' in a distinctive ideological sense. Rather, they were driven by a form of 'enlightenment rationalism' – precisely the mode of political thinking denounced by Burke. Gray argues that far from pursuing a conservative policy programme after 1979, a Conservative Party addicted to economic liberalism deliberately 'hollowed out' most of the institutions which conservatives hold dear – even the market itself, which cannot operate without some sense of community and widely shared social values. Thinking in terms of abstract individuals and ignoring the critical social dimension, Conservatives have applauded the corrosive effects of the free market instead of trying to resist them.[2]

As Gray's argument makes clear, the use of the same word in upper and lower cases respectively to denote a party and an ideology is an important source of confusion where conservatism is concerned. To make matters more complicated for students of this subject, many conservatives claim that ideology is a regrettable affliction which they have fortunately escaped. Oakeshott himself thought that it was worse than futile to seek the 'core principles' of conservatism, and he was particularly unhappy with the veneration of Burke as some kind of founding father. Oakeshott's preference for speaking of a conservative 'disposition', rather than appealing to a list of core beliefs, can lead to some implausible conclusions. On his criteria Charles James Fox and Michael Foot would have to be regarded as far more 'conservative' than Pitt the Younger or Thatcher. In the absence of any clear definitions there has recently been a tendency for commentators to use their own interpretations of conservatism as a means of discrediting their political opponents, or of defending their own allies within the Conservative Party (this trend was at its height during the controversy over Thatcherism).

If all definitions of ideology are themselves ideological, it might be argued that discussions of this kind are bound to generate more heat than light: and the present contribution to the debate is particularly vulnerable on this score. Yet when senior politicians are so anxious to 'prove' their own orthodoxy, it would be pusillanimous for commentators merely to provide uncritical reports of the various conflicting claims. Some have tried to resolve the terminological problem by ignoring it, blithely assuming that conservatism is whatever the Conservative Party happens to stand for at any given time. But this seems singularly unprofitable as a tool for those who wish to explore and explain the clear divisions among the various party factions – or, for that matter, among people who call themselves 'conservative' regardless of their partisan allegiance (and Blair's strictures). The same objection applies to the argument that conservatism is multi-faceted. Describing free market enthusiasts like Thatcher and Sir Keith Joseph as 'liberal conservatives' is at best an invitation for others to scrutinise their stated beliefs for evidence of liberalism and conservatism; and this inevitably brings back into play the question of ideological 'core principles', which Oakeshott and others have rejected. Talking of 'traditions' or 'doctrines' rather than 'ideologies' seems equally unprofitable; if we want to categorise these beliefs we cannot avoid referring to the central propositions, and occasionally lumping together thinkers and politicians who might have resented being placed in each other's company. The price of avoiding these pitfalls is the production of work which is equally arid and unenlightening.

The 'core tenets'

Pace Oakeshott, those wishing to understand conservatism after the 1997 defeat would be served best by examining stated principles, rather than extolling the conservative 'disposition'. In a recent survey of the party's prospects after Hague, Anthony Seldon and Peter Snowden have adopted this approach, identifying seven 'core tenets of British Conservatism'.[3] These are 'a belief in the imperfection of human nature and the limits to the power of reason'; an 'organic' theory of society and a desire for 'orderly' change; a conviction that liberty must be safeguarded by the rule of law; a desire for a strong but limited state; the maintenance of a prosperous economy; respect for property; and an attachment to the Nation. According to the authors, their list demonstrates that British Conservatism displays 'both constancy and continuity in a tradition enriched by the contributions of thinkers and politicians over 200 years'.

The list can be taken as representative for the sake of argument: unusually for those who write on this subject, the authors have no obvious axe to grind. The first point of interest is the use of the upper-case 'C' for 'conservatism'. Seldon and Snowden seem to be rejecting any distinction between the ideology and the policies or pronouncements of Conservative Party leaders. This is also suggested by the ordering of the tenets. The first two − on human nature and social change − are actually *three* distinct propositions (which in itself is slightly suspicious, suggestive of a desire on the authors' part to get them out of the way as quickly as possible). They are frequently advanced by writers on conservative ideology; indeed, they are often cited as the key principles underpinning all the rest. Even Oakeshott, who denies that there is any *necessary* connection between these ideas and a conservative 'disposition', accepts that some people have 'believed their disposition to be in some way confirmed by them'.[4]

In short, by giving top billing to these 'tenets' the authors are trying to prove that the ideas of today's Conservative Party do indeed show 'constancy and continuity' with traditional expositions of 'conservatism'. Yet even those who reject Gray's analysis would have to admit that a belief in 'orderly change' is scarcely characteristic of the contemporary party. Unsurprisingly, instead of listing examples of recent Conservative *practice* to illustrate their argument, Seldon and Snowden fall back on quotations from Burke and T. B. Macaulay – neither of whom could speak with much authority on Kenneth Baker's education reforms or the introduction of an 'internal market' to the National Health Service. No doubt Thatcherites will argue that when the Conservative government came to office in 1979 drastic and wide-ranging reform – amounting to something like a revolution – was urgently required. For example, in his notorious speech to the 1977 party conference, the young William Hague urged that the Conservatives should become the party of 'radicalism'. But while the ensuing changes which affected the trade unions (for example) could be described as 'orderly', this was more the exception than the rule. A more relevant case-study would be Thatcherite policy towards local government, which was driven by ideology and partisan considerations, and culminated in the poll tax fiasco.

On the conservative view of human nature, Oakeshott and Quintin Hogg (later Lord Hailsham) are quoted. In each case the source is around half a century old; and the Oakeshott quotation comes from an essay (discussed earlier) which suggested that conservatism was out of tune even with a relatively peaceful period of modern history. Only in their exposition of the 'organic' view of society do Seldon and Snowden produce examples from more recent writing; but even there they advance no supporting evidence from Conservative Party *practice*. The alarm bells start clanging when one reads in this section that 'Conservatives' are 'Imbued with a sense of historical continuity'. It is difficult to see how a party leader who was determined to reverse what she saw as decades of 'betrayal' could be said to have been so 'imbued'. If Mrs Thatcher and her allies thought about history at all, they hoped for a decisive break with post-war trends and took their inspiration from an anachronistic vision of the Victorian period. And rather than identifying belief in an 'organic society' as a characteristic of the party, the authors could have filled several volumes with recent quotations from Conservative politicians in praise of the abstract individual (like Thatcher's remark that 'there is no such thing as society'). Some Conservative politicians do at least pay lip-service to the notion of an organic society; but as in the case of David Willetts (who is quoted), they produce no concrete evidence to show that such a belief has any relevance to the policies of the contemporary party.[5]

Thus, although the approach taken by Seldon and Snowden suggests a concerted attempt to square recent Conservative Party practice and pronouncements with familiar expositions of conservatism, they are quite unconvincing in their treatment of three central propositions. Their presentation, indeed, inadvertently draws attention to the stark *dis*-continuity between politicians like Burke, Disraeli or Baldwin and today's leadership. This, it must be stressed, is not necessarily a *bad thing* for the Conservative

Party; it may have happened for perfectly respectable reasons. But at any rate the evidence suggests that it has indeed happened.

For the next four points on the list, the authors' task of linking ideas to practice is more straightforward. In the way that they are presented, at least, all of these 'tenets' are characteristic of nineteenth-century liberalism rather than conservatism. It might be thought that no serious political thinker actively opposes prosperity; but nineteenth-century conservatives like Samuel Taylor Coleridge acknowledged the possibility that this could be maintained at too high a cost to society. Coleridge's concerns arose from the industrial revolution which was an unequivocal boon to liberals; unlike Burke (who is quoted by Seldon and Snowden to suggest that support for economic liberalism has always been a conservative tenet) he belonged to the first generation to be confronted with the social damage caused by unrestrained industrial capitalism. On liberty, too, conservatives since Burke have differed from liberals in their emphasis on the context, rather than upholding freedom as an abstract idea. The same contrast between liberals and conservatives applies on the question of property; while the former uphold the right of possessors to do what they will with their own, the latter have stressed the obligations of property-holding, regarding ownership as a trust.

This leaves us with the 'nation'. As Seldon and Snowden concede, patriotism 'is upheld to varying degrees across the British political tradition'. But they argue that 'the most passionate defence of national identity and sovereign nationhood' has come from Conservatives. Equally, of course, some members of the Conservative Party have argued that sovereignty can be shared; and even die-hard opponents of the European Union have been happy for the USA to dictate British policy on defence and international relations.[6]

If we accept that 'defence of national identity and sovereign nationhood' really is a long-established 'core tenet' of conservatism, that still leaves us with only one out of the eight items which might indicate some sort of 'continuity' between the tradition of conservative thought and recent Conservative practice. The contemporary party is at best indifferent to three of the key propositions of traditional conservatism; but it broadly upholds four other tenets which have a much more intimate association with liberalism. Seldon and Snowden argue that conservatism has been 'embellished by the absorption of *periphery* values and concepts' with a 'distinctly liberal and libertarian flavour'. Yet on their own showing, these 'distinctly liberal' values have become the predominate 'core tenets' of what they choose to call 'Conservatism'; they are scarcely 'peripheral'. The only realistic conclusion is that today's Conservative Party is a liberal organisation, with a nationalistic twist.[7]

Some might think that this is merely a semantic point, but it helps to clarify some key developments in twentieth-century British politics, and provides the proper context for understanding Conservative Party ideology in the Hague years. In *The Case for Conservatism*, Hogg defended his party against the charge of inconsistency. There was nothing odd, he thought, in the fact that Conservatives were currently engaged 'in fighting the battle of Liberalism against the Socialists who attack *laissez faire* from almost exactly the same angle as [did] the Conservatives in 1948'.[8] Hogg felt that his party should always oppose prevailing political trends. This tactical outlook has been endorsed by several thinkers normally described as conservatives, notably the seventeenth-century Marquess of Halifax. Evidently Hogg believed that his party could remain distinctively conservative while performing this new version of its old balancing act; and, if circumstances changed, it would be free to resume the attack on abstract individualism. In other words, even if the party talked for a while as if liberalism provided it with its 'core tenets', it would only be borrowing them to meet a temporary challenge.

But Hogg had overlooked two crucial dangers. First, if the Conservative Party took the liberal side against 'the Socialists' in a tactical battle of ideas, was there not a chance that its members – particularly younger ones with little interest in the party's traditions, like the then Margaret Roberts – would absorb the tenets of *laissez-faire* as if these represented 'true' conservatism? *The Responsible Society*, a pamphlet published by the One Nation Group in 1959, gives a contrary impression; eight years after the defeat of the Attlee government some of the party's brightest young thinkers felt able to distance themselves equally from *laissez-faire* and socialism, and deployed Hogg's balancing-act argument to support their 'middle way'.[9] Yet at least one of the authors, Sir Keith Joseph, was later to repent of his moderation in those halcyon days.

Second, the eclipse of the Liberal Party as an electoral force had already deprived ambitious liberals of their natural home. Even before 1900 Joseph Chamberlain's supporters had defected to the Conservatives over Home Rule; and the reforms under Henry Campbell-Bannerman and Herbert Asquith, which offended against the principles of *laissez-faire*, provided an additional spur. Keeping faith with the declining Liberal Party, or trying to change the Conservatives from within, could be seen by believers in *laissez-faire* as a mirror image of the 'progressive' choice which David Marquand has analysed – a 'Regressive Dilemma', as it were.[10] Once they had taken the more promising option of infiltrating the Conservatives, there was every chance that Hogg's tactical switch would be institutionalised.

The analysis of 'core tenets' provided by Seldon and Snowden suggests that this process has occurred. Until 1975 Conservative Party leaders continued to prefer Disraeli to Samuel Smiles, but on this interpretation it can be argued that a fundamental change of direction was always inevitable once the party hit serious trouble; and after the leadership had been taken by a convinced liberal for the first time, conservatives would have found it difficult to regain control whether or not developments in the global economy had added practical force to their arguments. Hogg himself remained a Cabinet minister until 1987; but throughout the Thatcher years he was preoccupied with the defence of at least one traditional institution, the British legal system. However, in 1977 his pupil and friend Ian Gilmour repeated his warnings against doctrinaire politics, with particular reference to *laissez-faire*; unlike Hogg he persisted in his public protests, and was one of the first ministers to be sacked by Thatcher on ideological grounds.

Despite all the competing arguments and methodological objections, the most telling evidence of ideological allegiance within a political party seems to be the vision of state and society which is either made explicit in political rhetoric, or implied by the tendency of policy pronouncements. Even the most scrupulous self-denying commentators seem fated to fall back on some 'core tenets' when discussing different ideological traditions. As a general rule, however, the broader the definition the less useful it is as an analytical tool; and economic ideas still seem to be the most fruitful focus for investigation, given their obvious dependence upon conceptions of the individual, society and the state. Thus the dispute between 'wets' like Gilmour and the Thatcherite 'dries' during the 1970s and 1980s was an unmistakable symptom of ideological division. The foregoing discussion has necessarily involved much corner-cutting; but if the outlines are accepted it would follow that any ideological friction within the Conservative Party between 1997 and 2001 could only be interpreted as family disputes, among liberals rather than 'conservatives'. The ironic conclusion is that the party won elections when it was ideologically riven, and lost disastrously when the dispute had been settled in favour of the liberal 'dries'. This line seems worth pursuing, to see if it adds to our understanding of Hague's party and the prospects for the immediate future.

The legacy of Thatcherism

It has been argued here that whatever the ideological nature of the Conservative leadership up to 1975, it was unquestionably liberal after Thatcher succeeded Heath in that year. While it is obviously a mistake to assume that a party automatically follows the ideological preferences of any leader, we have also suggested why the Conservative Party was likely to swing behind Thatcher, even if at first she lacked much support among senior colleagues. On this view, Thatcher was not an alien intruder who hijacked the party; rather, she brought an end to an increasingly awkward period in which a series of 'pragmatic' politicians had risen to the head of a strongly ideological body. On paper, her enforced departure in November 1990 opened the possibility of a new 'Hoggite' tactical switch; after all, the poll tax which helped to topple Thatcher was a remarkable product of liberal rationalism, and there was powerful evidence that the popularity of the ex-premier's ideas had been gradually eroded since her first election victory in 1979.[11] But although he was certainly no radical, John Major was unwilling to challenge the new orthodoxy, to which the Conservative Party had wedded itself for better and for worse. The editors of a recent book on the party plausibly claim that in practice Major proved more Thatcherite than Thatcher herself, pushing privatisation into areas which his predecessor had left untouched.[12]

Until the ERM fiasco of September 1992 threw them a convenient concrete objection, in Thatcherite eyes Major's problem was not his record but his rhetoric. For them his visions of a 'classless society' and a country 'at ease with itself' were dismal departures from the ideological edge which Thatcher gave to almost everything she said (at least after her promise to replace 'discord' with 'harmony' when she first entered 10 Downing Street). Major's later attempt to sound like Baldwin (invoking the supposedly more relaxed society of the 1950s) was ridiculed, and his 'Back to Basics' speech of 1993 can also be seen as an ill-fated appeal to residual conservatism within his party. Given the true nature of his audience (whether in the hall or watching on television) his words could only be misinterpreted. As Andrew Gamble has suggested, Major's 'Citizen's Charter' initiative could also be seen as part of a search for some stability; but this fared no better.[13] When Hague took the leadership he seemed well placed to overcome Major's difficulties. In *The Times* Peter Riddell claimed that with his victory 'the Thatcherites have taken charge'.[14] Hague was obviously a product of the Thatcher years, and unlike both of his predecessors he was a natural orator. Under his leadership, it seemed, style and substance would be reunited; and there would be none of the bickering of the 1970s and 1980s in a fully 'Thatcherised' party.

Against this background the speech delivered by Hague's policy chief, Peter Lilley, at the Carlton Club in April 1999, was an unpleasant shock to many loyal Thatcherites. There could not have been a more fitting venue for conservatism's final fling; but Lilley was a most unlikely champion. As he remarked in the speech, he had been one of the party's foremost advocates of free market thinking, even before it became fashionable. But now he felt that, 'Conservatives seem to be on the intellectual back foot.' They had to remind the electorate that, 'Belief in the free market has only ever been a part of Conservatism.' In particular, while many people assumed that the party's ultimate goal was the privatisation of the health service, Lilley argued that 'the free market has only a limited role' in that sphere.

Some phrases in Lilley's speech echoed Burke, and thus evoked the 'historical continuity' claimed by Seldon and Snowden. For example, Lilley asserted that: 'We have an obligation to transmit to the next generation the heritage of learning and culture which we have inherited and developed.' He also claimed that: 'The Conservative tradition of pragmatism means that we believe in judging by results.' There was even a complaint about the intrusion of business language into inappropriate areas, and an emphasis on obligations to others rather than individual rights. In short, like Seldon and Snowden Lilley was drawing on the tradition of *conservative thought* to support propositions about the *Conservative Party*. Yet even in this context he was anxious to retain his liberal credentials, and not just in the economic sphere. 'Freedom is good in itself', he argued, 'it encourages personal responsibility and it promotes prosperity more effectively than any other system known to mankind.' [15]

To some extent, at least, it seems that Lilley immediately fell victim to some hostile 'spinning' by members of Hague's entourage. Yet the angry reaction to his speech was genuine for the most part. His offence was to confront unquestioning believers with concrete evidence that, despite all their efforts, the Thatcher and Major governments had failed to make Britain into a free market Utopia. While Lilley tried to make a virtue of this failure – notably by applauding the fact that the Conservative governments had never matched their harsh rhetoric on public spending – a party which was obsessed with the idea of differentiating itself from Labour could now only seek 'clear blue water' by embracing ever-more extreme forms of economic liberalism. In short, although his leader had endorsed the speech in advance, Lilley had no powerful allies within the party to protect him from the backlash. It was not just that there were no conservatives left within the Conservative Party; there were not even many *moderate* economic liberals. As one might have expected in these circumstances, despite the temporary storm aroused by Lilley's speech the main ideological split in the party concerned not economic policy, but competing approaches to social questions.

However, a speech by one leading Conservative politician during the Hague years apparently contradicts this argument. In July 1998 Iain Duncan Smith angrily denied that New Labour was 'conservative', as Tony Blair had implied with his 'One Nation' rhetoric. Rather, he argued, 'They can't see a British institution without reaching for the drawing board.' Blair was accused of ignoring 'the organic nature of society and British institutions'. Duncan Smith had obviously been reading Burke, whom he quoted against Blair. But whether or not Burke's assault on French Revolutionary principles as, 'This barbarous philosophy ... the offspring of cold hearts and muddy understandings' could have much relevance to New Labour as Duncan Smith assumed, he seemed wholly unaware that (on Burke's premises, at least) it was a reasonable description of the abstract ideas purveyed by the New Right since the 1970s. If Britain really had survived the upheavals of the Thatcher years as a society that could still be described as 'organic', it would surely prove robust enough to see off the Blair offensive – which at worst could be seen as 'more of the same'.[16]

There were only two possible explanations for Duncan Smith's speech. Either his own prosperous background had blinded him to the real social effects of Conservative government since 1979 — or his appeal to Burke's social ideas had been entirely cynical. Whatever the explanation, in the Shadow Cabinet after Lilley's speech Duncan Smith was reported to have joined Michael Howard and Ann Widdecombe in leading the attack, even asking for a face-to-face meeting with Lilley to spell out his objections. Whether or not Lilley fought back with talk of 'cold hearts and muddy understandings' is not recorded. Now that the party had rejected the possibility of a 'Hoggite' switch back to something which even vaguely resembled traditional conservatism, the real faction fights could begin.[17]

'Mods' and 'rockers'

Duncan Smith, Howard and Widdecombe were later identified as leading figures in the new Tory split. After the party conference of October 2000, commentators began to refer to the factions as 'mods' and 'rockers'. The 'mods', exemplified by Michael Portillo, wanted to transform the image of the party by reaching out to social groups which had previously regarded the Conservative Party as deeply intolerant. The 'rockers', by contrast, upheld 'traditional' social institutions and practices, exemplified by their tough policy ideas on law and order.

Andrew Gamble, Stuart Hall and others have drawn attention to the apparent contradiction in Thatcher's combination of economic individualism with social authoritarianism. It might be argued that the uneasy mixture proves the continuing relevance of conservatism under Thatcher: on this view, even if she was a liberal in economics, she remained deeply conservative in her approach to social questions.

It is certainly the case that Thatcherism, as generally understood, was an incoherent (if not self-contradictory) set of ideas. Yet the identification of *conservatism* with hard-line policies on law and order deserves closer examination. Certainly conservative scepticism about human nature indicates the permanent necessity of a strong police force, and deep suspicion of those who claim that offenders can be reformed. But liberals have always been quick to defend life and property; to suggest otherwise is to confuse liberalism with anarchism. In fact, during the regular crime 'scares' of the Thatcher years the Prime Minister and her ideological soul mates usually responded by asserting individual responsibility, in approved liberal fashion. By contrast, after the inner-city rioting of 1981 her sceptical Home Secretary, William Whitelaw, included references to social conditions when denouncing the offenders. From this perspective Whitelaw contrived to prevent some of the wilder ideas emanating from Downing Street, such as the introduction of an updated Riot Act. Whitelaw and other traditional conservatives in the first Thatcher cabinet were regarded as hopelessly 'wet' on crime as well as on economics; the activists who regularly bellowed for the return of capital punishment at Conservative Party conferences also tended to be 'hawkish' in their attitude to the welfare state and government intervention in general. With hindsight, the ready identification of hard-line views on law and order with conservatism seems to have no sounder basis than the traditional anxiety of the left to lump all the attitudes they dislike into this much-abused and misunderstood category.

In short, it seems unnecessary to attribute Thatcher's apparent inconsistency to an inner conflict between liberalism and conservatism. While sceptics predicted that her economic policies would inevitably increase social conflict, leading (for example) to more crime and marriage breakdowns, the Prime Minister herself genuinely seemed to think that social malaise was actually a product of well-meaning but misguided policies, which had been generally accepted both by Labour and by One Nation Conservatives since the time of the Churchill coalition. She apparently thought that once individuals were liberated from the 'dependency culture' they would be trained by the discipline of the market place; afterwards they would covet their neighbours' goods, but only to the extent of hoping to emulate their hard-earned affluence. Obviously there would still be some crime; but once the 'do-gooders' had been banished, offenders would be made to face up to their individual responsibilities.

Widdecombe, the rocker-in-chief, fully shares Thatcher's outlook. She was taught by her father that there was a 'very stark choice' in politics. 'You could not be a mix of both. I believed that individuals had to be free to grow economically, to make the most of their talents ... and that the state should interfere minimally.' 'The individual must, as far as possible, take responsibility for himself', she argues.[18] Her well-publicised views on drugs are fully compatible with this general approach. Even if addiction does not lead directly to crime, in her view it diminishes individual responsibility. Contrary to her retributivist caricature, after Widdecombe's exposure to conditions within Britain's jails she became a strong advocate of rehabilitation. If she had ever become Home Secretary her policies might have increased the prison population, but she believes that the experience should be 'constructive' for individual inmates.

In short, Widdecombe is a liberal. Her differences with Portillo and co. arise from their conflicting assessments of the effects of certain practices – their different applications of John Stuart Mill's 'harm principle'. On subjects such as drugs and homosexuality, the 'mods' are obviously not conservatives in the traditional mould; they are *libertarian*. Equally, the fact that Widdecombe applies her liberal principles across a narrower range of practices probably reflects her strong religious convictions; but it does not make her a conservative. Unfortunately for the Conservative Party – and for Widdecombe herself – she chose to underline her rejection of libertarianism at the 2000 party conference, at precisely the time when the 'Portillistas' were booting up their attempts to show a more 'caring' (or rather, tolerant) image. The resulting argument might have sounded like a clash between conflicting ideologies – and the media might have presented it in that way – but it was a family quarrel about the proper limits of liberalism, accentuated by competing political ambitions and personality clashes.

This does not belittle the importance of the dispute – after all, family quarrels often end in something worse than tears, dragging in distant relatives as well as the main protagonists. And the fiasco over drugs in October 2000 was not the end of the story. Two months later Hague stumbled into the debate between the 'mods' and the 'rockers'. In November 2000 Britain was shocked by the murder of Damilola Taylor. Hague decided to turn the tragedy to partisan advantage, by alleging that the Macpherson Report was hampering the police. In a speech to the Centre for Policy Studies, he claimed that 'the liberal elite have seized on the report as a stick with which to beat the police'. At first Hague consulted only Widdecombe, his Home Affairs spokesperson, about this form of words. But when Michael Portillo was asked for his views he expressed dissent, jesting that he was a member of the 'liberal elite' himself. According to Simon Walters, 'Hague replied instantly: "Well I'm not a liberal, nor am I a member of any elite".' [19]

In Walters' book this anecdote is related at Portillo's expense. But in the British context, at least, there is something unsettling about the argument on both sides. Presumably Hague thinks that a Yorkshire birthplace automatically rules out membership of 'any elite'; otherwise he would not have tried to play up his self-image as an 'outsider' in his response to Blair's 'forces of conservatism' speech. Others will take a different view of Oxford graduates (not to mention the serving leaders of any major political party). But Hague's obvious confidence that 'liberal elite' would be a damaging label to stick on the government was, ironically, itself a clear sign that he was accustomed to speaking in terms that would cause serious confusion outside the increasingly narrow confines of the political 'elite'. The British public might have been more responsive had Hague spoken of 'socialism', which has a far longer history of misrepresentation in Britain. Most British voters have yet to follow the US Republicans – and Conservative members of the 'Westminster village' – in responding like Pavlov's dog to the word 'liberal'. Hague had obviously been misled by his exposure to the US political scene (at this time, of course, George W. Bush's Presidential campaign was providing the British Conservatives with a misleading source of optimism). Yet instead of pointing out Hague's glaring category mistake, Portillo apparently responded as if he were a proud US Democrat. The whole incident might as well have been a conversation between spin-doctors in Washington. The contagion seems to have spread to the author of *Tory Wars*, who does not remark on the transatlantic flavour of the conversation (and generally follows the US model, by 'reconstructing' the private conversations of senior politicians and their advisers).

Judging ideological traditions from the very different British perspective, for all the abuse heaped on 'liberals', both of the main US political parties are members of that family. Whatever they might call him in the USA, Hague is himself a liberal – indeed, compared to Widdecombe, at least, he should be classed as a member of the libertarian wing of his party. But by the autumn of 2000 he felt outflanked by the 'Portillistas', and he was already tempted to throw in his lot with the 'rockers' to shore up his position. It might be too fanciful to claim that Hague spent the months leading up to the 2001 general election fighting the wrong battle, and trying both in public and in private to distance himself from people who would be denounced as 'liberals' in the USA. But certainly that was one way of uniting in his own mind his twin enemies – Portillo and Blair. Hague hoped to portray himself as a plucky outsider, the champion of the 'little man'; but in the absence of clear ideological distinctions in Britain, he could only adopt the vocabulary and mind-set of a Republican candidate, attacking the Washington elite. Thus Hague's attack on the 'liberal elite' was a red herring, but no less fascinating for that. Two decades after the party went to war with itself over the meaning of 'conservatism', it was now riven by a dispute over rival definitions of liberalism. The only constant factor was that the battle-cries and slogans of the competing camps still made life very difficult for students of ideology trying to get a fix on what was really going on.

The Conservative Party and the 2001 general election

It is often said that by accepting so much of Conservative policy after 1994, Tony Blair stole his opponents' clothes and restricted their room for ma-noeuvre in any future elections. This is undoubtedly true. But the Conservative Party conspired with Labour by boxing themselves in. In 1996 Andrew Gamble rightly characterised them as 'an ideological party'. The change in the nature of the party since Thatcher's term of office is best gauged by comparing its situation after the 1997 general election with previous periods of opposition. In 1950, 1951, 1966, 1970, October 1974 and even 1979, it could persuasively pose as a pragmatic alternative to Labour. From this position it was a relatively straight-forward task to stigmatise the government's mistakes, whether or not the voting public took the hint. Policy differences could easily be highlighted by reference to 'socialism'. Only in 1979 was Labour faced by a doctrinaire Conservative leader, and on that first outing it was possible for campaign managers to disguise Thatcher's true nature.

But the fact that the Conservative Party was seen as 'ideological' after 1979 meant that all of its mishaps could be interpreted from this perspective. During Thatcher's first two terms the public seemed unwilling to adopt this viewpoint; hence the consternation of Labour activists when she was re-elected, and their depression when the emollient image of Major temporarily staved off the inevitable reckoning in 1992. But by 1997 the chapter of ideological accidents was too bulky to ignore, and the right-wing press might have been forced to switch sides even without the Blair factor. The slump of the early 1990s was a fitting nemesis for a party which had boasted that its free market reforms had produced an 'economic miracle'. The poll tax, too, was rightly seen as a product of ideology; and financial 'sleaze' could easily be traced to Thatcherite presuppositions about acquisitive human nature. The botched privatisation of the railways would have been unthinkable under a 'pragmatic' government. In this context, it was inevitable that commentators should see other problems, like the split over Europe, as ideological conflicts whereas in reality they were conducted in terms which showed that all of the antagonists were working from distinctively liberal premises. So by 1997 the general post-war pattern had been reversed; a newly 'pragmatic' Labour Party was always likely to improve on its previous performances, but its prospects were vastly improved by the fact that it was attacking an 'ideological' government. In 2001 its task was even more straightforward; a tactfully reticent Thatcher might have won in the unusual circumstances of 1979, but Foot's fate four years later is far more typical of British opposition leaders whose parties are perceived to be strongly ideological, all other things being as equal as they can be in an uncertain world.

If the Conservative Party had really been the adaptive organisation of old, capable of following the advice of Hogg and Halifax 'the Trimmer', it would have stopped bragging about its 'victory' in the 'battle of ideas' shortly after the destruction of the Berlin Wall. The fact that global conditions clearly favoured economic liberalism would have been taken into account; but on the same principle which had led it to oppose 'socialism' in its post-war heyday the Conservative Party would at least have posed as the champion of the insecure voter against the unsettling effects of the market. The fact that it did no such thing is further evidence of its distance from one aspect of the conservative tradition. But the *reason* for its failure to change is even more telling. The Conservatives had adopted a dogmatic mind-set – the very trait which their leaders still persisted in denouncing in 'socialists'. The truth is that after Thatcher, a retreat from hard-line economic liberalism, however limited, would have deprived the party of its *raison d'être*.

If Major can be forgiven for his failure to stem the Thatcherite tide after 1990, his successor as leader had no such excuse. The ill-starred Lilley initiative was an attempt to slay the ideological dragon, allowing the Conservative Party to return to its habitual post-war pose of a pragmatic government in waiting. At best, the crushing defeat of 1997 could be taken as evidence that the British people had learned to live with economic liberalism, but preferred to take mild doses disguised by a generous coating of Blairite sugar. But people in the advanced stages of ideological addiction are doomed to deny any evidence which disturbs their view of the world – a malady aptly described in a recent paper by Pippa Norris and Joni Lovenduski as 'selective perception'.[20] As one Shadow Minister put it after the Lilley speech, 'One of the few things that held us together was the belief in Thatcherism, yet he appeared to be throwing that out too.' In these circumstances it seemed much safer to throw out Lilley instead; at the same time, though, any chance of a vigorous Tory fightback was extinguished.[21]

When the Conservative Party subsequently published its draft manifesto, *Believing in Britain*, its ideological albatross loomed over almost every page. Hague's foreword contained one shock admission. Instead of claiming that all Britain's troubles stemmed from the previous four years, he wrote that: 'We could have greater stability and stronger communities than for many years past'. But this diagnosis prescribed the kind of radical shift from Thatcherite individualism which had been ruled out. So in his closing remarks Hague explained the problem in terms that were impeccably liberal, and quite irrelevant: 'Our sense of community is threatened by increased centralisation and the increasing size of government'. The main text urged that: 'The key to a strong and stable society is to trust local communities and institutions.' Burke would have agreed with that. But the document continues: 'We have to resist those who respond to every problem with another scheme for central government intervention and another excuse for political interference'. In substance this would have committed Hague's party to all-out opposition against the Thatcher and Major governments, which for narrow partisan reasons had interfered in local government far more than any of their predecessors. But instead of admitting that the party had a great deal to live down in these areas, strategists thought that they could erase the past by dressing up the complaint in hard-line liberal language. There can hardly be a better illustration of 'selective perception' in (futile) action.

In the run-up to June 2001 Hague promised faithful Tories that: 'Labour's high taxes and broken promises will be at the centre of the Conservative election campaign.' But even ideologues have to recognise the power of opinion polls, and on these subjects the party had made no progress since 1997. Hague's only hope was the final item of the Seldon and Snowden list – the nation. This, after all, had arguably been Thatcher's most effective weapon, which had secured her easy re-election in 1983. Even here, of course, the Conservative Party ought to have had mixed feelings. Officially at least, the 'nation' in question was Britain; but Conservative governments after 1979 had neglected the 'Celtic fringe' to the extent that the party had been wiped out outside England. Devolution was the inevitable consequence, once the Tories had lost power in 1997. Thus when Hague toured the country in a last-ditch attempt to save the 'nation' of Britain, he was battling on behalf of an abstraction that his own party had hollowed out.

Conclusion

At the time of writing, the Conservative Party does seem to be addressing its past, even if a 'Hoggite' shift is now out of the question. On economics, Willetts has repeated (almost verbatim) Peter Lilley's attempt to draw a line under Thatcherism, without being sacked. This time there was no ill-intentioned intervention by the spin doctors; it was obvious that Willetts was only offering the token reassurance which had failed to register with the public between 1997 and 2001. Meanwhile, almost as soon as the polls had closed, social libertarians like Alan Duncan seized the initiative; and although Duncan Smith is the archetypical 'rocker' he seems to have accepted the 'mod' case that the intolerant image was a vote-loser for the party.

Conservative Party practice after 1979 supports the view that electoral recovery need not bear any relation to ideological clarity, or even unity. Yet the Conservatives have been an 'ideological party' for so long that they may feel queasy at recent developments. Under Thatcher they were taught to admire extreme economic liberalism, but to distrust libertarianism. Now, it appears, they are being advised to reverse this balance. If the present line lasts longer than the Lilley initiative, it will certainly provide a stern test of grass-roots loyalty.

There is, though, one idea which might keep the activists entertained while the party re-positions itself. In more than one interview conducted for this chapter, Conservative MPs wondered aloud about the current purpose of their party. These doubts could be erased by the explicit adoption of English nationalism as the rallying cry. Devolution, and developments within the European Union, could easily permit the Conservative Party to exchange their hollowed-out abstraction for something which – superficially, at least – can be made to look like a living reality. Advocates of English nationalism, like Simon Heffer and Teresa Gorman, might not have thought through the economic implications of their idea. But it seems that, if the unsavoury choice were presented, they would prefer flinty independence to prosperity. The possible ramifications are intriguing; for example, under conditions of autarchy, economic liberalism would have to go at last. The only certainty, as members of the party face yet another period in which there is 'little to be enjoyed', is that realistic lists of 'Conservative principles' will have the 'nation' in its proper place – at the top.

Notes

1 M. Oakeshott, *Rationalism in Politics and Other Essays* (London, Methuen, 1962), pp. 169, 174, 175, 178.
2 See, for example, J. Gray, *Enlightenment's Wake: Politics and Culture at the Close of the Modern Age* (London, Routledge, 1995), pp. 87–119.

3 A. Seldon and P. Snowden, *A New Conservative Century?* (London, Centre for Policy Studies, 2001), pp. 18–25.

4 Oakeshott, *Rationalism in Politics*, p. 183.

5 See D. Willetts, *Modern Conservatism* (Harmondsworth, Penguin, 1992) for an account which carefully avoids any discussion of the real social impact of Thatcherism.

6 Seldon and Snowden, *A New Conservative Century?*, p. 25.

7 Seldon and Snowden, *A New Conservative Century?*, p. 18.

8 Q. Hogg, *The Case for Conservatism* (Harmondsworth, Penguin, 1947), p. 53.

9 One Nation Group, *The Responsible Society* (London, Conservative Political Centre, 1959), pp. 7–8.

10 D. Marquand, *The Progressive Dilemma* (London, Heinemann, 1992).

11 I. Crewe, 'Values: the crusade that failed', in D. Kavanagh and A. Seldon (eds), *The Thatcher Effect: A Decade of Change* (Oxford, Oxford University Press, 1989), pp. 239–50, remains the best exposition of this view.

12 See S. Ludlam and M. J. Smith (eds), *Contemporary British Conservatism* (London, Macmillan, 1996), Ch. 14.

13 A. Gamble, 'An ideological party', in Ludlam and Smith (eds), *Contemporary British Conservatism*, p. 32.

14 P. Riddell, 'King William inaugurates the Thatcherite Restoration', *The Times*, 21 June 1997.

15 P. Lilley, 'Butler Memorial Lecture', the Carlton Club, 20 April 1999, www.peterlilley. co.uk/speeches.phtml?action=show&id=16.

16 I. Duncan Smith, speech to the Centre for Policy Studies, London, 28 July 1998.

17 P. Riddell, 'Welcome to the collapse of the Conservative Party', *The Times*, 21 April 1999.

18 Quoted in N. Kochan, *Ann Widdecombe: Right from the Beginning* (London, Politico's, 2000), pp. 237 and 240.

19 S. Walters, *Tory Wars: Conservatives in Crisis* (London, Politico's, 2001), pp. 106–7.

20 P. Norris and J. Lovenduski, 'The Iceberg and the Titanic: electoral defeat, policy moods and party change', paper presented at the EPOP annual conference, University of Sussex, 15 September 2001.

21 Walters, *Tory Wars*, p. 118.

7

Conservative policy under Hague

Peter Dorey

> The Tories have published any number of pre-manifesto documents, only to rip them up and start all over again in the manner of a panic-stricken student sitting an exam that he knows he will fail.[1]

The Conservative Party encountered considerable difficulty in crafting a coherent package of policies once in opposition after the 1997 election defeat. Much of this difficulty derived from the ideological uncertainty which afflicted the Conservative Party during this period, as discussed in the previous chapter. Conservatives were uncertain as to whether their response ought to be a more vigorous advocacy of Thatcherism, thereby placing 'clear blue water' between them and New Labour, or whether they should embrace a more 'compassionate conservatism', in order to recapture the One Nation terrain that the party occupied so successfully until the 1970s. In the context of such uncertainty, Conservative policies often lacked coherence, clarity and consistency.

These problems were compounded by differences of interpretation concerning the significance of New Labour's 1997 election success. Whilst the proponents of a more 'compassionate conservatism' were inclined to view the Blair government's victory as reflective of a definite and significant change of public mood after eighteen years of 'permanent revolution', the continued adherents of Thatcherism maintained the view that New Labour was all spin and no substance, so that the Blair government's policies and popularity would dissipate once hard choices had to be made, and Labour's policies either proved ineffective or unpopular (or both). The former perspective clearly implied the need for a major rethink of Conservative policy, and a shift back towards the centre ground, whilst the latter view seemed to suggest that rather than panic, and ditch the policies so successfully pursued during the previous eighteen years, the Conservative Party ought to hold its ground, thereby regaining political and electoral support once the New Labour 'project' unravelled, whilst also demonstrating firmness and consistency of both principles and policies.

Consequently, the Conservatives evinced both intra-party disagreement over general policy direction, and shifts and U-turns concerning a number of specific polices. This chapter will examine Conservative policies in seven main areas: the economy, 'tax and spend' (including public services), law and order, the family and sexual politics, welfare reform and pensions, asylum seekers, and rural affairs. The vital and vexatious issue of Europe is addressed in Chapter 8.

The economy

Throughout most of the 1980s successful stewardship of the economy had been the Conservative Party's trump card, and one which was played with devastating effect against Labour in the 1992 election especially. In spite of having presided over two recessions during this period, general elections saw the Conservatives lead the Labour Party by large majorities when opinion polls asked voters who they most trusted to manage the economy. During a period when the nationalized industries were deeply unpopular and government intervention in the economy was widely deemed to be excessive and inimical to entrepreneurial innovation and wealth-creation, the Conservative Party's advocacy of 'rolling back the state', rewarding risk-takers, and reducing inflation, proved highly popular, even though voters were less enamoured with the social consequences (high unemployment, under-funded public services). Thus psephologists during the 1980s developed the notion of 'pocket voting', whereby perceptions of material well-being, and judgements about the economic competence of the political parties, often proved the decisive criteria in shaping the outcome of a general election. The Labour Party might have proffered more popular social policies, but on the all-important issue of economic trust the Conservatives seemed unassailable.

This changed irrevocably on 16 September 1992 ('Black Wednesday'), when Britain was obliged to withdraw from the Exchange Rate Mechanism. Literally overnight, the Conservatives' previous reputation for economic competence was destroyed, and thereafter, right up until the 1997 election (and beyond), the party trailed Labour in the polls, often by 15–25 per cent. Even though the British economy was in relatively good health – hence the Conservatives' poster campaign proclaiming 'Britain's booming; don't let Labour ruin it' – the electorate seemed unwilling to grant the Conservatives much credit or gratitude for this renewed prosperity. Indeed, there seemed to be a tacit view amongst many voters that if the British economy was now booming, it was in spite of, not because of, the Major government's economic policies. Furthermore, the sense of economic well-being actually seemed to have made more voters willing to risk voting Labour (whereas in previous elections, when the economic situation was often rather poor, much of the electorate was inclined to 'cling to nurse, for fear of something worse').

Having lost the 1997 election, the Conservatives continued to find it difficult to challenge the trust which New Labour now enjoyed from much of the electorate over successful management of the economy. One reason for this difficulty derives from the extent to which the Labour Party under Tony Blair's leadership has embraced 'the market', and accepted the need to prioritise low inflation and fiscal prudence. Indeed, on many aspects of economic policy, the first Blair government seemed explicitly to adopt many of the measures formerly pursued by the Major government. In this context, the Conservative opposition led by William Hague found it difficult to launch an effective or sustained attack on the Blair government on many economic issues, particularly because strong criticism might have been interpreted as a repudiation of the economic strategy followed by the Conservatives themselves up until 1997.[2]

Previous Conservative oppositions were used to attacking Labour governments for their formal commitment to public ownership and concomitant nationalisation measures, along with their punitive levels of taxation, alleged hostility to enterprise and entrepreneurship, and high levels of public expenditure. However, the Conservatives after May 1997 were perplexed by a Labour government which rejected nationalisation, refused to increase income tax and actually reduced corporation tax, and contemplated further privatisation (as well as private sector involvement in public services via Public–Private Partnerships, and the continued application of Private Finance Initiatives, initiated by the previous Conservative government). The Blair government posed a further problem for the Conservatives by adhering to the outgoing Major administration's public spending plans for the first two years in office. New Labour's stance on such economic issues made it extremely difficult for the Conservatives to attack it, and thereby articulate an alternative Conservative economic policy agenda.

The second reason why the Conservatives found it so difficult to attack the Blair government on economic affairs was that the British economy remained unexpectedly robust throughout Labour's first term of office. Whereas the Conservatives had historically benefited from the tendency for Labour governments to be fatally weakened by economic crises, the Blair government presided over unprecedented (for a Labour government) economic prosperity and stability, which, in turn, enabled it to benefit from 'pocket voting' in the 2001 election, whilst warning voters that their prosperity and the return to near-full employment would be seriously jeopardised by the return of the Conservatives. Even a widely predicted economic down-turn in 1998 failed to materialise, thus further depriving the Conservatives of ammunition with which to attack the government on the issue of economic management.

Admittedly, various Shadow Ministers attacked the government for the rise in interest rates which occurred during 1997 and 1998 (peaking at 7.5

per cent in the autumn of 1998), claiming that such 'high levels' were deeply damaging to British industry, although from 1999 onwards rates were in the 5 to 6 per cent range, falling further to 4 per cent in early 2002. Also deemed damaging to British industry were the new regulations and additional red tape which Labour ministers imposed on businesses, often in the guise of either employment or environmental protection. Hague's Conservatives also lamented the high value of sterling, which was rendering British exports uncompetitive, yet it was difficult for Conservative critics to proffer credible alternatives in these areas. Quite apart from the fact that interest rates were now set by the (independent) Bank of England's Monetary Policy Committee, the Conservatives themselves had relied heavily on interest rates as a central tool of macro-economic strategy, with the rate often considerably higher than it was under the Blair government. Meanwhile, reducing the value of sterling to aid British exporters implied either devaluation, which would have resulted in a corresponding increase in the cost of imports (and more expensive goods in the shops), and thus a worsening of Britain's balance of payments, or British membership of the European single currency (which would effectively entail devaluation anyway). As these options were clearly anathema to most Conservatives, their criticisms of the government's macro-economic policies were somewhat lacking in credibility and coherence.

Furthermore, on a couple of economic issues, the Conservatives performed U-turns, the most notable of these being the announcement that a future Conservative government would retain the statutory minimum wage introduced by the Blair government. Hitherto, the Conservatives had repeatedly denounced the minimum wage, alleging that it would seriously damage the competitiveness of the British economy and deter inward investment, thereby jeopardising up to one million jobs. However, once the minimum wage, set at £3.60 per hour, was on the statute book, Michael Portillo (appointed Shadow Chancellor in February 2000, having won a by-election in Kensington and Chelsea in November 1999) announced that it was no longer formally opposed by the Conservative Party, and would thus not be repealed by the Conservatives when next in office. Other economic U-turns performed by Portillo included abandonment of the party's opposition to independence for the Bank of England (the Blair government having made it independent within days of winning the 1997 election), and a pledge that the Conservatives would henceforth accept the pursuit of full employment as a policy objective.

As such, by the time of the 2001 election campaign, Hague's Conservatives were unable to offer little that was distinctive or original in the sphere of macro-economic policy (beyond continued rejection of the euro), their main pledges being to reduce the inflation target from 2.5 per cent to 2 per cent, and further increasing the independence of the Bank of England, coupled with the establishment of a Council of Economic Advisers to offer advice on the

Chancellor's fiscal policies. Such measures, though, were hardly likely to enthuse disaffected voters or persuade them to return to the Conservative fold.

However, it was over the twin issues of taxation and public expenditure (commonly referred to as 'tax and spend') that Hague's Conservative Party encountered the most difficulties in opposition, to the extent that this particular policy area warrants consideration in its own right.

'Tax and spend'

The Conservatives' difficulty in challenging the Labour Party's new-found reputation for economic competence and fiscal prudence was compounded by the problems which arose over the twin issues of taxation and public expenditure (commonly referred to as 'tax and spend'). When the Blair government refused to renege on its pledge not to raise income tax rates, the Conservatives found it necessary to switch focus, firstly by pledging further cuts in direct taxation, and secondly by attacking the government's apparent penchant for increasing indirect taxation instead, which the Conservatives labelled 'stealth taxes'. However, whereas taxation had once been a clear vote-winner for the Conservatives, from 1997 onwards the party struggled to reassert its former dominance over Labour on this issue.

In the autumn of 1999, at the party's annual conference, Hague pledged – in accordance with proposals drafted by his then Shadow Chancellor, Francis Maude – that a future Conservative government would reduce taxes as a proportion of GDP, over the lifetime of a Parliament: the much-vaunted 'Tax Guarantee'. However, more prescient Conservatives recognised that cutting taxes as a proportion of GDP might not prove feasible if the economy entered recession, for, in such a situation, higher unemployment would entail lower income tax and National Insurance revenues combined with an unavoidable increase in social security expenditure, thereby leading to a proportional increase in overall taxation *vis-à-vis* GDP.

This discrepancy was acknowledged more explicitly when Portillo replaced Maude as Shadow Chancellor in February 2000. Recognising that the policy was a hostage to fortune, Portillo suggested that it might be better viewed as an aspiration (rather than a guarantee), which would clearly give a future Conservative government much more flexibility and mean that if taxes did increase the political damage would be rather more limited. Indeed, Hague and Portillo jointly announced in July 2000 that the 'Tax Guarantee' was being abandoned, due to recognition that the Conservatives could not promise categorically than taxes would definitely not rise when the party was next returned to office.[3]

However, the 'tax and spend' issue was never satisfactorily resolved, and, indeed, was to prove uncharacteristically problematic for the Conservatives during the 2001 general election campaign. At the start of the campaign, the party promised tax cuts totalling £8 billion, these to be financed by 'efficiency savings', cutting bureaucracy and further action on social security fraud. However, Labour was able to question whether such savings were genuinely feasible, and would yield the £8 billion savings necessary to fund the promised Tory tax cuts. Implicit in such criticism was the question of why the Conservatives had not effected these savings during their eighteen years in office up until 1997.

Worse still, though, was the apparent lack of agreement in the Conservative Party over the envisaged level of tax cuts which would be offered following an election victory. Against the official target of £8 billion, a BBC *Newsnight* interview on 11 May heard the Conservatives' social security spokesperson David Willetts intimate that £7 billion might be a more realistic target. Rather more damaging, however, was the claim, three days later, by the Shadow Chief Secretary to the Treasury, Oliver Letwin, that a Conservative government would actually cut taxes by £20 billion, whereupon Labour gleefully pointed to a £12 billion 'black hole' in the Tories' 'tax and spend' figures.[4] Labour also alleged that the Conservatives had a secret tax-cutting agenda which could only be financed by significant cuts in public expenditure, even though the Conservative Party was pledging to match Labour's promised increases on education, health and law and order. Ultimately, it was the Conservative Party which was forced on the defensive over the issue of 'tax and spend' during the 2001 election campaign, with Labour claiming that 'their sums don't add up'. Thus an ICM poll conducted during the election campaign revealed that on the question of which party was most trusted over taxation, Labour led the Conservatives by 34 per cent to 21 per cent (whilst on the issue of economic competence, the corresponding figures were 49 per cent and 29 per cent).

In emphasising tax cuts (albeit with increased spending on key public services), the Conservatives perhaps failed to appreciate the extent to which the British electorate had become more concerned about reviving the country's ailing public services. The public might not have been clamouring for actual increases in taxation, particularly not direct taxation – although countless opinion polls during the previous decade had suggested that a majority of people would be willing to pay higher taxes if the money was spent on improving public services – but there did seem to be a widespread view amongst the electorate that increased investment in such areas as education and health ought to take precedence over further tax cuts. In this respect, the Conservatives appeared to be fighting the battles of yesteryear, seeming to assume that what had been a highly effective strategy in 1992 would reap dividends once again. It was a major miscalculation.

Inextricably linked to the Conservatives' pledge to reduce the overall tax burden during the lifetime of a Parliament was the party's attack on the government for raising indirect taxation. This offered the Conservatives scope to claim that New Labour was little different from Old Labour in its instinctive inclination to raise taxes, except that instead of directly taxing people, it was doing so by stealth, via a range of indirect taxes. As such, it was variously claimed, the overall tax burden increased for many people under the Blair government, even if income tax rates themselves had not been raised. Indeed, as the 2001 election approached, the Conservatives could claim that since May 1997, the level of taxation overall had increased from 35.2 per cent to 37.2 per cent of GDP.

What appeared to be a major breakthrough for the Conservatives on the issue of 'stealth taxes' occurred in the guise of the 'fuel protests' in September 2000. These entailed road hauliers and farmers blockading oil refineries in protest at the high levels of duty charged on petrol in Britain. These protests, combined with rapidly ensuing shortages in the shops (as deliveries dwindled, and panic-buying spread), threatened to bring Britain to a complete stand-still, and alarmed Labour ministers who fearfully envisaged another 'winter of discontent'.

The petrol protests enabled the Conservatives to claim that the Blair government had finally been exposed over its reliance on raising indirect taxes, and that the British people were finally beginning to revolt over ever-increasing 'stealth taxes'. Although the blockades were in clear breach of anti-trade union legislation introduced by the Conservatives themselves during the 1980s (involving as they did more than six pickets at the entrances to the oil refineries, whilst also constituting 'secondary picketing'), and would doubtless have been fiercely condemned by the Conservative Party (and pro-Conservative newspapers) if any other group of workers had sought to 'hold the country to ransom' in such a manner, Hague expressed his clear support by describing the fuel protesters as 'fine, upstanding citizens'.[5] Opinion polls suggested that the 'fuel protests' were also supported by the overwhelming majority of the British public, in spite of any inconvenience they might have experienced, which further heartened Conservatives who now felt that they had found a clear issue with which to 'reconnect' with the electorate.

Against the backdrop of the fuel protests, Hague pledged that a Conservative government would cut fuel duty by 3p per litre, and was rewarded by a short-lived surge of support in the opinion polls – the Conservatives' first lead over Labour since 'Black Wednesday' in September 1992. This lead swiftly dissipated, though, partly reflecting Labour's apparent success in challenging the viability of Hague's promised 3p per litre reduction in fuel duty, for the question was once again raised about where the money would come from to finance such a cut. It was also suggested that any reduction in fuel duty might simply be cancelled out by the petrol companies raising fuel prices by the same amount, thereby further undermining the initial attractiveness of Hague's pledge on cutting fuel duty; motorists might find themselves paying exactly the same amount on the garage forecourt regardless, whilst Conservative ministers found themselves having either to raise taxes elsewhere to cover the reduced fuel tax revenues, or further cutting public expenditure.

With the exception of their short-lived lead in the opinion polls following the fuel protests, the Conservatives found themselves uncharacteristically on the defensive over taxation issues, desperately seeking to wrest the agenda back from the Blair government. Public disquiet over increases in 'stealth taxes' did not translate into anything but the most fleeting popularity for the Conservatives, for every Conservative pledge to reduce indirect taxation was countered by Labour allegations that such tax cuts could only be financed, ultimately, by further reductions in government expenditure, thereby further damaging Britain's ailing public services.

Law and order

Traditionally another policy area which had seemed inextricably associated with the Conservative Party, and which had so successfully connected with a significant strand of social authoritarianism in British society – particularly during the 'authoritarian populism' of the Thatcher years – law and order was also an issue over which Hague's Conservatives often struggled to re-establish the party's traditional dominance over Labour. This dominance had been successfully challenged during the 1990s, when – as Labour's home affairs spokesperson – Tony Blair had coined the phrase 'tough on crime, tough on the causes of crime', thereby signalling that a Labour government would no longer appear to exonerate criminal activity on the grounds of socio-economic deprivation or disadvantage. In so doing, the Labour Party shifted from a somewhat 'structuralist determinist' account of crime, to a stance which accepted that irrespective of background or environment, an individual still had to be held responsible for criminal acts, even though in the longer term, improving social conditions would continue to play a part in reducing crime. This revised stance on law and order enabled Labour to neutralise the Conservative Party's traditional dominance in this area, making it much more difficult for the Conservatives to depict Labour as 'soft on crime' or of being 'the criminal's friend'.

This is not to say that they did not try, of course, but it did mean that Conservative attacks on the Blair government's law and order record failed to reap the political dividends that had traditionally accrued to the Party on this policy issue. One line of attack which Hague and his Shadow Home Secretaries pursued was to criticise the government for a decline in police numbers, whilst also denouncing the amount of time and effort which police officers (like most other public sector workers) were obliged to expend on paper work and form filling.

The February 1999 publication of the Macpherson Report was also seized upon by Hague as part of his attempt at regaining the initiative on law and order.[6] An inquiry chaired by Sir William Macpherson had been established by the Labour Home Secretary, Jack Straw, in response to disquiet about the manner in which the police had investigated (or, according to critics, failed properly to investigate) the murder of a black teenager, Stephen Lawrence in 1993. The Macpherson Report was indeed critical of the Metropolitan Police's handling of the case, claiming that it was permeated by a culture of 'institutional racism'. Hague subsequently claimed that the Report had seriously damaged morale in the police force, thereby adding to the problems of recruitment and retention. Yoking together the alleged impact of the Report with the volume of paperwork which police officers were apparently over-burdened with, William Hague called, at the Conservatives' 1999 conference, for 'more PCs, and less PC [political correctness]'.

Another event which offered the Conservatives an opportunity to seize the initiative on law and order was the high-profile court case of Tony Martin, a Norfolk farmer. Martin had been subject to numerous burglaries and attempted break-ins at his farm – many of which were attributed to gypsies and 'travellers' in the area – and eventually shot dead a sixteen-year-old intruder (himself part of a gypsy family, and who, it was revealed, already had numerous convictions, having been in trouble with the police throughout his teens). Martin was consequently found guilty of murder – rather than manslaughter – and thus sentenced to life imprisonment. This verdict caused a public outcry, and was also widely condemned by many newspapers, due to the sympathy which people felt for Martin; an ordinary person repeatedly the victim of crime, yet himself given a life sentence for having decided to fight back against criminals, and defend his property against yet another break-in: a plucky 'have-a-go hero'.

The Conservative Party, too, depicted the punishment meted out to Martin as a travesty of justice, also subscribing to the view that he was the victim of crime, rather than a criminal himself. As such, Hague made clear his view that the law needed to be reviewed (in spite of the fact that a mandatory life sentence for murder had hitherto been strongly supported by Conservatives – and pro-Conservative newspapers – as part of their tough stance on law and order), so that a sentence other than life imprisonment could be imposed in certain circumstances. To this end, Hague pledged that the next Conservative government would amend the law, so that 'the state will be on the side of people who protect their homes and families against criminals',[7] a pledge reiterated by the Shadow Home Secretary, Ann Widde-combe, when she informed delegates at the Conservatives' 2000 conference that it 'cannot be common sense to arrest the householder instead of the burglar'. Consequently, in the 2001 election campaign, the Conservatives promised a Victims First initiative, which would include a new legal right to 'self-defence' for victims of crime.

The Conservative Party also sought to link the plight of Tony Martin to the problems of the countryside in general, alleging that crime in rural areas was another manifestation of New Labour's neglect of rural issues and citizens (see below).

Meanwhile, in citing drug abuse as a major factor underpinning much criminal activity in Britain, Widdecombe announced (with Hague's approval), at the 2000 conference, that she favoured a 'zero tolerance' policy towards the possession of drugs – any drugs – which would entail an automatic £100 fine in the first instance, with an automatic court appearance for a second offence.[8] Having previously derided Blair's suggestion that drunken yobs should be subject to a £100 on-the-spot fine (or escorted to the nearest cashpoint machine), Widdecombe was taken aback by the rather lukewarm response of the police to such a policy. Rather more damaging, though, were the subsequent announcements by several Shadow Cabinet colleagues that they themselves had imbibed soft drugs when younger or at university, yet none of them had progressed to hard drugs or crime. Not surprisingly, perhaps, the policy proposal was rapidly retracted for reconsideration.

The family and sexual politics

Hague's Conservatives were afforded ample opportunity to re-emphasise their self-appointed role as *the* party of the family in the context of New Labour's commitment to 'gay rights', and the Blair government's abolition of the married person's tax allowance in April 2000.

With regard to the issue of 'gay rights', Hague's initial intimation that the Conservative Party ought to become more 'socially inclusive' and less prescriptive about people's lifestyles was not reflected in the Division Lobbies when the Blair government sought – via the 1998 Crime and Disorder Bill – to reduce the age of consent for gay sex to sixteen, thereby ensuring legal equality with heterosexuals. Although Hague himself had previously supported such a change in the law in 1994, only sixteen Conservative MPs voted in favour of equalisation four years later, the legislation subsequently being obstructed in the House of Lords, with the Conservative Baroness Young denouncing it as a 'paedophile's charter'.

That Hague's 'socially inclusive' Conservatism was a short-lived phenomenon, and one which was not widely or enthusiastically endorsed by many other Conservative MPs, was subsequently indicated by the party's staunch opposition to the government's attempt (via the 1999 Local Government Bill) at repealing Section 28 of the 1988 Local Government Act, which prohibited the 'promotion of homosexuality' in schools. The Conservative leadership imposed a three-line whip on its peers – the Bill having been introduced in the House of Lords, rather than the Commons – to oppose repeal of Section 28, and this opposition was maintained in spite of various modifications and measures proposed by Labour ministers to assuage the objections of the Conservatives. Faced with implacable opposition from Conservative peers in the Lords (this being prior to the removal of the majority of hereditary peers), and unable to invoke the 1949 Parliament Act – which does not apply to Bills introduced in the House of Lords – the government was obliged to abandon its initial attempts at repealing Section 28, although New Labour remained formally committed to such reform.[9]

For Hague's Conservative Party, however, the successful opposition to repeal of Section 28 could be depicted as a victory both for 'common sense', and for traditional Conservatism, with its strong emphasis on the importance of marriage, as well as the conviction that sex education in schools ought to be more morally prescriptive. However, the party's stance on 'gay rights' also resulted in the defections to New Labour of Shaun Woodward (who had been sacked from the Shadow Frontbench because of his refusal to support the party's stance in opposing repeal of Section 28), and a wealthy Conservative businessman, Ivor Massow, both of whom alluded to the 'bigotry' still prevalent in much of the Party, whilst Marc Cranfield-Adams, a Conservative 'gay rights' campaigner, warned the leadership that: 'Society has moved on. The Conservative Party must move on too.'[10]

This reinvigorated emphasis on the centrality of marriage and the 'normal' family was further emphasised through key speeches by Hague, and by the party's response to the government's abolition of the married couples' tax allowance. Having successfully resisted legislation which would allegedly have permitted the 'promotion of homosexuality' in schools via sex education lessons, the Conservatives returned to a theme from Major's era, namely the innate superiority of (married) couples over single parents, particularly with regard to child-rearing. Whilst insisting that the Conservative Party was not seeking to demonise lone parents – a more contrite Portillo had even made a speech shortly after losing his Enfield and Southgate seat in 1997, acknowledging that some single parents did an excellent job in raising their children in very difficult circumstances – various speeches made by senior Conservatives towards the end of the 1990s indicated that most of them continued to believe strongly in the moral superiority and social necessity of marriage, and joint parental responsibility for raising children.

Indeed, in a speech to the Social Market Foundation in January 1998, Hague intimated that the Conservatives had not done enough to assist traditional families during their eighteen years in office.[11] Although he insisted that the Conservative Party had to become more tolerant of personal and sexual relationships other than marriage, he remained convinced that marriage was the best institutional arrangement for raising children, to the extent that divorce was often more traumatic for children than being brought up by parents who were no longer happily married. Furthermore, Hague claimed that whilst 'People who cohabit presumably have taken a legitimate decision not to marry ... we should respect the decision of people who wish to cohabit by not extending to them the full panoply of marriage law.' In other words, cohabiting couples should not be entitled to the same pension rights, or rights pertaining to division of property, as married couples. Whilst cohabitation was a matter for the individuals concerned, Hague believed that the state was entitled to make clear its preference for marriage by offering married couples tax allowances, particularly in respect of their children. Clearly, greater acceptance of alternatives lifestyles and sexual relationships did not mean moral neutrality or indifference.

Later the same year, in his speech to the party's 1998 conference, Hague alluded to the apparent link between the welfare state and family disintegration, when he insisted on the need for 'welfare reform that encourages families to stay together and doesn't discriminate against marriage'. To this end, Hague pledged that the Conservative Party would 'develop policies on welfare reform which strengthen family responsibility and support for the institution of marriage'.

The Conservatives thus condemned the government's April 2000 abolition of the married couples' tax allowance, which Hague deemed 'vital to a stable, healthy society', on the grounds that children were 'nearly always' best raised by a married couple. Restoration of this tax allowance henceforth became a clear commitment of the Conservative Party, and was reiterated in the 2001 election manifesto.

Welfare reform and pensions

Having spent eighteen years in office seeking to reform and curb Britain's welfare state, there was no diminution by the Conservatives in their efforts to detect fraud and identify those who constituted an 'undeserving poor'. Again, however, their task was rendered more difficult by the government's own tougher stance against those who abused the welfare state, and New Labour's 'third way' insistence that rights had to be matched by reciprocal responsibilities; the unemployed could no longer expect 'something for nothing' under a Labour government, with Blair insisting that welfare provision should be about providing 'a hand-up, not a hand-out'.

In this context, the Conservatives sought to outflank the government by promising even stronger measures to combat welfare abuse and the workshy. Hague promised delegates at the 1999 Conservative conference that when the party was next in office, 'any unemployed person who can work, and who is offered a job, either takes that job or loses their unemployment benefits'. Furthermore, Hague pledged that a system of payment-by-results would be imposed on job centres, thus making clear that they 'are not there to pay people benefits for doing nothing'.

Meanwhile, for many Conservatives, single parents continued to straddle the boundary between revival of traditional (family) morality and retrenchment of the welfare state, with the party's social security spokesperson, David Willetts, unveiling proposals for further tightening-up eligibility criteria for lone parents. In a 1999 speech to the Social Market Foundation, Willetts announced that under a Conservative government, once their only or youngest child had reached eleven years of age, single parents would be given thirteen weeks in which to find paid employment, after which their benefit would be reduced (although they would continue to receive social security payments for their children). This, Willetts claimed, would ensure that rather than receiving welfare benefits 'simply by virtue of not having an income and being a single parent', lone parents would 'instead be expected ... to be actively seeking work – seeking the sorts of jobs which their married counterparts are doing'.[12]

The Conservatives might have expected more success on the issue of old age pensions, partly because of the traditionally higher levels of support the party attracted amongst the elderly, and also because of the outcry which followed the government's announcement of a derisory 80p increase in the state pension for April 2000 (the rationale being that this was in line with the then very low rate of inflation, to which pensions and other welfare benefits were generally linked – another policy which New Labour inherited from previous Conservative governments).

Apart from condemning the government over this insultingly low increase in the state pension, the Conservatives also criticised the introduction of free TV licences for the over seventy-fives, along with the system of one-off Christmas bonuses and winter fuel allowances, claiming that these were another manifestation of New Labour's 'nanny state' tendencies, with pensioners being told that certain payments were for specific purposes only. Against this, Willetts, argued that these 'special payments' should be consolidated into an overall increase in the state retirement pension, whereupon pensioners would be able to exercise their own choice and individual responsibility in deciding how to spend the money.

However, when Chancellor Gordon Brown subsequently announced a significant increase in the state pension – well above the rate of inflation – the Conservatives responded by suggesting that pensioners should be permitted to decide whether they wanted to have a higher 'consolidated' pension, or to retain the various 'one off' payments and bonuses. What was perhaps not fully appreciated, though, was that this would yield two parallel systems of state retirement pensions, leading to considerable administrative complexities for a Conservative Party committed to cutting red tape. More important, however, was that in spite of the outcry over the 80p increase in the state pension in 2000, Labour still led the Conservatives in the 2001 election campaign, when an ICM poll asked voters which of the parties had the best policies on pensions, although this may have owed something to Brown's contrition in increasing pensions by £5 per week in the April 2001 budget. Furthermore, in the general election itself, support for the Conservative Party amongst the sixty-five plus age cohort declined slightly, from 44 per cent in 1997 (having been 53 per cent back in 1983) to 42 per cent in 2001, whilst amongst the fifty-five to sixty-four age group (the next generation of pensioners, in effect), Labour led the Conservatives by 40 per cent to 34 per cent.

Asylum seekers

Faced with consistently low opinion poll ratings (the false dawn of early autumn 2000 notwithstanding), one of the few policy areas where Hague's Conservatives believed they could garner significant support, and thereby force the Blair government onto the defensive, was that of asylum seekers, or, more particularly, 'bogus' asylum seekers. Just as ministers in the Major government had sought to posit a distinction between legitimate refugees and mere 'economic migrants', so too did the Conservatives after 1997 draw a distinction between genuine asylum seekers literally fleeing for their lives from tyrannical political regimes, and 'bogus asylum seekers' who were deemed to be illegally entering Britain in search of a more prosperous lifestyle or 'easy' welfare benefits. In spite of this distinction, however, the phrase 'bogus asylum seekers' was used so routinely that many people instinctively viewed asylum seekers as 'bogus' *per se*.

From the Conservatives' perspective, highlighting the alleged problem of 'bogus asylum seekers' provided scope for connecting a number of themes which were traditionally advantageous to the party. Firstly, the party could appeal – however vehemently Hague might deny it – to racist and xeno-phobic sentiments amongst the least-educated sections of British society, by identifying the 'alien other' or 'outsiders' who were threatening to overwhelm the country. Secondly, but following directly on from this, the Conservatives invoked the numbers game, by claiming that 'bogus asylum seekers' were 'flooding' Britain, so great was the increase in their numbers under the Blair government – official figures indicating that the number of asylum seekers had increased from 29,640 in 1997 to 76,035 in 2001 – thereby reviving echoes of Margaret Thatcher's notorious 1978 'swamping' speech. Thirdly, but again, following on from this point, Hague and many of his colleagues directly blamed the government, insisting that it had rendered Britain 'a soft touch' due to its inability or unwillingness to address the issue properly. Fourthly, some Conservatives alluded to the apparent drain on resources, either in terms of welfare payments, or the costs incurred by some local authorities in having to house asylum seekers whilst their applications were being considered. Fifthly, there was occasional criticism of the Home

Office for its apparent tardiness in processing claims for asylum, and the delay in reaching decisions. Finally, there were occasional attempts at linking the issue to Euro-scepticism, on the grounds that other European countries (France especially) ought either to be more vigilant in apprehending 'bogus asylum seekers' *en route* to Britain, or should themselves be accepting more of them, so that they did not target Britain in such apparently large numbers.

The Conservatives' response was to invoke the phrase 'a safe haven, not a soft touch', claiming that a Conservative government would deal sympathetically with genuine asylum seekers, but severely with those deemed 'bogus'. What was also urgently required, the Conservatives insisted, was a much more swift and efficient procedure for processing applications for asylum, thereby reducing the growing backlog of cases, whilst ensuring that those whose applications were rejected could be deported much more quickly (thereby also alleviating the growing burden on taxpayers and local authorities). Meanwhile, whilst their applications were being processed, the Conservative Party suggested that asylum seekers should be detained in secure 'reception centres'.

Rural affairs

Britain's status as an advanced industrial society (now post-industrial, many would claim) has ensured that, in contrast to some other European countries, an urban–rural cleavage had never been particularly prominent or politically significant during the twentieth century, even though the shires have generally been Conservative heartlands. However, from 1997 onwards, 'rural politics' did become a more discernible issue, and one onwhich the Conservatives sought to capitalise under Hague's leadership.

In recent years, Britain's rural communities have faced a number of problems, most notably: the continued decline of the farming industry (exacerbated by the BSE crisis of the mid-1990s, and the foot-and-mouth epidemic in the spring of 2001); the closure of rural schools and post offices (previously endorsed by many Conservatives on the grounds of cost-effectiveness and lack of economic viability); the paucity of public transport in rural areas (particularly in the wake of deregulation or privatisation of transport, whereupon many rural routes were deemed 'not commercially viable'); the high cost of housing in many villages, which many younger people raised in them cannot afford, in which case they often move away, leaving the villages either to atrophy, or be 'colonised' by former urban dwellers and 'townies' buying second homes or retiring to the countryside.

Although these trends had emerged or accelerated under the Major governments during the 1990s, Hague's Conservative Party sought to claim that the plight of Britain's countryside was largely the responsibility of the

Blair government, constituting as it allegedly did a 'metropolitan elite' which was ignorant of, or indifferent to, the vicissitudes of village life in rural areas of Britain. Having spent two decades denouncing subsidies to inefficient or outdated industries, condemning the demands of producer interests, insisting on the need for flexibility and adaptation to change, and extolling the virtues of self-help, the Conservatives suddenly rediscovered the virtues of government intervention and investment, at least in relation to the farming industry and protection of rural communities. Compared to the relentless neo-liberalism and individualism of the 1980s and most of the 1990s, it was a truly remarkable U-turn.

Another apparent U-turn manifested itself in the Conservatives' defence of 'green belts' against further urban sprawl. Having itself presided over extensive 'out-of-town' housing developments during the 1980s and much of the 1990s, the post-1997 Conservative Party demanded that two-thirds of new houses should henceforth be built on 'brownfield' sites (such as derelict land) in urban areas, thereby simultaneously reviving inner-city districts whilst protecting the countryside from further urban encroachment.

What really crystallised ruralism as a political issue, though, was the Blair government's avowed intention to outlaw fox-hunting. Indeed, a Private Members' Bill introduced in the 1997–98 parliamentary session, to prohibit hunting with hounds, prompted the formation of the Countryside Alliance, which held a high-profile rally in London in March 1998. Although this body purported to be concerned about a wide range of rural problems, it was clear that defence of fox-hunting was its primary motivation, with other issues conjoined in order to attract wider support.

Furthermore, whilst the Countryside Alliance purported to be non-political (and even ostentatiously highlighted a few Labour politicians amongst its ranks), it was clear that it shared a very close affinity with the Conservatives, with the latter echoing many of the Alliance's grievances and attacks on the government. With regard to New Labour's desire to ban fox-hunting, Conservatives (and the Countryside Alliance) deployed various arguments, most notably that it was an issue of individual liberty, that a ban would lead to further job losses in rural areas, and that fox-hunting was a traditional and cultural component of rural life in Britain – something which was beyond the comprehension of a urban, metropolitan Labour government. It was also occasionally claimed that thousands of hounds would have to be destroyed if fox-hunting was outlawed. For many Conservatives, the government's antipathy to blood-sports was a manifestation of a rather 'Old Labour' class warfare, on the grounds that fox-hunting was perceived to be enjoyed primarily by wealthy landowners and squires, rather than rural dwellers of all social and occupational backgrounds.

That the Blair government was seeking to outlaw fox-hunting, whilst also infuriating many landowners by legislating for a statutory 'right to roam' across their land, at a time when the countryside was already in crisis, was cited by the Conservatives as evidence of the Labour Party's contempt for rural people and their traditional way of life. New Labour, it seemed, was unable or unwilling to see beyond the bistros and wine-bars of Islington, and with Hague himself representing a market town in rural North Yorkshire, the Conservatives clearly aligned themselves with the 'simple folk' of the shires against Blair's 'liberal, metropolitan, urban, elite'.

Conclusion

Hague's Conservative Party faced a particularly difficult task in developing a coherent and popular raft of policies in opposition after the 1997 election defeat. The party's uncertainty and lack of agreement over the most appropriate ideological response (discussed in the previous chapter) to New Labour's landslide victory at the polls was itself a major inhibition in developing consistent policies. Hence the Conservative Party oscillated between advocacy of more tolerant and 'socially inclusive' policies at some junctures before resorting to more authoritarian populist measures at others. This inconsistency was itself a consequence not merely of the long-standing ideological divisions in the parliamentary party between Thatcherites and remnants of One Nation Toryism, but of the apparent recantation of former Thatcherites like Lilley and Portillo, who sought to reposition themselves away from the right of the party, particularly on social issues.

The Conservatives' difficulties in developing a coherent and consistent set of policies were further exacerbated by the traditional problem facing a party which has just lost office, namely the time needed to reconsider and regroup. To embrace new policies too quickly would not only increase the likelihood of ill-judged or incoherent measures being adopted, but would also appear to many voters as blatant opportunism. It would either imply that the party was prepared to say virtually anything in order to return to power at the earliest possible opportunity, with scant regard to its political principles, or it would lead sceptical voters to enquire why the new policies had not been considered or implemented whilst the party was still in office, in place of the unpopular policies which had presaged the election defeat. Furthermore, if policies were hastily adopted which looked like proving popular, then they were likely to be appropriated by the government, which would then take the political credit if they were successful, a fact recognised by Lilley when he was allocated responsibility for overseeing a review of Conservative policies in June 1998.[13]

A further problem facing the Conservative Party after May 1997 directly relates to the success of the Labour Party in repositioning itself during its eighteen years in opposition. On the basis that much of the British electorate preferred or trusted the Conservatives' economic policies – at least up until

September 1992 – whilst liking Labour's social policies, New Labour sought to meld the two, so that nationalisation and higher income taxes were jettisoned, and a more business-friendly stance adopted, whilst commitments remained to social justice, reviving public services and eradicating poverty – the much-vaunted 'third way'. Given the range of economic principles and policies which the Blair government inherited, maintained and even developed further, the Conservatives found it difficult to level consistent or convincing criticisms against the government, particularly as these might be construed as criticisms against some of the measures that Conservative ministers themselves implemented prior to 1997. On the other hand, Conservative criticisms pertaining to the state of public services under the Blair government merely served to remind voters of how education, health and public transport had been allowed to deteriorate for eighteen years in the first place. Similarly, when Conservatives denounced the government for the mountain of red tape and bureaucracy in schools, universities and hospitals, Labour ministers could readily point out that these were invariably associated with reforms – internal markets, quality audits, etc – introduced by the Thatcher and Major governments.

Finally, and perhaps most importantly, the post-1997 Conservative Party has found it difficult to come to terms with the world as it is today (even though it played a notable part in shaping it when in office) and thereby to formulate an appropriate range of policies in response. During the 1990s, the excesses of the unfettered free market and the relentless drive for more competitiveness proved profoundly destabilising for much of the British middle and professional classes, who had previously looked to the Conservative Party to provide them with security and stability.[14] The 'labour market flexibility' which Conservative ministers extolled so enthusiastically was instead experienced by millions of people as increased job insecurity, fixed-term contracts and longer working-hours. Yet in remaining wedded to the alleged virtues of globalisation and the free market, and thus denouncing the meddling 'nanny state', the Conservative Party since 1997 has remained unable or unwilling to address the problems of job insecurity and excessive working hours, which themselves appear to be having an increasingly damaging impact on people's health, whilst also being inimical to family life.

An indication of the problems facing the post-1997 Conservative Party in developing new policies was indicated when Hague announced a 'Listening to Britain' exercise in the summer of 1998, involving Shadow Ministers attending up to 150 meetings throughout the country, attended by 40,000 people, with a view to discerning what ordinary citizens were thinking and asking for *vis-à-vis* a whole range of policy issues. In announcing this consultation exercise, Hague claimed that apart from the party's stance on the single European currency, every previous Conservative policy was subject to review and potential revision. However, he was also emphatic that Conservative principles were non-negotiable, so that the party's commitment to a low-tax, private enterprise economy remained inviolate, as did its belief in the importance of the family, the constitution, and the nation state.[15] It immediately became apparent, therefore, that the scope for new policies was actually rather limited, and that many existing commitments would not be ditched after all.

The 'findings' of the 'Listening to Britain' exercise were published a year later in a document of the same name, by which time Hague was proclaiming a 'Common Sense Revolution' to provide the basis of Conservative policies for the next general election. What was pledged (via an eponymous forty-two page document) was a series of policy proposals – half populist, half prosaic – which variously promised empowerment for families and 'the community' against 'the nanny state', a reduction in the overall tax burden (albeit during the lifetime of a Parliament), and measures to create a more secure society, whilst defending Britain's interests *vis-à-vis* the European Union. These pledges were reiterated in 2000 in yet another policy document (albeit more brief, at twenty-nine pages), *Believing in Britain*.

Yet Hague's Conservative Party found that neither the more 'socially inclusive' stance of the early period in opposition – a stance which continued to be urged by former Thatcherites like Portillo and Lilley – nor a reversion to a more populist stance during the latter period, elicited a discernible or durable increase in popularity. Indeed, in spite of the Blair government's arrogance, obsession with 'spin' and self-confessed failure to 'deliver', the Conservatives proved unable to regain public support, beyond their core 30 to 32 per cent.

Hague and his senior colleagues were in an unenviable position throughout the Conservatives' period in opposition. Adopting a more 'socially inclusive' and 'social liberal' stance, in order to challenge New Labour for the centre One Nation ground, incurred the wrath of the homophobes, xenophobes and petit-bourgeois curtain-twitchers on the party's right, who still yearned for the social authoritarianism and moral absolutism of Thatcherism. It has always been an irony that those Conservatives most critical of the drab grey conformity which socialism would allegedly impose – 'they'd make us all the same' – are invariably the very Conservatives most intolerant of any social group which is different to the majority, and is thus deemed deviant or dangerous for not conforming. Such Conservatives call for an increase in individual liberty and less government interference, yet then instinctively mutter 'it shouldn't be allowed … the government ought to put a stop to it' when confronted by a lifestyle or socio-cultural minority of which they disapprove – 'why can't these people just be like everybody else?'. Yet, on the other hand, when Hague's Conservatives retreated to right-wing authoritarian populism to bolster the party's 'core support', it found itself being denounced for succumbing to extremism, and of being out-of-touch with mainstream centrist opinion, even though on issues like retaining Section 28, anxiety about asylum seekers and opposing the euro, the Conservatives' stance broadly reflected public opinion. Yet this did not yield any notable increase in electoral support, largely because on most issues – and especially the most salient ones – the government retained a lead over the Conservatives in terms of trust and competence. Even in policy areas where New Labour had evidently 'failed to deliver', it was still generally preferred to the Conservatives, and deemed more likely to deliver if granted a second term. By contrast, the Conservatives found that on a range of policies, they were either disliked, or simply not trusted, particularly on those pertaining to the public services, although even on their traditional trump card, the economy, they trailed New Labour by a considerable margin.

The consequent election defeat in June 2001, when the Conservatives gained just one additional seat overall, means that Hague's successor, Iain Duncan Smith, will have to grapple with all of the same policy issues, whilst simultaneously hoping either that the Blair government's 'luck' will run out before the next general election, or that the electorate will tire of New Labour's 'spin' and continued failure (perceived or proven) to 'deliver' on asylum, crime, education, health and transport, even if the economy remains relatively robust.

Notes

1 T. Baldwin, 'The polished prose that is written by many and read by few', *The Times*, 24 February 2001.
2 See J. Bush, 'Bare-faced cheek of Brown's critics', *The Times*, 28 October 1998.
3 G. Jones, 'Confident Tory leader enters enemy territory with tax weapon', *Daily Telegraph*, 11 July 2000.
4 A. Sparrow and G. Jones', 'Tories "aspire" to cut taxes beyond the £8bn promise', *Daily Telegraph*, 15 May 2001.
5 G. Jones, 'Firms must keep the fuel flowing', *Daily Telegraph*, 18 September 2000.
6 'The Stephen Lawrence Inquiry Report' ['the Macpherson Report'] (London, HMSO, 1999) Cm 4262-I.
7 N. Watt, 'Hague joins outcry over jailed farmer', *Guardian*, 26 April 2000.
8 G. Jones, 'Tory crackdown on cannabis', *Daily Telegraph*, 4 October 2000.
9 For a detailed analysis, see M. Waites, 'Regulation of sexuality: age of consent, Section 28 and sex education', *Parliamentary Affairs*, 54:3 (2001).
10 A. Pierce, 'Threat of revolt forces Tory U-turn on gays', *The Times*, 11 December 1999.
11 See J. Sherman, 'Hague calls for tax aid to boost family values', *The Times*, 30 January 1998.
12 See A. Frean, 'Conservatives plan jobs deadline for single parents', *The Times*, 23 November 1999.
13 D. Butler and D. Kavanagh, *The British General Election of 2001* (London, Palgrave, 2002), p. 48.

14 See P. Dorey, 'Despair and disillusion abound: the Major Premiership in perspective', in P. Dorey (ed.), *The Major Premiership: Politics and Policies under John Major* (London, Palgrave, 1999), pp. 218–49, and J. Gray, 'Conservatism R.I.P.', in J. Gray and D. Willetts, *Is Conservatism Dead?* (London, Social Market Foundation, 1997).

15 A. Pierce, 'Tories go on tour as Hague pledges wholesale changes', *The Times*, 15 July 1998.

8

The Conservatives and Europe, 1997–2001

Philip Lynch

As Conservatives reflected on the 1997 general election, they could agree that the issue of Britain's relationship with the European Union (EU) was a significant factor in their defeat. But they disagreed over how and why 'Europe' had contributed to the party's demise. Euro-sceptics blamed John Major's European policy. For Euro-sceptics, Major had accepted developments in the European Union that ran counter to the Thatcherite defence of the nation state and promotion of the free market by signing the Maastricht Treaty. This opened a schism in the Conservative Party that Major exacerbated by paying insufficient attention to the growth of Euro-sceptic sentiment. Membership of the Exchange Rate Mechanism (ERM) prolonged recession and undermined the party's reputation for economic competence. Finally, Euro-sceptics argued that Major's unwillingness to rule out British entry into the single currency for at least the next Parliament left the party unable to capitalise on the Euro-scepticism that prevailed in the electorate.

Pro-Europeans and Major loyalists saw things differently. They believed that Major had acted in the national interest at Maastricht by signing a Treaty that allowed Britain to influence the development of Economic and Monetary Union (EMU) without being bound to join it. Pro-Europeans noted that Thatcher had agreed to an equivalent, if not greater, loss of sovereignty by signing the Single European Act. They believed that much of the party could and should have united around Major's 'wait and see' policy on EMU entry. But the activities of a small number of hardline Euro-sceptics undermined the government's domestic authority and its influence in Europe. An electorate that had little interest in the European issue – but which responded most favourably to the 'wait and see' position on EMU and continued membership of an intergovernmental EU – recoiled from a divided party and punished it at the polls.

Given this background, Europe was going to be one of the most important and difficult issues facing William Hague as Conservative leader. This chapter examines Conservative policy on Europe under Hague, arguing that, despite the pragmatism of Hague's position, the Conservatives took significant steps in a Euro-sceptic direction. The term 'Euro-scepticism' is conceptually loose and contested. In their work on Euro-sceptic parties, Taggart and Szczerbiak distinguish between a 'hard Euro-scepticism' of principled opposition to EU or to the integration project as currently conceived and a 'soft Euro-scepticism' that supports membership but opposes further economic and political union.[1] The post-1997 Conservative Party is situated somewhere between the two. The pragmatic 'In Europe, but not run by Europe' platform and 'two Parliaments' position on EMU entry suggest a 'soft' scepticism but they masked demands for major reform of the EU and a renegotiation of the Nice Treaty. If these were not forthcoming, Conservative support for fundamental renegotiation or withdrawal was no longer inconceivable. Though the party did not cross the Rubicon under Hague, it adopted a Euro-sceptic position considerably 'harder' than both its stance in the mid-1990s (when withdrawal was unthinkable for most Tory MPs) and those adopted by other mainstream centre right parties in the EU. Yet this stance did not bring great electoral rewards and Europe remained a significant faultline in Conservative politics.

Hague and Europe

Europe featured prominently in the 1997 leadership election. At the outset, eventual winner William Hague had the least clearly defined position on Europe of the five candidates. Michael Howard, Peter Lilley and John Redwood – who had challenged Major in 1995 on an anti-EMU platform – were on the Euro-sceptic right. Kenneth Clarke was the standard bearer of the pro-European Tory left. Most committed Euro-sceptics and significant numbers of sceptic-leaning MPs from the 'party faithful' voted for the candidates of the right.[2] Redwood finished third on the first ballot; Lilley and Howard withdrawing after poor performances. Hague won forty-one votes, mainly from the centre right, and trailed Clarke by eight. Hague recognised that to pick up votes from supporters of Lilley and Howard (both of whom now endorsed him), he must convince them of his Euro-sceptic credentials. But his inconsistency and prevarication on the single currency question sowed further seeds of doubt in the minds of many Euro-sceptics.[3] Hague first indicated that he was opposed to EMU entry in principle, then declared that he would oppose British entry for the 'foreseeable future', suggesting this meant a period of two Parliaments or ten years. He was also criticised for stating that accepting the policy on EMU would be a precondition of membership of his Shadow Cabinet.[4] This show of virility worried pro-Europeans but did not fully convince Euro-sceptics. Hague gained ground on Clarke in the second ballot, which eliminated Redwood. Clarke's attempt to clinch the leadership by brokering a deal with Redwood that promised a free vote on EMU entry backfired. Euro-sceptics like Iain Duncan Smith, Redwood's campaign manager, recoiled from the pact, doubting its durability and fearing it would institutionalise rather than bridge the party's Euro-divide.

Hague was the beneficiary, coming through to win by ninety-two votes to seventy on the third ballot. But the victory was not resounding: only on the final ballot had Hague secured the backing of the bulk of the Euro-sceptic right.[5] There were uncomfortable parallels with Major's win in 1990. In both contests, an ideologically shallow candidate with little political baggage and few enemies had come through to win. Hague appeared to offer a European policy (or form of words) that could draw support from across the party, but had not convinced committed Euro-sceptics and had antagonised pro-Europeans. After his victory, Hague gave Euro-sceptics prominent positions in the Shadow Cabinet. Within a year, three pro-Europeans had left the Shadow Cabinet – Ian Taylor and David Curry resigned in October 1997 after policy on the euro was hardened; Stephen Dorrell left in June 1998.

A number of factors shaped Conservative policy on Europe, offering opportunities to forge a new position but also constraints on its effectiveness. The first factor was the position inherited from Major: the 'wait and see' policy had run its course allowing Hague to develop his own position, while he could also build on the moderate Euro-sceptic position formulated for the 1996–97 Intergovernmental Conference (IGC). Policy would also be forged in response to a pro-European Labour government and to developments in the EU. Considerations of party unity and electoral impact would also be significant. Major's 'wait and see' position was replaced by a tougher line that ruled out British entry for two Parliaments but not for all time. The 'In Europe, not run by Europe' platform envisaged a new relationship between Britain and the EU based on flexibility and renegotiation.

Economic and monetary union

Election defeat and Major's resignation nullified the 'wait and see' policy and the pledge to hold a referendum on EMU. Cast from office, the Conservatives no longer had to take the decision on whether Britain would join EMU at its launch, taking some of the heat out of the party's Euro-divisions. Hague sought to bring party policy in line with his pledge to oppose EMU entry for the lifetime of the current Parliament and the next one. But he toned down his message at the 1997 party conference as the Shadow Cabinet had not reached a firm policy decision, in part because three pro-European members missed a meeting at which the issue was to have been resolved.[6] But the Shadow Cabinet approved the 'two Parliaments' position soon after, signalling that the Tories would campaign against the euro at the next general election and in a referendum held in the period in question. A Conservative government elected at the next election would oppose EMU entry and would not hold a euro referendum. Hague weathered the pro-European storm that followed, cementing his authority and the legitimacy of the new policy by holding a ballot of party members that produced an 84.8 per cent vote in favour of the 'two Parliaments' line in 1998. Critics noted that the ballot did not seek opinions on alternative policies and that 40 per cent of members did not return their ballot papers.

In October 1997, Chancellor Gordon Brown announced that Britain was unlikely to enter EMU in the current Parliament but should join in future if the single currency proved a success. A decision on membership would be taken on the basis of five economic tests: sustainable convergence, sufficient flexibility and EMU's impact on investment, the financial services and employment. Brown declared that the government supported British membership in principle and saw 'no over-riding constitutional bar to membership'. Hague thereafter presented the choice facing the British people as one between a Labour Party committed to EMU entry and a Conservative Party that had major economic and political objections to membership – even though it did not rule out entry in the long term. Labour's National Changeover Plan, the slide in the value of the euro against the dollar, Commission proposals for tax harmonisation (resisted by the government) and the 2000 Danish referendum 'No' to EMU entry reinforced Conservative opposition. As Shadow Chancellor, Michael Portillo maintained the 'Sterling Guarantee' outlined in the 1999 *Common Sense Revolution* and backed Bank of England independence. In February 2000 Hague launched a 'Keep the Pound' campaign, stepping aboard a flatbed truck to take his pro-sterling message around the country.

The Conservatives focused on the economic case against EMU, though political and constitutional concerns also surfaced. In his first party conference speech, Hague apologised for ERM membership and warned that EMU would bring greater dangers. A month later he developed a wide-ranging economic case against entry.[7] The EU lacked the labour market flexibility needed to survive economic shocks. There was little evidence of sustained economic convergence: the British and German business cycles were diverging. Sustainable convergence appeared unlikely given the 'fundamental differences in the structure of the British economy compared to other European economies'. Britain had a larger equity market and financial services industry, more homeowners with mortgages and funded pension provision and was a net exporter of gas and oil. It also had a more flexible labour market and lower taxes than many EU states, plus a higher proportion of trade with non-EU countries. Finally, there were important differences between British and European welfare, fiscal and regulatory regimes. Britain could be more influential as a low tax, free enterprise economy outside the euro zone.[8]

Hague established a commission of supportive economists and businessmen, chaired by former Cabinet minister Lord Nott, to examine the case for retaining sterling. The Nott Report highlighted the economic dangers of joining EMU and claimed that as the fifth (later fourth) largest economy in the world, the UK would prosper outside EMU.[9] Yet the commission went beyond its remit and Hague's 'two Parliaments' line by presenting political arguments against EMU entry at any time.

The Conservatives built up a relatively coherent case against EMU entry despite inconsistencies in policy and poor presentation. But, as Major had discovered, a pragmatic position based on compromise did not stand up well to rigorous analysis. The single biggest flaw of Hague's formula was the tension between a case against entry based on economic and *constitutional* grounds and the official policy of ruling out EMU entry for just two Parliaments.[10] Given his grave concerns about the economic and political costs of EMU entry, was Hague opposed to membership in principle? If not, under what circumstances would he support entry? Hague had struggled to effectively answer such questions in the leadership contest and continued to do so.

To limit the damage, Hague focused on the economic case against entry but he and senior Conservatives regularly alluded to the adverse implications of EMU for democratic self-government. The 'two Parliaments' position reflected a compromise between the party's rival wings, but would allow more time to assess the performance of the euro zone, and reflected the conservative disposition towards the tried and tested. However, Conservative opposition to EMU on political and constitutional grounds was principled rather than time constrained. The political implications of membership — the loss of national control over key economic decisions and the erosion of self-govern-ment — were long-term and likely to become more pronounced if, as Hague predicted, EMU entailed further harmonisation. The Blair government had a principled answer on the question of EMU membership but its enthusiasm waned when faced with the practicalities of entry. The Conservatives did not agree on a principled anti-euro position, despite the leadership being more convinced of its position than their Labour counterparts. It was difficult to envisage any circumstances in which Hague, Portillo, Maude and others would recommend or support EMU entry, but they were unwilling or unable to say as much in public.

'In Europe, not run by Europe'

Hague had come up with the phrase 'In Europe, not run by Europe' in 1997 and it featured in that year's manifesto. After private polling revealed the phrase struck a chord with voters, it was widely used and became the title of the 1999 European election manifesto.[11] The policies it encompassed were gradually fleshed out, the leadership emphasising flexibility and renegotiation from 1999, committing itself to legislation on 'reserved powers' the following year, then proposing significant EU institutional reform in 2001.

The 'In Europe, not run by Europe' platform had its roots in the Euro-sceptic position adopted for the 1996–97 IGC. Hague went further, seeking not only to halt the integrationist tide but also to row back from Treaty commitments and radically reform the EU. Unlike his predecessor, Hague made little effort to back up his claim that he wanted Britain to remain in the Union by highlighting the benefits of membership. Instead, he argued that Europe had to choose between an integrationist path leading to a European 'superstate' or a flexible 'network' Europe.

FLEXIBILITY AND RENEGOTIATION

Flexibility became a central plank of Conservative policy. In the mid-1990s, Major had envisaged a 'multi-track, multi-speed, multi-layered Europe' in which Member States would be bound by single market rules but could opt-out of other policy areas.[12] A small group of Member States could pursue closer cooperation provided that any arrangement allowing them to use Community institutions to promote new measures was agreed by all states, open to all and did not force reluctant states into further integration.

Under Hague, the Conservatives held that 'new members should have the right to accept some EU policies on a selective basis in perpetuity and ... existing Member States too should be free to develop a mix and match approach'.[13] The new policy had three main elements. Firstly, a Conservative government would press for a new Treaty provision on flexibility. All Member States would have to accept the 'rights and responsibilities of the single market' and the 'core elements of an open, free-trading and competitive Europe'. But, outside the core areas, a new Treaty provision 'would allow countries not to participate in new legislative actions at a European level which they felt they wished to handle at national level'.[14] Little detail was given as to how this provision might be arrived at or how it would work in practice. Shadow Foreign Secretary John Maples claimed it would neither block those countries that wanted to go ahead with new legislation, nor affect existing legislation.[15] But the Tories also sought to repatriate policies, opposed many commitments entered into by the Blair government and demanded the renegotiation of the Nice Treaty. Determining which new legislative proposals fell within the 'core areas' would be a fraught process. Hague indicated that 'things that cross national boundaries' like trade and the environment might be considered core areas, but that taxation would not.[16]

A second, related element was 'two-way flexibility'. The Conservatives accepted the Amsterdam provisions for enhanced cooperation by which some Member States could forge ahead with new legislation using EU institutions and procedures without requiring the involvement of all states. But during the 2000 IGC, Hague's third Shadow Foreign Secretary, Francis Maude, opposed proposals on flexibility that were ultimately included in the Treaty of Nice. These were that enhanced cooperation, using EU institutions, include as few as eight Member States; be established by qualified majority voting (QMV); and that the 'emergency brake' be abolished. Britain had no desire to prevent states from pressing ahead with new policies just because it was not in its national interest to move with them. But Maude demanded that Member States retain the veto, though he 'would expect the presumption to be against Britain exercising its veto, save where necessary to protect our national interests'.[17] Whereas Major had rejected the idea of a hard core, Maude felt that, should a core emerge, Britain might not block it. He dismissed Europhile claims that Britain would lose influence and Euro-sceptic fears that opt-outs would ultimately be surrendered. Finally, the Conservatives argued that the EU should grant Central and Eastern European applicant states derogations from the *acquis*. In a flexible EU, new Member States should not be compelled to join EMU, defence arrangements and the like.

Policy on flexibility was coupled with renegotiation. A future Conservative government would aim to renegotiate any Treaty resulting from the 2000 IGC that did not include their favoured 'flexibility clause'. But a key problem would be the likely opposition of other Member States to the party's proposals on flexibility and renegotiation. No matter how attractive and coherent policy might appear domestically, translating it into practice would prove difficult and divisive. Both sides of the party's Euro-divide speculated on the extent of renegotiation the leadership envisaged. Pro-Europeans argued that a flexibility clause allowing states to opt-out of new policy areas was unnecessary as Treaty changes required unanimity. They feared that 'renegotiation' was code for eventual withdrawal. Euro-sceptics felt that a flexibility clause covering only new policy areas was insufficient, pressing instead for renegotiation of existing commitments or, if this was not forthcoming, withdrawal. Senior Conservatives denied that they were seeking a renegotiation of existing EU legislation or Britain's terms of membership. But their opposition to a raft of recent EU policies and the difficulties of securing agreement from other Member States for the Conservative position encouraged speculation that the leadership saw withdrawal as a possible scenario if renegotiation failed.

At the 1996–97 IGC, the Major government had sought a limited renegotiation of existing Treaty commitments and the repatriation of some competences to the nation state. Demands included an end to the Common Fisheries Policy, an exemption from the Working Time Directive and curbs on the power of the European Court of Justice. The signing of the Amsterdam and Nice Treaties fuelled Euro-sceptic demands for renegotiation and EU reform, though the leadership was cagey on how it might deal with new areas of the *acquis* that it opposed. Following the signing of the Nice Treaty, Maude signalled that the Conservatives would call for two IGCs. The first would be a brief affair, coinciding with the next European Council meeting. Its remit would be to produce a Treaty stripped of its 'integrationist' elements but containing those clauses deemed essential for enlargement. A second, more thorough IGC would renegotiate other areas of the Treaty, the intention being to reverse the extensions of QMV, include a new flexibility clause and overhaul EU institutions.

The Euro-sceptic thrust of Conservative policy was evident in two further developments. *Believing in Britain* included a proposal to create reserve powers, guaranteeing Parliamentary sovereignty in some policy areas by ring fencing them in new legislation. This would prevent EU law from overriding the will of Parliament in areas currently excluded from the treaties – such as defence, education, health and direct taxation. Future governments could participate in new EU initiatives but would require the express approval of Parliament to do so. The legislation would also prevent EU law overriding Parliament where unanimity had been replaced by QMV, countering the 'Treaty creep' that forced Britain to accept the Working Time Directive. Secondly, the 2001 manifesto stated that any future government that wished to 'surrender any more of Parliament's rights and powers to Brussels' should be required to secure approval for the transfer of competencies in a referendum. This echoed demands for referendums on the Amsterdam and Nice Treaties.

REFORMING EU INSTITUTIONS AND POLICIES

The Conservatives opposed the Treaty of Amsterdam (agreed in 1997) and the Treaty of Nice (agreed in 2000), claiming that they pursued an integrationist agenda rather than focusing on enlargement. These were the first cases in which the Conservatives issued a three line whip against legislation amending the 1972 European Communities Act. The party proposed major changes to the role and powers of the main EU institutions. The resignation of the Santer Commission following a damning report into fraud and mismanagement provided extra ammunition, Hague issuing a ten-point plan for reform that featured in the European election manifesto. In May 2001, Maude unveiled new proposals designed to strengthen the Council of Ministers and weaken the Commission, the latter becoming 'an impartial civil service' with its right of initiative constrained.[18]

Hague took up the Major government's proposals for reform of the European Court of Justice, demanding Treaty changes to ensure that the Court did not extend the powers of other EU institutions. Legislation that the ECJ had interpreted in a way different from that originally intended should be subject to rapid amendment, while Member States' liability for damages should be limited to the most serious cases. The goal of eliminating 'unnecessary bureaucracy' threatened a number of EU bodies, including the Committee of the Regions. The principle of subsidiarity – understood as shifting decision-making to the national, rather than regional or European level – should be strengthened by a new Treaty provision on its application and the creation of a 'subsidiarity panel' to screen draft laws.

As for the Council of Ministers, the Conservatives supported the Nice Treaty provisions for a re-weighting of votes in the Council to reflect the population of large Member States. But they rejected any extension of QMV. Under Maude's proposals, senior ministers from Member State governments would be appointed to the Council, taking direct control of EU negotiations and spending half the week in Brussels. The British Minister for Europe would be accountable to Westminster, perhaps through a weekly Question Time. Parliament's powers of scrutiny over EU matters would be strengthened, for example by the establishment in statute of the scrutiny reserve by which ministers should not approve proposals in Council until parliamentary scrutiny is completed.

Hague argued that the Union had almost reached the end-point of acceptable integration and should concentrate on market liberalisation and enlargement. The Conservatives continued to promote a deregulatory agenda, urging the completion of the Single Market, the liberalisation of protected sectors and tougher competition policy. They were uncomfortable with parts of the EU's regulatory regime and employment policy framework.[19] Their free trade agenda extended beyond the EU, looking to strengthen the World Trade Organisation and achieve global tariff-free trade by the year 2020. The Common Agricultural Policy was 'indefensible socially, economically, ecologically, environmentally and morally', and the Common Fisheries Policy should end with responsibility for British territorial waters transferred to national or local level. The communitarisation of parts of the Common Foreign and Security Policy (CFSP) and Justice and Home Affairs (JHA) intergovernmental pillars was opposed. The Conservatives were wary of the post-Amsterdam adoption of parts of the Schengen *acquis* and sought intergovernmental and bilateral cooperation (rather than extended EU competence) on asylum and immigration. Blair's initiatives on a Rapid Reaction Force and enhanced European defence were strongly criticised by Shadow Secretary of State for Defence Iain Duncan Smith who took his message about the dangers of a 'European army' undermining NATO to Washington in 2001. Finally, the Conservatives also opposed the Charter of Fundamental Rights agreed at Nice.

A Euro-sceptic party

For many Conservative MPs and party members, Euro-scepticism has become the defining feature of their political identity and the defence of British sovereignty the over-riding mission of their party. The Conservative parliamentary party has become significantly more Euro-sceptic over the last decade. This increase in Euro-sceptic sentiment is a result of changes in both personnel and attitudes. Pro-European MPs have stood down and been replaced by MPs who are more Euro-sceptic while election defeats have also removed sitting pro-Europeans. Additionally, a number of Conservative MPs who were in Parliament for some or all of the period have hardened their position on Europe, becoming more sceptical as integration moves on apace and its impact becomes more pronounced.

Surveys of the attitudes of Conservative MPs reveal that a sizeable majority of the parliamentary party hold Euro-sceptic beliefs that go beyond official party policy. The party became more Euro-sceptic after 1997: two-thirds of MPs responding to a 1998 survey believed that joining the single currency would 'signal the end of the UK as a sovereign nation', 80 per cent favoured an Act of Parliament to establish the ultimate supremacy of Parliament and 26 per cent felt that Britain should withdraw from the EU.[20] A disproportionate number of pro-European or loyalist MPs stood down at the 1997 election, many being replaced by Euro-sceptic candidates. Philip Norton calculated that 30 per cent of Conservative MPs belonged to the Euro-sceptic right, 21 per cent to the pro-European left and 50 per cent to the party faithful, though 29 per cent of the party are 'sceptic-leaning' party faithful.[21]

Activists on both sides of the debate have published surveys of the attitudes of Conservative candidates. The internet-based Candidlist compiled by Sean Gabb used a range of information to classify candidates, including a questionnaire asking if candidates would oppose entry into the euro-zone even if it were recommended by the party leadership, and vote for withdrawal from the EU if forced to choose between this and accepting the supremacy of EU law. Candidates who replied 'yes' to both questions were classified as 'Sceptic'; those accepting the party line, providing vague answers or about whom little was known were put down as 'Don't Knows', while others were dubbed 'Europhiles'.[22] In May 2001, more than eighty Tory MPs were listed as Sceptic implying that they opposed euro membership in principle and supported either renegotiation or withdrawal.

The Pro-Euro Conservative Party claimed that 57 per cent of Conservative MPs opposed EMU entry, listing eighty-seven as 'Ultra-Sceptic' (opposed in principle) and thirty-four as 'Sceptic' (opposed to entry in the next Parliament).[23] Eighteen MPs 'might' be in favour of entry in the next Parliament; just three 'would' support it. Both the Pro-Euro and Candidlist data showed that Euro-sceptics heavily outnumbered pro-European candidates in target seats.[24] Euro-scepticism had also spread at grass roots level: a majority of party members are opposed to further integration and EMU.[25]

After the tumult of the 1992–97 Parliament, divisions over Europe abated somewhat. Hague imposed a three-line whip requiring Tory MPs to vote against the ratification of the Treaty of Amsterdam. No Conservatives voted

with the government though a number of pro-Europeans were absent from
the vote on the Second Reading of the European Communities (Amendment)
Bill. There were no Tory dissenting votes on European issues during the
first three sessions of the 1997–2001 Parliament. In the fourth session, four
votes saw very low levels of dissent.[26] The relative absence of rebellions
suggests that Euro-sceptic MPs were more comfortable with party policy
and recognised that the tide was moving in their direction. But the party
was not quiescent: some Euro-sceptics favoured tougher positions on EMU
and renegotiation than those adopted by the leadership, while pro-Europeans
were publicly critical of Hague's stance.

PRO-EUROPEANS

Conservative pro-Europeans became more openly critical of the party's drift
towards Euro-scepticism. Three (Curry, Dorrell and Taylor) left the Shadow
Cabinet. Peter Temple-Morris lost the Whip in November 1997 after holding
discussions with Blair about his possible defection, sitting as an Independent
before joining Labour in 1998. The new policy on EMU provoked a chorus
of criticism from ex-ministers including Lord Howe, Lord Hurd, Chris Patten,
Kenneth Clarke and Michael Heseltine. Heseltine warned a 1999 conference
fringe meeting that the party was being pushed towards the 'incalculable
folly' of withdrawal. He and Clarke then shared a platform with Blair and
Brown at the launch of the 'Britain in Europe' group. They urged the Prime
Minister to present a positive case for British membership of the EU
(which he was willing to do) and EMU entry (on which he was more wary,
sticking to the five economic tests mantra). The Positive European Group
and the Tory Reform Group presented a Conservative case for the euro.
Pro-Europeans were critical of the Keep the Pound campaign, but stayed
largely silent during the European election and general election campaigns.

Former Conservative MEPs John Stevens and Brendan Donnelly set up
the Pro-Euro Conservative Party in 1999. The breakaway party failed to win
the endorsement of heavyweight Conservatives (Clarke was highly critical).
However, Lord (Ian) Gilmour and Sir Julian Critchley had their Conservative
membership 'terminated' as ten former Conservative MPs and MEPs gave
their support. Nor did the Pro-Euro party attract large numbers of disillusioned Conservative voters, winning just 1.4 per cent in the 1999 European
election. In December 2001, it was wound up and its small band of members
joined the Liberal Democrats.[27]

The 1999 European election was contested under a regional list variant
of proportional representation. Stevens and Donnelly had gained lowly positions on the South-East list before resigning from the party, but the selection
procedures did not produce a uniform Euro-sceptic slate.[28] The thirty-six-
strong Conservative representation in the European Parliament included a
mix of pro-Europeans and hardline sceptics, the latter being reluctant to sit

with the centre right European People's Party. Discussions eventually saw the MEPs allied to the newly christened European People's Party and European Democrats under a deal allowing them to oppose policies that ran counter to the Conservative line.

EURO-SCEPTICS

Conservative Euro-sceptics are not a homogeneous group, exhibiting differences in ideological positions, policy proposals and favoured political tactics. Many are ideologically Thatcherite but differ in the importance they attach to the twin foundations of Thatcherism, neo-liberal economics and defence of the nation state. Neo-liberals tend to view the EU as a threat to their favoured scenario of a low tax, deregulatory and free-enterprise-driven British economy competing successfully in a global free trade regime. But in the early 1990s neo-liberal Thatcherites differed on the merits of ERM membership and in the late 1990s on the prospects of achieving their economic goals within a reformed EU. Baker, Gamble and Seawright distinguish between a 'hyper-globalist' position that advocates national economic independence outside the EU and a 'national political economy' perspective that opposes the euro but supports continued membership of a reformed Union.[29] 'National' or 'constitutionalist' Euro-sceptics, meanwhile, emphasise the threat integration poses to national sovereignty and self-government, emphasising the importance of institutions and the constitution to British identity. On European policy, Conservative Euro-sceptic positions range from greater EU flexibility, through renegotiation to outright withdrawal.

Hague's refusal to advocate principled opposition to the single currency and his claim that Britain could be 'in Europe' without being 'run by Europe' was questioned by hardline sceptics. Leading 'constitutionalist' sceptic Bill Cash advocated a fundamental renegotiation of the treaties and left open the possibility of withdrawal.[30] The Conservatives Against a Federal Europe group had, in the mid-1990s, advocated withdrawal unless membership terms were radically altered. The group, which boasted eleven frontbench spokespersons including Duncan Smith among its members, was slow to fall into line with Hague's policy.[31] Redwood argued that greater economic independence would be possible through an enhanced relationship with the North American Free Trade Agreement (NAFTA).[32] Lady Thatcher advocated both fundamental renegotiation and NAFTA membership.[33]

A few Tories flirted with Euro-sceptic fringe parties. Christopher Gill, one of the Whipless Eight in the mid-1990s, left the party (but did not resign the Whip) shortly before he was due to stand down as MP, becoming chair of the Freedom Association which advocated withdrawal from the EU. The Whip was withdrawn from retiring MP Charles Wardle who, like Gill, campaigned for the UK Independence Party (UKIP) in the general election. Former MPs Roger Knapman and John Browne stood as UKIP candidates.

In the 1997 general election campaign, more than 200 Conservative candidates declared their opposition to EMU. Many candidates issued anti-European personal manifestos in 2001 but Hague limited dissent by reportedly allowing candidates to state that they would vote to keep the pound without having to limit this pledge to a single Parliament. Thatcher provided the highest profile break with the official line, telling an election rally in Plymouth that she 'would never be prepared to give up our own currency'.[34] But fear of being made scapegoats for a second landslide defeat ensured that pro-European and Euro-sceptic candidates largely kept their counsel.

Europe and Conservative electoral strategy

The leaders of Britain's main political parties have tended not to prioritise European issues at general elections, recognising that the issue is not easy to exploit as it does not figure highly among voter concerns and can expose divisions in their own ranks. Hague, however, put the Keep the Pound message at the heart of the 2001 Conservative election campaign. Opinion polls suggested that the Conservative's Euro-sceptic message was closer to public opinion than Labour's, making Europe a potential vote winner for the Tories. The same had been true in 1997 but Europe did not bring significant electoral benefits as the Conservatives were viewed as divided and the Referendum Party competed for Euro-sceptic votes.[35] Hague hoped for more in 2001 but after another Labour landslide, critics blamed his focus on the euro.

Since 1999 Hague had increasingly – though not exclusively – focused on issues such as Europe and asylum that appealed to traditional Conservative supporters. This 'core vote' strategy shored up Hague's position and brought greater media coverage. The 1999 European election provided encouragement as the Conservatives topped the polls on the back of a concerted Euro-sceptic campaign. It provided a section of the electorate with a low-cost opportunity to vote on the basis of their opposition to EMU, but this scenario was unlikely to be repeated at a general election. A leaked document written by Labour strategists identified Europe as a 'life preserver' for the Conservatives that could make the party 'relevant and electable'.[36] But time would show that the 35.8 per cent of the vote the Conservatives won in a low turnout election dominated by a single issue should not have suggested that a Euro-sceptic campaign offered the optimal route to electoral salvation.

Post-mortems conducted after the 2001 election pointed to short-term tactical errors in the presentation of policy on Europe and posed questions about the impact of Europe on voting behaviour and support for the Conservatives. The Keep the Pound campaign had been running for over a year and hit centre stage in late May when, after Blair suggested that voters could be persuaded to accept the euro, Hague began to countdown the number of days left to 'save the Pound'. Despite advance planning, the Tory campaign did not play out as anticipated. Hague invested more energy into the single currency issue than some of his campaign team would have liked, while party strategists also complained that the media focused on Europe despite their efforts to direct attention elsewhere. With the opinion polls showing little movement and members of Hague's team voicing their concerns, plans to focus on the euro in the final days of the campaign were scaled back.

The Keep the Pound message might have been delivered more effectively. Hague concentrated on the constitutional arguments for retaining Sterling, brandishing pound coins on the hustings. A bruising BBC *Newsnight* interview with Jeremy Paxman exposed the tensions between Hague's message and his policy of opposing entry for the next Parliament. A claim that the Commission planned to harmonise taxes hit the buffers when scrutiny of the document in question indicated this was not the case.[37] Two issues might have been further developed. Hague claimed that a changeover to the euro would cost £36 billion but more might have been made of the government's preparations for entry. Secondly, the campaign did not highlight the impact of membership of the single currency on UK public spending effectively. In an election in which public spending featured prominently, Hague only linked EMU entry with potential constraints on investment in health and education late in the campaign.

More significantly, Hague claimed that a vote for the Conservatives at the general election provided the last chance to save the pound. Labour's commitment to holding a referendum should it recommend entry did not provide a sufficient safeguard as the government could not be trusted to produce a 'fair' question and had formulated the rules for the conduct of the referendum so that the 'Yes' campaign could heavily outspend the 'No' side. Independent Euro-sceptic groups feared that association with a failed Tory campaign would cause lasting damage to their prospects. The No Campaign group, made up of Business for Sterling and New Europe, hastily dissociated itself from Hague's fatalistic message and stressed that a cross-party 'No' campaign could win a referendum.

Defenders of the campaign note that the single currency issue was a strong one for the Conservatives, the Keep the Pound message shaped the agenda and maximised media coverage of the Conservative case, and that the campaign had some success in getting Euro-sceptic Conservatives out to vote. Two of the architects of the campaign, Andrew Lansley and Tim Collins, point out that the single currency 'was a powerful issue for us; there were not many other policies we had which were supported by over 70 per cent of the public'.[38] Opinion polls suggested there was a two to one majority against membership of the euro, though the decline in the 'no' figure when voters were asked how they would vote if government and business urged a 'yes' vote suggested that opinion was fickle. The 'wait and see' position (condemned as a vote loser by Euro-sceptics) was the preferred position of a plurality of voters. But more voters chose Labour (50 per cent) than the Conservatives (33 per cent) as the party that best represented their views on Europe; only 8 per cent of Labour voters and 27 per cent of Liberal Democrat voters picked the Conservatives.[39] A majority of Conservative supporters were also unaware of their party's precise position on the euro, some believing it had ruled out entry for all time and others that it would hold a referendum.[40]

Europe did not rank highly among voters concerns: ICM found only 40 per cent of voters saying Europe was important to them, the issue coming bottom of a list of eleven issues even among Conservatives voters.[41] Although Mori reported an increase in the number of people citing Europe as an important issue as the campaign progressed, the figure still totalled just 14 per cent.[42] Furthermore, Europe was not a key issue among floating voters and was unlikely to be a swing issue. Existing Conservative voters were more likely to be receptive to a Euro-sceptic message. The issue played better with older and less-well-educated voters than with the university-educated, middle-class voters whose votes were crucial in many target seats.[43] The Keep the Pound message may have persuaded some hesitant Tories to vote, but for others, it reinforced their perceptions of the party as extreme and out of touch. A post-election Gallup poll reported that 65 per cent of those surveyed believed the party focused too much on Europe.[44] An overwhelming majority of those who switched to the Conservatives in 2001 were Euro-sceptic, but not enough people changed their allegiance to give the party a decisive electoral boost.[45] The Tories were, though, the main beneficiaries of the decline of the UKIP which, after causing Conservative strategists some concern, polled just 1.5 per cent of the vote.[46]

Conclusion: from Hague to Duncan Smith

Hague's record on Europe was a mixed one. The 'two Parliaments' position and 'In Europe, not run by Europe' platform reflected his desire to develop a more authoritative Euro-sceptic position while also holding together much of a fractious parliamentary party. Although these pragmatic positions were not wholeheartedly endorsed by Euro-sceptics, Hague's policy was the one most likely to find most favour in a party where Euro-sceptics were predominant. The new position was also significantly more Euro-sceptic than that of Thatcher or Major. From being the 'party of Europe' in the 1980s, the Conservatives were now the most Euro-sceptic mainstream party in Britain and perhaps the EU. Their agenda of flexibility, renegotiation and reserved powers, plus opposition to many EU developments, suggested a radically different relationship between Britain and the EU. The transition would be an acrimonious one as there was minimal support for this vision in the EU.

Special status for the UK in an enlarged EU or British withdrawal emerged as possible future scenarios. Ultimately, Hague's emphasis on Europe failed to deliver the votes he required and contributed to his downfall.

Europe was again prominent in the leadership election that followed Hague's resignation, especially in the second stage when Clarke and Duncan Smith competed for the votes of party members. Duncan Smith denied claims that he backed withdrawal but confirmed his support for renegotiation and indicated that he would never support EMU entry. His record of rebellion on Maastricht became a virtue rather than a vice. Clarke reiterated his opposition to federalism, indicated he would appoint a majority of Euro-sceptics to his Shadow Cabinet and would allow all Tory MPs free speech in a euro referendum. However, he would be prominent in the 'Yes' campaign and would abstain in the vote on the Nice Treaty even though party policy was to oppose it.

In the MPs-only stage of the election, Duncan Smith's support came mainly from the Euro-sceptic right. Clarke topped the second ballot of MPs, winning votes mainly from the pro-European left, but also from some sceptics who believed he offered the best prospect of a Conservative revival. In the party membership stage, twenty-seven Euro-sceptic MPs publicly backed Clarke. An ICM survey poll of four constituency parties showed 37 per cent of members identifying Europe as the most important policy area when deciding how to vote, with 76 per cent saying it was 'very important' or 'quite important'. However, two-thirds said that the most significant factor was which candidate was most likely to win the next general election.[47] Ultimately the question that Clarke set himself – whether a largely Euro-sceptic party could be successfully led by a staunch pro-European – was answered in the negative by party members as Duncan Smith won 60.7 per cent of the final ballot. A predominantly Euro-sceptic party had followed its instincts, choosing the candidate that most reflected its views.

Notes

1 P. Taggart and A. Szczerbiak, 'The party politics of Euroscepticism in EU member and candidate states'. Opposing Europe Research Network Working Paper No. 6 (Brighton, University of Sussex, 2002), p. 7.

2 P. Cowley, 'Just William? A supplementary analysis of the 1997 Conservative leadership contest', *Talking Politics*, 10:2 (1997/8) 91–5; P. Norton, 'Electing the leader: the Conservative leadership contest 1997', *Politics Review*, 7:4 (1998) 10–14.

3 H. Williams, *Guilty Men. Conservative Decline and Fall, 1992–97* (London, Aurum Press, 1998).

4 J.-A. Nadler, *William Hague. In His Own Right* (London, Politico's Publishing, 2000), pp. 36–7.

5 Cowley, 'Just William', p. 94.

6 Nadler, *William Hague*, pp. 238–40.

7 W. Hague speech to the CBI, Birmingham, 10 November 1997.

8 W. Hague, speech to the European Research Group's Second Congress for Democracy, London, 8 July 1999.

9 'Britain and the pound: a prosperous future for Britain' (London, Report of the Commission on the Pound Sterling, 1999).

10 M. Holmes, 'William Hague's European policy' (London, The Bruges Group, Occasional Paper No. 40, 1999).

11 D. Butler and M. Westlake, *British Politics and European Elections 1999* (London, Macmillan, 2000), p. 55.

12 J. Major, 'Europe: a future that works', William and Mary Lecture, Leiden, 7 September 1994.

13 W. Hague, 'No to a federal Europe', speech in Budapest, 13 May 1999.

14 *In Europe, not run by Europe* (London, Conservative Party, 1999), Ch. 2.

15 J. Maples, 'Flexibility in Europe', *Financial Times*, 8 November 1999.

16 'Hague: transcript of interview', *Financial Times*, 1 November 1999.

17 F. Maude, 'Nations and networks: towards the new Europe', speech to the Humboldt University, Berlin, 8 June 2000.

18 'Conservatives unveil EU reform plans', Conservative Party press release, 3 May 2001.

19 J. Maples, 'A Europe for the 21st century', lecture to the Centre for Policy Studies, London, 6 December 1999.

20 D. Baker, A. Gamble, and D. Seawright with K. Bull, 'MPs and Europe: Enthusiasm, Circumspection or Outright Scepticism?', *British and Elections Parties Review, Vol. 9* (London, Frank Cass, 1999), pp. 170–85.

21 Norton, 'Electing the Leader'.

22 At www.candidlist.demon.co.uk. Gabb's motives and methodology are problematic. A number of MPs challenged their classification or refused to respond to the questionnaire, while the criteria saw a number of MPs not usually considered pro-European included as 'Europhile'.

23 Pro-Euro Conservative Party, 'Views of William Hague's candidates on Europe', www.proeuro.co.uk (accessed May 2001).

24 A. Heath, 'No, No, No: Thatcher's grandchildren reject the superstate', *The European Journal*, October (2000), 13–15.

25 P. Whiteley, P. Seyd and J. Richardson, *True Blues. The Politics of Conservative Party Membership* (Oxford, Clarendon Press, 1994), pp. 57–8.

26 Seven sceptics voted against an EU budget vote, four voted for an EU take note motion on sport and five against; seven voted against an EU customs vote; and three voted for and three against on an EU companies (political exemptions) vote. Thanks to Mark Stuart for the data.

27 J. Stevens, 'Why the Pro-Euro Conservatives are joining the Liberal Democrats', *Independent*, 10 December 2001.

28 Butler and Westlake, *British Politics and European Elections 1999*, pp. 82–5 and 206–7.

29 D. Baker, A. Gamble and D. Seawright, 'The European Exceptionalism of the British Political Elite', paper presented to the ECPR Joint Sessions, Mannheim, March 1999.

30 B. Cash, *Associated, not Absorbed – the Associated European Area* (London, European Foundation, 2000).

31 R. Shrimsley, 'Hague faces clash with "extremist" EU group', *Daily Telegraph*, 5 August 1999.

32 J. Redwood, *Stars and Strife* (London, Palgrave, 2001).

33 M. Thatcher, *Statecraft. Strategies for a Changing World* (London, Harper Collins, 2002), Chs 9 and 10.

34 M. Thatcher, 'Above all, we must keep the Pound', *The Times*, 23 May 2001.

35 G. Evans, 'Euroscepticism and Conservative electoral support: how an asset became a liability', *British Journal of Political Science*, 28:4 (1998), 573–90.

36 P. Gould and S. Greenberg, 'Why Labour is losing the euro argument', *The Times*, 27 July 2000.

37 I. Black and M. White, 'Tory tax ploy misfires', *Guardian*, 24 May 2001.

38 A. Lansley and T. Collins, 'We now have a foundation for the future', *Daily Telegraph*, 14 June 2001.

39 A. King, 'Fatalism may pave way for "yes" vote in single currency referendum', *Daily Telegraph*, 31 May 2001.

40 D. Butler and D. Butler, *The British General Election of 2001* (London, Palgrave, 2002), pp. 246–7.

41 A. Travis, 'Voters fail to share Hague's euro obsession', *Guardian*, 30 May 2001.

42 J. Curtice, 'Tories' campaign strategy a flop, latest poll reveals', *Sunday Telegraph*, 3 June 2001.

43 J. Curtice and M. Steed, 'Appendix 2: the results', in Butler and Kavanagh, *The British General Election of 2001*, p. 313.

44 A. King, 'Electors fed up with spin and soundbites', *Daily Telegraph*, 11 June 2001.

45 G. Evans, 'The Conservatives and Europe: waving or drowning?', in A. Park *et al.*, *British Social Attitudes. The 18th Report* (London, Sage, 2001), pp. 245–62.

46 Curtice and Steed, 'Appendix 2: the results', p. 327.

47 D. Cracknell, 'Poll shows Europe is the main issue for Conservatives', *Sunday Telegraph*, 26 August 2001.

9

The Scottish Conservatives, 1997–2001: from disaster to devolution and beyond

Peter Lynch

William Hague's four years of leadership of the Conservative Party coincided with a revolution in the political opportunity structure of Scottish Conservatism. First, the Scotish Tories were wiped out at the 1997 general election, their worst electoral performance of all time and their lowest share of the vote since 1865. Second, the party's constitutional position was heavily defeated at the devolution referendum of September 1997, so that Conservative opposition to a Scottish Parliament became an anachronism and devolution was set to become a reality. The party's prospects took an upward turn when it gained seats in the new Scottish Parliament in the May election of 1999 and from then on, it has faced a radically different political environment to that which existed previously. After 1999, bereft of Westminster representation, the devolved parliament was the only show in town for the Tories north of the Border, with an untested leader, a weakened party organisation, declining levels of political support and a reduced status in that Parliament as the Scottish National Party (SNP) were the main opposition party. Adjusting to this new environment was a major task for the Scottish party.

The combined impact of the 1997 general election wipeout and the onset of devolution brought three fundamental challenges for the Scottish Tories. First, the party had to adjust to devolution within Scotland in terms of party organisation, policy, autonomy and campaigning. It was required to act as an autonomous entity in the Scottish Parliament and gain credibility as a Scottish party – and reverse its image as an anti-Scottish party.[1] Organisational change and a reinvention of the Tories as a Scottish party were high priorities after 1997. Second, the electoral wipeout of 1997 required the party to rebuild electoral support in Scotland and do so rapidly because of the proximity of the devolved elections of 6 May 1999. Third, the lack of Scottish Conservative representation at Westminster, the onset of devolution and the election of William Hague as UK party leader markedly altered the relations between the Scottish and UK Conservatives. Hague's attitude to devolution and to a more autonomous Scottish Conservative Party was not easy to discern in 1997. Were he to have been a centralist, it would have undermined the efforts of the Scottish Tories to appear 'Made in Scotland' in advance of the 1999 elections. Similarly, were Hague to play the English nationalist card through excessively deploying the West Lothian Question or Barnett formula, then Scottish Conservatism would have faced major strategic problems. This third challenge therefore had the potential to seriously undermine Scottish Conservative efforts to recover from the 1997 wipeout.

Dealing with devolution

Since the 1960s, the Scottish Conservatives struggled to deal with the rise in national consciousness in Scotland that manifested itself in electoral support for the SNP and support for a Scottish parliament. The mood of Scottish voters has travelled very far in recent decades, yet Conservatives – the party of the nation – failed to deal with the onset of Scottish Nationalism with a capital 'N' or the more widespread nationalism with a smaller 'n'. The essential Conservative error was to treat these nationalisms as the same thing, which would lead to the break-up of Britain. Whilst Labour came to a *rapprochement* with rising national sentiment in Scotland, through electoral and internal pressure and attitudinal change, Conservatives stuck to a hard-line position of opposition to constitutional change after the 1979 devolution referendum which contributed to the party's unpopularity and anti-Scottish image. This image has proven difficult to shift and will likely prove a long-term legacy for Scottish Conservatives regardless of the impact of devolution in actually establishing a more 'Scottish' Conservative Party north of the Border.

Active Conservative management of the Union was almost non-existent during the 1980s. Indeed, with the exception of the establishment of the Select Committee on Scottish Affairs and some slight rejigging of the Scottish Grand Committee in 1979, there were no distinct Scottish initiatives until the Major government's 'Taking Stock' process from 1992 to 1993. The 'Taking Stock' exercise was a minimalist reform which briefly raised expectations but failed to address public demand.[2] It transferred some policy areas to the Scottish Office and gave more powers to the Scottish Grand Committee, neither of which impressed a Scottish electorate seeking 'actual' devolution as opposed to symbolic initiatives that retained centralised control. The second set of reforms under Major were the much-trumpeted changes to the Scottish Grand Committee instituted by former Scottish Secretary, Michael Forsyth, in 1995, which strengthened the role of the committee whilst taking it on a high profile (and extremely expensive) tour of Scotland in order to bring the government of Scotland closer to the people. Forsyth was also responsible for adopting a range of consensual and symbolic concessions during his tenure as Scottish Secretary through an all-party anti-drugs campaign, more open appointments to non-departmental public bodies, various initiatives for the crofting community, the Council for the Highlands and Islands and the Scottish Economic Council, as well as the return of the Stone of Destiny. However, though these initiatives were an indication that the Conservatives had learned from some of their previous mistakes, they came too late to restore much semblance of a Scottish identity amongst an electorate distrustful of the party, especially when efforts at accommodating Scottish opinion excluded more substantive concessions such as devolution.[3] The party therefore had severe image and identity problems to deal with after 1997 which directly clashed with devolution and the onset of 'Scottish' politics.

A new pragmatism?

Despite an uncompromising Unionist stance at the 1997 election, Scottish Conservatives demonstrated a more pragmatic and cautious face in dealing with constitutional issues ever since. The party supported the 'No' campaign at the devolution referendum in September 1997, but took a backseat role in the campaign.[4] The fact that *Think Twice* emerged as an umbrella organisation for the 'No' campaign allowed the Tories to sit back from the 'No' campaign and focus on the second referendum on tax-raising powers rather than simple hostility to a Scottish parliament. Of course, realistically, the Scottish Tories had no money, no elected representatives and a grass roots still shattered by 1 May 1997. The extent to which they were willing or able to involve themselves in the 'No' campaign was always going to be problematic. However, by sitting back from the campaign itself they did not make things worse for themselves in Scotland by appearing more anti-Scottish, though equally, they didn't make things much better either as they were the sole party identified with the 'No' campaign.

Post-referendum, the Scottish Conservatives sought to demonstrate a new-found populism in relation to Scottish issues in a calculated attempt to fly the flag for Scotland on as many occasions as possible to erase its anti-Scottish past. For example, the party sought to capitalise on the divisions within Labour over the temporary siting of the Scottish Parliament in Edinburgh or Glasgow by proposing the decentralisation of the Scottish Office throughout Scotland – with the Scottish civil service departments moving to Aberdeen, Perth, Inverness and Glasgow.[5] In addition, Conservative peers in the Lords sought to amend the Scotland bill to allow the Scottish Parliament's First Minister to nominate a Scottish representative to the monetary policy committee of the Bank of England. In time, such efforts led to more consistent Conservative stances in Scotland, such as those over tuition fees and state-funded care for the elderly, but it is interesting to note how Tories were keen to demonstrate a break with the past very early on after the 1997 general election. Of course, under Hague's leadership, the

Conservative Party entered its 'apologetic' phase in an attempt to distance itself from the Thatcher era and the fact that it lost touch with the public in different parts of the UK. However, saying 'sorry' to Scottish voters for eighteen years of rule by an insensitive Conservative steamroller – which delivered the poll tax – and expecting to be forgiven in time for the first elections to the Scottish Parliament seemed optimistic to say the least.

Moreover, in contrast to moderating its position towards devolution and to Scotland, the Conservatives also sought to make political capital from the rise of the English question. And this situation illustrated the Conservative political dilemma: how to appear pro-Scottish in Scotland when the party at Westminster resembled an English nationalist party in terms of political composition, outlook and opportunities. Thus, achieving some form of accommodation with devolution and lessening the anti-Scottish image of the party was partly undermined by efforts to exploit the West Lothian Question, Barnett formula and Scotland's share of UK public expenditure. Such incoherence in territorial politics was hardly likely to assist the Scottish Conservatives, even though it may have assisted Tories in England. Though Scottish and Westminster priorities were in direct conflict under Hague, he did loosen the ties between the two sets of parties to allow the Scottish Tories to act autonomously in the devolved policy areas. Similarly, as a result of devolution and the 1997 general election, the Conservatives at Westminster become more Anglo-centric in policy orientation as a result of the migration of Scottish and Welsh issues to Edinburgh and Cardiff. Allowing some Scottish and Welsh autonomy was easier to do in opposition than in government, but Hague did so nonetheless. Whether Iain Duncan Smith adopts a similar approach to devolution remains to be seen.

Made in Scotland: reorganising the party after 1997

One substantial development within the Scottish Conservatives from 1997 to 2001 involved the reorganisation of the party in Scotland. The main reason for organisational reform was the establishment of a Scottish Parliament, and the need to prepare the party for life after devolution, though other factors were also important. For example, the Scottish reforms of 1997–98 have to be considered in light of Hague's reform agenda for the UK party generally, though devolution gave these reforms a very specific context and form. Similarly, organisational reform has been a characteristic response to electoral failure amongst Scottish Conservatives for many years and the 1997 general election certainly marked a substantial electoral failure. The 1997 reforms were in the tradition of the reforms of 1965 which created the Scottish Conservative and Unionist Party, and removed the Scottish Unionist Party label,[6] the Fairgrieve reforms of 1977 that instituted closer relations between the Scottish and UK Conservatives with a Scottish Party Chairman and increased central funding for the Scottish party,[7] and the 1987–88 reforms which sought to make the Scottish Conservatives more autonomous from the UK organisation with the appointment of a Chief Executive and financial autonomy for the Scottish party.[8]

The post-1997 Scottish Conservative reorganisation offered an interesting insight into the party's internal life and factional intrigues. Within a week of the 1997 election defeat, both the Scottish leadership and the small band of pro-devolution dissidents within the party had begun to consider the future of Scottish Conservatism. This included organisational reform and some kind of *rapprochement* with devolution as a means of restoring the party's fortunes in Scotland – even though the party remained committed to opposeing devolution at the 1997 referendum. Jackson Carlaw, the party's deputy chairman, expressed the deep-seated reforms necessary:

> There needs to be a complete redefinition of the party, including a different approach to the constitution, to the electoral system and to party funding. There has to be a comprehensive realignment of the party in Scotland. I look forward to the time when the leader of the Scottish Conservative group in the Scottish Parliament is elected by One Member One Vote. I am very firmly of the view that the party which emerges should, to coin a phrase, be 'New Tories, New Scotland'.[9]

However, rather than wait for the party leadership to address the issue some party activists sought to kick-start the party's organisational reorientation by presenting an agenda for radical reform. Prominent figures from the (small and shrinking) devolutionist wing of the party proposed that Conservatives should found a completely new party in Scotland by making a unilateral declaration of independence from London and break links with the UK party.[10] This proposal was modelled on the relationship between the Bavarian Christian Social Union (CSU) and Chancellor Kohl's Christian Democratic Union.[11] Under this proposal the Scottish party would set itself up as a party standing solely in Scotland, with Scottish policies and interests, which would form a coalition with English and Welsh Conservatives at Westminster. The rationale for the year-zero option was outlined in stark terms by one of the pro-devolution dissidents, Brian Meek:

> We need a new party with a changed name, linked but not handcuffed to the English Conservatives. It would be a party which raised all of its own finances, paid its own workers, elected by one member one vote all its own office-bearers from the leader down, wrote its own contract/manifesto with the people. Consider the alternatives. We could simply stick with the status quo.[12]

However, the radical Bavarian option was widely dismissed within the party, not least by the leadership. The Bavarian option was unpopular for a number of reasons. First, it involved a Downsian strategy to reconnect the party with the bulk of the Scottish electorate similar to the old cross-class, centrist Scottish Unionist Party. This suggestion was opposed by the right wing of the party and a renewed bout of faction-fighting ensued. Second, the fact that the Bavarians were pro-devolutionist fed into a more substantial issue than party reform – namely, dropping opposition to a Scottish parliament at the devolution referendum and reversing Conservative policy which had existed since 1976: something that Tory activists could not stomach. Third, many party members opposed the proposals because they would break-up the Conservative Party and there was a general feeling that the Bavarian wing had jumped the gun on party reform at the Scottish and UK levels. The fact that the Bavarian wing sought financial support from the Konrad Adenauer foundation to institute a study of the CSU's political and organisational autonomy,[13] with the intention of setting up a Scottish CSU as a rival to the Conservatives only enflamed passions within the Tory leadership and rank and file.

The party leadership responded to the fractious debate through establishing a party commission under former junior Scottish Office minister, Lord Strathclyde, to examine the changes needed to be made to the party organisation with devolution. The Strathclyde Commission comprised key figures associated with the party leadership, a large number of parliamentary candidates from 1997 and a few councillors and constituency activists: most of whom were identifiable as party loyalists rather than dissidents. The Commission issued its recommendations in January 1998, which were discussed at seven consultative roadshows for party members around Scotland from 16 to 31 January before deliberation at the party's special conference on 7 March, which would institute the new party structures in time for the main conference in June which would herald a new organisation. The Strathclyde Report made recommendations in seven main areas, most of which were adopted at the party conference in March. These changes were of both major and minor importance. The minor issues involved the merger of the professional and voluntary wings of the party, new procedures for consulting party members over the Scottish manifesto and the creation of centralised membership lists (all UK-wide Conservative reform initiatives) as well as the establishment of a Scottish Conservative Executive with its own elected convenor.[14] The major reforms proposed by the Strathclyde Report involved the election of a Scottish leader, candidate selection procedures for the Scottish Parliament election and the creation of a Scottish Policy Commission to research and consult on policy for the first devolved elections: though this latter initiative was only partly instituted and Tory policy was generated by the leadership in consultation with grass roots activists.

Before devolution, the leadership of the party in Scotland was in the gift of the party leader in London: who appointed the party chairman in Scotland and the (Shadow) Secretary of State for Scotland who also acted as the party leader. After devolution, the Scottish party leader was to be a member of the devolved parliament and elected by an electoral college of party members and MSPs. However, party members were to have only 30 per cent of votes within the electoral college, with the remaining 70 per cent going to the MSPs. This division was to look extremely bizarre given the limited numbers of Conservative MSPs elected at the devolved election in 1999. As only eighteen Conserative MSPs were elected, it meant that this small number controlled 70 per cent of the vote: hardly an exercise in intra-party democracy. Moreover, the Strathclyde proposals for electing the Scottish leader were deficient as they ignored the fact that the party needed a leader in advance of the devolved election in 1999 – unless it was to be completely leaderless in the year before the election and throughout the campaign.

Therefore, the Conservatives had to amend the Strathclyde proposals to conduct an ad hoc Scottish leadership contest in September 1998. This contest involved David McLetchie and Phil Gallie. McLetchie was President of the party in Scotland from 1994–97, but never held public office. Gallie was the former MP for Ayr from 1992–97 and a combative right-wing populist who stood in the leadership election to ensure a proper contest. Neither of these two contenders were substantial figures in the party: a fact indicative of the state of the party itself.[15] Moreover, the special electoral college established to elect the Scottish leader was hardly an exercise in intra-party democracy. The college comprised constituency delegates plus parliamentary candidates, rather than an OMOV ballot of party members, with McLetchie winning with ninety-one votes to Gallie's eighty-three. The fact that only 174 people took place in the leadership election – as opposed to the 176,391 members who participated in Hague's 1997 membership ballot – was an illustration of the gap between the rhetoric and reality of party democracy in Scotland that contrasted with the UK reforms.

The proposals for candidate selection to the devolved parliament were the second main change proposed by the Strathclyde Commission and in-tended to produce an entirely autonomous selection process and to ensure that candidates reside in Scotland. This latter aspect caused some controversy – as it banned English candidates from selection in Scotland – however, the move was long overdue. The large number of hopeless seats in Scotland requiring a candidate and the competition for safe(r) seats in the Conservative south,[16] tended to make Scotland a proving-ground for English Conservatives who descended, fresh from the candidates list, on areas they had never heard of, at short notice. This development further contributed to the party's image as anti-Scottish and pro-south-east. Continuing this practice in the context of devolution would have provided a rather unique solution to the West Lothian Question – English residents standing for a Scottish parliament – but was absurd in relation to the devolution issue. However, the problem for the Scottish Conservatives, which to some extent underlay the proliferation of non-Scots serving as parliamentary candidates, was a lack of candidates at various electoral levels from local government to national and European elections. Scottish Conservatism does not have the quantity or quality of personnel to compete in elections in Scotland at any level, so that limiting candidate selection for the Scottish Parliament had the potential to illuminate the threadbare nature of the party's Scottish candidates list, despite allowing the party to adopt a more distinctly Scottish face. The low profile and limited impact of many Conservative MSPs in the Scottish Parliament since 1999 seems to have illustrated this problem rather well.

The Scottish Conservatives also debated changing the party's name as part of a strategy to make it more Scottish. From 1912 to 1965, the party was known as the Scottish Unionist Party. This name was replaced because of the demise of Unionism (as in Ireland) as a mobilising force and the preference for a more middle-class, modern Conservatism that developed with Heath's leadership of the Tory Party in the 1960s. Options for a new name post-1997 included a return to Scottish Unionist Party, the Scottish New Unionist Party (proposed by Malcolm Rifkind), the Scottish Conservative Party, the Progressive Conservative Party, the Scottish Tory Party and the Scottish Democratic Conservative Party.[17] This fixation on a new name was intended to allow the party a symbolic break with the past and a more distinctly Scottish identity – even if the best ones have already been taken by the plethora of Unionist parties in Northern Ireland. The party also sought to emerge as 'New' in a similar style to New Labour, with some assumption that the key to electoral success was to place 'New' somewhere in the party's title. However, as there was not consensus on a name change, the party decided to stick with the Scottish Conservative and Unionist Party. Rebranding had its limits.

The 1999 Scottish election

The 1999 Scottish election was a unique and ironic experience for Scottish Conservatives. With few exceptions, the party's candidates went into the campaign seeking election to an institution they vehemently opposed and likely to succeed through a proportional electoral system they abhorred. The campaign had a degree of novelty, as it was the first Scottish election in which all parties were faced with the additional member system of seventy-three first-past-the-post (FPTP) and fifty-six regional list members. Given the Scottish Conservative performance in 1997, in which the party lost all of its Scottish seats (on FPTP), it was likely to be the regional lists that saw Conservatives elected. And, this situation was exactly what transpired on 6 May 1999, with the Tories winning eighteen seats on the regional list system and none by FPTP (see Table 9.1).[18]

Table 9.1 The 1999 Scottish election

| Party | First-past-the-post | | Regional list | | |
	% Vote	Seats	% Vote	Seats	Total seats
Labour	38.69	53	33.64	3	56
SNP	28.72	7	27.31	28	35
Conservative	15.55	–	15.35	18	18
Liberal Democrat	14.23	12	12.43	5	17
Others	2.81	1	11.27	2	3

The Scottish Conservatives were effectively marginalised at the 1999 election, which may become their fate at subsequent Scottish elections too. As a contest, the election was fought out between Labour and the SNP, much as Westminster elections are viewed as two-party affairs between Labour and Conservatives. Support for the Nationalists had risen dramatically in the year before the Scottish election to challenge Labour to be Scotland's leading party.[19] Thus, much of the political focus of the campaign dealt with the SNP-Labour contest and issues such as Chancellor Gordon Brown's budget, the use of the Parliament's tax powers (especially after the SNP announced its 'Penny for Scotland' policy), student tuition fees, Alex Salmond's controversial stance over NATO's bombing of Kosovo (which he described as 'unpardonable folly'), Labour's plans for private finance initiatives, etc. Even though these issues were of the 'tax and spending' variety which Conservatives had utilised in the past, the party itself was marginalised from such questions by the dominance of Labour and the SNP in the media. Second, the Conservatives marginalised themselves from the election campaign by ruling themselves out of participation in any post-election coalition. As coalition was the only game in town and Tories were not going to play it, then there was little scope for the party to promote itself in 1999. Instead, political attention focused on the Liberal Democrats and whether they would align themselves with the SNP or Labour after the election.

Where the Tories did do well in the 1999 campaign was in TV debates, where party leader McLetchie performed well. Expectations of McLetchie were low, largely because he was an unknown quantity within Scottish politics, so his sharp performances came as a surprise. Also, in such debates, the Tories found themselves in an entirely new political position. Pre-1999, the Tories had found themselves on the wrong end of the anti-Conservative alliance of Labour, Liberal Democrats and Nationalists. In 1999, this position had changed markedly. The Conservatives were no longer in government and no longer subject to the three-against-one arithmetic. Indeed, if anything, it was the SNP, which suffered from an anti-Nationalist alliance amongst the other parties.[20] The Tories also distinguished themselves in a very surprising way at the 1999 campaign: with their sense of humour. The party's leaflets and billboards poked fun at the other parties, especially in their depiction of Alex Salmond as a Tellytubby. Humour, combined with 'attack politics', as opposed to constructive policy engagement, gave Scotish Tories some prominence in the campaign, though this profile did not translate into too many votes.

Conservatives had prepared for the 1999 election by composing a manifesto through the medium of the 'Listening to Scotland' meetings. Hague had convened 'Listening to Britain' meetings with party members and supporters to discuss the Conservative policy platform and this practice were adopted in Scotland as a means to produce the 1999 manifesto. It was designed to show a more open and inclusive Scottish Conservative organisation, which adopted policies through consultation and widespread discussion with supporters and non-supporters alike. The exercise involved over 500 'Listening' meetings across Scotland, with 15,000 participants and sought to demonstrate that the Conservatives were 'a new party'.[21] Such a claim was an essential outcome of the party's rebranding efforts since the Strathclyde Commission and an attempt to give credence to the party's claim that it was 'Made in Scotland'. Moreover, the title of the party's manifesto was 'Scotland First', which aped the SNP's former slogan of 'Put Scotland First', which had first surfaced at the Kilmarnock by-election in 1946 before being used widely in the 1960s.

The content of the 1999 manifesto was not notably Scottish however, despite the quasi-Nationalist sloganeering. Out of the party's seven main pledges, only one – to lift the ban on beef-on-the-bone – was a distinctly Scottish initiative. The remainder, were largely UK-wide initiatives on taxation, health and education: such as no tax increases, the re-introduction of matrons on to hospital wards and the abolition of student tuition fees though this latter policy had a strong Scottish dimension.[22] The Scottish Conservative manifesto contained a range of other specific policy pledges, though often other parties shared such pledges. Thus, the Tories supported zero tolerance of crime and drugs, directly elected council leaders and council house stock transfer, which were also Labour policies and its position on student tuition fees was shared by the SNP and Liberal Democrats. In a positive vein, the party committed itself to the decentralisation of Scottish Executive departments, an enhanced road-building programme, establishing a voucher system for post-sixteen education and training, restoring a voucher system for nursery schools and removing schools from local authority control. The Tories also committed themselves to opposing road tolls, tourist taxes, stealth taxes, abolition of the pound and seeking lower fuel prices: with the latter two policies being UK initiatives. However, none of these policies or initiatives were particularly bold or original and, moreover, as the Tories had put themselves out of the coalition game, none were given serious attention at the election.

Autonomy in action: Scottish Conservatism, 1999–2001

Conservatives in the Scottish Parliament face a very different political opportunity structure to their colleagues at Westminster. For example, the
party in Scotland exists in a multi-party legislature in which it is the third
or fourth party rather than the government or opposition. This situation has
two facets. First, as the Tories are *persona non grata* in Scottish coalition
politics, ruled themselves out of coalition and are electorally weak in Scotland
they have no prospect of power. Exclusion from government office and
permanent status as an opposition contrast with the party's prospects at
two-party Westminster. Second, the Scotish Tories found themselves as the
second opposition party in the Parliament after the 1999 election rather than
capable of filling the shoes of Her Majesty's Loyal Opposition as at Westminster. The SNP are the official opposition with priority at First Minister's
question time, Scottish Executive question time, more time for party-spon-
sored debates in the Parliament, shadow Ministerial portfolios, more time
speaking in debates, the leading role as opposition and a host of other
advantages denied to the Conservatives. In addition, not only are the Tories
the second opposition, but they face a coalition government of Labour and
Liberal Democrats. This is an advantageous position compared to Westminster, as it allows the Scotish Tories to attack two opposing parties at once,
rather than finding themselves outflanked or undermined by the Liberal
Democrats taking a middle-way position of opposition to Labour. However,
all of these factors make for a complex, multi-party politics.

The Scottish Conservatives in the Scottish Parliament are very much a
mixed bag as a parliamentary group. Very few had Westminster experience
and, those that had were the very ones that lost their seats in 1997: Phil
Gallie and Lord James Douglas Hamilton. The MSPs thus have few links
with Westminster, with implications for relations with the UK party as a
whole. Two further distinguishing characteristics of the parliamentary group
are notable. First, the Tory group is middle-aged to elderly, with an average
age of forty-nine at the 1999 election: joint highest amongst the parties with
the Liberal Democrats. Second, the Tory parliamentary group is predominantly male, with only three female MSPs. Though the party has one more
female MSP than the Liberal Democrats, the SNP and Labour easily eclipse
it, with much more equal (and numerous) numbers of male and female
representatives. Thus, the MSP's group does not resemble the inclusive party
that Conservatives modernisers have sought to promote in recent years,
which is important as it is the MSPs who are the leading figures within the
party in Scotland.

The political activities of the Tories within the Scottish Parliament have
had four distinct characteristics. First, the party has concentrated on acting
as a strong opposition to the coalition parties in the Scottish Executive. This

has meant playing 'attack' politics on a large number of occasions to oppose most of the Executive's legislative programme but not making common cause with the SNP. At times this approach has pitched the Tories against all other parties in the Parliament – such as over the proposal to abolish Section 28 and land reform – and further enhanced the party's unpopularity. However, this strategy allowed the party to set out distinctive positions and avoid the soggy centre-ground of political consensus in the Parliament: providing it with a clear, uncompromised political identity and a cutting edge. Second, the party also sought to focus on public services and the failure of the Scottish Executive in delivering adequate public services: the type of sensible position that the Tories at Westminster have adopted post-Hague. This focus on issues of everyday concern to voters – as opposed to ones which get party activists hot under the collar – does not show any great strategic perceptiveness that set Scotish Tories aside from their British counterparts. Rather, it is the logic of devolution itself, which established a Parliament responsible for education, health, transport, local government etc. However, the situation allowed the Tories to connect with the everyday concerns of Scottish voters.

Third, the Tories sought to push particular policy positions that were shared by other parties in the Parliament, were capable of dividing the Executive and could assist the Tories to develop a new image in Scotland. For example, the Conservatives' support for state-funded personal care for the elderly – and thus the implementation of the Sutherland Royal Commission on Care for the Elderly – was an issue supported by a majority in the Parliament but initially opposed by the Scottish Executive. Conservative support for the issue enabled it to appear pro-pensioner, pro-public services, capable of supporting a policy that was not supported by Tories at Westminster and also in a position to force the Executive to adopt the policy through parliamentary pressure. Fourth, the party has engaged in ideological repositioning to some extent through support for the abolition of student tuition fees and for funded care for the elderly. Similarly, the issues the Scotish Tories have not picked up in the Parliament have helped the party to attempt to renovate its image. For example, the MSPs adopted a moderate stance over immigration and asylum seekers that contrasted with the more fevered approach of Hague and the Westminster party. Indeed, Scottish Conservatives avoided adopting a populist approach to such issues and took a more centrist ideological position in Scotland, in spite of the presence of right-wing MSPs within the Scottish parliamentary group.

However, such limited repositioning did not constitute a substantial ideological change. The party remains committed to attracting a centre right electorate, even though it constitutes a very limited electoral 'hunting ground' for the party in Scotland.[23] Indeed, the party's low level of electoral support and the electoral system for the Scottish Parliament seem set to cement the Tory's position as a party representing a limited constituency rather than seeking support from a broader electorate.[24] Such representation, without the prospect of government participation appears an unattractive prospectus over the medium to long-term as it leaves the party bereft of a coalition potential.[25] Unless the Tories can find a viable coalition partner, then it is likely to remain marginalised in the devolved parliament and only capable of exercising influence through one-off coalitions on specific issues such as care for the elderly. And yet, even then the party's abilities are limited by its lack of flexibility. Two issues illustrate this point. Despite some of the party's MSPs expressing support for fiscal autonomy for the Parliament, the Tories have not picked up this issue officially and sought to form alliances with the SNP, Liberal Democrats or sympathetic Labour MSPs to promote the issue. Thus, an issue which could trump Labour over devolution and commit the Tories to improve the Parliament and appear pro-Scottish has been neglected. Second, in spite of the damage it could do to the Liberal Democrat-Labour coalition, the Tories retained an entirely dogmatic approach to electoral reform in local government. Rather than support a reform which would wreck Labour's local one-party states, generate a coalition crisis and lead to the election of scores of Conservative councillors, the party retained its opposition to any electoral reform for fear of what it might mean at Westminster.

The 2001 general election and after

The 2001 election was almost as disappointing for the Tories as that of 1997. Whilst the party won back Galloway and Upper Nithsdale in the face of a collapse in the SNP vote and came close to retaking Perth, results in most other seats were disappointing. The party saw small rises in Ayr, Dumfries and Edinburgh Pentlands but a decline in their support in the key seats of Aberdeen South, Aberdeenshire West and Kincardine, Eastwood, Edinburgh West and Tayside North. These latter constituencies may now be lost to the Conservatives on a permanent basis: the case with the seats lost in the electoral collapse of 1987. More fundamentally, popular support for the Tories in 2001 was 15.58 per cent (1.93 per cent less than the 1997 disaster) and the Tories came fourth behind the Liberal Democrats: an all-time low for Scottish Conservatism. Winning a seat in what was an apocalyptic election seems nothing short of miraculous, however, the general election did not presage any great Conservative recovery in time for the 2003 Scottish election. The 2001 results pointed to an improved ability to win FPTP seats compared to 1999, but any gains will be offset through the corrective mechanisms of the regional lists. The party will therefore continue as a marginal force at Holyrood in terms of seats and coalition-potential (see Table 9.2).

The post-Hague Conservative leadership election had a negative impact on the party in Scotland, not so much in terms of who was actually elected as leader in September 2001, but in the manner in which the debate over the

Table 9.2 The 2001 general election in Scotland

	% Vote	Seats	Change
Labour	43.26	55	−1*
SNP	20.06	5	−1
Liberal Democrat	16.37	10	−
Conservative	15.58	1	+1
Speaker	−	1	+1

Note: * Former Labour MP, Michael Martin now sits as the Speaker.

leadership fanned the flames of factional conflict within the Scottish party. Given there was only one Scottish Conservative MP elected to Westminster in 2001, there was little Scottish influence on the MP's ballots at the leadership contest. However, the ballot of party members brought a much greater opportunity for Scottish involvement and influence over the leadership contest. Both Kenneth Clarke and Iain Duncan Smith made forays to Scotland during the campaign and each addressed the Scottish Conservatives' one-day conference on 1 September 2001. Prominent MSPs took a stand as supporters of each candidate and the focus of the leadership campaign in Scotland began to revolve around the impact either candidate would have on the Scottish party. Of the two candidates, it was Clarke who sought to make political capital amongst Scottish Conservatives by addressing Scottish issues. However, such efforts were extremely ill-informed and self-destructive. Initially, Clarke promised that he would seek to give more powers to the Scottish Parliament to increase the extent of devolution.[26] However, Clarke provided no serious proposals to back this statement up. Next, Clarke proposed to give more autonomy to the Scottish party's MSPs to make policy: apparently ignorant of the fact they had enjoyed such autonomy in devolved areas since 1999. Third, Clarke produced an entirely muddled position on public expenditure in Scotland. His leadership manifesto promised a review of the Barnett formula to address 'budgetary unfairness' and reduce Scotland's share of public spending: a proposal to attract support in England. However, this policy was retracted quickly in favour of arguing for a needs assessment of regional spending in the UK:[27] a policy which could still involve reducing Scottish spending and undermining the Scottish Parliament. This latter position invited and received considerable ridicule from the Scottish media.

In contrast to Clarke's manoeuvring, Duncan Smith adopted a more relaxed approach to Scotland and to devolution. Indeed, Duncan Smith eschewed any attempt to court Scottish opinion through Scottish issues. Rather, he came to Scotland with an open mind about devolution and the role of the Scottish Conservatives, concentrated on dialogue with the Scottish party and talked about the general campaign themes such as public services.

Duncan Smith's only foray into devolved politics involved his suggestion that the Scottish party leader should sit in his shadow cabinet at Westminster: a complete reversal of devolution that disappeared from view after July and was not implemented following Duncan Smith's success in the leadership ballot.

However, the significance of the leadership campaign was not how the two candidates handled Scottish issues, but what the contest itself did to the Scottish Conservatives as a party. The leadership contest inevitably led to increased tensions within the Scottish Tories as leading MSPs and party office-bearers moved to support the opposing candidates. Prominent right-wingers such as new MP Peter Duncan, Phil Gallie MSP, Brian Monteith MSP and former Scottish chairman Raymond Robertson supported Duncan Smith, whilst left-wing and centrist Tories such as Murray Tosh MSP, Struan Stevenson MEP and Malcolm Rifkind supported Ken Clarke. However, as the internal politics of the Scotish Tories has traditionally been extremely fractious and personalised, the leadership contest brought about a period of intense faction-fighting between the left, right and centre of the party in Scotland. The faction-fighting was not confined to policy issues or the ideological positioning of the Conservatives under Clarke or Duncan Smith, but was about the effect of a change of leadership on the balance of power within the Scottish Tories. Such issues included the performance of the Scottish party leader, David McLetchie;[28] the effectiveness of the MSPs in the Scottish Parliament; the selection procedures for candidates at the 2003 election;[29] and factional sympathies of the person who would be appointed as Scottish party chairman by the Westminster leader.

The leadership campaign was not aided by the decision by Nick Johnston, regional list MSP (Mid-Scotland and Fife), to resign from the Scottish Parliament amid accusations of weak leadership by McLetchie and factional conflicts amongst the MSPs.[30] The leadership contest also generated uncertainty about McLetchie's role as Scottish leader, with speculation that a Duncan Smith victory would lead to pressure on McLetchie to stand down as Scottish leader and briefings against McLetchie from MSPs from various wings of the party. There was even speculation that Duncan Smith would appoint a party chairman in Scotland who would effectively undermine McLetchie.[31] The Scottish conference therefore took on an entirely different complexion. It was no longer an opportunity for the two leadership candidates to impress the party faithful, but an event overshadowed by internal conflict and instability which damaged the party's image in Scotland.

Of course, such faction-fighting and internal conflict is exactly how the Scottish Conservatives operate. One newspaper report of the conference was headlined 'Blood on the agenda at Perth',[32] whilst another read 'Back-stabbing and blood-letting ... it's party time for the Tories'.[33] Prominent Conservative and newspaper columnist, Brian Meek, remarked that:

The Tory party, particularly the Scottish version, has a lot of similarities with the Balkans. No sooner is one regional revolution quelled – peace proposals accepted, handshakes all round – than a grenade from another faction re-opens hostilities. What happens next is equally predictable: the media are blamed for stirring up trouble, though in back-stabbing terms, the party's ever-declining number of MPs, MSPs and leading members could teach old Brutus a slash or two.[34]

Thus, to find the Scottish Conservatives descending into factional in-fighting seemed an entirely natural state of affairs. And, yet when the leadership contest was over, McLetchie survived as Scottish party leader and a factionally neutral member, David Mitchell, was appointed as Scottish party chairman by Duncan Smith.[35] The in-fighting had no outcome barring the destabilisation of the Scottish Conservatives and little effect on the leadership election itself.

Conclusion

The years between 1997 and 2001 were a difficult period of adjustment for Scottish Conservatives, though one which they coped with reasonably well. The party made no great strides in terms of electoral success, but settled into the Scottish Parliament and sought to carve an opposition role for itself in the new devolved Scotland. Hague's *laissez-faire* attitude to the Scottish Conservatives clearly assisted the party's period of adjustment.[36] At a time in which Labour was heavily criticised for political and organisational cen-tralisation that flew in the face of devolution – in Wales and London for example – Hague allowed the Scottish Conservatives a substantial degree of freedom. On the one hand, this freedom was exactly what devolution was supposed to be about. Furthermore, the Scottish Conservatives needed such freedom to seek to establish themselves as a credible political force in Scotland which gave some truth to the party's claims to be 'Made in Scotland'. On the other hand, such freedom was permissible because the Scottish Conservatives were unimportant as an opposition party with no prospect of government: with clear similarities to the party at Westminster during the 1997–2001 period. Therefore, there was little to lose from allowing the Scottish Conser-vatives to go their own way.

Whilst Scotland-London conflicts were few and far between from 1997 to 2001, despite the deployment of controversial issues such as the West Lothian Question and Barnett formula at Westminster, the domestic position of the Scottish Conservatives in this period was not a particularly happy one. Gaining representation in the devolved parliament in 1999 and carving a role as a strong opposition is one thing, but the prospect of power is very much another. The Scottish Conservatives seem set to exist as a party representing a small, centre right electorate, with little prospect of broadening its support and gaining a share of power in the Parliament. The party's coalition potential is severely limited in a multi-party system in which the Scottish Conservatives remain *persona non grata* to the other parties and therefore permanently excluded from power. Whilst the party's prospects in the Parliament are extremely limited, its electoral future remains uncertain. If Iain Duncan Smith and the Conservatives at Westminster increase their credibility and political support, this will feed into the popularity of the Scottish Conservatives, especially at Scottish elections: a very ironic position for the Scottish Conservatives to be in.

Notes

1 D. Seawright, *An Important Matter of Principle. The Decline of the Scottish Conservative and Unionist Party* (Aldershot, Ashgate, 1999), p. 29.

2 HMSO, 'Scotland in the Union: A Partnership for Good' (Edinburgh, Scottish Office, 1993). Cm 2225.

3 See J. Rudolph and R. Thompson, 'Ethnoterritorial movements and the policy process: accomodating nationalist demands in the developed world', *Comparative Politics*, 17:3 (1985) 291–311.

4 See D. Denver, J. Mitchell, C. Pattie and H. Bochel, *Scotland Decides* (London, Frank Cass, 2000).

5 This move was entirely populist – they had completely ignored the issue when in office from 1979 to 1997 – though had some precedent in the Tories' Next Steps initiatives which had a marginal effect on the Scottish Office.

6 D. Urwin, 'Scottish Conservatism: a party organisation in transition', *Political Studies*, 14:2 (1965) 145–62.

7 C. Stevens, 'Scottish Conservatism: a failure of organisation?', in A. Brown and R. Parry (eds), *Scottish Government Yearbook* (Edinburgh, Unit for the Study of Government in Scotland, 1990).

8 Seawright, *An Important Matter of Principle*, p. 29.

9 'Tories set for a u-turn on devolution position', *The Scotsman*, 8 May 1997.

10 'UDI call to Scots Tories', *The Herald*, 29 May 1997.

11 The CSU had already been aired as a model for the Scottish Tories as far back as 1996 but only became prominent after the 1997 election. See P. Dwyer, 'Conservatives need to create a true Scottish identity', *The Herald*, 9 May 1996.

12 B. Meek, 'Taking the bold step', *The Herald*, 19 May 1997.

13 The Foundation was reported to have provided finance for a breakaway Scottish Tory Party, even though in reality it had only agreed to fund a study group of CDU-CSU relations by Conservative dissidents. *The Herald*, 26 June 1997.

14 This reform provided for five executive members, including the Convenor, to be directly elected by an OMOV ballot of party members. However, the majority of the executive remained nominated, co-opted and ex-office members, with three of them actually appointed by the UK party leader.

15 Former Scottish Tory Cabinet Ministers such as Michael Forsyth, Ian Lang and Malcolm Rifkind demonstrated no interest in standing for the Scottish Parliament or Scottish Conservative leadership.

16 A situation made more competitive by former Scottish MPs heading South following electoral defeat in Scotland: Michael Ancram, Gerry Malone and Ian Sproat are examples of this trend.

17 The Strathclyde Commission, *Made in Scotland* (Edinburgh, Scottish Conservative and Unionist Party, 1998), p. 7.

18 This position improved slightly in 2000, when the Tories won the Ayr by-election to give them one FPTP seat in the Scottish Parliament.

19 See the polls in G. Hassan and P. Lynch, *The Almanac of Scottish Politics* (London, Politico's, 2001).

20 See P. Jones, 'The 1999 Scottish Parliament elections: from anti-Tory to anti-Nationalist politics', *Scottish Affairs*, 28 (1999) 1–9.

21 D. McLetchie, 'Introduction', *Scotland First: Scottish Conservative Manifesto for the Scottish election 1999* (Edinburgh, Scottish Conservative and Unionist Party, 1999).

22 Scottish Conservatives, *Scotland First.*

23 See A. Panebianco, *Political Parties: Organisation and Power* (Cambridge, Cambridge University Press, 1988).

24 See H. Kitschelt, *The Logic of Party Formation* (Ithaca, NY, Cornell University Press, 1989).

25 See G. Sartori, *Parties and Party Systems* (Cambridge, Cambridge University Press, 1976).

26 *Scotland on Sunday*, 29 July 2001.

27 *The Scotsman*, 31 August 2001.

28 *The Scotsman*, 1 September 2001.

29 *Sunday Herald*, 12 August 2001.

30 *The Herald*, 11 August 2001.

31 *The Scotsman*, 1 September 2001.

32 *The Herald*, 21 August 2001.

33 *Sunday Herald*, 2 September 2001.

34 *The Herald*, 4 September 2001.

35 Though, this situation was illustrative of the weakness of the Scottish party itself as a key Scottish appointment was still made in London in spite of devolution.

36 Indeed, there were no major cases of disagreement between the Scottish and UK Conservatives in this period over policy, organisation or strategy.

10

Nationhood and identity in Conservative politics

Philip Lynch

Identification with the nation and nation state has been a central theme in Conservative politics for over a century. The party's status as a patriotic party safeguarding the constitution, Union and, for much of its history, the Empire was an important factor in its political success. The appeal of the Conservative politics of nationhood rested upon three main pillars: (i) a coherent vision of nationhood and conservative state patriotism; (ii) effective use of a patriotic discourse, which portrayed the Conservatives as a national rather than sectional party, popularised its vision of nationhood and questioned the patriotic credentials of its rivals; and (iii) a political strategy which accorded the defence of the nation state and national identity a leading place.[1] But the politics of nationhood has also proved divisive periodically – tariff reform, the Irish question and European integration produced damaging intra-party divisions over British identity and party strategy in the last century. This chapter examines the Conservative politics of nationhood under William Hague, focusing on the 'English Question' and the politics of 'race'. Policy towards the European Union (EU) is examined in Chapter 8.

The end of Empire, moves towards membership of the European Community (EC), devolution and immigration posed significant challenges to the dominant One Nation perspective in the 1960s. Two contrasting positions on how to adapt the Conservative politics of nationhood emerged. Edward Heath proposed EC membership, Scottish devolution and a liberal perspective on race relations. Enoch Powell offered a post-imperial, Tory nationalist strategy that aimed to safeguard parliamentary sovereignty and national identity from the perceived threats posed by European integration, devolution and immigration. Later, the revival of British nationhood was a prominent theme within Thatcherism. The Thatcher governments made effective use of patriotic discourse, claiming to promote British interests and identity by defending the Union, limiting immigration and promoting a vision of a free market, intergovernmental EC, but also presided over a significant erosion of sovereignty and fuelled demands for devolution.

The challenges facing the Conservatives in this area were apparent in the 1990s as divisions emerged over Europe and the government failed to stem the pro-devolution tide. Rather than contributing to effective Conservative statecraft, problems in the politics of nationhood provoked intra-party disputes, undermined governing competence and issue hegemony, and contributed to election defeat.[2] John Major adopted a holding position but this proved akin to plugging leaks in a dyke. Whereas the Euro-sceptic right urged Major to shore up the defences against a perceived rising tide of European integration and sub-state nationalism that threatened the nation state, One Nation Tories looked to adapt pragmatically to EMU and devolution.

The politics of nationhood under Hague

Contemporary conservative thinking on the concept of the nation has coalesced around two general approaches: a civic account of the nation which looks to a limited politics of state patriotism and a cultural account (evident in the work of Roger Scruton) which stresses the pre-political basis of nationhood and a common culture.[3] In the 1990s, the influence of the civic account has been apparent in Conservative discourse, but the cultural conservative perspective informs the Tory right's critique of European integration and multiculturalism. Conservative state patriotism sees a shared civic culture, allegiance to common institutions and membership of a historic community as the bedrock of national identity. The authors of a 1996 Conservative Political Centre report, *Strengthening the United Kingdom*, depicted Britishness as a form of constitutional patriotism denoting allegiance to the constitution and its underlying principles, but allowing for diverse identities within this framework.[4] Both the civic and cultural accounts view further European integration as a threat to national sovereignty, but sovereignty is a contested concept in Conservative politics. Euro-sceptics equate it with national self-government and parliamentary authority, both of which were central to a British identity rooted in state patriotism. Pro-Europeans, for their part, see sovereignty as a capacity for influence that can be enhanced by constructive engagement in the EU.

Hague emphasised the importance of the nation to British Conservatism and sought to renew the party's position as the champion of the nation in the light of new challenges.[5] To restore their political fortunes, the Conservatives had to be a national party, understanding and drawing upon British identity and values. The defining features of British identity were individualism, a spirit of enterprise, social mobility – with Hague praising the contribution of immigrants to British culture – and attachment to locality and the 'little platoons' of civil society. But common political institutions are central to British identity as they both reflect and shape these other values. With its programme of constitutional reform, support for further European integration and efforts to 'rebrand' Britishness, New Labour threatens the

'British Way'. Hague rejected claims that Britishness was an historical invention now ripe for modernisation, arguing that it continued to be a unifying force.

Hague's Conservative nation draws upon a traditional Tory attachment to political institutions, a Thatcherite emphasis on individuals and markets, plus a belief in the virtue of local communities and civil society that underpins the 'civic conservatism' of David Willetts. Indeed, Hague's speech on the 'British way' drew on an earlier speech by Willetts on British identity.[6] Willetts recognised that the Conservatives' traditional strength in the politics of nationhood was being challenged by a New Labour government determined to align itself with and modernise British identity, and by claims from historians that Britishness was a now outdated 'invented' identity. Following Michael Oakeshott, Willetts believes that the nation state should provide a framework which protects the intermediate institutions and loyalties of civil society, but should not be an 'enterprise association' striving for a homogeneous national identity. The nation state is one among a series of communities: 'a shared cultural tradition, limited government, the free market and loyalty to the central institutions of the nation state, are the integrating forces in which a conservative trusts'.[7] The state's role in upholding the shared political culture and an integrative, state patriotism is a limited one – 'the nation state can command our loyalty as the protector of these communities but we certainly cannot look to it as one organic whole embodying detailed moral purposes which we all share'.[8]

The significance of the nation in Conservative politics was evident in policy on Europe, constitutional reform and race relations. European integration was perceived as a threat to self-government and national identity. For Hague a nation is: 'a group of people who feel enough in common with one another to accept government from each other's hands. This is why democracy functions best within nations.'[9] Historic identities and allegiance to national institutions endure because 'national identity fulfils a basic human need to belong'. The EU does not enjoy such legitimacy or popular allegiance. Labour's programme for constitutional reform – reform of the House of Lords, incorporation of the European Convention on Human Rights, proportional representation for some elections and devolution – challenged a Conservative constitutional or state patriotism that depicted parliamentary sovereignty and the Union as bedrocks of the British state and identity. Although staunch opponents of devolution under Major, the Conservatives now accepted the 'Yes' votes in the Scottish and Welsh referendums, and backed the Good Friday Agreement though this support was eroded by the limited progress on IRA decommissioning. Predictions of a post-devolution 'break up of Britain' no longer figured prominently, but the leadership argued that the constitutional anomalies of devolution had destabilised the Union and made an English nationalist backlash more likely. On 'race', Hague described

Britain as a 'nation of immigrants' to which ethnic minority communities had made important contributions but was uncomfortable with some aspects of multiculturalism.

In New Labour, the Conservatives faced a party more confident and adept in the use of patriotic discourse than previously. The Blair government depicted itself as representing modern patriotism, revitalising both the nation state and national identity through its programme of constitutional reform, devolution and constructive engagement in the EU. The 'cool Britannia' message of creativity in the arts added more heat than light but symbolised efforts to 'rebrand' Britishness.[10] The appointment of Michael Wills as the government's 'patriotism envoy' also illustrated a desire to counter Tory patriotism.

More significant were a series of speeches by ministers outlining their vision of British identity and championing New Labour as the patriotic party.[11] Rather than being redundant, Britishness was being modernised through constitutional reform and a positive role in the EU. Constructive engagement in the EU was an expression of modern patriotism. Devolution would strengthen the Union by enhancing the sense of mutual interest and shared values, and bolster British identity by recognising that Britishness is a plural identity that embraces local and national allegiances. As a plural rather than ethnic identity, British culture had been enriched by immigration. Importantly, New Labour rejected Conservative claims that British identity was rooted in traditional institutions. Instead, ministers argued that nationhood arose from the collective experiences and shared values of the British people. Among the values identified were creativity and adaptability; tolerance and fair play; an outward looking rather than insular approach to the world; a commitment to both individual liberty and mutual responsibility; and a belief in the virtues of decentralisation, strong communities and civic engagement. New Labour thus blended elements of the conservative nation – Brown cited Burke's attachment to local communities and reform – with an own emphasis on community and constitutional reform to foster its 'outward looking modern patriotism'.

England and the Union

The Conservatives claimed that national institutions were central features of British national identity and thus presented constitutional reform as a threat to the 'British way'. The new leadership initially took a pragmatic position on Labour's devolution legislation before pledging to work constructively within the new institutions. As Peter Lynch discusses in Chapter 9, the Scottish Conservative Party gained greater autonomy and sought, with

limited success, to shed its anti-Scottish tag. Reworking Conservative Unionism was a tricky task, particularly as Conservative MPs were uneasy with
the perceived unfair treatment of England in the new settlement.

THE ENGLISH QUESTION

The 1997 general election defeat left the Conservatives without representation at Westminster from three of the UK's four component nations.
They looked still more like an English national party and under Hague's
leadership promoted English values and interests prominently. The Conservatives thus identified themselves with the countryside and rural way of life
on issues such as rural crime, threats to services, the plight of farmers and
fox-hunting. This was though a narrow view of English values which, coupled
with the party's tone on asylum and the family, did not accord with the
cultural outlook of many young urban voters. The Conservatives did not
become an explicitly English nationalist party. Hague defended the Union,
spoke of Britishness and the 'British way' rather than English identity (his
speeches on the 'English Question' were notably reticent in defining Eng-
lishness), rejected proposals for an English Parliament and shied away from
advocating major reforms to the Barnett formula. At the 2001 election, the
Conservatives pledged to retain the positions of Secretary of State for
Scotland and Wales but to merge the posts with other UK Cabinet roles.[12]

The English dimension of devolution emerged as an important theme
in Conservative politics, though not the guiding principle that some predicted. Conservatives claimed that devolution to Scotland and Wales had
unbalanced the Union by maintaining their preferential treatment while
disadvantaging England. Constitutional anomalies such as the West Lothian
Question – why should Scottish MPs at Westminster be able to vote on
English matters when English MPs had no say on equivalent matters
devolved to the Scottish Parliament? – undermined the Union and raised
the spectre of an English backlash. Hague believed that an emerging English
political identity might be productively harnessed, but was wary of both
breaking too sharply with the party's Unionist tradition or lurching towards
an extreme English nationalist position. A review of policy on constitutional
reform would explore four options: strengthening local government; reducing the number of Scottish MPs at Westminster; restricting the voting rights
of Scottish MPs; and creating an English Parliament with similar powers
to those in Scotland.[13]

The creation of an English Parliament was the most radical option, but
was rejected. Hague declared himself 'as yet unpersuaded' by the arguments
in July 1999.[14] The UK was 'not easily suited' to a federal model as England,
with over 80 per cent of the UK's population and revenue, would be
predominant. An English Parliament could undermine Westminster and
further destabilise the Union. Nonetheless it found some favour within the

party, though there was little consensus on how it might fit into the UK's institutional architecture. Lord (Kenneth) Baker's scheme proposed that an English Parliament of members from existing English constituencies would meet at Westminster for three days a week. The majority party would appoint a First Minister and Executive with responsibility for 'domestic' English law. A UK Parliament of 350 members would handle economic, foreign and defence policy.[15] Others proposed 'devolution in the round' with an English Parliament operating within a federal United Kingdom, or an independent English state.[16]

Those MPs most critical of the 'unfair' treatment of England and supportive of an English Parliament came from the Euro-sceptic right. The disproportionate number of Scottish MPs at Westminster, their participation in votes on 'English' matters, the number of Scottish Cabinet Ministers and the higher levels of public spending per head of population in Scotland than in England were cited as examples of bias against England. Teresa Gorman felt that the Conservatives should no longer make compromises for the sake of the Union, but should champion English rights and identity. She launched an unsuccessful Bill, supported by David Davis and Eric Forth, to provide for a referendum on an English Parliament.[17] However, few Conservative heavyweights lent their support: Iain Duncan Smith, Kenneth Clarke, Ann Widdecombe and Peter Lilley all expressed doubts.[18]

The official Conservative position, announced in July 1999, was that 'English votes for English laws' provided the optimal answer to the West Lothian Question. Under Hague's plan, Scottish MPs would lose their right to vote on legislation on non-Scottish 'domestic' matters, leaving English MPs an exclusive say over English law and spending plans. The Speaker would identify those Bills that related only to English matters as 'English Bills'. They would be debated and voted on by English MPs at each stage of the legislative process in the House of Commons. In practice, as the National Assembly for Wales does not have primary legislative power, Bills on health, education and the like would be certified as 'English and Welsh Bills' with MPs representing English and Welsh constituencies voting. Removing the right of Scottish MPs to vote on English legislation would be among the first actions of a Conservative government.[19]

Hague claimed that his scheme was the optimal solution to the 'West Lothian Question', requiring neither an English executive nor special 'English days' at Westminster. However, there were potential problems with the 'English votes for English law' plan. The withdrawal of voting rights from Scottish MPs could leave a future UK government without sufficient support to pass English legislation. Hague argued that Parliament would then be able to check the executive effectively, but Labour would suffer under this scenario given the low levels of Conservative support in Scotland. Furthermore, it would not be easy to identify exclusively English legislation as under the Barnett formula decisions on spending in England impact upon the size of the block grant allocated to the Scottish Parliament. Denying Scottish MPs a say on English legislation would reduce their influence over public expenditure in Scotland.

The government opposed the proposal, though the House of Commons Procedure Committee did recommend that existing provisions allowing the Speaker to designate legislation as relating exclusively to Scotland be adapted to provide for English (or English and Welsh) Bills.[20] These would be referred to a Second Reading Committee made up entirely of members of the appropriate territory. However they would have to be approved by the House as a whole. The Conservatives did not fully support this plan; the government rejected it. Nor was Labour's plan to revive the Standing Committee on Regional Affairs – consisting exclusively of English MPs – wholly endorsed, as its remit would be regional affairs rather than English matters. Four Conservatives became standing members of the Committee but, when it finally met in May 2001, only one Tory turned up even though all English MPs were entitled to attend.[21]

The Conservatives supported a reduction in the number of Scottish MPs sitting at Westminster but saw this as an insufficient answer to the 'English Question'. Scotland has some fourteen seats more than it would have if Scottish constituencies were of equivalent size to the English average of 72,000 constituents per seat. The government indicated that the number of Scottish seats at Westminster would be reduced to between fifty-seven and sixty, but this would not take effect until the general election after next, whereas the Tories sought immediate change.

Finally, the Conservatives opposed both the Regional Development Agencies (RDAs) established by the government and Labour's proposals for elected regional assemblies in England. The RDAs were condemned as costly and bureaucratic, duplicating or taking over functions best carried out by local councils, and would be abolished. Regional government was not the answer to the 'English Question': few parts of England had a strong regional identity and those that did (for example, Cornwall) might find themselves part of an artificial entity.

Hopes that the Conservatives might benefit from a re-awakening of English identity and backlash against the anomalies of devolution were largely unfulfilled. Surveys suggested that since devolution British identity had weakened, as the number of people describing themselves as being more Scottish, Welsh or English than British increased.[22] Although a greater number of people in England were now more likely to identify themselves as English rather than British, there were few signs of either widespread or deeply felt resentment about the treatment of England.[23] Support in England for Scottish and Welsh devolution increased but only a minority – even of those identifying themselves as English rather than British – wanted devolution for England, either in the form of regional assemblies (15 per cent support) or an English Parliament (18 per cent). Those with a strong English identity were more Euro-sceptic but this did not produce a strong identification with the Conservatives. Although the Tories were seen as more English than Labour, they scored less than 30 per cent support among those with a strong English identity, trailing Labour.[24]

The politics of 'race'

It was a case of 'one step forward, but two steps back' for Conservative policy on 'race' issues during Hague's leadership. On a positive note, Hague continued efforts to attract greater ethnic minority participation in, and support for, the Conservatives. But the net results were disappointing, largely because of the negative signals that emanated from Hague's tough position and populist rhetoric on asylum, and by evidence of continued hostility to multiculturalism on the Tory right.

Early in his leadership, Hague stressed his social liberal credentials, praising the contributions made by immigrants to British life and promoting a 'patriotism without bigotry'. He firmly rebuffed Lord Tebbit's claim that 'one cannot … be loyal to two nations … it perpetuates ethnic divisions because nationality is in the long term more about culture than ethnics'. The new leader and his fiancée also made a symbolic visit to the 1997 Notting Hill carnival but media coverage focused on unsuccessful efforts to improve Hague's public image. Despite the early promise, the Conservatives would develop a hardline policy and populist rhetoric on asylum and fail to tackle racism in the Conservative Party by the end of his tenure.

ASYLUM

Asylum emerged as a central theme in Conservative politics midway through Hague's leadership when it became part of a 'core vote strategy' aimed at shoring up traditional Tory support and using populist themes to maximise coverage of the Conservative agenda. The government had introduced a number of measures to tackle the increase in asylum applications – a voucher system, the dispersal of asylum seekers across the UK and civil penalties on hauliers caught bringing illegal immigrants into the UK – some of which the Conservatives opposed. Policy on 'bogus asylum seekers' was only briefly mentioned in the 1999 *Common Sense Revolution* which promised to reinstate the 'safe countries' list, end amnesties and 'use more detention'.

Within a year asylum had moved close to the top of the Tory agenda as applications continued to rise and Ann Widdecombe established her position as Shadow Home Secretary. The Conservatives made asylum a key issue in the 2000 local elections, accusing Labour of making Britain 'a soft touch for the organised asylum racketeers who are flooding our country with bogus asylum seekers' and highlighting the costs of asylum support borne by some local authorities.

In a keynote speech mixing reasoned argument and populist prescription, Hague set out his plans for tackling abuse of the asylum system.[25] He claimed that a Conservative government would uphold Britain's 'proud tradition of offering sanctuary to those who are fleeing injustice and wrong'. But this tradition of hospitality was now at risk – not from racism or an unwillingness to accept genuine refugees in Britain, but from a flawed asylum regime. The international system for dealing with refugees put in place by the 1951 Geneva Convention was no longer working effectively in a world of mass emigration – a view shared by the government. Hague claimed that up to 80 per cent of those claiming asylum had manifestly unfounded cases but few were speedily removed from the country. Furthermore, the asylum system was being abused by human trafficking and organised provision of false documents. But Hague also blamed the government for the pressure on the asylum system, attacking the cost and effectiveness of its policies. (Though at least some of the blame for the backlog of cases could be traced to a troubled contract to update the Immigration and Nationality Directorate computer system agreed by the Major government.)

The most draconian of the Conservative proposals on asylum was that all new applicants be detained in secure reception centres until their cases had been determined. Though costly, it was argued that detention would ensure that asylum seekers had access to support without the need for a voucher system and would make it easier for a new Removals Agency to deport those whose cases had been turned down. Decisions on asylum cases and the appeals process would be speeded up. A list of 'manifestly safe' countries (from where the cases of asylum seekers would normally be deemed unfounded) would be restored. Finally, the Conservatives would press the other signatories of the Dublin Convention – under which asylum seekers should be dealt with by the first safe country they reach – to implement the Convention.

This hard-line position was welcomed by the Tory right and by the (former) Tory press but liberal and One Nation Conservatives – including Steven Norris who as party vice-chairman was responsible for improving ethnic minority participation – were critical of the authoritarian nature of party policy and of Hague's populist rhetoric. Questions about the cost and practicality of housing all asylum applicants prompted speculation about a policy rethink, but Hague stuck at the general election by his position of detaining 'all new applicants for asylum, whether port applicants or in-country applicants, in reception centres until their cases have been heard'.[26] Widdecombe was also critical of Labour's proposals for changes to the migration system allowing more skilled workers to settle in the UK, claiming that the existing work permit system was sufficient.

In his most controversial speech, Hague warned the 2001 Conservative spring forum that Britain after a Labour second term would be a 'foreign land'.[27] The phrase did not appear in the section of the speech dealing with asylum (on which Hague said nothing new), but referred primarily to the abolition of sterling. The media, encouraged by Conservative spin doctors, did though connect the 'foreign land' warning with Conservative policy on asylum. The speech was widely condemned in the press; even the *Sun* dubbed it extremist. Asylum remained an important theme in the party's general election campaign – Hague and Widdecombe visited Dover – but Hague was reported to have vetoed an election broadcast focusing on the issue.

There were significant parallels between Margaret Thatcher's policy on immigration and that of Hague on asylum. Both criticised the existing migration regime and sought firmer rules limiting entry into the UK while claiming to be acting in the interests of Britain's ethnic minority community. Hague's populist rhetoric echoed that of Thatcher – both claimed to be pursuing a 'common sense' agenda that reflected the views of the British people, depicted Labour as a 'soft touch' and used phrases such as 'flooding'.

MULTIETHNIC BRITAIN

Hague stressed that the Conservatives were committed to an inclusive, tolerant society in which racism had no place, and praised the contributions ethnic minorities had made to British life. Campaigning in Bradford, he said:

> The fact that the United Kingdom is made up of different communities with a variety of different cultures and traditions greatly enriches our national life. Whatever our religious beliefs or ethnic background, I believe passionately that the United Kingdom belongs to us all. It has never mattered to me whether people are Muslim, Christian, Hindu, Sikh, Jewish, White, Black or Asian. As far as I am concerned we are all as British as each other.[28]

The Thatcher and Major governments had adopted a pragmatic, non-interventionist approach to race relations. Good race relations were best achieved through equality of opportunity in a meritocratic free market economy, backed up by existing anti-discrimination legislation. In tandem with this market liberal approach, however, many Conservatives held a cultural integrationist perspective in Conservative thought which believed that successful integration required that ethnic minorities accept the primacy of British values. Both strands of thought were evident during Hague's leadership. While recognising that Britain contained diverse cultures, Hague noted that Britain had a 'predominant national culture' and rejected the Parekh Report's suggestion that national identity be 're-imagined' as a 'community of communities' because 'Britishness has systematic racial connotations'.[29]

The Conservatives initially welcomed the Macpherson Report into the handling of the Stephen Lawrence case by the Metropolitan Police and for the most part backed the action proposed by the government, including the 2000 Race Relations (Amendment) Bill. The leadership accepted the Report's definition of 'institutional racism' but was concerned that it would undermine the police.[30] But in December 2000, Hague claimed that the Report had 'contributed directly to a collapse of police morale and recruitment and has led to a crisis on our streets' with street crime increasing as the police shied away from 'stop and search'.[31]

'RACE' AND THE CONSERVATIVE PARTY

Since the late 1970s, the Conservative Party has tried to increase its black and Asian membership and attract greater ethnic minority electoral support. Hague followed Major in pledging to increase party membership from ethnic minorities and boost the number of black and Asian Conservative candidates. He established a Cultural Unit (replacing the One Nation Forum) to increase ethnic minority participation, change attitudes in the party and offer advice on multiculturalism. But its efforts brought only limited success. The Conservatives fielded sixteen candidates from ethnic minorities at the 2001 election (up from ten in 1997), but only one candidate, Shailesh Vara in Northampton South, was selected for a winnable seat and he was narrowly defeated.[32] Two Asian candidates – Bashir Khanbai and former MP Nirj Deva – were elected in the 1999 European parliamentary election. But Andrew Lansley and John Bercow (a former Monday Club member) recognised that not enough had been done to promote ethnic minority candidates and tackle racism in the party.[33]

Major had courted ethnic minority votes, particularly those of middle-class Asian voters who were said to share Conservative values of enterprise and authority. Although this strategy was of dubious merit, the party won some 25 per cent of the British Asian vote in 1997.[34] Hague told an audience of British Muslims that:

> We can all share the emphasis that members of the Muslim community place on enterprise, on hard work, on education, on respect for others, on standing up for what is right, on carrying out our obligations to others, on the importance to society of marriage and the family, of community and tradition, and, through your religion, the need for a spiritual dimension to our lives.[35]

The prospect of greater ethnic minority support has been adversely affected by the persistence of cultural conservative views on the Tory right and the negative experiences of potential black and Asian candidates.[36] The anti-immigration nationalist wing of the party has been in retreat for some years, but was still able periodically to embarrass the leadership. The most damaging example occurred shortly before the 2001 election when retiring MP John Townend told a local association meeting that: 'our homogeneous

Anglo-Saxon society has been seriously undermined by the massive immigration – particularly Commonwealth immigration – that has taken place since the war'.[37]

Townend also blamed asylum seekers for rising crime and said that Enoch Powell's predictions about immigration had been proved right. Hague denounced the comments as 'wholly unacceptable'. The leaders of the main parties had meanwhile signed a Commission for Racial Equality (CRE) compact not to exploit race issues in the election. Michael Ancram sent a memo to Conservative parliamentary candidates warning them to 'avoid using language which is likely to generate racial or religious hatred', but did not give clear guidance on whether they should individually sign the CRE compact. Although Hague had technically signed on behalf of his party, the CRE revealed that a number of Conservative MPs had refused to sign.

The controversy was fuelled when Townend wrote that 'the concept of a multicultural, multiethnic, multilingual society is a mistake and will inevitably cause great problems', then said that Robin Cook saw the British as a 'mongrel race'. This provoked a furious response from Lord Taylor of Warwick, a black life peer who experienced racism in the party when standing as parliamentary candidate for Cheltenham in 1992. Taylor accused Hague of weak leadership, demanded that Townend be expelled from the party and intimated that he might defect to Labour if action wasn't taken.[38] Hague belatedly forced Townend to apologise and withdraw his remarks or be expelled from the party, while Taylor was asked to confirm his loyalty. Eleven black and Asian candidates also signed an open letter, drawn up by Ancram, declaring that the Conservatives were an 'open and tolerant party' in which racism had no place. Thatcher warned that 'a multicultural society will never be a united society' during the election campaign but her comments did not attract much attention.[39]

There is little evidence to suggest that asylum policy brought electoral dividends. The Tories did not regain any seats in Kent where the pressures on the asylum system were particularly apparent. A Gallup poll taken shortly after the Townend affair gave the Conservatives only a narrow lead: 43 per cent identified them as the best party to handle the asylum issue compared to 36 per cent choosing Labour.[40] Other polls showed public concern about levels of immigration and support for tough action on asylum, but a lack of faith in the policies of either main party.[41] Conservative supporters were more likely to believe that Britain was a 'soft touch' on asylum and that there were too many immigrants in Britain.[42] But liberal attitudes on race relations and skilled migration were becoming more prevalent. Gallup reported that 73 per cent agreed that Britain was a 'multicultural, multiracial society' with 69 per cent believing this was a 'good thing', while Labour enjoyed a healthy 56–27 per cent lead over the Conservatives on race relations. This, together with Conservative divisions on race and the limited impact of its asylum message, allowed Labour to promote a positive message on race without suffering an electoral backlash.[43]

Conclusion

Two broad visions of British identity are evident in contemporary British political discourse. The first is a pluralist perspective on Britishness that emphasises the multinational character of the UK state and seeks an updated British identity. It supports constitutional reform, devolution, constructive engagement in the EU and government action to improve race relations. One Nation Conservatives embraced a similar vision in the 1970s, but this perspective is now most clearly associated with New Labour. The second is an authoritarian individualist perspective, primarily associated with That- cherite Conservatives, which views enterprise, individual liberty and state authority as the key attributes of British identity. It supports the Union but in seeking to safeguard parliamentary sovereignty and the constitutional status quo, has tended to treat the UK as a unitary state. The focus has now shifted to the 'English dimension' of devolution with authoritarian individ- ualists advocating English interests and identity. This is also a Euro-sceptic perspective: European integration is viewed as a threat to the nation state and national identity. The authoritarian individualist perspective does not prioritise cultural homogeneity like the old Tory right, but is wary of multiculturalism and holds that ethnic minorities should accept British values.

The trend in the Conservative politics of nationhood under Hague's leadership was clearly towards a stronger authoritarian individualist perspec- tive though there were limits to this. The party accused New Labour of undermining Britishness, adopted a firmer Euro-sceptic line by ruling out EMU entry for two Parliaments and calling for greater flexibility, and demanded 'English votes for English laws'. But Hague did not move as far in this direction as some on the Tory right would have liked – he did not rule out membership of the single currency as a matter of principle and did not support the creation of an English Parliament. The Conservatives also embraced parts of the pluralist perspective on Britishness. The party had to abandon its implacable opposition to devolution after the Scottish and Welsh referendums, and sought to develop a more pragmatic Unionism that accepted devolution in principle – though urging fairer treatment of England – and continued to make a positive case for the Union. Hague also recognised that Britain was a multiethnic society and that British identity should embrace cultural diversity, though concerns about the implications that multicultu- ralism may have upon shared values were also apparent.

The nation and nation state regained a central place in Conservative politics after the 1997 election defeat. However, each of the three core elements of an effective Conservative politics of nationhood – a coherent concept of the nation, effective use of patriotic discourse and a political strategy that offers an electorally attractive and politically viable defence of the nation state and national identity – posed difficult questions for the party. Firstly, the Conservatives have yet to address fully questions about the nature of Britishness, particularly the relationship between English and British identities, and the appropriate balance between cultural diversity and shared values. Secondly, the party found that its discourse of identity and patriotism lost some its potency as New Labour became more adept at employing the language of nationhood itself. Finally, the Conservatives need to consider the lessons of the failure of Hague's brand of patriotic politics. A populist Tory nationalist strategy built around Euro-scepticism, defence of English interests and a tough line on asylum did establish a distinctive, high-profile Conservative strategy, but it had little electoral appeal beyond the party's core support.

Notes

1 See P. Lynch, *The Politics of Nationhood: Sovereignty, Britishness and Conservative Politics* (London, Palgrave, 1999).
2 On Conservative statecraft, see J. Bulpitt, 'The discipline of the new democracy: Mrs Thatcher's domestic statecraft', *Political Studies*, 34:1 (1986) 19–39.
3 R. Scruton, 'In defence of the nation', in J. C. D. Clark (ed.), *Ideas and Politics in Modern Britain* (London, Macmillan, 1990), pp. 53–86.
4 CPC National Policy Group on the Constitution, *Strengthening the United Kingdom* (London, Conservative Political Centre, 1996), pp. 15–16.
5 W. Hague, 'Identity and the British way', speech to the Centre for Policy Studies, London, 19 January 1999.
6 D. Willetts, 'Who do we think we are?', speech to the Centre for Policy Studies, London, 8 October 1998. He outlined five features of British identity: individualism, a spirit of enterprise, social mobility, identification with the local and political institutions.
7 D. Willetts, *Modern Conservatism* (London, Penguin, 1992), p. 184.
8 Willetts, *Modern Conservatism*, p. 106.
9 W. Hague, 'The potential for Europe and the limits to union', speech to INSEAD Business School, Fontainebleau, 19 May 1998.
10 See M. Leonard. *Britain^TM. Renewing our Identity* (London, Demos, 1997).
11 G. Brown, 'Spectator/Allied Dunbar Lecture – Outward bound', *The Spectator*, 8 November 1997; G. Brown, 'This is the time to start building a greater Britain', *The Times*, 10 January 2000; T. Blair, 'Speech on Britishness', London, 28 March 2000; R. Cook, 'Celebrating Britishness', speech to the Centre for the Open Society, London, 19 April 2001.
12 W. Hague, 'Play the Scottish card', *Scotland on Sunday*, 4 March 2001.
13 W. Hague, 'Change and tradition: thinking creatively about devolution', speech to the Centre for Policy Studies, London, 24 February 1998.
14 W. Hague, 'Strengthening the Union after devolution', speech to the Centre for Policy Studies, London, 15 July 1999.
15 Hague, 'Strengthening the Union after devolution'.
16 Compare J. Barnes, *Federal Britain – No Longer Unthinkable?* (London, Centre for

Policy Studies, 1998) and S. Heffer, *Nor Shall my Sword. The Reinvention of England* (London, Weidenfeld & Nicolson, 1999).

17 T. Gorman, *A Parliament for England* (Cheltenham, This England Books, 1999). The Referendum (English Parliament) Bill, No. 9, 1997–98. The Second Reading Debate took place on 16 January 1998.

18 A. Sparrow, 'Big guns shoot down English Parliament', *Daily Telegraph*, 9 October 1998.

19 W. Hague, 'A Conservative view of constitutional change', speech at Magdalen College, Oxford, 13 November 2000.

20 'The Procedural Consequences of Devolution', Fourth Report of the House of Commons Procedure Committee 1998–99, HC 185.

21 See R. Masterman and R. Hazell, 'Devolution and Westminster', in A. Trench (ed.), *The State of the Nations: The Second Year of Devolution in the United Kingdom* (London, Constitution Unit, 2001), pp. 218–20.

22 J. Curtice and B. Seyd, 'Is devolution strengthening or weakening the UK?', in A. Park *et al.* (eds), *British Social Attitudes: The 18th Report* (London, Sage, 2001), pp. 227–44.

23 J. Curtice and A. Heath, 'Is the English lion about to roar? National identity after devolution', in R. Jowell *et al.* (eds), *British Social Attitudes. The 17th Report* (London, Sage, 2000), pp. 155–74.

24 Curtice and Heath, 'Is the English lion about to roar?', pp. 169–71.

25 W. Hague, 'Common sense on asylum seekers', speech to the Social Market Foundation, London, 18 April 2000.

26 P. Wintour, 'Tories retreat on asylum detentions', *Guardian*, 29 November 2000; W. Hague 'Conservatives will make Britain a safe haven for genuine refugees', speech at Dover, 18 May 2001.

27 W. Hague, 'The last chance election for Britain', speech to the Conservative Party Spring Forum, Harrogate, 4 March 2001.

28 W. Hague, 'We will renew Britain's civil society', speech in Bradford, 1 June 2001.

29 W. Hague, 'Why I am sick of the anti-British disease', *Daily Telegraph*, 13 October 2000; *The Future of Multi-Ethnic Britain* (London, Profile Books/The Runnymede Trust, 2000), Part One.

30 'The Stephen Lawrence Inquiry Report' ('The Macpherson Report'), Vol. 1 (London, HMSO, 1999) Cm 4262-I. The Report (para. 6.34) defined institutional racism as 'the collective failure of an organisation to provide an appropriate and professional service to people because of their colour, culture or ethnic origin. It can be seen or detected in processes, attitudes and behaviour which amount to discrimination through unwitting prejudice, ignorance, thoughtlessness and racist stereotyping which disadvantage ethnic minority people'.

31 W. Hague, 'Common sense on crime', speech to the Centre for Policy Studies, London, 14 December 2000. See also W. Hague, 'Where was Jack Straw when Damilola died?', *Sunday Telegraph*, 17 December 2000.

32 D. Butler and D. Kavanagh, *The British General Election of 2001* (London, Palgrave, 2002), pp. 197 and 191.

33 See the comments by A. Lansley in R. Sylvester and P. Johnston, 'Racism endemic in Tory party', *Daily Telegraph*, 3 September 2001; and by J. Bercow at the 2000 Conservative Party annual conference fringe meeting 'Being Blue and Black in an Inclusive Society', www.millenniumb.f9.co.uk/Tory_fringe2000.htm.

34 S. Saggar, 'A late, though not lost, opportunity: ethnic minority electors, party strategy and the Conservative Party', *Political Quarterly*, 69:2 (1998) 148–59.

35 Hague, 'We will renew Britain's civil society'.

36 On the latter, see R. Ali and C. O'Cinneide, *Our House? Race and Representation in British Politics* (London, Institute of Public Policy Research, 2002).

37 'We should have acted sooner – extracts from John Townend's speech', *Daily Telegraph*, 29 March 2001. Subsequent events are described in S. Walters, *Tory Wars. Conservatives in Crisis* (London, Politico's, 2001), pp. 146–63.

38 J. Taylor, 'The Conservative Party cannot contain Townend and people like me', *The Times*, 30 April 2001.

39 Walters, *Tory Wars*, pp. 174–9.

40 A. King, 'Voters support Hague's stand on immigration and asylum seekers', *Daily Telegraph*, 12 May 2001.

41 MORI poll in the *Mail on Sunday*, 7 January 2001, www.mori.com/polls/2001/ms010106.shtml; A. Travis, 'The way we see it', *The Guardian*, 21 May 2001. Here, ICM found that 51 per cent would support a 'green card' style system for economic migration to the UK.

42 MORI poll, 'Britain today – are we an intolerant nation?', 23 October 2000. www.mori.com/polls/2000/rd-july.shtml.

43 See S. Saggar, 'The race card, again', in P. Norris (ed.), *Britain Votes 2001* (Oxford, Oxford University Press, 2001), pp. 195–210.

11

The 2001 general election:
so, no change there then?

David Broughton

A week is a long time in politics, as former Prime Minister Harold Wilson once noted. A year can seem like an eternity, especially when a party makes negligible progress in advance of a second successive general election drubbing. To follow such a humiliation with an occasionally bitter and long drawn out leadership contest – in which one candidate calls the other an 'extremist',[1] and the other retorts by dubbing his opponent 'a right wing hanger and flogger'[2] – provides incontrovertible evidence of a party in turmoil.

For these reasons, amongst others considered elsewhere in this volume, the current state of the Conservative Party remains one of inherent and considerable interest as the party slowly mounts a recovery effort under Iain Duncan Smith. There appears, at last, to be a degree of recognition within the party leadership at least that the terrain of successful electoral politics in Britain has changed radically since the halcyon days for the party in the 1980s. With a very different terrain, the need for a very different route map inevitably arises. Duncan Smith will have to force through major changes in the way in which the Conservative Party presents itself to the electorate if he is to restore the party's credibility and reputation. In this task, he will need to show much more imagination and commitment to the process of substantive change than his predecessor, William Hague, who flirted with the requirements of the process but too briefly and too superficially.

The enforced retirement from public life of Margaret Thatcher in March 2002 provides Duncan Smith with a vital opportunity (denied to Hague) to move on by acknowledging the legacy of Thatcherism in the 1980s, but grappling simultaneously with the existence of a radically different socio-political context. Such a context has been shaped and sustained by the electoral success of the Labour Party in 1997 and 2001. The context has also been guided in practical terms by the instincts of Tony Blair as a leader in control both of his party and of the country at large, even if a lack of open enthusiasm for his efforts has increasingly characterised public perceptions. But this does not necessarily make the task of the opposition any easier.[3]

At the Conservative spring conference in March 2001, Hague had made his widely criticised 'foreign land' speech that seemed a tacit admission of impending electoral defeat, in its failure to make any attempt at widening Conservative Party support beyond its 'core'. Allegedly focusing upon the future relationship between Britain and Europe, the speech was instead widely interpreted as a coded pandering to Conservative loyalists on questions of asylum seekers and race.

In sharp contrast, Duncan Smith's speech at the 2002 spring conference attracted conditional and partial praise from some unlikely sources,[4] as a step in the right direction of setting out a broader, more inclusive Conservatism with a better chance of being effective in challenging the overall record in office of the second Blair administration.

This chapter will consider the second successive Conservative election defeat in 2001 in the light of the previous four years of the party attempting to adjust to the first landslide mauling of 1997. Given the striking similarities in outcome between the two elections of 1997 and 2001, it might be tempting to assume a case of 'no change'. In some ways, the task facing the new Conservative leader were indeed the same as those which confronted his predecessor, but Duncan Smith at least had more widespread willingness within the party to enact substantive change than Hague was ever able to muster. It was inevitably very difficult indeed for party activists and sympathisers to comprehend the Conservatives' rapid fall from political grace, when the party had largely dominated the British political landscape throughout the twentieth century.[5]

However, even given this more favourable context, the sheer electoral arithmetic and the unavoidable approach to re-gaining national power, based on a genuine re-appraisal of what the party stands for, is certainly similar both in magnitude and in the inherent difficulties involved in actually succeeding.

The 2001 general election

The raw statistics of the 2001 general election paint a stark picture of the parlous electoral state of the Conservative Party. Overall, the party made a net gain of just one seat (up from 165 to 166), gaining nine seats, but losing eight. In three of those nine gains, the Conservative majority is less than 1,000 votes.

Hague's position as leader was thus untenable, and he resigned the following morning. His exact target for net seat gains in order to stay on as party leader was never revealed, but it was widely felt to be a minimum of thirty net gains, with a hope of gaining roughly fifty seats.[6] Much more optimistic scenarios envisaged cutting Labour's 1997 overall majority of 179 in half, to somewhere between 70 and 100 seats.

The Conservatives in fact won 31.7 per cent of the vote, their second worst result since 1832, following on from the previous trough of 1997. The Labour–Conservative swing was 1.8 per cent in favour of the latter, but a national swing of 11.6 per cent was needed for Hague to ensure that he avoided the unfortunate fate of being only the second Conservative leader not to become Prime Minister.

Highly variable swing in particular key marginal seats further undermined the notion of uniform national swing. Whilst the Conservatives performed well in south Essex, regaining Romford from Labour with a swing of 9 per cent, smaller swings to the party only reduced Labour's majority rather than winning back the seat (as in Birmingham Perry Barr and Barking). In addition, Labour often performed relatively well in seats it had first won in 1997 such as Birmingham Edgbaston, Enfield Southgate and Harrow West. In seats which the party already held, the Conservative vote share rose by an average of 2.6 per cent but it only rose by 0.17 per cent in Labour-held seats. The Conservative vote actually fell by 0.15 per cent in seats held by the Liberal Democrats.[7]

In 1997, the Conservatives ended up with no seats in either Scotland or Wales. In 2001, they gained one seat in Scotland from the SNP (Galloway and Upper Nithsdale), although very narrowly with a majority of just seventy-four votes. The party still finished in overall fourth place in Scotland behind the Liberal Democrats for the first time. The Conservatives won 15.6 per cent of the vote in Scotland compared to 16.3 per cent for the Liberal Democrats. Once more, the Conservatives failed to win any seats in Wales, despite winning 21.0 per cent of the vote and remaining the second most popular party behind Labour (which won 48.6 per cent).

Table 11.1 The 2001 general election

Party	Vote		Change	Seats	
	2001 (%)	*1997 (%)*	*01–97 (%)*	*2001*	*1997*
Con.	31.7	30.7	+1.0	166	165 (+1)
Labour	40.7	43.2	−2.5	412	418 (−6)
Liberal Democrats	18.2	16.8	+1.4	52	46 (+6)
Others	9.4	10.3	−0.9	29	30 (−1)

Source: Adapted from Electoral Commission, *Election 2001. The Official Results* (London: Politico's Publishing, 2001).

The 2001 election outcome (see Table 11.1) effectively renders the Conservatives a party of rural, suburban, middle England, with a vote heavily concentrated in the south. Even here, though, in the main region of traditional Conservative electoral strength, Labour has made inroads since 1997 as a 'catch-all party'. In the north of England, the Conservatives failed to win any seats at all in cities such as Liverpool, Leeds, Sheffield and Newcastle.

The Conservatives remain the party of the professional classes, the self-employed, the elderly, homeowners and readers of the *Daily Mail, Daily Telegraph* and *The Times*. In addition, the largest Conservative vote gain in 2001 was amongst the unemployed, although this 'success' still only produced a vote share of 23 per cent within this particular category, still leaving a lead of 31 per cent for Labour.[8]

However, in a 'post-ideological' age marked by partisan and class dealignment, these figures do not provide any real comfort for the Conservatives because socio-economic background as a whole is no longer a major determinant of electoral choice. Instead, questions of overall policy competence, leader images and issue saliency are now assuming that role.

The 2001 defeat was the first time that the Conservative Party had suffered a second successive landslide. After the 1945 defeat, the party achieved a near miss in 1950 and its heavy defeat in 1966 was followed by immediate victory in 1970. Between 1992 and 2001, the party lost nearly 6 million votes (down to 8.3 million from 14 million), a trend reinforced by tactical voting by Liberal Democrat voters which remains, as in 1997, helpful to Labour in key marginal seats. The exact degree to which tactical voting affected the overall outcome of the election is disputed but it is generally agreed that, in 2001, tactical voting by Labour supporters enabled the Liberal Democrats to retain some of the seats they first won in 1997 while Liberal Democrat voters returned the favour for Labour to do the same.[9] The Conservative Party also simultaneously suffered from the workings of the first-past-the-post electoral system, as we shall see later on.

Given this outcome in 2001, and looking ahead to the next general election in 2005/6, the Conservatives will need a uniform national swing to them of at least 6.5 per cent. A swing of 9 per cent will make the Conservatives the largest party, but winning the next election will require a Labour-Conservative swing of 10.5 per cent to produce an overall Conservative majority of one seat: this is twice the size of any swing achieved in the post-war era. The Conservatives will require a 13 per cent lead in votes over Labour to form the next government.[10]

These results and predictions, stark as they are, should not have been such a surprise to many, since in the period between 1997 and 2001, the Conservative Party had suffered much more than simply at the ballot box. The party had also to confront a greater degree of organisational and strategic disarray in terms of dissension within the Shadow Cabinet, an increasing financial deficit, a decline in the level of party activism, falling membership figures and widespread press scepticism. In addition, the Conservatives made little progress in terms of the gender composition of the parliamentary party, with only fourteen of their 166 MPs (8.4 per cent) elected in 2001 being women. The party has no ethnic minority MPs. These statistics remain important in terms of any Conservative 'message' regarding its wish and claim to represent the whole of British society in a more inclusive way than in the recent past.

Given these simultaneous and very serious challenges, it was not surprising that the party made little ground in the opinion polls, although the rock-like stability in the party's poll rating over the four-year period from 1997 to 2001 is still utterly remarkable. In the period between May 1997 and April 2001, the Conservative opinion poll rating for vote intention ranged between 23 per cent and 36 per cent. This latter maximum is an exaggeration however. The rating was only attained for a very brief period in the autumn of 2000 during the protests against increases in fuel prices and the government's handling of the issue. More usually, over the four-year period, the Conservatives were stuck at around 30 per cent, although even this rating, mainly in the latter part of the period, represented an improvement on the first eighteen months of Hague's leadership when the party's national poll rating often panned out at about 28 per cent.[11]

In the election campaign polls of 2001, the Conservative vote range was still stuck between 28 and 33 per cent. Fully twenty-six out of thirty-two polls placed the Conservatives in the range 28–32 per cent and thirty out of thirty-two polls in the range 27–33 per cent.[12]

The recovery strategy of the Conservatives after 1997

Whilst hindsight is always a wonderful luxury, it was partially apparent, even at the time, that the Conservative leadership was unable to agree in crucial ways why they had crashed to such an electoral humiliation in 1997 and, in particular, what needed to be done to rebuild the party before the next election. The 1997 defeat was seen as a 'blip', one that could be put right four years later with renewed organisational effort and reforged party unity. The main lessons of the Labour Party's four successive election defeats between 1979 and 1992 in terms of policy renewal, pragmatic party leadership and a careful re-shaping of the party's image were ignored.

Under Hague's leadership, various forms of 'new' conservatism (a 'fresh start', 'common sense', 'caring', 'compassionate', 'kitchen table') were first floated rhetorically but then not followed through in detail. Towards the election campaign of 2001, populist policies on issues such as 'bogus' asylum seekers and tackling crime crowded out any serious and sustained attempt to take on the Labour government and its occupation of the political centre ground. As a strategy to secure the party's core, loyalist vote and to establish 'clear blue water' between the main parties, this may have made sense. As a strategy to increase the party's attraction to floating voters and those who were disaffected and distrustful of the party after eighteen years in power, it appeared to be an admission of inevitable defeat. The implicit basis for this approach was that there was a 'silent majority' of voters simply waiting for and wanting to be mobilised by right-wing populism. The empirical evidence underpinning this assumption was never produced.

Regardless of any policy renewal and development, Hague's immediate task was to rebuild unity within a party still scarred by recent memories of the seemingly endemic party dissent over European integration under John Major which almost became a defining feature of his government.[13] The common assumption is that divided parties do not win elections. Hague seemed to accept this concern but he did not find the means to deal with it. Internal referenda on policy might give the impression of party unity but, on the key policy question, Hague was not master in his own house.[14] The 'European issue' was not going to be confronted until the Blair government held a referendum on membership of the euro. Until then, virtually any mention of 'Europe' inevitably harked back in the minds of the voters to the Major days of repeated turbulence and ever-increasing exasperation, a febrile condition dominating the party to such an extent that it contributed considerably to the 1997 landslide election defeat.

Mid-term elections, 1997–2001

Throughout his leadership of the party, Hague anxiously sought 'proof' that his overall strategy for recovery was working in terms of interim election results and opinion poll ratings. As mentioned earlier, the latter showed no evidence whatsoever of success (and they were thus routinely dismissed as not being 'real'). The former source of empirical evidence of potential Conservative recovery was patchy and unclear in terms of its political significance.

The Labour government under Blair did not lose a single by-election of the fifteen head-to-head contests between the main two parties during the 1997–2001 Parliament. In addition, the Conservatives contrived to lose the seat of Romsey in Hampshire to the Liberal Democrats in a by-election held in May 2000. Although the Conservative vote only decreased by 4.0 per cent – not in itself enough to lose the seat – compared to the 1997 general election, the collapse in the Labour vote by nearly 15 per cent via tactical voting was enough for the Liberal Democrats to win. As a reliable sign of things to come, the Conservatives managing to lose a safe seat in the mid-term of a Labour government was hard to beat.

The Conservatives were also hammered by the Liberal Democrats in the re-run general election contest in Winchester in November 1997. The Liberal Democrat share of the vote rose from 42.1 per cent to 68.0 per cent between May and November 1997. Even the return of Michael Portillo to the House of Commons after winning the by-election in Kensington and Chelsea in November 1999 was to prove a double-edged sword for Hague in terms of forging a good working relationship with a supposed leadership rival, someone deemed to have the backing of important sections of the Conservative Party.

In his constant search for evidence that the Conservative Party was on the mend, Hague latched quickly on to the outcome of the elections to the European Parliament (EP) held in June 1999, claiming that the Conservatives had 'won' the election. He presumably meant that the Conservatives had won more seats than Labour since no government is formed as the result of European Parliament elections. The Conservatives won thirty-six seats compared to twenty-nine for Labour and this did indeed contrast sharply with the outcome of the previous EP election in 1994 (Labour sixty-two, Conservatives nineteen). However, the 1999 EP election turnout was a pitiful 24 per cent, much more an indication of voter apathy and alienation than of renewed support for the Conservatives. The 'success' of the Conservatives in the EP election was at least partly related to the introduction of a closed list system of proportional representation rather than the first-past-the-post electoral system used for Westminster elections. This had also proved important for ensuring Conservative representation in the Scottish Parliament and Welsh Assembly.

In local elections, the overall picture for the Conservative Party was one of a quiet and modest advance, with net gains in terms of council control and seats recorded each year between 1998 and 2001. At the end of the Parliament, however, the party had a majority in only ten of the thirty-four shire counties, and they controlled no local authorities at all in either Scotland or Wales. In England, the Conservatives controlled only ninety-six of the 380 local authorities, mainly in the small towns, suburbs or rural areas.[15]

The official Conservative candidate, Steve Norris, came second to the independent candidate, Ken Livingstone, in the election to be the mayor of London held in May 2000. Norris succeeded in pushing the official Labour candidate, Frank Dobson, into third place, winning 27 per cent of the vote compared to 38 per cent for Livingstone. In addition, the Conservatives won the same number of seats on the Greater London Authority as Labour (both winning nine seats).

The main lesson of all these interim elections was that the Conservatives could still perform well, if erratically, at sub-national, supra-national and 'second-order' elections of various types. However, given the fact that these elections are often marked by very low turnout, interpreting their outcomes as evidence of a likely recovery of the party in elections to Westminster, with national power at stake, was unduly complacent and wishfully over-optimistic.

William Hague's opinion poll ratings

The Conservative Party was bound to fight the next national election with Hague as its leader, given that he had only been at the helm for four years since succeeding Major. The problem for the party was therefore how best to create a credible 'narrative' around Hague's strengths and how best to deal

Table 11.2 William Hague as (i) Leader of the Opposition and (ii) the best person for Prime Minister

	(i)	*(ii)*
Period when average rating measured		
1997 (July–December)	−18	10
1998	−28	12
1999	−26	14
2000	−22	20
2001 (January–April)	−29	19

Note: The data in column (i) are the net score of positive minus negative responses to the question, 'do you think that Mr Hague is or is not proving a good leader of the Conservative Party?'. The data in column (ii) are the percentage of the respective sample respondents who chose Hague as the best Prime Minister.
Sources: *British Elections and Parties Review*, 1998, 1999, 2000, 2001 (published by Frank Cass). Original data published in the monthly 'Gallup Political and Economic Index', or Gallup 'snapshot' polls.

with the widespread concerns regarding his image. Hague's debating strengths at Prime Minister's Question Time in the House of Commons were noted and often applauded within the confines of the 'Westminster village' but they made little impact with the voters where it mattered most. Blair's predictable refusal to agree to a television debate with Hague (probably also including Charles Kennedy, the leader of the Liberal Democrats) on television during the election campaign, despite the argument that such a debate might stimulate turnout at the election, effectively neutralised one of Hague's acknowledged strengths.

The available polling evidence asking about perceptions as to whether Hague was doing a good job as the Conservative Party leader or how he fared in terms of evaluating the best Prime Minister told a story of persistent weakness rather than strength.

The satisfaction ratings of Hague from the time he took over as Conservative leader were virtually always negative throughout the Parliament. His 'honeymoon period' as leader lasted for precisely three months (with ratings of +3, 0 and −2 between July and September 1997) but after that, his rating was always heavily negative, reaching a lowpoint of −40 in October 1997. After that, his rating settled at a range of −11 to −29 in 1998, between −21 to −36 in 1999, between −10 to −37 in 2000 and between −27 to −31 in the first four months of 2001 (the annual averages for this particular indicator are shown in Table 11.2).

Hague's 'best' period was around the time of the fuel crisis of September 2000, with ratings of −10 in July and −14 in August. For most of the overall period, he made little impression against a Prime Minister chalking up satisfaction ratings of between +30 and +40. Even when Blair's rating slipped dramatically, becoming mildly negative for six months from July 2000 onwards, Hague was unable to exploit the rare opportunity. Blair's rating recovered slightly to enter the election campaign just about positive, but Hague's rating had slipped back again to −29 as the formal election campaign got under way.

These feelings of satisfaction or otherwise about the party leaders also fed through into perceptions as to which party leader would make the best Prime Minister. The percentage of respondents who chose Hague as the best Prime Minister is shown in the second column of Table 11.2. Blair's dominance is very apparent here as well, with the incumbent often winning the support of between 50–60 per cent of the sample. This preference dipped somewhat in late 2000 but, even then, Blair remained the choice as best Prime Minister of 40 per cent of the voters. This period also saw Hague's highest popularity rating but he was unable to chalk up more than a maximum preference of 24 per cent.

We can also 'unpack' the available data to note the particular problems that Hague took into the election campaign. Table 11.3 gives a general insight into the mix of personality and policies affecting the performance of any party leader. There appeared to be 'deficits' on both aspects, with fully 37 per cent saying that they neither liked Hague as a person nor his policies. In contrast, only 25 per cent gave this response for Blair. Whilst 34 per cent liked both Blair as a person and his policies, only 15 per cent said the same regarding Hague. Even after nearly four years as Conservative leader, 17 per cent still had no opinion about Hague.

Table 11.3 Views on William Hague (%, January 2001)

I like him and I like his policies	15
I like him but I dislike his policies	15
I dislike him but I like his policies	16
I dislike him and I dislike his policies	37
No opinion	17

Source: www.mori.com/polls/2001/t010122.shtml.

More specifically, MORI offered its respondents a list of both favourable and unfavourable things said about politicians and asked them to pick the ones they felt best fitted the party leaders. The percentage scores for William Hague are shown in Table 11.4. The first column contains data from April 2001 and the second the results from the same question back in October 1997.

Hague scored best on 'being patriotic' and as someone who 'understands the problems facing Britain' but he was also regarded as 'inexperienced', 'out of touch with ordinary people' and 'rather narrow minded'. In contrast, Blair

Table 11.4 Perceived attributes of William Hague (%) April 2001 and October 1997

	April 2001	*October 1997*
Rather inexperienced	33	(52)
Out of touch with ordinary people	28	(29)
Rather narrow minded	24	(16)
Tends to talk down to people	23	(21)
Patriotic	21	(18)
Understands the problems facing Britain	17	(10)
A capable leader	12	(9)
Good in a crisis	6	(3)
Has got a lot of personality	5	(5)
Has sound judgement	5	(5)

Source: 2001 – www.mori.com/polls/2001/t010424.shtml. 1997 – P. Cowley and S. Quayle, ' The Conservatives: Running on the Spot', in A. Geddes and J. Tonge (eds), *Labour's Second Landslide: The British General Election 2001* (Manchester, Manchester University Press, 2002), p. 59.

was seen as 'a capable leader' (33 per cent) and as someone who 'understands the problems facing Britain' (25 per cent). In terms of negative attributes, Blair was also regarded as someone who 'tends to talks down to people' (25 per cent) and who is 'out of touch with ordinary people' (36 per cent).

It is always easiest to blame the messenger and to assume that the party leader is a significant influence on how people vote. The debate over 'leader effects' is largely a question of which came first: did voters like Hague because they support the Conservative Party or did they support the Conservative Party because they like Hague? Untangling this web of politically relevant attitudes and opinions is always complex.

For most voters, this particular web will encompass a range of judgements and evaluations relating to their social background, general partisan views based on party identification, retrospective evaluations of the incumbent government's performance, prospective evaluations of the different parties (both government and opposition), evaluations of specific leadership traits and, finally, overall evaluations of the various parties and their leaders. Anthony King lists twenty-six personal attributes that might have a bearing on voting decisions.[16] Actual and potential effectiveness in political office are often seen as being more important than likeability as a human being, the qualities the voters would prefer to perceive in a Prime Minister rather than in their next-door neighbour.

These various influences inevitably interact and overlap with one another in a continuous and dynamic process of evaluation to such an extent that it is especially problematic to ascribe to any *single* influence the predominant role in voter decision-making. Most recent research on this theme suggests there is little direct impact of leaders and their personalities on electoral choice that is net of values, policy preferences and assessments of the state of the economy.[17]

In terms of coverage in the campaign itself, Blair appeared in 35.4 per cent of election news items and Hague in 26.4 per cent, a considerably wider gap than between Major and Blair in 1997 (34.1 per cent against 35.5 per cent). The 'lead' of Blair in 2001 was particularly apparent in the press. The overall campaign in 2001 was seen as being 'presidentialised', post-partisan and narrow in focus.[18]

The 2001 general election campaign

For some commentators, the Conservative election campaign of 2001 was partially successful so far as it went, from an admittedly low level of expectations, but it was one ultimately fought on the wrong issues and the wrong overall agenda.[19] Concentrating upon issues such as the euro and 'saving the pound', asylum seekers, tax cuts and crime, and not upon public services such as schools and hospitals, represented a sustained misperception by the party of the attitudes and priorities of the electorate. The data in Table 11.5 show clearly that the voters thought the state of the public services was the most important issue in the months immediately prior to the 2001 election.

Table 11.5 Issue saliency at the 2001 general election (%)

	NHS	*Education*	*Law and Order*	*EU*	*Unemployment*
January	50	32	30	21	12
February	48	37	25	23	12
March	37	29	16	17	10
April	41	32	19	14	12

Note: The percentages in the table total more than 100 per cent because the data are a combination of more than one answer (the most important issue and then other important issues).
Source: www.mori.com/polls/trends/issues.shtml.

One very interesting omission from the top of the list of most important issues is the overall state of the economy. On average, only 10 per cent chose this as the most important issue. This is ample testimony to widespread perceptions that Labour Chancellor Gordon Brown had managed the economy assiduously and competently in their first term of office. This is borne out by the finding that Labour was seen as having the best policy for managing the economy by 44 per cent to the Conservative rating of 18 per cent.

Not only were the Conservatives choosing to emphasise the 'wrong' issues based on the views of the voters, they were also not seen as the party with the best policies on the issues that voters cared about most (see Table 11.6). In terms of health care and education, the two issues deemed to be most important, Labour was seen as the best party by a long way – as it was on managing the economy.

The issues on which the Conservatives were seen as the best party, were all relatively 'low salience' issues compared to questions of the state of public services. The question of Europe and the euro, for example, had been effectively neutralised for many voters by the government promise to hold a referendum before any possible entry to the single currency. The Conservatives were seen as the best party very narrowly on defence policy/foreign affairs (26 per cent to 25 per cent for Labour) but this was seen as an important issue by only an average of 4 per cent of the voters in the lead-up to the election campaign.

Table 11.6 Best party policy on problems facing Britain today (%, February 2001)

	Con.	Lab.	LD	None	Don't know
Healthcare	14	42	7	11	24
Education	17	44	8	7	23
Law and Order	26	30	5	11	27
EU	26	27	5	9	31
Unemployment	12	48	2	11	26

Source: www.mori.com/polls/2001/t010220.shtml.

In addition to emphasising the wrong issues and not having the best policies on the issues which the voters cared about most, the Conservatives were equally unable to make a variety of sleaze and incompetence charges against the government stick. There was a wide choice of possible foci here: the foot and mouth crisis delaying the election by a month, the continuing expenditure on the Millennium Dome, the underlying issues which had sparked the anger of the fuel protesters in the autumn of 2000, and the mobilisation potential of the Countryside Alliance in terms of Labour's stated intention to ban hunting with hounds. It should equally not have been too onerous to home in on a variety of more minor examples which showed the Blair administration at its worst, exuding a general air of smugness and an instinctive preference for extensive, if occasionally unsure, control of the overall political process.

Instead, the Conservatives seemed to believe that more and more effort should be targeted at less and less of the electorate. They never did find an overarching theme for their 2001 campaign. This failure contrasts sharply with Mrs Thatcher's clear-sighted depiction of her 'enemies of choice' such as the trade unions within a context of a Labour Party flirting with electoral suicide. Hague had none of these options available to him with which he could position and structure his campaign on a much firmer foundation. Instead, he concentrated upon the less credible, less important issues that did not resonate with the British voters.

This is not to say that Labour was overwhelmingly popular. Its 2001 vote share of 41 per cent was hardly a ringing endorsement of the achievements in its first term and a turnout crashing to below 60 per cent does not merit the description of a 'culture of contentment'. The main problem the Conservatives faced was not that Labour was fireproof and backed enthusiastically by the electorate. It was that their campaign missed the essential point of changing voter priorities and they did not manage to dispel the uneasy feeling that they would do even worse than Labour if re-elected. Evidently a second term in the electoral wilderness was needed before the Conservatives could hope to be trusted with national office again.

It seems unlikely that the four-week formal election campaign changed many votes, particularly in terms of the overall outcome. The Liberal Democrats were often seen as having run the 'best' campaign in terms of their focus on public services and 'honest taxation'.[20] Overall leader perceptions or the specific events of the election campaign did not appear to change much either. The main reasons for the 2001 election result lay further back in time than Hague's election as party leader. Arguably, the 2001 election campaign was more about the state of the Conservatives than the achievements of the government.

The Conservatives were regarded as having fought the campaign as the opposition rather than as a government in waiting in that they were reported by the media as attacking their opponents' policies nearly twice as frequently and presenting their own policies roughly half as frequently as Labour. The Conservatives were also twice as often reported as presenting policies in the context of internal disputes within the party.[21]

The chaotic memories of the Major years remained too sharp for many to seriously contemplate supporting a party that continued to labour under the disadvantages derived from such deep-seated and seemingly intractable conflicts between 1990 and 1997. Appealing to voters towards the end of the 2001 campaign to reduce Blair's impending landslide majority was utterly typical of the Conservative Party's defeatist strategy rooted in implicit acknowledgement of severe weaknesses within the party. There were a number of good reasons for not voting for Blair a second time in 2001 but there were no compelling reasons at all for voting Conservative.

The workings of the electoral system

If the above problems and challenges were not enough for the Conservatives, we must also look at the ways in which the party is disadvantaged electorally by the workings of the first-past-the post electoral system which the party continues to defend stoutly for elections to the House of Commons. At the 2001 election, Labour won 41 per cent of the votes but 63 per cent of the seats, whilst the Conservatives won 32 per cent of the votes but only 25 per cent of the seats. The Liberal Democrats won 18 per cent and 8 per cent respectively.

There are two main reasons for this bias towards Labour, some of whose effects might be mitigated by changing the constituency boundaries in time for the next general election, but much of which will still remain.

Firstly, Labour benefits from winning seats that have smaller electorates and lower turnouts. Labour seats tend to be in the inner cities but the population drift to the suburbs and countryside, which should favour the Conservatives, is only taken into account intermittently with the periodic revision of the constituency boundaries. These boundaries are only reviewed at 8–12 year intervals, which means the data are often out-of-date when any boundary changes based on them are actually implemented. In addition, future projections of population growth are not taken into account. Both the 1997 and 2001 elections were fought on the basis of the 1991 electorates in England and the 1992 electorates in Scotland and Wales. Both Scotland and Wales also have more constituencies by law than they should have, purely in terms of population, and Labour's electoral strength in these two areas also works to the party's benefit.

Secondly, the increasing use of tactical voting has also benefited Labour. Anti-Conservative tactical voting by both Labour and Liberal Democrat voters has, in the last two general elections, ensured that both parties have retained seats they might well otherwise have lost back to the Conservatives. In 2001, the Conservatives only gained four of Labour's thirty most vulnerable seats, although they moved close in three others; in the remaining twenty-three seats, Labour moved even further ahead of the Conservatives. The Liberal Democrats lost only two of their eighteen most vulnerable seats to the Conservatives, whilst in two others, the Conservatives performed better than in 1997. In the remaining fourteen seats, the Liberal Democrat vote share increased even further.[22]

The combined effect of these two factors is that Labour, at the last three general elections, has gained a substantial 'seat bias' based on assumptions of equal vote shares producing an equal number of seats for each main party and the same lead in votes over the other main party in order to obtain an overall majority of seats. However, this is far from the case in reality. If both the Conservatives and Labour won 37.4 per cent of the vote, Labour would still have a lead of 140 seats. Even if the Conservatives had won a 9.3 per cent lead over Labour in 2001, they would still have been twenty-five seats short of an overall majority.[23] In 1992, the Conservatives were denied a comfortable majority due to this bias within the system. Instead, despite their record vote, they only achieved an overall majority of twenty-one, which was eventually whittled away to nothing through by-election losses – thus increasing the potential for serious backbench revolts, particularly on the issue of European integration.

In a close election, the possibility exists of the party winning the most votes not winning the most seats, thus opening up the current electoral system to further criticism regarding its 'unfairness'.

This seat bias may be reduced by the introduction of new constituency boundaries to take account of population movements and the number of seats in Scotland may equally be reduced. However, the degree of bias is not likely to be changed in any major way by these technical alterations if anti-Conservative tactical voting remains effective in key marginal seats, if Labour continues to chalk up above-average performances in the marginal constituencies it already holds, and if it also continues to draw benefit from unequally sized constituencies. In this context, the already enormous challenges facing the Conservatives at the next election are made substantially more difficult.

Conclusion

A few days before the 2001 general election, one unnamed senior Conservative suggested, on the basis of private canvassing evidence, that 'news from our target marginals is good. Forget predictions about Labour increasing its majority. We will make net gains.'[24] Two out of three predictions correct is certainly not a bad score but they were only correct at the utterly minimal and very pessimistic end of the scale of expectations. There were crumbs of comfort for the Conservatives in that they did not actually go backwards in 2001, but that represented scant and wholly inadequate reassurance for a party once instinctively sure of its inalienable and commanding role in shaping the contours of British politics.

The academic analyses published since the election have all swung much more towards varieties of the 'mountainous climb' metaphor than assessments founded on one 'last push' in four years time. For example, Butler and Kavanagh believe that any claims that the 2001 election outcome was not so bad for the Conservatives, in terms of providing a platform for the next election, require 'some heroic assumptions and the acceptance of questionable analogies'.[25] Norris and Lovenduski compare the belief that the 2001 election outcome for the Conservatives was not that bad to being similar to 'saying that the Titanic voyage was a success because a few people survived on life rafts'.[26]

Looking forward, Ivor Crewe has set out the six main options, which the Conservatives could adopt as their latest recovery strategy.[27] Firstly, the party could go down the road of economic Thatcherism, including more privatisation of areas such as welfare. However, this might lose more votes than it could gain.

Secondly, the party could adopt populist authoritarianism on cultural and citizenship issues such as the family, crime and asylum seekers. The danger here would be to divide the party once more on issues that are of limited issue saliency.

Thirdly, social libertarianism could be adopted in order to move to the left on cultural and citizenship issues akin to the position of Michael Portillo in his 2001 leadership campaign. The Conservative Party would become more liberal but such policies would only appeal to minorities in both the party and the country at large.

Fourthly, the party could adopt an agenda of constitutional reform. This would involve establishing an elected House of Lords, endorsing electoral reform and agreeing to grant further powers to the Scottish Parliament and the Welsh Assembly. This would have the advantage of reducing the present distance from the Liberal Democrats for potential electoral advantage and improved, if still wary, inter-party relationships. Reversing such long-held and stubbornly defended positions in terms of the structure of the British state would be seen by many in the party as too radical this side of another heavy election defeat in four years time.

Fifthly, the party could implement a U-turn on policy towards the euro, adopting a more neutral position akin to that of the government. This would certainly mark the party out as 'new' and 'pragmatic' but would also engender severe internal party divisions, exacerbating the already existing image amongst the voters of the Conservatives being a divided party.

Finally, the Conservatives could become the party of public services, by challenging Labour on its own territory and holding Blair to account on his promise to 'deliver'. This will certainly provide a lot of useful material with which to attack the Blair government, given the long time span needed to improve the quality of the public services. The main problem with this approach lies in establishing the credibility of the Conservatives in terms of being able to 'deliver' better than Labour and not, in the process, to alienate even more voters from the political process by indulging in a slanging match of statistics which sheds much more unfocused, intemperate heat than light. This broad approach is supported by Collings and Seldon who recommend that, 'the next Tory leader should spend the next four years saying, "Labour will not deliver its promises on health, education and transport"'.[28] It is an approach that Iain Duncan Smith seems to be adopting as well, concentrating more on actual output than precise mechanisms.

Duncan Smith's leadership of the party will be severely tested by the host of interrelated challenges we have considered in this chapter. In particular, how he tackles the legacy of Thatcherism and adapts the Conservative Party to the very changed circumstances in which he leads them will lie at the core of his task.[29] To a great extent, the Conservatives have still not really steadied themselves after the turbulent and profoundly divisive events of the Premiership of John Major in which the party's overall credibility, particularly in terms of a reputation for economic competence, was lost, its image severely tarnished and its policy direction buffeted and blown off course.

During this period, the Conservatives became largely defined in terms of negatives: 'boom and bust' economics and strongly associated with tax cuts, leading to cuts in public services, tags which Labour has managed to keep pinned to the Conservative Party breast ever since. Whilst we should always be sceptical of exaggerated claims of 'newness' in politics, the Conservative Party desperately needs a major overhaul in terms of its credibility and image. Proposing serious reform to the electoral system to Westminster would be one way of doing this. This would partly be related to party self-interest of course, as we explained earlier, and it would undoubtedly be met with widespread scepticism. But such a change would, if carried through, give some genuine substance to claims of being 'new', 'inclusive' and 'modern'.[30]

In the absence of such an admittedly radical approach to defining new policies, the Conservatives will inevitably be flirting with more electoral defeats. The structural disadvantages of their present unenviable electoral position are utterly stark, although being overtaken by the Liberal Democrats as the main opposition to Labour now seems much more unlikely than in the immediate aftermath of the 2001 election. Nevertheless, the Conservatives cannot ignore the obvious threats, to the extent that no change is no option.

The 'deficits' which the party currently faces can only be overcome by a renewed and thoroughgoing practical understanding that, for most ordinary voters in Britain, politics is an elemental process of only passing interest. For many electors, their key focus is upon a narrow range of simplified issues and personalities, mediated as broadly perceived 'performance' in opposition rather than a grasp of detailed policies.

New policies are certainly important and the 'devil', as always, will certainly lie in the detail. However, the main consideration for the Conservatives must be to ensure that the very likely increasing disenchantment with the Blair administration can be steadily converted into electoral support for a changed Conservative Party, by concentrating as much on the 'small' picture of everyday lives as the 'big picture' of policy development. This must also be a party whose credibility has been restored and which has instituted the indispensable changes soberly designed to lead the party firmly back on to the path where it re-discovers its 'ruthless, visceral appetite for power'.[31]

Notes

1 Duncan Smith describing Clarke because of the latter's views on Europe were at odds with those of most Conservative Party members. A. McElvoy, 'Iain Duncan Smith: extreme? I'll tell you what's extreme', *Independent on Sunday*, 29 July 2001.

2 Clarke describing Duncan Smith on the *Jimmy Young Show* on BBC Radio 2, reported in N. Watt, 'Clarke dismisses Tory rival as "hanger and flogger"', *Guardian*, 30 August 2001.

3 Stephen Bayley believes that 'we have no effective opposition, because there are no real beliefs for them to oppose', in N. Walsh, 'How was Blair's first term for you?', *Observer*, 6 May 2001. R. Skidelsky, 'Five years Labour', *Prospect*, May 2002, p. 22, characterised the Blair government as being, 'Britain's first truly representative government ... Its very mediocrity of language and ambition reflects the land it governs – a second-class country with a great past, a comfortable present, and modest prospects.'

4 A. Grice, 'New approach preaches power of being positive', *Independent*, 25 March 2002. Grice noted that 'Duncan Smith poses a far more dangerous threat to Tony Blair than Labour realises' and 'his unspun image is a deliberate contrast to Mr Blair and may prove popular with the voters if Mr Blair cannot stem the tide of public and party discontent'. Grice also noted the 'little or no flesh on the party's policy bones'.

5 Of the 111-year period 1886–1997, non-Conservative governments with parliamentary majorities had been in office for less than twenty years. A. Seldon, 'Thatcher's legacy distorts the Tory vision', *Financial Times*, 24 August 2001.

6 R. Shrimsley and B. Groom, 'Hague defiant as polls put Tory share of vote at 32%', *Financial Times*, 4 May 2001.

7 P. Norris, 'Apathetic landslide: the 2001 British general election', in P. Norris (ed.), *Britain Votes 2001* (Oxford: Oxford University Press, 2001), p. 13.

8 Data taken from www.mori.com/polls/2001/election.shtml.

9 J. Bartle, 'Why Labour won – again', in A. King (ed.), *Britain at the Polls, 2001* (New York, Chatham House Publishers, 2002), p. 195. See also I. Crewe, ' Things can only get worse for the Tories', *New Statesman*, 30 April 2001.

10 Norris, 'Apathetic landslide', p. 4.

11 See *British Elections and Parties Review*, 1998, 1999, 2000 (published by Frank Cass); data for 2001 calculated from *Elections, Public Opinion and Parties in Britain*, (EPOP) Newsletter and MORI polling data available on www.mori.com.

12 I. Crewe, 'The opinion polls: still biased to Labour', in Norris (ed.), *Britain Votes 2001*, p. 94.

13 D. Broughton, 'The limitations of likeability: the Major premiership and public opinion', in P. Dorey (ed.), *The Major Premiership: Politics and Policies Under John Major, 1990–97* (London, Macmillan, 1999), pp. 199–217.

14 P. Norton, 'The Conservative Party: is there anyone out there?', in King (ed.), *Britain at the Polls, 2001*, pp. 81–8.

15 D. Butler and D. Kavanagh, *The British General Election of 2001* (London, Palgrave, 2002), p. 15.

16 A. King, 'Do leaders' personalities really matter?', in A. King (ed.), *Leaders' Personalities and the Outcomes of Democratic Elections* (Oxford, Oxford University Press, 2002), p. 9.

17 J. Bartle and I. Crewe, 'The impact of party leaders in Britain: strong assumptions, weak evidence', in King (ed.), *Leaders' Personalities and the Outcomes of Democratic Elections*, pp. 70–95.

18 P. Golding and D. Deacon, 'An election that many watched but few enjoyed', *Guardian*, 12 June 2001.

19 R. Shrimsley, 'Looking Back on Election 2001', *Representation*, 38 (2001) 187–91; Butler and Kavanagh, *The British General Election of 2001*, p. 255.

20 Bartle, 'Why Labour won – again', p. 173.

21 Golding and Deacon, 'An election that many watched but few enjoyed'.

22 I. Crewe, 'A new political hegemony?', in King (ed.), *Britain at the Polls, 2001*, pp. 218–19.

23 J. Curtice, 'The electoral system: biased to Blair?', in Norris (ed.), *Britain Votes 2001*, p. 243.

24 D. Smith, 'Four years on, the Tories are just one point up in the polls', *Sunday Times*, 3 June 2001.

25 Butler and Kavanagh, *The British General Election of 2001*, p. 242.

26 P. Norris and J. Lovenduski, 'The iceberg and the Titanic: electoral defeat, policy moods and party change', paper presented to the annual conference of the Elections, Public Opinion and Parties (EPOP) specialist group, University of Sussex, September 2001.

27 Crewe, 'A new political hegemony?', pp. 221–4.

28 D. Collings and A. Seldon, 'Conservatives in opposition', in Norris (ed.), *Britain Votes 2001*, p. 72.

29 A comparison between the Conservative Party and *Fawlty Towers* makes the point neatly. The similarities between the two are based on 'faded gentility, a suspicion of foreigners and the continuing influence of a powerful and fearsomely coiffured woman', J. Guthrie, 'Putting humour into "Tory Towers"', *Financial Times*, 24 August 2001. Steve Norris was more blunt in describing the Conservatives as the 'nasty, exclusive, rather angry and backward-looking party', J. Ashley, 'The NS interview', *New Statesman*, 25 June 2001, p. 18.

30 Above all, as Chris Patten put it, the Conservatives under Duncan Smith must 'demonstrate that the Conservative Party isn't simply a wholly-owned subsidiary of the *Daily Telegraph*', quoted in C. Newman and P. Norman, 'Rightwing nature of top team angers Tory left', *Financial Times*, 15 September 2001.

31 D. Macintyre, 'Has the Conservative Party lost its appetite for power', *Independent*, 12 July 2001.

The reform of the Conservative Party

Lord Parkinson

When William Hague appeared on the platform at the 2001 Conservative Party conference, he was greeted by a wave of sympathy which extended far beyond the audience at Blackpool. This was more than the usual reaction to a plucky underdog: it was a well-deserved testimony to the dignity which had marked William's conduct since the 2001 general election. Perhaps the public had begun to appreciate some of William's qualities. The pity is that the truth dawned on most of them far too late.

As someone who witnessed at close hand William's courage and good humour during some of the darkest days the Conservative Party has known, I feel strongly that the disappointing result in June 2001 should be seen in its true context. When a defeated party chooses a new leader it is always tempting to write off the old regime and hope for better times ahead. But although I supported Iain Duncan Smith and wish him every good fortune for the next battle, I hope that he realises what a hard act he has to follow. The reality is that although the last fight ended badly, without William we would have been in no condition to fight at all.

William asked me to be his first Party Chairman before the final round of the leadership ballot, as part of his contingency planning. When he first contacted me on the telephone I was reluctant to get involved. I had many outside commitments, and as I pointed out I hardly knew him. But any doubts disappeared at our first meeting. I knew that it would be a pleasure to work with William. It was not just that he seemed to have an inexhaustible stock of good humour and optimism. More important, he knew what he wanted and he had the determination to see things through. Instead of having to boost his morale, in the early days I felt that it was almost necessary to curb his enthusiasm for the task ahead.

One of the first gatherings of party members I attended in my new capacity proved to me how difficult it was going to be to knock us back into shape. I arrived just in time to hear a prominent activist delivering a tirade of abuse against the parliamentary party. At the first conference after the 1997 general election the atmosphere was nearly as bad. I had suggested that as a demonstration of our joint determination to produce a united, democratic party, the Chairman of the 1922 Committee, Archie Hamilton, the Chairman of the National Union Executive, Robin Hodgson and Archie Norman, the Vice-Chairman of the party, should all speak in the debate on the Green Paper on reform, which I would wind up. When Archie Hamilton spoke, he was heckled by the audience. He was not troubled, raised himself to his full height of about six foot six inches and raised the volume of his voice. He was then heard by a more respectful, if not intimidated audience!

William had decided to make reform of the party the central plank of his leadership campaign. This was the right response to the grievances, real or imaginary, of our grass roots membership. The ballot to endorse his reform programme and his own position was the perfect way to stabilise the situation. Later he decided with my support to hold a similar ballot on his policy towards the single currency in the run up to the 1998 Conference. He proved to be right again, and the issue which had caused us so much trouble for so long was pretty well neutralised for the rest of the Parliament. Obviously a subject which arouses so much passion on both sides could not disappear entirely, but if anything William's tactics worked too well. As soon as something like peace was restored, people began to take it for granted. I doubt that any other leader, or any other policy, could have come so close to complete success, and this major achievement should not be forgotten now.

People also should remember the state of our finances after the 1997 general election. We were very near to bankruptcy, and the voluntary party was particularly exercised by our expenditure of £28 million during the 1997 election campaign. William offered full support for the difficult decisions I felt we had to take and this, coupled with his brave decision to appoint Michael Ashcroft as Party Treasurer, resulted in Iain Duncan Smith inheriting a much more healthy financial situation. Obviously we would have all preferred a substantial increase in party membership, and here William was unlucky. The temporary unpopularity of the party in the country, combined with a mood of apathy created by Labour's spin doctors, has made recruitment very difficult for all parties. It will take some time to hit the targets William set, but by aiming high he showed his confidence in the party he had supported since childhood, and in the ideas which have served this country so well. Even so, he left the party with a larger membership than either the Labour or Liberal Democrat parties (and possibly bigger than the pair put together if the truth were known).

Although there were a number of necessary and far-reaching reforms during my time at Central Office, in my view the most important was the replacement of the previous tripartite structure of the party with a single, unified system. In this volume, Richard Kelly has criticised the eventual composition of the Party Board on the grounds that it was insufficiently democratic. It may be true that we were unduly influenced by New Labour's example in some other respects, but there was nothing surprising in this. As Kelly himself notes, every party tends to look for organisational defects after a heavy defeat, and it is quite natural to see if anything can be learned from the winning side. But the Party Board was, in my view, a wholly appropriate response to the unique problems of the Conservative Party.

The old system tended to exaggerate existing tensions between the parliamentary party, the National Union, and Central Office. In the early days of my second spell as Chairman, I found that each section of the party was anxious to avoid its own responsibility by blaming everyone else. Having decided to get rid of institutional divisions, we had to ensure that the new body would represent the party as a whole. So we included representatives of the party in the House of Commons and the House of Lords; in Scotland and in Wales; in the European Parliament; in local government; and at Central Office. Obviously there also had to be a place for the Party Treasurer. In the *Blueprint for Change* we were imprecise about the number of Board members who would be elected, but at that stage we envisaged that it would be 'about half'. Yet given that twelve people who had to be on the Board *ex officio*, this would have resulted in an unwieldy body of twenty-four. So on further reflection we reduced the number of elected representatives to five out of the seventeen. But although the others are nominated, this hardly guarantees the leader an automatic majority. Many of the remaining twelve are themselves elected – like the Chairman of the 1922 Committee – and they represent interests which could be in conflict. Hopefully, since the various representatives now deliberate in the same room, a viable consensus will usually emerge. But I am convinced that the present composition of the Board ensures creative tension, where the old system caused destructive tension and the alternatives threatened deadlock. This has never been true of Labour's National Executive Committee, which has either been a rough house or a rubber stamp. At the first meeting of the Board I was able to canvass opinion around a single table – a refreshing change from the position I had experienced as Party Chairman between 1981 and 1983. From the Chairman's point of view it is a great advantage to feel that everyone is bound in by the decisions; but thanks to the reforms the voluntary party can be confident – for the first time – of having a meaningful role in the process of arriving at those decisions.

Kelly claims that the effect of the new Board was to 'nourish the party's top-down mentality', 'stifle grass-root initiatives' etc. I believe that this verdict can only rest on an unrealistic vision of how a political party can operate. Kelly does allow that the reforms as a whole have made party members feel that their voice counts for more. There might be a case for tinkering with the system of choosing the leader, but the principle of One Member One Vote is here to stay. The turnout in the ballot on the draft manifesto was indeed disappointing, and it may be the case that members will need time before they grow accustomed to the new situation. On the other hand, the ballots on the reform programme and on European policy produced a big response. William did his best to encourage participation, and he has introduced new fora for policy input. If the members do not take advantage of these opportunities they will only have themselves to blame. At the same time, it would be ludicrous if the party leader had responsibility without any power.

After the election William was prepared to admit that he had not convinced the public that he was a Prime Minister in waiting. I remain convinced that the election would have been broadly similar, whatever he had said or done. But a potential Prime Minister has to take many crucial decisions on his own initiative, and even if William did make occasional mistakes he never flinched under the burden imposed by his office.

We should also be grateful to William for having inspired a revival of our fortunes in local government. When he took over we had sunk below the Liberal Democrats and it looked as though the only way was down. Now we are the second party of local government and on the same day as the disappointing general election we took control of six county councils. This is an essential platform for a lasting recovery, an unmistakable sign that under William's leadership we were recovering the trust of the voters. Again, it seems that William has actually suffered from this. Seeing the green shoots spring up, some members of our party expected the whole garden suddenly to look rosy again. But it was absurd to think that we could overcome our negative image of 1997 overnight, or even in a single Parliament.

Perhaps the same was true of the situation in Parliament itself. Everyone agrees that William got the better of Tony Blair day after day. His skill in overcoming the disadvantages faced by any opposition leader on these occasions will have led some people to think that it was all rather easy. It makes me wonder what would have happened if the arithmetic in the Commons had been different. If only William could have displayed his talents in a debate where the government looked in danger of defeat. That, after all, was the position when Margaret Thatcher forged her reputation as a damaging debator back in the 1970s.

As it was, William's regular victories over Blair have been written off as meaningless. I could understand his decision to lay down the leadership after such a dispiriting election result. I did not agree with all of his decisions. At times I felt that he listened to people who lacked the necessary experience of political life, and some of his very early photo-opportunities were ill-advised. It would be a tragedy if his abilities are lost to the party, and I hope that he will return to play a prominent role in the future. What is remarkable is his total lack of bitterness and acrimony.

From values to policy: the Conservative challenge[1]

Andrew Lansley MP

In the wake of the 1997 election defeat, very few Conservatives spoke of the fear which gripped them: of a party which splits apart and consequently hands power to Labour for a generation. William Hague was elected leader for his youth and for a fresh start, undoubtedly because he had abundant talent, but not least because he was the candidate with the least number of enemies. This, as we have seen regularly, is the best predictive factor in recent Conservative leadership elections.

Two years later, in the local and European Parliament elections of 1999, the leap into the unknown which the Conservative Party had taken by abandoning all those who had been prominent in its preceding generation, appeared to be justified. In early 1999 a 35 per cent share of the vote in the European election was our target. We hit it. The campaign was fought on European issues. From a critical source of internal division two years before, Europe and the euro in particular, had been turned into a source of apparent electoral advantage. Solid diplomatic effort by Hague, Michael Howard and John Maples, as well as the strategic coup of the euro ballot of party members in 1998, delivered a party willing to see Europe form part of its attack and, given the press sympathy, it acquired resonance. As we have found before and since, if it seems to be working, the 'tea room' pundits keep their alternative 'strategies' to themselves.

So, now fast-forward the tape to mid-2001. The Conservative Party had convinced itself that the previous four years had been wasted. To defend the achievements of the preceding four years was to attract near-pariah status. Yet, two things are clear: first that compared to the threat in 1997, the party had been saved from schism and collapse; secondly, that the promise of 1999 had not been fulfilled. We need to recognise both.

The raw figures of 2001 offer scant comfort: no real increase in our total of seats: barely a percentage increase in our share of the vote. Yet if the parallel case was the Labour Party after 1979, we polled a better share of the vote than Labour did in either 1983 or 1987 and only one percentage point less than Labour polled in 1992. Over the four years, the Conservatives had won some 3,000 additional local council seats and had doubled their representation in the European Parliament. The kind of swing required to give the Conservative Party a plurality over Labour at the next election is not only possible but far from exceptional. It is, however, the current distribution of votes for seats – which delivers parliamentary seats far more efficiently in relation to votes for Labour than for the Conservatives – that presents the greater technical obstacle.

Will these challenges be met and overcome? The answer lies in whether we suffer the same fate as in the run-up to the 2001 election. It was not a matter of the campaign itself. Even Labour's professional campaigners have recognised that, from where we were in April 2001, we fought the campaign we had to. Issues of tax, law and order, and Europe were the only ones on which we enjoyed a comparative advantage, or nearly so, in relation to Labour. To fight a campaign focused on health and education would have been to fight on ground of Labour's choosing. Election campaigns – the last five weeks at most – can never be more than a contest to win the agenda of debate and, by focusing it on one's strengths, to allow the public's prejudices about the parties (positive or negative) to be activated. In 1992, we activated negative views of Labour on tax to dramatic effect. In 1997, Labour neutralised their negatives and focused the agenda on health and education. By the end of the 2001 campaign, public attention was again on health and negative perceptions of the Conservatives were re-activated. Helpfully, the Tory press and a significant number of prominent Conservatives contributed to the increasingly prevalent view that the only issues which mattered were health and education. Yet one can see that we had campaigned on public services earlier in 2001. Most of our expenditure on posters was on 'You paid the tax, so where are the nurses?' etc. It had no effect then on Labour's lead, nor would it have done during the four weeks of the campaign.

The lesson of this is: by early 2001, we were in no position to win. The issues which were better for us were not the ones which mattered most to voters, and we could not make them so. On the issues which did matter, and where Labour's past strengths had hardly diminished, we were not trusted – and trust is a vital ingredient for electoral success. (I well remember in 1991, how sure we were that Labour were not trusted and the Conservatives still were – pre-Black Wednesday – hence the 'You can't trust Labour' campaign in early 1992.)

It is axiomatic that elections are won in four years, not four weeks. So we proved again between 1997 and 2001 and, despite stabilising a party in decline, we were unable to gain the trust which would have unlocked gains in 2001. Why?

After 1997 we set out to change and renew the Conservative Party. To double our membership, with many more young people, involving the party membership directly in policy through, for example, policy ballots. To 'Listen to Britain' so we should never be out of touch again; to put public service reform, and health and education in particular, at the forefront of our policy renewal. The *Common Sense Revolution* in October 1999 had flagship policies on education ('free schools' and a Parents' Guarantee) and on health (the Patients' Guarantee). In October 2000, our party conference was introduced by a policy initiative on reform in our cities and a message of tolerance and inclusiveness.

These were right things to do *then*. It is right to be stressing the same policy objectives *now*, but we must not delude ourselves. Look at what happened before. After the party conference in 1999, we made progress in the public's mind for several weeks, then the Section 28 row, Shaun Woodward's defection and the Lord Archer debacle took over and by January 2000 we were worse off than ever. At the 2000 party conference our message of tolerance lasted three days until the row over zero tolerance of cannabis took over and internal division and intolerance was left as the enduring image of the party.

These are painful recollections, but they are necessary. Unity and discipline would have limited these problems, but we have to understand that what they demonstrated was that in a matter of moments, resurrected negative images of our party can undo the work of months of positive policy formulation.

By the time of the election campaign in 2001 we had literally hundreds of policies. The electorate hardly knew any of them. Many of our policy ideas had already been taken by Labour. We called for budget delegation to schools – Labour followed. We called for abandonment of school exclusions targets – Labour followed. We called for Partner Schools with a range of school providers – Labour followed with their City Academies. We called for the Patients' Guarantee – Labour offered the pledged time for cancer referral. We called for stand-alone surgical units – Labour followed. We called for waiting time targets – Labour followed. We called for a cull of health authorities – Labour followed.

It was never true to say that the Conservative Party under William Hague's leadership did not put health and education reform at the fore. We did. But the public believed otherwise, denying us trust and credibility on these issues. Labour could misrepresent us as committed to cuts and privatisation – and the electorate believed it.

In government, you are judged by what you do. In opposition, you are judged for who you are. From here to the next election, we have to tell the public who we are and what we stand for. We have to renew the image of the Conservative Party. We have to articulate consistently the values of Conservatism which reflect and reinforce that image. Then as opportunities arise and with a limited number of carefully chosen policy initiatives, we have to announce policies which consistently reflect and reinforce those values.

Let me start with image. We are like a major brand which has lost the confidence of its customers. Without stretching the analogy too far, perhaps we are like Marks and Spencer before its recent recovery: a declining number of loyal customers, some products seen as worth buying, but overall perceived as out of date, out of touch, and with products which just won't sell. Like Marks and Spencer, we have to win customers back through a new image and improved products. As yet, however, the act of buying into our brand is not seen as a positive, forward-looking, exciting statement of who you are.

New product lines are not the only answer. Quality in product design is necessary, but not sufficient. Renewing the brand's appeal is the only way; bringing the customer through the door is the only way. A brand with values which people identify with. We now have to bring voters through the door of the Conservative Party. We have to make membership of the Conservative Party an exciting option. We have to make being a Conservative a source of interest and respect. We have to make voting Conservative a positive statement of who we are and what we want from our lives.

These are hard truths about where the Conservatives are. We need to recognise our faults so that we can promote real change – that recognition is the prerequisite to a process of change. If we say there is nothing wrong, then each time intolerance emerges in our party it will say we are out of touch. As a key example, recognising our need to change does not diminish us – it says we live in the real world. Recognising the reality of discrimination in British society and in the Conservative Party does not change us – it is the only way to be acknowledged to be living in the real world, to achieve the tolerance and inclusiveness we need so much and which is the mark of democracy. We are fighting for democracy: the treatment of minorities is a mark and test of civilisation and democracy.

The issue of image should not be discussed in terms of personalities within the Conservative Party; the issue is the personality *of* the Conservative Party. So, to start with, when the public see the Conservative Party, they should see people with whom they can identify.

One senior colleague said to me that the need was for the Conservative Party to start liking itself again. Nonsense. We have never suffered from a lack of mutual liking. The issue is that those outside our party need to like us again, and to respect us. Not just the former Conservatives coming back. Our objective must be to reach out by the next election to the twenty-somethings and thirty-somethings who have never voted Conservative, but who – as they acquire interests and responsibilities – are thinking long-term about who represents them.

They will be like Chris and Debbie, the characters in the Conservative party political broadcasts before the 1999 European election – young, aspirational, interested in issues (but not much in politics), concerned, socially liberal, caring about schools, transport and local health services, but also sceptical about bureaucracy (especially European bureaucracy), and conscious of how much tax they pay and what it buys for them.

It means younger members speaking for the Conservative Party in public and in the media. The party should bring forward those in local government, including younger people, women and those from ethnic minorities who are better represented there than in Parliament. It means giving leadership to councillors who are tackling real-life issues; rebuilding our city organisations.

It means a new system for the selection of parliamentary candidates so that the Conservative parliamentary party after the next election has a large number of women MPs and a substantial number drawn from the ethnic minority communities. It means adopting equal opportunities policies inside the Conservative Party and in each Association. It means building a younger party and enabling networks of members to grow and recruit others. It means recreating the NHS Task Force and, with an education equivalent, creating networks of committed professionals who speak with credibility from a Conservative viewpoint.

But it means more than these important organisational changes. It means a break with the past. We don't have to denigrate past achievements in order to recognise that elections are fought about the future, not about the past. I detect that, even if our party resents any repudiation of the past, it is well recognised from the top–down that we have to live in the future and leave behind the past, including all its internal divisions.

For Labour, the break with the past was symbolically achieved through the abandonment of Clause IV. A new leader for Labour brought forward in Tony Blair someone who was, to all intents and purposes, a blank sheet of paper on which they could write. Labour's project was clear: new image, new values, then *some* new policies.

Of course, it is right to say that the Conservative Party shouldn't try to ape Labour. Our task is more complex. Conservatism has brand values which we should not abandon. We have to retain the positive values of our brand while creating a new perception of the party and its future.

One helpful way of thinking about who we are and our values is to approach it from the public's point of view. What do they want from a political party? In varying degrees, the public want three things: opportunity, security and hope in the future. We have to show how *our* values will offer these directly.

Conservatism is an organic political philosophy; it grows and changes. It has appeared in the recent past to be dominated by economic liberalism. That is not enough. We are also a party of social progress; of recognition of our responsibilities to others. We are the party of the British constitution, favouring pragmatic, tested and incremental change. The Conservatives are the party of freedom and the rule of law, seeing liberty as an ideal but recognising the need to constrain abuses to liberty. None of these are principles we need to abandon. However, these are all part of the philosophy of Conservatism that needs to be translated into values with which people can identify.

So let us be clear about those simple values: of freedom, of community, of security, of opportunity and of respect.

Freedom because it is at the heart of the Conservative Party's distinctive appeal, and setting people free is a value to which young people can respond. Freedom is the incentive; *community* the mechanism, distinct from the state and bureaucracy; *security* the result of offering protection to those most vulnerable in our community; *opportunity* our means of identifying with aspirational young people; and *respect* our means of showing that we are open to the cultures and lifestyle differences which are so much a part of our life in Britain today.

It is important to speak of our values consistently; not to chop and change. The mission of the Conservative Party is not changed annually. Our task in giving the people of Britain new opportunity, security and hope in the future is enduring and has to be restated, continually and consistently. Restating Conservative values implies structuring the continuing review of policy explicitly around these values:

For freedom, it means a policy of tax simplification and of the transfer of funding and control out of the state bureaucracy and into the hands of individuals and their families. It means challenging the growth of state bureaucracy and of 'political correctness' (which is not about respecting differences, but about patronising control of language and attitudes).

Community means the dismantling of central government control and direction and creating local agreements between local government, business organisations, community bodies, voluntary groups, charities, faith communities, committed to joint working and agreed local service design, including the diverse local design of how traditional central government services (such as benefit systems, health and education) are provided.

For security, it means big increases in local policing and commitments to health service standards. This is not just about choice but also about equity in health, so that there is no 'two nations' in health care. It also means effective welfare, through community institutions, for vulnerable people.

Opportunity means commitment to standards in education and to a focus on skills. It also means the opportunity for participation in further and higher education. This may mean, for example, recognising that if families or individuals meet their costs of maintenance in higher education, then the costs of tuition should be met by the taxpayer. Opportunity means providing real and substantial help to parents in looking after children, making real their choice of whether to look after young children at home or to go out to work.

Respect means not being colour-blind, but aware and active in designing services and policies in response to cultural differences, faith communities and lifestyle choices. It means stopping the gratuitous offence of treating gay couples as if theirs is a 'pretended' family relationship. It means reaching out to support development internationally and promoting an environmental agenda domestically and internationally.

All of these policy changes mean that we, like a modern newspaper, can continue to be Conservative at the front of the book, but we must have our own lifestyle sections – issues without politics: talking about real health and schooling issues, responding to the experiences of individuals in their own terms, open to change and new ideas.

We are as yet in the early stages of this Parliament. Indicative electoral movements have yet to come. As in 1999, they may flatter to deceive. Mid-term results, especially on a poor turnout, are generally an opportunity to register a protest against the government. These are not an accurate prediction for the outcome of a subsequent general election. Of greater significance are the 'foundation' measures, which indicate a change in image: for example, the extent to which a party is seen as trustworthy, in touch, to be trusted on the issues, and able to offer leadership.

It is always true that in the early stages of a Parliament, the opposition gets much less attention than towards an election so it is more difficult to secure the share of voice necessary to control the agenda. It is even more difficult both to use the media opportunities available to attack the government, whilst also ensuring that the positive definition of a changed party is heard and understood.

The necessity of repetition when in opposition is often ignored. The Conservative Party leadership since 2001 has not done so. It has understood that for the party's values to be understood, powerful 'counter-scheduling' is needed; that is, to behave in ways which are opposed to one's perceived image, thus attracting strong attention. The Conservative focus on the needs of the vulnerable in society are just such examples. They need to be reinforced and repeated. The changes in candidate selection, and extending the reach of the party, geographically and demographically, have to be seen through to truly substantive effect. Those in the Conservative Party, those who represent us, those who speak for us, must all be different and tell the story of change in our party. That story should be driven home by the party's specific positions on emblematic issues.

All of this has to happen by the middle of 2004. By that time, four things will have happened: first, the mid-term election results will create a higher level of election anticipation, raising the pace of the partisan contest, which will mean that Conservatives will increasingly be defined as 'not Labour'. Secondly, the space in which to establish a reformed Conservative image and values will be largely used up. Thirdly, the Conservative Party will have to have policies. They will succeed or fail not because of their intellectual rigour, still less on grounds of originality, but far more to the extent to which they are consistent with the Conservative message and a reformed image of who Conservatives are; and therefore carry credibility. But if the image and message has not been established, the policies will not succeed. Fourthly, the Conservatives will have to know whether or not they can seek to drive the election agenda towards public services, or tax, or law and order or even – if the euro referendum remains a 'will he, won't he?' mirage – towards European issues.

Time is our most precious asset. It should not be wasted. The reason to have a protracted policy review is not principally for fear of having policies which are ill-thought through or stolen by Labour, but to *use* that time, to achieve the reform of values and image which must precede policy presentation.

In the first year after the 2001 general election, the sense of disillusionment with Labour's lack of policy delivery strengthened greatly. The risks to Labour of economic reversal, higher taxes and rising interest rates mean the 'sheet anchor' of Labour performance could fail; and the disquiet at Labour's 'spin' has undermined the values on which its initial electoral appeal was based.

If this creates a decline in Labour support and, in particular, in trust in Tony Blair, then the opportunity is obvious for the Conservative Party. But it is there for the Liberal Democrats too. It is only if the Conservative Party, 'unspun', honest and trustworthy, reformed, representative and united, can articulate its distinctive values of freedom and respect, consistently expressed through policies which offer realistic prospects of successful delivery, that those opportunities can be realised in election success.

I heartily hope we will succeed in this. Labour's 'project' has failed to deliver – other than to give them access to power. It has not delivered for the British people and has left a public cynical and disillusioned about politics and politicians. Conservatives have to be as ruthless as Labour were in understanding the processes by which elections are won, but we must be wholly different from them in our approach to government. Extending freedom, in the context of a society which recognises the role of community, of interdependence, and of respect for diversity, is the centre right philosophy which is winning through in elections across the world – the Conservative Party can win too.

Notes

1 This chapter draws on 'Image, values and policy – from here to the next election', a speech to the Bow Group, Blackpool, 9 October 2001, published as a Bow Group Policy Brief, www.bowgroup.org/pub/lansley.pdf.

The Conservatives, 1997–2001: a party in crisis?

Ian Taylor MP [1]

Coming out of the worst election defeat since the Liberal landslide of 1906, there was a remarkable sense of optimism amongst Conservatives in the summer of 1997. People felt that the party could not go any lower; that the nadir of our misfortunes had been reached. The difficulties of the Blair government in its first few months created a feeling that it might not be long before we would return to government. John Major made this point in his conference speech that October: 'The tide will turn, perhaps more speedily than anyone imagines.' [2]

The election of William Hague as the new leader gave focus to this growing sense that the party was beginning its renewal. Bright, articulate, at thirty-six our youngest leader since the eighteenth century, Hague embodied the hopes of a party that desperately wanted to embrace a new generation of British voters. Yet, looking back, it is clear that the events of the 1997–2001 Parliament were a disaster for the Conservative Party.

Far from undergoing a great revival, the party slipped back further. Struggling to break the thirty percentage points barrier all through the Parliament, the result of the 2001 general election was technically an improvement on 1997 – it gained one seat overall and increased its share of the vote by one per cent – but in reality it was a catastrophic defeat far worse than 1997. The party may have gained nine seats but it had lost eight others. To fail to capitalise on Labour's poor performance in government was bad enough; to lose seats was an indication that the party, far from being renewed, had lost ground since 1997.

The aftermath of the attacks on the USA on 11 September 2001 distorted the first few months of Iain Duncan Smith's leadership.[3] The first leader elected by the whole Party and not just MPs, Duncan Smith had more time to attune himself to the demands of being Leader of the Opposition without the barrage of attacks he would have faced from other parties. When normal politics resumed in the spring of 2002, Duncan Smith was perceived to have made a solid start. His emphasis on 'helping the vulnerable' caught the Labour Party off guard and pleased the moderate wing of his own Party.

This renewed mission to regenerate the party begs the question: why did it all go wrong last time? What went wrong for Hague? After all, there was no doubting his intellectual and political ability; Hague had been singled out as one of the party's rising stars before he went to university.[4] The youngest Cabinet Minister since Harold Wilson, as a fresh face, and one not closely associated with the defeat of 1997, Hague seemed ideally placed to lead the party. As a non-ideological figure, not linked to the factional battles of the 1990s, he was in a good position to unite the party and lead its revival. Yet it did not happen.

A party without direction

Of all the problems facing the party in 1997, one was startlingly apparent. It was regarded by a large section of the electorate as harsh and uncaring. This was attributed to various factors including the public's perception that not only were Conservatives not committed to the improvement of public services but they were obsessed with further tax cuts. Labour was said to have the best policies on the top three issues of concern by an overwhelming margin in early 1997.[5] The vociferous denunciations of gays by some; perceptions of racism in the party; and a feeling that anti-Europeanism was a reflection of xenophobia rather of than an intellectual disagreement with the European Union, all made things worse. The right-wing image stemmed partly from the survey of 3,000 party members conducted in 1992. It found that 70 per cent of members believed that a future Conservative government should encourage the repatriation of immigrants; 69 per cent wanted to bring back the death penalty for murder and only 1 per cent described themselves as non-white.[6]

The alarming nature of this information and the result of the 1997 general election, galvanised Hague to address this lack of appeal. During the election campaign Tory candidates had been shocked at the level of hostility shown to the party. The fact that younger women felt particularly alienated from Conservatives was alarming to a party that depended on a veritable army of women workers to get out the vote, and had come to take for granted its lead over Labour amongst women voters.[7] Indeed, that lead over Labour amongst female voters was the reason why the party had won the 1992 general election.[8] This alienation from the electorate and the unrepresentative party membership was swiftly recognised by Hague. He said that the voters, 'decided that our party across the country had become unrepresentative of society at large and irrelevant'.[9]

This distance from the cares and concerns of ordinary voters was well reported by Rupert Morris. At the Benton Conservative Club on Tyneside, Morris found that women were not admitted as full members and jackets had to be worn at all times unless a green light came on above the bar to indicate that they could be removed.[10] The Tory Party had come to inhabit a world utterly remote from that where most voters resided.

Given that the 1992 survey had found that the average age of members was sixty-two and only 5 per cent were under thirty-five, Hague was brave to take on the more reactionary sections of the party.[11] He had always been liberally minded himself; as a junior minister Hague had been one of only forty-two Tory MPs to vote in 1994 for the equalisation of sexual consent at sixteen.

This reform agenda began with internal party matters – the crucial merger of the three separate parts of the party: MPs, volunteers (the National Union) and Central Office – was endorsed in principle by a ballot of members in September 1997. But it was also meant to encompass wider changes. Lord Freeman was brought in to advise on the reform of the candidates' selection procedure. Peta Buscombe, an Oxfordshire councillor with ambitions to get into Parliament, was appointed a party Vice Chairman with responsibility for developing more women candidates. A Cultural Unit was established inside Central Office to build bridges with ethnic communities. Hague himself admitted that what he was seeking was 'nothing short of a cultural revolution in the way this party conducts itself'.[12] It was ambitious but it was right.

Dr Jekyll and Mr Hague

It is now painfully obvious that this 'cultural revolution' may not have been as destructive as Chairman Mao's but it was no more successful in advancing reform. Of course, the structural changes needed to create a modern, integrated party were carried through. But despite promising to bring the three separate parts of the party together, the new constitution of June 1998 did not mention Conservative Central Office. Buscombe achieved her ambition to get into Parliament but as a life peer rather than an MP. Her career path seemed all too typical of that offered to prominent women in the party.

At the 2001 general election the party had no women candidates at all in Conservative-held seats where the sitting MP was retiring. Far from broadening our range of candidates, the modest reforms in the selection process did not prevent deeply damaging rows over selections in a number of constituencies. Simon Walters' book *Tory Wars*, exposes the way some activists were able to manipulate the selection procedure to exclude those they did not want. It must make painful reading for those who claimed that Hague was going to make the Tory Party more inclusive, show a greater professionalism and be more representative of society than we had been in the past.[13] In our candidate selection process, we achieved none of those things.

The desire to make the party more inclusive fared little better. Despite having previously voted for equalising the age of consent, Hague absented

himself from the debates when the issue returned to the Commons after the
1997 election. He might well have changed his view – and why not? But by
appearing to hide from the issue, he only raised the salience of it. Attitudes
to homosexuality are not the sole measure of a person's liberalism but by
appearing to change the party's position on the issue and then failing to
deliver, Hague raised and then dashed the expectations of supporters of a
more liberal approach. This apparent vacillation undermined his credibility
as leader.

More extraordinary was the handling of Section 28. This clause in local
government legislation banned the 'promotion' of homosexuality in schools
but was largely redundant because new provisions relating to sex education
in schools had superseded it. Astonishingly, the Shadow Cabinet decided to
continue support for Section 28 in a discussion lasting under two minutes
for which no policy papers had been tabled for consideration.[14] If it was felt
necessary to produce a consultation paper on future roads' policy, why did
we not take a similar approach on an issue that divided Conservatives and
gave us a bad press? Apart from anything else, such an open approach might
have prevented the loss of Shaun Woodward MP to Labour over the issue.
Woodward sought to get the leadership to change its approach but was
sacked from his post despite not having gone public with his objections to
the policy. Even if the party had continued with the same policy, an open
consultation process would have given supporters and critics alike the sense
that we were prepared to consider the issue seriously.

It appeared to many that Hague, faced with implacable hostility to his
'modernisation' of the party from some on the right and in the press, retreated
wholesale. The young liberal had become an old fogey. This was not wholly
fair; Hague had always been vocal in his support for the institution of the
family and he appears to have undergone a change of heart on equalising the
age of consent.[15] But an opportunity to take the party in a new and more
inclusive direction had been lost.

There was another aspect to inclusiveness that was important but was
evaded; the task of making the Conservative Party a welcoming place for all
who share the Tory tradition. The Woodward affair demonstrated a personal
intolerance on the part of Hague that shocked many people in the party.
Sacking someone from the frontbench by means of a message to his pager is
extraordinarily insensitive. Many of us began to sense that Hague's party
would prefer to shrink further rather than continue to house those with
different views. There was a process of purification going on in which those
who came from the One Nation tradition were the enemy – a sort of Tory
Bennism. Hague encouraged this atmosphere with his aggressive responses
to criticism. When twelve senior figures, including Chris Patten, signed a
letter calling for Britain to prepare for a single currency, Hague called them
'yesterday's men'.[16] When later there was talk of de-selecting pro-European

MPs, some people at the grass roots level clearly felt that they were doing the leader's bidding.

The absence of ideas

The difficulty was that the libertarian agenda Hague pursued and his attempts to reform the party were conceived in isolation from mainstream policy-making. This agenda was not followed through in a logical manner. Without a philosophical substructure on which fresh policies could be built, the party drifted intellectually. Hague's correct vision of a party that judged people by what they could do, not by what they are, could not stand on its own as the party's policy platform. It needed to be linked into a One Nation agenda that emphasised the restoration of public services and a greater sense of community.[17]

In October 2000 my parliamentary colleague Damian Green and I sought to establish the meaning of a One Nation agenda in the twenty-first century.[18] The argument that we deployed was that the party needed to stop sounding as if it believed that 'there is no such thing as society' and demonstrate that individual liberty was the building block of society and not an end in itself. The party had to focus on improving public services but before it could advance radical ideas for change, it had to convince the public that it genuinely believed in those services. This meant an end to disparaging remarks about public sector workers and to the centralising approach to public services. There needed to be a better balance between the responsibilities of individuals, family and the community. The social implications of taxation and economic policy needed to be articulated.

The publication of our paper was greeted with horror by some of Hague's advisers. Green, a junior frontbench spokesman at the time, was threatened with the sack for writing such treasonous material.[19] It is ironic indeed that the agenda that we set out has now largely been adopted, judging by Shadow Cabinet speeches, under Duncan Smith, and Green is now Shadow Education Secretary.

To his critics outside the party, Hague's focus on individual liberty suggested that the Conservatives were still orientated towards a 'me-first' culture that they associated with greed and selfishness. The party appeared (however unjustifiably) wedded to private affluence surrounded by public squalor. In short, the approach to ideas convinced few, with inevitable consequences for morale within the party and electoral support outside it.

The decision to replace the party's internal policy-making arm, the Conservative Political Centre (CPC), with something sounding almost the same but in reality with a lower profile, was accompanied by a virtual abandonment of the tradition of publishing policy papers. The CPC had produced a stream of policy papers on a variety of topics. Their authors were sometimes groups of MPs – such as the One Nation or the 'No Turning Back' groups – leading party figures or policy experts. The CPC may not have been the engine of a great Tory intellectual revival but involved the wider party in the ideas process and demonstrated that there was intellectual life in the party.

Europe: the Achilles Heel

'Divided parties don't win elections'. So wrote experienced pollster Bob Worcester in his account of the 1997 Labour landslide. Worcester noted that the number of electors thinking the Conservative Party divided had risen from 17 per cent in July 1992 to half of all voters a year later.[20] The cause of this dramatic reversal – only 14 per cent of electors had thought us divided at the 1992 election, compared to 24 per cent for Labour – was the issue of Europe.[21] Curiously, in one respect the public was not divided. They largely thought it a second-order issue. (I recognise that the public see it that way but, although I disagree with them, it is certainly not the only issue.) In February 1997, just 26 per cent of voters thought Europe the most important issue. In other words, three-quarters of voters didn't think it very important.[22]

It was obvious to Conservative MPs after 1997 that we could not go on with the divisions over Europe; they had almost destroyed the party. Two different factions emerged in the argument around how best to deal with the dispute; the leadership election ended with one of those factions triumphant. The decision by Kenneth Clarke and John Redwood to combine together for the final ballot of the leadership election was portrayed by many as an act of cynicism; a version of the Ribbentrop-Molotov Pact.[23] This was far from the truth. Both Clarke and Redwood knew all too well how profound their differences were over Europe but they also knew that what united them as Conservatives was greater than that which divided them. They had concluded that for the party to govern again, the two sides had to reach an accommodation with one another. Their 'deal' was an attempt to demonstrate that apparently warring factions could come together in the wider interests of the party. It was what ordinary party members had asked for. But it was not to be. Redwood was unable to deliver the votes of his former supporters as, led by Duncan Smith, they switched to Hague.

Hague won the leadership election on a clear platform on the European issue. He had stated that he would not take Britain into a single European currency for two parliaments and that all members of the Shadow Cabinet would have to support this policy.[24] Hague went further and actually declared that members of his frontbench team would have to sign a piece of paper stating their support for this policy. When this was raised at a meeting between Hague and members of the Positive European Group of MPs during the leadership election, his position was strongly attacked. When the leadership election was over, he had to retreat from his hardline position in order to put his Shadow Cabinet together. When I saw Hague and he offered me a post on the frontbench, I only agreed to serve on the condition that I was not expected to sign up to his single currency policy. He readily accepted that I could not be asked to do so.

Interestingly, in Chapter 8 Philip Lynch does not think that Hague's position was clear at the time of the leadership election and that this was one of the reasons why Michael Howard and Redwood stayed in the ballot. What was clear was that Hague was not going to allow a free vote for the whole party on the single currency issue, as Clarke had offered. His 'take it or leave it' approach might have been less damaging had the European question not come to dominate the party's policy agenda. I became sharply aware of the drift in thinking when I found it necessary to resign from the frontbench in October 1997. Hague had adopted the line after the leadership election that the party would not support joining the single currency 'for the foreseeable future'. This had the merit that it was vague and open to a variety of interpretations. For that reason, the policy came under attack from Euro-sceptics in the Shadow Cabinet who saw it as weak. At a heated meeting of the Shadow Cabinet on 23 October 1997, Hague sought to change the policy.[25] He succeeded in going back to the one he had called for in the leadership election: outright opposition in that Parliament and the next.

Hague attempted to deal with the European issue by saying, 'this is my policy: back it or else'. This was not an approach that could unite the party. Like it or not, the supporters of the single currency within the party were led by Clarke and Heseltine, two senior Conservatives highly respected by the public. They could not be ignored and attempts to marginalise them backfired. Hague's dismissive reference to them as 'retired Cabinet ministers' appeared childish and petulant. Hague clearly believed that strong leadership meant giving orders; the European issue was one that defined his authority as leader: 'this is a challenge my authority will survive'.[26]

I could not support this approach. Apart from anything else, I had been appointed to the frontbench on a different basis. I resigned on 29 October and so for the same reason did David Curry, the Shadow Minister for Agriculture four days later. The decision to abandon a compromise policy on the single currency and switch to an ideological one, was a harbinger of what was to come. It meant two things: firstly, no real attempt was to be made to unite the party on the key issue that divided it; and, secondly, that Europe was to play a more central role in the party's platform than was either politically necessary or electorally desirable. As I said in my resignation letter, I did not 'believe that hard line Euro-scepticism will be a basis for us to regain the trust of the electorate'.[27]

The next act in the seemingly never-ending European drama was the ballot of party members, called nearly a year after the Shadow Cabinet's

U-turn on the single currency. Although this was an opportunity for party members freely to express their views, it was self-evidently a motion of confidence in the leader; if William had lost it, he would undoubtedly have had to resign. It is hardly surprising that the leadership ran a ruthless campaign but this approach only raised tensions in the party.

When one party activist opposed to the ballot was summoned by his local Conservative association officers to justify his stance, he was astonished to find a senior Central Office official at the meeting who made various (false) allegations about his behaviour. The Party Chairman also dismissed Heseltine's reservations about holding such a ballot at short notice and without a real debate. Those who were unhappy at the outcome of the ballot, the Chairman said, clearly presuming that Hague would win, were the 'most arrogant of the old autocratic hierarchy'.[28] This hardly encouraged party members to unite behind the outcome of the ballot.

The margin of victory for the leadership was clear enough: 84.4 per cent of those who voted supported the new line. But in total, more members had either voted against or not voted at all. It was a hollow victory and the holding of the ballot, far from healing divisions, only made them wider. A pamphlet written by Geoffrey Howe, Heseltine, Clarke, Curry and myself and published the day of the result was dismissed as the 'last roar of the dinosaurs' by anonymous party sources.[29] Pro-Europeans noted the rough tactics used by some of William's supporters while those opposed to Britain ever joining the euro thought the policy a fudge.

The failure of our European policy was not that it reflected the majority view in the party – which was clearly intensely Euro-sceptic – but that it did so without proper debate or discussion. Hague had emphasised at the beginning of his leadership the need to be open to new ideas: 'we have to genuinely welcome new ideas'.[30] Except on Europe of course. The Shadow Cabinet took refuge behind opinion polls showing a majority against joining the single currency. Yet that reflected the fact that the government had not argued the case for the new currency and, anyway, some of the most important issues facing the European Union were not to do with the single currency. There was no recognition by the leadership that our policies isolated us from the bulk of the business community. Hague had promised to 'lead and to heal'; his European policy did not live up to that promise.

Hague's people

The stance on European policy pre-determined who would serve the new leadership. The effective exclusion of pro-Europeans confirmed divisions within the party, denied us the service of some our most talented MPs and gave the outside world a one-sided impression of the party. The essential failure was to construct a team of all the talents from across the party. Such an approach would have forced parliamentarians to work together in a constructive way. It would not have been without difficulties but it would have avoided some of the conflicts that resulted from the conscious parking on the backbench of colleagues whose talents were sorely missed from the front bench.

By basing himself at Central Office, Hague chose to isolate himself from his parliamentary colleagues. The practical reasons for the decision are obvious in an age when the House of Commons no longer feels as if it is the centre of national political debate. But switching to a media-focused strategy for communication always suffered from the weakness that Labour's slicker and larger machine could always outgun us and that Hague's own best performances were not on television. Our 'war room' never quite seemed to match Labour's. They had, after all, years of practice at operating through the media because they were not in control of the Commons. We were so used to working in isolated government departments, each operating with its own agenda, that we found it difficult to work as a team.

Hague made a valiant effort to get his colleagues to work together. He sought to bring together MPs on a regular basis and his own managerial style was mostly consensual. But his age and lack of experience undermined his authority from the beginning. After all, William had had no prior experience of leadership on a significant scale before or after he became an MP. A section of the party (and more dangerously, the media) could never quite take him seriously. He was to some of his critics, a boy doing a man's job. While that view was rarely articulated at first, it was an undercurrent that ran through the entire Parliament. Each slip-up was seen in the context of Hague's perceived inexperience and not necessarily judged fairly.

Over time, a bunker mentality developed. Often, when criticism began to raise questions as to whether he would survive as leader, he put in a bravura performance in Prime Minister's Question Time to uphold his position. But there was tension amongst backbenchers who feared for their seats. Hague's team took a very harsh view of those who were critical of what he was trying to do. But those criticisms were inevitable because some of those advising Hague were second-rate. Bad advisers do not like criticism because they feel threatened by it. There were times when Hague's leadership was under threat, with serious rumblings of discontent (mostly on the right of the party) but the aggressive 'you are with us or you are against us' attitude of a number of Hague supporters only made the situation worse. It appeared divisive for its own sake.

I had first-hand experience of the divisive attitude of some the Hague entourage when I faced an attempt to de-select me in my Surrey constituency. Although I had been already re-adopted as the candidate in 1998, a year later a group of party members sought to remove me. Their grounds for doing so were revealing. My views on Europe were 'tantamount to heresy' one of them

told the local paper.[31] Although Hague's stated policy was to allow backbenchers the freedom to express their views on Europe, this was not the
externally perceived line to take. As a result, some association members
demonstrated a shocking intolerance of differing views within the Conservative Party. Fortunately, I found that many MPs, including Euro-sceptics such
as Iain Duncan Smith and David Davis, rallied openly to my support because
they saw the dangers to the party if an MP could face de-selection because
of his views on a policy issue.[32]

Flatlining

For ten years the Conservative Party has struggled to break the 30 percentage points barrier in the opinion polls. Since the battles over Maastricht and
the hurried departure from the ERM, the party has stagnated in the polls.
Occasionally we have drifted down and much more rarely up, but never more
than few points either way. We have been 'flatlining' in the jargon of US
pollsters. The aim of the leadership was to break out of that polling ghetto
and start to rebuild our electoral base.

Oppositions, it is invariably said, don't win elections; governments lose
them. John Smith's strategy as Labour leader in the early 1990s was based
upon that theory – and we gave him plenty of evidence to back it up. The
situation was very different for the Conservatives in 1997 because we had
suffered our worst defeat since 1906 and morale within the party collapsed.
Large numbers of activists walked away.

Hague's initial strategy had been not to oppose for the sake of doing so.
This was surely right; we had been humiliated at the polls and were in no
position to start lecturing Labour. But somehow, when we did seek to expose
Labour's failings, our criticisms did not resonate with the public. The 'stealth
taxes' tag stuck for a time but the decision of the Chancellor to put a tax on
personal pensions, for example, was never fully exploited. This was due in
part to factors beyond the control of the party. The BBC's decision to abandon
the practice of giving the opposition the right of reply to ministers on current
affairs programmes, a change of practice brought in after the 1997 general
election, meant that representatives of pressure groups were often chosen to
appear instead of our spokesmen. There was also a general media waning of
interest in politics. The run-up to the 1997 general election had seemed
interminable and the slanging match between the parties over 'sleaze' unedi-
fying. Newspapers felt that their readers were not that interested in political
stories. We were just not being reported.

While the media was losing interest in politics, the Conservative Party
was becoming more obsessed with the media. The 'war-room' at the centre
of party headquarters, where media monitoring, press officers and research
staff come together, was an idea that had become out of date by the time the

new facility was constructed. It was no good responding rapidly to every announcement the government made if the BBC would not broadcast your comments anyway.

The decision to borrow Labour's opposition technique of attacking almost everything the government does and to do so through instant, pithy phrases ('soundbites'), was not only copying an idea just as it was going out of fashion but it made the party look cynical and opportunistic. After all, we had attacked Labour for behaving in the way we were now behaving.

Our whole agenda became media driven. There was no strategy for the party, no sense of purpose. The lack of a Tory narrative that would explain to the public what we stood for and where we were going was compounded by the sense that we did not know ourselves. The confusion over our policy towards reform of the House of Lords, highlighted by the dismissal of Lord Cranborne in December 1998, was one example of what could happen if the party did not get down to the hard business of thinking policy through. This 'seat of the pants approach' may have been exhilarating for those in the war room but it did not impress the public.

When the government was genuinely in trouble, as over the National Health Service in January 2000, the mistake was to allow ministers to regain the initiative. In that instance, it was the extraordinary decision that Hague should make a speech in support of expanding private healthcare that enabled the government to recover its position. Had there been a long-term strategy to argue that the NHS had to be supplemented by some kind of private involvement in healthcare provision, such a speech would have been timely. It could have effectively exploited the situation to develop the argument further. In reality, it was a blatantly opportunistic one-off and it backfired.

The one attempt to break out of the media-driven agenda was the 'Listening to Britain' exercise. This was a series of meetings around the country to which the public were invited. All too often, the audience was dominated by party members who turned up in order to be supportive, but who in fact outnumbered ordinary members of the public. 'Listening to Britain' became an exercise in listening to ourselves and, as such, served only to confirm existing prejudices. It did not move the party leadership on from an agenda focused on anti-Europeanism rather than public service reform. It did not educate party members in the need for us to change. And it did not convince the media or the public that we really were trying to listen to what they had to say.

The party needed a more long-term approach to fighting the government. It can take time for the failings of an administration to sink in. It usually takes several instances of failure to be highlighted before it becomes obvious that the underlying policy does not work. This requires patience and tenacity on the part of the opposition; in the last Parliament that did not always appear to be there.

A bandwagon to nowhere

In the autumn of 1998, Hague underwent a change of heart that was not immediately obvious but the drift of policy gradually became clear. The decision to hold a referendum of party members on the euro that September marked a shift in emphasis back to European issues. The failure of the party to make significant headway on other policies probably contributed to this switch in emphasis.

What appears to have happened is that Hague and his advisers felt that their strategy of inclusiveness had failed to win back support for the party and that they needed an approach that focused on issues where they could beat Labour. Crime, asylum and Europe all became central issues in this campaign. The tactic recognised that Labour had huge leads over us as the party perceived to have the best policies on the top two issues of public concern – health and education. Its leads were enormous: thirty-eight points for health and twenty-three points for education.[33] By switching the attack to topics where we had a lead over Labour or were close behind, there was an opportunity to establish an electoral bridgehead. The problem with this strategy was that however popular our policies were, the issues on which we could 'win' were not the most important issues to the public. In other words, we were fighting on the wrong ground.

Hague's approach contrasted markedly with the way Tony Blair as Shadow Home Secretary in the mid-nineties had decided to take on the Conservative Party, despite its traditional lead over Labour as having the best policies on law and order. This approach was widely perceived to have undermined the Conservatives' strong position in this area and enhanced Blair's own reputation.[34]

Some thought that this switch of emphasis from party inclusiveness to a batch of issues clustered around the idea of national identity, constituted a new narrative for the Conservatives. They felt that Hague was carving out a new position for the party, exploiting the traditional Conservative identity with the nation state. Labour were being portrayed as the cosmopolitan liberal elite, obsessed with political correctness, slavishly pro-European and destroying the United Kingdom. The weakness of this approach was said to be that its logical conclusion was to express support for withdrawal from the EU and for English autonomy.[35] It also had the defect that many Tories supported much of what the right-wing press labelled 'political correctness', while Michael Portillo apparently considered himself to be part of the 'liberal elite' that Hague criticised.[36]

Hague's new strategy was entirely a short-term one; it was not a new narrative for the party. He seized opportunities as they came along. Policy became opportunistic – the politics of the cheap thrill. The problem with this approach was that Hague was inevitably accused of jumping on every bandwagon. The party was always on the move but without necessarily having a clear idea of the destination. The support given to Tony Martin, a Norfolk man who had shot a burglar and then been charged, was an example of this opportunistic approach. 'Hard cases make bad law', as the old adage puts it, and yet Hague pursued such matters without any sense of where they might lead us. Not only did this approach trigger a great deal of critical media comment – much of which Hague clearly revelled in – but, more fundamentally, it split the party.[37]

One of Hague's closest supporters, Archie Norman MP, has described what he saw as a change in personality on the leader's part. Hague had seemed 'genuinely progressive' to him but, then, 'he went back to his roots and became a Yorkshire Poujadiste, a tub-thumping little Englishman'.[38]

The distaste many in the party felt for Hague's new approach inevitably provoked a row. Many moderate and pro-European MPs like myself had taken, if not a vow of silence, certainly a restrained approach to expressing our concerns about the direction in which the party was going. Resentment against what William had been doing had built up over time and when he switched to the issues of race and asylum, it was no longer possible for many of us to keep our counsel. Both Stephen Dorrell and I spoke out over Easter 2000, hitting the front page of *The Times*. I agreed with Dorrell's observation that Hague appeared to be exploiting the asylum issue for electoral reasons and that in doing so, 'he may unleash dangerous forces in society and that is not in keeping with the traditions of generous Conservatism'.[39] A short while afterwards, David Davis echoed these comments.

The 1999 European elections and the myth of Tory success

The right-wing turn that Hague had taken in the run-up to the June 1999 European Parliament elections became accentuated afterwards. So successful had the anti-European agenda supposedly been, that it became the dominant theme for the next two years. All talk of 'inclusiveness' or the centre ground disappeared completely. A new policy position was constructed around the three pillars of Europe, asylum and crime.

This was a house built on foundations of sand. The party had not scored much more than a propaganda triumph in the European elections. Of course, it was excellent that we had finished up with thirty-six seats, seven more than Labour, and that their vote had fallen to 28 per cent, but our vote was in fact the lowest we had obtained at any national election since 1918.[40] The results were distorted by the breathtakingly low turnout – just 23 per cent. This should have been a warning; only one in eight of the electorate had voted for us. It was foolish to base our electoral strategy for the general election on the outcome of elections that were not only warped by the low turnout but by the fact that they were mid-term elections and Labour had not delivered the improved public services that they had promised. The party drew completely the wrong conclusions from the results; they were a warning of impending disaster, not a prediction of future glories.

The hostility to Hague's right-wing shift led to some rowing back. At the 2000 party conference an attempt was made to promote some sensible policies on inner cities. But it was little more than a fig leaf to conceal the nakedness of our xenophobic agenda. In any case, what benefits we might have obtained by the promotion of One Nation policies were lost because of the row about drugs that dominated the conference. The dispute between Ann Widdecombe and the supporters of Portillo was most significant for its effects on the 2001 leadership election where Widdecombe's opposition to Portillo becoming leader made his ambition more difficult to achieve.

Any suggestion that we were serious about broadening our appeal was fatally undermined by Hague's 'foreign land' speech at the March 2001 meeting of the party's Spring Forum, a few weeks before the general election. It remains a source of complete bewilderment to many Conservatives that so intelligent, gentle and sophisticated a man as Hague could have delivered a speech of that kind. Hague is no racist. He is not intolerant. Yet he made a speech that deeply ashamed many Tories and produced howls of outrage. Our opponents were given an opportunity that they could not turn down, to accuse us of 'playing the race card'. By making this speech, Hague crossed a line. He raised questions as he had never done before about his decency. But the most worrying aspect of this speech was that his internal alarm bells had not rung. Hague gave the clear impression that he did not understand the enormity of what he had done. It was a truly extraordinary misjudgement and it made a leadership election contest inevitable if he did not win the general election.

The Harrogate speech opened the floodgates; it gave racists within the Conservative Party the signal that they could openly express views that they had kept largely hidden for years. John Townend's offensive remarks were no surprise to many of his parliamentary colleagues but Hague's decision not to withdraw the whip from him left critics and friends of Hague alike completely astounded.[41]

A missed opportunity

A period in opposition has many downsides but it provides one significant opportunity for a political party: the time to focus on questions of party organisation. By 1997 our membership, which had peaked at 2.5 million in the 1950s, was down to less than half a million. We had never been truly solvent in the 1992–97 Parliament and our whole campaigning machine was rusty, slow and ineffective.

Hague set about reform with gusto. He carried out the largest reorgani-sation of the party since 1867. But did it improve our performance in the election? Richard Kelly in his chapter believes it did not. Jennifer Lees-Marsh-ment and Stuart Quayle, writing before the results of the 2001 general election were known, concluded that it could.[42] There were positive improvements. The start of our campaign was faster than before, the new Area Campaign Directors covered the ground well and many marginals were better organised than in 1997. We did have the upper hand at times during the election campaign; Blair's bizarre decision to launch the campaign at a girls' school in South London was widely condemned. Yet our electoral performance was unquestionably dismal. The fact that we failed to come second in any seat in Liverpool or Manchester – we held seats in both cities until 1983 and 1987 respectively – was particularly depressing.[43] That failure was symbolic of the collapse of our vote in the inner cities over the last decade and the failure to rebuild our electoral position there. The party did gain one MP in Scotland, but Wales again did not return a single Tory to Westminster.

The plain truth is that the reforms of 1998 were not sufficient to turn the party round. Of course, the continuing financial problems of the party made the situation difficult to tackle (unlike Labour during its 1980s nadir we do not have the trade unions to guarantee us income). The decision to close our regional offices and run everything from the centre was a mistake and needs to be reversed. Similarly, the Area Campaign Directors, each with responsibility for thirty to forty seats, lacked direction as the result of the abolition of the regional director posts. The media were very critical of our media operation. At one point we were so slow in finding Conservative speakers for the media that programmes sometimes started without the party's spokesman having turned up.[44] Such failings on their own are rela-tively minor; taken together they are very serious. It must not be ignored by party managers in their assessment of our performance in 2001 that the Conservative vote rose by no more in the seats we were targeting to win from Labour or the Liberal Democrats than those that were not targets.[45]

Over questions of 'sleaze' and the selection of candidates, the party got into further difficulty. This is inexcusable. Hague admitted that the failure to stop Lord Archer becoming the party's London mayoral candidate was his worst mistake.[46] The inability to prevent the 'sleaze' issue damaging the party by swift referral of disputes and complaints to the party's Ethics and Integrity Committee is one of the most extraordinary stories of the last Parliament. It is inexplicable because it was one of the first tasks Hague set himself on becoming leader.

Symptomatic of the organisational failures was the start of the party's election campaign. Hague appeared on the back of a truck in Watford addressing a crowd; as a contrast to Blair's stage-managed appearance, this was good. But giving local activists the wrong banners to carry in Watford ruined it. Placards saying 'Keep the Pound' surrounded Hague. That was not intended to happen and it was a tragedy because the pre-election campaign of posters saying 'You paid the taxes, where are the policemen etc.' had conveyed just the right message. But it became obliterated.

Meltdown

The 2001 general election produced the party's worst performance since 1906. It was much worse than 1997 because we had had four years to begin the ascent up the huge electoral mountain we have to climb and yet we failed to get to first base. Ken Clarke's description of the last Parliament as 'four wasted years' was tough but true. Our strategy of seeking to mobilise our core vote simply failed to work. We did do better than the other parties in rural areas but for the first time since 1922 our share of the vote in Scotland was below that of the Liberals.[47] In England, we now have just one seat in the five major northern conurbations. The Liberal Democrats took six seats off us (and retained Romsey which we had lost in a by-election) and Labour gained one. As Andrew Tyrie has pointed out, had the turnout been higher, it is likely that the election results would have been even worse.[48]

Despite winning one seat back in Scotland, and the seats we have in the Welsh Assembly and the Scottish Parliament, at Westminster we are not a national party. For a Unionist party that is horrifying. It cannot be anything other than depressing for Conservatives that the Liberal Democrats used the opportunities we gave them in the last Parliament to consolidate their hold on existing seats and to add further ones to their total.

Daniel Collings and Anthony Seldon see the results as suggesting that Hague was a good tactician but not a good strategist.[49] This is too generous an assessment; there was no strategy and the tactics were often lamentable. It is always unfair to personalise political disasters in this way – those that served with Hague in the Shadow Cabinet and their advisers clearly share in the blame. But it was Hague's decision after 1998 to try and put dark blue water between Labour and ourselves. This attempt to reposition the party on the right failed spectacularly. It neither mobilised our own core supporters nor did it attract back those voters we had lost since 1992.

Recovery or decline

If the Conservative Party wants to govern Britain again it will have to shift its electoral position. Out on the right flank we can score the occasional goal but we will not win the match. For much of the last decade the Conservative Party has been trying to convince itself that it can win by being more right wing than ever before. We have fought two general elections in a row on an anti-European ticket and we have been slaughtered. If the party cannot see the folly of this approach now, it is doomed to political extinction. The Liberal Democrats are flexing their muscles and re-positioning themselves to take advantage of Tory failures.

On his election as Leader, Duncan Smith took a pragmatic approach to policy. He avoided conflicts within the Party, except with the racist right, with whom he was commendably firm. He sought to lower the temperature on Europe and when a Labour MEP, Richard Balfe, joined the Tory Party in March 2002, he was welcomed wholeheartedly by Duncan Smith, regardless of Balfe's personal commitment to the UK joining the euro and his longstanding membership of the European Movement.

But by the summer of 2003, the situation looked very different. Predictions that Iain Duncan Smith would return to his anti-European roots appeared to have been realised. The success of the Conservative Party in the May 2003 elections, triggered a change in strategy by Duncan Smith that looked remarkably similar to that adopted by William Hague after his claims of success in the 1999 European Parliament elections. Abandoning his strategy of avoiding the divisive European issue, he launched a full-blooded attack on the proposals for a new structure for the European Union.

The sense of déjà vu in the Tory Party was palpable. Perhaps even more astonishingly, when Duncan Smith's leadership was challenged by Crispin Blunt MP in the aftermath of the May elections, Blunt suggested that William Hague might make a comeback in the future.[50]

Of course Duncan Smith could not avoid the European question forever but his aggressive stance simply re-opened wounds in the Party rather than moved it forward. He made no attempt to bridge the philosophical divide between the essentially Atlanticist anti-Europeans and the rest of us. At least Duncan Smith has stopped the party falling into one elephant trap Labour had been digging: he has said that if the country votes 'Yes' in the euro referendum, he will accept that result.[51]

It is not just that we have to stop blaming 'Europe' for all our troubles. The party has to break out of the damaging obsession that private is always better and public is always worse. Taxpayer funded public services deliver the goods in dozens of countries across the world: why isn't that possible in Britain? In recent years, Tory spokesmen have given the impression that reform of public services was more to try to save money than to improve the quality of outputs. Duncan Smith is absolutely right to switch the emphasis from copying everything from the USA and looking at the successful policies of our near neighbours.

There is still a damaging fixation in the party that our fundamental aim should be to create a 'small state'. This is driven by the belief that the USA is the model society that we should seek to copy. Elements of US life and society are indeed attractive but Britain is a European country. That does not mean that the British people aspire to pay significantly higher amounts of taxation but they do believe in public services largely funded through a redistributive tax system. And they want a Conservative Party that will provide those things and do it better than Labour ever could.

As Chris Patten has observed of the success of the Partido Popular in Spain, it is perfectly possible to advocate a liberal economic agenda without being driven by dogma or falling into the clutches of special interest groups.[52] At various times Hague used the language of One Nation politics but he never adopted the policies to go with it. He seemed increasingly obsessed with the so-called core vote. As a result, he inspired a coalition against him larger than the one behind him. That way, madness lies. If Iain Duncan Smith is to claw his way into government, then the way forward for our party has never been clearer.

Notes

1 I am grateful to Nicholas Kent for carrying out much of the research for this chapter and to Sarah Clee-Charlton for commenting on drafts. The views are my responsibility.
2 John Major, speech to the Conservative Party conference, 7 October 1997.
3 See Nicholas Kent's inside story of the leadership race, 'The party I joined was full of nice old people; today it is full of nasty old people', *Guardian*, 5 December 2001.
4 J.-A. Nadler, *William Hague. In His Own Right* (London, Politico's, 2000), pp. 86–9.
5 R. Worcester and R. Mortimore, *Explaining Labour's Landslide* (London, Politico's, 1999), p. 49.
6 P. Whitely, P. Seyd and J. Richardson, *True Blues: The Politics of Conservative Party Membership* (Oxford, Clarendon Press, 1994), pp. 253, 265 and 277.
7 In fact, Whiteley *et al.*, *True Blues*, p. 106, did not find that women were more active as party workers than men.
8 Worcester and Mortimore, *Explaining Labour's Landslide*, p. 245.
9 W. Hague, speech to London and Southern Region, Central Office, London, 15 September 1997.
10 R. Morris, *Tories, From Village Hall to Westminster: A Political Sketch* (London, Mainstream Publishing, 1991), pp. 96–7.
11 Whiteley *et al*, *True Blues*, p. 42.
12 Hague, speech to London and Southern Region.
13 P. Waugh and B. Russell, 'Hague: I should have insisted on women and black candidates', *Independent*, 21 January 2002.
14 A. Pierce, 'Threat of revolt forces Tory U-turn on gays', *The Times*, 11 December 1999.
15 See Nadler, *William Hague*, pp. 284–5 for a discussion of this.
16 'Hague tells Patten to toe the line', *Daily Telegraph*, 7 January 1998.
17 I. Taylor, 'The Tory recovery – a hard climb', *The House Magazine*, October 2000.
18 D. Green and I. Taylor, *Restoring the Balance* (London, Tory Reform Group, 2000).
19 *Sun* 10 October 2000.
20 Worcester and Mortimore, *Explaining Labour's Landslide*, p. 70.
21 Worcester and Mortimore, *Explaining Labour's Landslide*, p. 90.
22 Worcester and Mortimore, *Explaining Labour's Landslide*, p. 49.
23 Nadler, *William Hague*, p. 40.

24 Nadler, *William Hague*, pp. 37–8.
25 A. Pierce, 'Shadow Cabinet backs sceptical line on EMU', *The Times*, 24 October 1997.
26 P. Webster, 'Hague warns Heseltine to keep clear', *The Times*, 31 October 1997.
27 Ian Taylor MP, resignation letter, 29 October 1997.
28 'Ancram defends consulting party members', Conservative Party press release, 26 September 1998.
29 Quoted in G. Jones, 'Hague wins 84 per cent vote on the euro', *Daily Telegraph*, 6 October 1998.
30 Hague, speech to London and Southern Region.
31 Quoted in the *Esher News and Mail*, 22 November 1999.
32 See P. Oborne, 'An accurate autopsy', *The Spectator*, 3 November 2001.
33 Worcester and Mortimore, *Explaining Labour's Second Landslide*, table on p. 30.
34 The Conservative lead over Labour on crime was down to 2 per cent by 1997.
35 'A new narrative for the Tories?', *Political Quarterly*, 71:4 (2000) 383–5.
36 S. Walters, *Tory Wars: Conservatives in Crisis* (London, Politico's, 2001), p. 101.
37 Walters, *Tory Wars*, p. 55.
38 Quoted in Walters, *Tory Wars*, p. 57.
39 Quoted in T. Baldwin, 'Tory mutiny over asylum rocks Hague', *The Times*, 22 April, 2000.
40 Worcester and Mortimore, *Explaining Labour's Landslide*, p. 66.
41 See Walters, *Tory Wars*, pp. 150–3.
42 J. Lees-Marshment and S. Quayle, 'Empowering the members or marketing the party? The Conservative reforms of 1998', *Political Quarterly*, 72:2 (2001) 204–12.
43 See R. Kelly, 'The party didn't work: Conservative reorganisation and electoral failure,' *Political Quarterly*, 73:1 (2002) 38.
44 Nadler, *William Hague*, p. 216.
45 D. Butler and D. Kavanagh, *The British General Election of 2001* (London, Palgrave, 2002), p. 320.
46 On the Archer case, see A. McSmith 'A Tory disaster waiting to happen', *Daily Telegraph*, 20 July 2001.
47 Butler and Kavanagh, *The British General Election of 2001*, pp. 315–16.
48 A. Tyrie, *Back from the Brink* (London, Parliamentary Mainstream, 2001), p. 6.
49 D. Collings and A. Seldon, 'Conservatives in opposition', *Parliamentary Affairs*, 54:4 (2001) 624–37.
50 For Blunt's comments see, http://news.bbc.co.uk/1/hi/uk_politics/2994993.stm.
51 D. Charter, 'Duncan Smith to accept euro vote', *The Times*, 21 January 2002.
52 C. Patten, 'Spanish lessons', *Guardian*, 13 February 2002.

Conclusions: the Conservatives in crisis

Philip Lynch and Mark Garnett

Recent British political history has been, to borrow Labour Chancellor Gordon Brown's beloved phrase, one of 'Tory boom and bust'. The change in the fortunes of the Conservative Party since 1992 is remarkable. Holding office alone or in coalition for two-thirds of the twentieth century, the Conservatives were considered the 'natural party of government'. Even when they met serious setbacks in 1945, 1964 and 1974 (twice), they managed a rapid return to power. Defeat was predicted in 1992, but instead the party won a record 14 million votes.

In the post-war period, the Conservatives regularly won elections because of their dependable middle-class majority, plus support from a significant section of the numerically dominant working class. In 1997 and 2001, New Labour achieved cross-class appeal, securing many direct conversions among those 'upwardly mobile' voters who supported Mrs Thatcher in the 1980s. The Conservatives were also a national party with support across Great Britain and (until 1974) an alliance with the Ulster Unionists at Westminster. After 1997, they had no MPs in Scotland, Wales and most large cities, Conservative parliamentary representation being largely confined to its southern English heartlands. A party that had fought successfully on the electoral centre ground in the 1950s and 1960s then steered elite and (to a lesser extent) public opinion towards its political agenda under Thatcher found itself trumped by a New Labour party that managed to do both. The Conservative reputation for sound political and economic management had been shattered, allowing a remodelled Labour Party to win votes on traditional Tory issues such as taxation and law and order. Europe and the single currency brought together a potent cocktail of strategic dilemmas concerning political economy and nationhood that re-opened a serious intra-party fault line. Unity was once (albeit erroneously) said to be the Tories' secret weapon, but now the party was bitterly divided. Finally, as Andrew Gamble has noted, the pillars of Conservative hegemony – the defence of property, the constitution, Union, and Empire then Europe – were 'hollowed out' during the Thatcher and Major period.[1]

Restoring the fortunes of a party at its lowest ebb was always going to be a difficult task for William Hague. To achieve political renewal, the Conservatives had to understand the reasons for the 1997 defeat, develop a distinctive and relevant narrative, draw up attractive headline policies, and be seen as a 'government in waiting' with an effective leader. Organisational reform was also overdue.

Organisational reform

In 1997 the Conservative Party appeared close to political and financial bankruptcy. John Major had lacked the authority to impose his will on a divided party. An ageing and demoralised membership bemoaned their lack of influence and had proved little match for Labour's constituency campaigning. Central Office was in debt, poorly managed and slow to utilise new campaign techniques. It was little wonder that Hague made reorganisation of the party's moribund structures a priority. His reforms brought about important changes, but produced mixed results in Hague's six areas of priority: unity, decentralisation, democracy, involvement, integrity and openness.[2]

The *Fresh Future* reforms created a single party structure and largely placated the voluntary party. Although divisions on Europe remained, the schism was not as all-pervading as in the mid-1990s. Morale in the parliamentary party was low and there was some dissatisfaction with the leadership, but outright dissent was limited. The reforms brought greater democracy to a traditionally hierarchical party. Party members were consulted on party reform and could contribute to policy forums. Ballots of the membership were held on policy and organisational issues. Constituency members could vote at final candidate selection meetings. Finally, the party leader was to be elected by a vote of all party members. Nonetheless, power remained concentrated at the centre. The policy forums were advisory bodies; it is difficult to pinpoint policy changes that resulted directly from them. Hague used the membership ballots to bolster his own authority, presenting 'take it or leave it' questions. Central Office drew up approved lists of potential candidates for all but local elections. Finally, members were given a choice of just two leadership contenders as MPs nominated and then reduced the number of candidates. The first election held under the new rules was not auspicious, in part because of ideological hostility between Kenneth Clarke and Iain Duncan Smith, but also due to dissatisfaction with the procedures.

The ambitious target of doubling party membership was not met, though a figure of 319,000 members in 2001 exceeded Labour at a time of disenchantment with politics. That the membership is predominantly elderly and concentrated in rural and southern England is a cause for concern: small, inactive local parties are unlikely to be effective campaigning bodies. Conservative members are also politically unrepresentative, tending to be more authoritarian and Euro-sceptic than target voters. The failure to recruit and force a cultural shift in the party means that an elderly, authoritarian membership can act as a drag anchor on wider reform. Unease in the voluntary party contributed to Hague's focus on the Tory core vote.

An Ethics and Integrity Committee was established, but Hague's endorsement of the Lord Archer as candidate for Mayor of London showed the limitations of its effectiveness. The party's parlous financial situation improved, but some donations brought unfavourable comment. Central Office extended its use of new campaign techniques in 2001 and managed local campaigns more actively but, as Kelly argued in Chapter 5, resources were overstretched.[3] Nor did the reforms have the impact of Labour's abandonment of Clause IV. However, as Ball noted in Chapter 1, organisational reform has rarely been the catalyst for a significant improvement in Conservative fortunes, tending instead to follow from or run in parallel with it.

Political renewal

Conservative political renewal required that the party: (1) recognise the reasons for election defeat and achieve some distance from its recent failings; (2) develop a distinctive narrative that provided a broad (and broadly agreed) sense of what the party stood for; (3) draw up a set of headline policies likely to attract target voters; and (4) foster the perception that it was a 'government in waiting' with a capable leader. The record in each was poor.

COMING TO TERMS WITH DEFEAT

As Ball noted in Chapter 1, assessing and addressing the causes of defeat is an essential first step to recovery. But after 1997 the Conservatives neither adequately came to terms with the reasons for the party's unpopularity nor achieved an effective break with the immediate past. No clear answer emerged to the key strategic question – whether the Conservatives should embrace elements of the New Labour agenda and compete on the electoral centre ground, or put 'clear blue water' between themselves and Labour by moving to the right. Some Conservatives argued that the party had to reposition itself on public services, gaining the trust of voters by moving away from the Thatcherite mantra of the market. They focused on winning back the support of those 'missing Conservatives' who had shifted allegiance to Labour or the Liberal Democrats in 1997. Others targeted former Conservative voters who abstained in 1997 or supported fringe Euro-sceptic parties, arguing that populist Tory policies – notably a firm line on Europe – would bring them back into the fold.[4]

Hague was advised to apologise for past mistakes before developing his own agenda.[5] He duly apologised for ERM entry but this could not erase voter memories of Conservative economic woes. By seeking a clean break with the past, the Tories also made it more difficult to gain credit for the healthy economic situation Labour had inherited. The 'Listening to Britain' exercise was intended to show that the Conservatives were addressing their unpopularity and consulting interested parties in their search for new policy ideas, but this could not substitute for a far-reaching policy review.

A DISTINCTIVE NARRATIVE

The Conservatives failed to develop a distinctive and compelling narrative that adapted its core values to a changed environment. They were unable to project an underlying sense of purpose or provide the electorate with a clear picture of what the party stood for. Instead, the quest for an effective narrative saw the Conservatives move from 'compassionate conservatism', through the *Common Sense Revolution*, to a 'core vote' strategy without successfully developing any of these. Previous spells in opposition suggested that a coherent policy review was an essential stepping-stone to recovery. But in 1997–2001, the policy review process was flawed.[6] The Conservative Research Department had been subsumed within a Central Office 'war room' and there were few fruitful exchanges with think tanks. Peter Lilley's review produced disappointingly little, undermined by funding constraints and differences over the way forward. The *Common Sense Revolution* was hastily drafted, containing a raft of policy commitments but little by way of a connecting theme. (It is, though, questionable whether there were would have been sufficient time for the results of a radical policy review to feed into party policy.) As Andrew Lansley noted in his contribution, producing detailed policy commitments at an early stage also allowed Labour to appropriate or neutralise many of them.

The 1997–2001 period can usefully be divided into two phases.[7] In Phase One (1997 to mid-1999), Hague sought to broaden the party's appeal by fostering a more inclusive brand of Conservatism, though this was apparent more in tone than policy. Hague looked at the political recoveries made by both the US Republican Party and the Canadian Progressive Conservatives, flirting with the 'compassionate conservatism' of George W. Bush and the 'common sense conservatism' of Mike Harris. These developed traditional right-wing themes of law and order, authority and the family but also focused on improving public services by extending choice and diversity in welfare delivery. Yet, as Ashbee argued in Chapter 2, neither agenda was developed or driven home consistently. In late 1998 the *Kitchen Table Conservatives* paper warned ominously that the party lacked a strategy and clear sense of direction.[8]

In Phase Two (mid-1999 to 2001), Hague sought to shore up the Conservative core vote by emphasising Europe, asylum and law and order. This phase was also characterised by short-term, populist initiatives and retreats from previously announced positions. Examples of the former included the response to the fuel crisis of September 2000 when Hague announced plans for a three pence per litre cut in petrol duty, albeit after opposition from Portillo,[9] and the conviction for murder of Tony Martin, after which Hague said that the Conservatives would amend the law so that it was on the side of those protecting their property. Populist positions on Europe and asylum brought additional media coverage but few newspaper endorsements. A number of policy changes followed Portillo's appointment as Shadow Chancellor: the 'Tax Guarantee' was watered down while Bank of England independence and the minimum wage were accepted.

This division of the 1997–2001 period conveys the main trends in policy and tactics, but caution is required. One should not exaggerate the divergence between the phases nor ignore developments that do not fit comfortably with a shift to the right. Thus the 2001 manifesto promised tax cuts of some £8 billion, but matched Labour's spending plans on health, education, transport, defence and law and order. The 2000 party conference was intended to broaden the party's appeal by promoting a message of tolerance and One Nation values, but this was derailed by Widdecombe's message of zero tolerance on cannabis use. Policy on Europe developed in a linear fashion: the tougher position on the euro was agreed in 1997, the 'Keep the Pound' campaign ran for over a year and the 'In Europe, not run by Europe' platform was fleshed out over time.

The move from Phase One to Phase Two was not a Dr Jekyll and Mr Hyde conversion. Nor was it the result of a strategic decision made at an identifiable moment, but rather a series of tactical adjustments. The shift in tone and policy took place over several months in 1999 and was the result of a combination of factors. These included the weakness of Hague's position, the limited impact of the early approach on the opinion polls, fears that Tory voters might desert the party, success in the 1999 European elections and Blair's attack on the 'forces of conservatism'. The critical backlash that followed Lilley's 1999 Butler lecture was particularly significant. Lilley believed that the negative public perception of the Conservative position on welfare was the main obstacle to revival and argued that the party should accept that the market had only a limited role to play in improving public services.[10]

HEADLINE POLICIES

As Lansley pointed out, for a party in opposition, what your policies say about you can often be more important than what you say about policy. The Conservatives got their tone and message wrong. The 1998 *Kitchen Table Conservatives* paper argued that the party had to employ a new language and address popular concerns about their attitude to public services. Yet by 2001 the Tories lacked positive symbolic policies on health and education, even though they had shifted to the left on public spending.[11] Labour was vulnerable on public services: many middle-class voters relied on public transport, the NHS and state education and were disappointed by Labour's record. But the Conservatives were not seen as credible: voters did not prioritise tax cuts and doubted that the Tories could reduce taxes without harming public services. The focus on the core vote may have brought some Euro-sceptics back into the fold, but it did not reflect the concerns of large numbers of 'missing Conservatives' who had deserted the party since 1992.[12] A campaign focused on a small and shrinking core vote was unlikely to bring net gains. It also cemented the caricature of a harsh, intolerant party: voting Conservative had negative connotations for too many young and middle-class voters.[13]

CREDIBILITY AND LEADERSHIP

The transition from government to opposition was not going to be easy for a Conservative Party that had been in power for eighteen years and whose members had little experience of opposition. Opposition parties find it difficult to set the agenda and are frequently at the mercy of factors beyond their control, hoping to profit from the misfortunes of the government. Two main tasks present themselves. On the one hand, the opposition must exploit the failings of the government with carefully-crafted attacks on their integrity and record, without themselves appearing excessively opportunistic or drawing unwelcome attention to their own past mistakes or uncertain future plans. On the other, the opposition must foster the impression that it is a credible 'government in waiting', ready to take the reins at the next election. It is invariably difficult to enjoy success in both – and to achieve an appropriate balance between the two. The Conservatives enjoyed little success in either. Labour benefited from low inflation and low interest rates, rarely appearing vulnerable to Tory attacks, while the Conservatives did not convince voters that they were ready for a return to office.

Hague did not prove an effective leader. He offered a fresh start and had the opportunity to restructure the party's policies, image and organisation. But a combination of external constraints and personal shortcomings left him short of real authority. Hague won the 1997 leadership election because he was acceptable to a majority of MPs, but he did not inspire great loyalty and had no particular constituency of MPs whose support he could rely upon. Party leaders rarely have a decisive impact on the election result but the leader does play a significant role in the presentation of a party's message. Hague's consistently poor showing in opinion poll surveys on his performance damaged his authority and the prospects of his party to the extent that he was soon perceived as an obstacle to Conservative recovery. Despite impressive performances in Parliament, Hague was unable to counter the negative opinions the public formed of him early in his leadership.

Hague was neither a particularly adept tactician nor a great strategist. His credibility was periodically undermined by tactical blunders and his judgement was questioned on a number of occasions. More significantly, he failed to settle on or develop a coherent strategy for recovery, retreating into a populism that saw him dubbed 'Billy Bandwagon'. After his resignation, many Conservatives highlighted courage as Hague's main virtue. While his endurance in the face of unenviable odds cannot be doubted, Hague brought to mind not a skilled and fearsome opponent, but a punch drunk boxer who carries on the contest without an effective game plan and fails to land any telling blows.

The 2001 general election

After Labour's 1997 landslide, the Conservatives had an electoral mountain to climb: they never, though, got much beyond the lower foothills. The party flatlined at around the 30 per cent mark in opinion polls for almost all the 1997–2001 period. Only during the fuel protests of autumn 2000 were they briefly ahead – and then because of government failings. They also failed to make any by-election gains, scored poorly in elections to the Scottish Parliament and Welsh Assembly (but won seats), and 'won' the 1999 European parliamentary election with 35.8 per cent of the vote on a low turnout.

At the 2001 election, the Conservatives made a net gain of one seat (winning nine but losing eight) and one percentage point (scoring only 31.7 per cent of the UK vote). Rather than marking a slight upturn in fortunes, taken in its context the result was worse than 1997.[14] The Tories fell further behind Labour and the Liberal Democrats in many of their top target seats. They made small gains amongst the elderly and working-class voters, and in rural areas. But Labour maintained or extended its support among professionals, the middle class and women, in urban and suburban areas. Tactical voting and strong Liberal Democrat performances in Tory target seats also damaged the prospects of a recovery in the near future. As Broughton noted in Chapter 10, the electoral system is biased against the Conservatives to the extent that they will require a double figure lead over Labour to gain a parliamentary majority at the next election.

A crisis of Conservatism

In the 2001 leadership contest, Kenneth Clarke called the period in opposition 'four wasted years'. The judgment is rather harsh. Hague earns some credit for the reform of the party organisation, for damping down the flames of division on Europe and for at least steadying the Tory ship – if this had not happened, the situation could have been worse still. But 1997–2001 was the Conservatives' most barren spell in opposition since 1906–14. Hague failed to bring about many of the basic requirements for political recovery, leaving the party in as parlous a state as he had found it. Another leader might have produced a better result in 2001, but a short-term reversal of fortunes was unlikely given the deep-rooted problems facing the Conservative Party. The Conservatives are not simply experiencing a temporary downturn in fortunes, with recovery inevitable once the current political cycle runs its course, but rather a period of crisis in which the bases of post-war Conservative domin-ance have been eroded. Five linked facets of this crisis of Conservatism provide a future research agenda and will be explored briefly.

THE IMPLOSION OF CONSERVATIVE STATECRAFT

The implosion of Conservative statecraft in the 1990s was a critical factor in the 1997 defeat; its shock waves continue to be felt. Statecraft is concerned with the maximisation of executive autonomy, the insulation of the govern-ment (so far as possible) from domestic and external pressures.[15] Governing competence, effective party management, political argument hegemony and a winning electoral strategy are required, but each was found wanting in the 1990s. The collapse of Conservative statecraft resulted from the unresolved contradictions of Thatcherism, the challenges of a new political environment and the record of the Major governments.

The legacy of Thatcherism has been a difficult one for the Conservatives. As Garnett argued in Chapter 6, the Conservatives became a more ideological party and one more prone to divisions in the Thatcher period, while the relationship between Thatcherism and conservatism was also an uneasy one. Despite its electoral success, Thatcherism did not bring about a sea change in public attitudes. The transformation of the economy and labour market accelerated social fragmentation and the erosion of class loyalty, loosening the ties between middle-class voters and the Conservative Party. Changes to the British state and nation undermined two of the traditional pillars of Conservative hegemony, while the end of the Cold War and acceleration of European integration necessitated new foreign policy thinking.

One of the most problematic elements of the Thatcher legacy was the relationship between Britain and the European Union (EU). Europe became a difficult and divisive issue given the explosive mix of strategic questions about Conservative statecraft, nationhood and political economy it engenders. The Single Market could cement Thatcherism's neo-liberal agenda while ERM membership offered an external economic strategy that could entrench low inflation and enhance the government's standing. But further European integration, and particularly EMU, threatened parliamentary sovereignty and British nationhood – and, significantly, would undermine executive auton-omy.[16] By the late 1990s, the centre right was divided between those favouring membership of a reformed, single-market-led EU but opposing EMU and those who want to pursue economic independence outside the Union.[17]

As well as fuelling the party's Euro-divide, the enforced exit from the

ERM in 1992 damaged the Conservatives' reputation for economic competence. Recession, tax increases and greater personal economic insecurity inflicted further damage. Meanwhile, New Labour courted business and the City by embracing the free market, resisting increases in direct taxation, giving the Bank of England independence to set interest rates, and supporting EMU. It also capitalised on sleaze and the Conservatives' lack of purpose, successfully targeting disillusioned voters in 'middle England'.

DISTANCE FROM PREVAILING SOCIAL ATTITUDES

While no party – not even New Labour – can be all things to all voters, the Conservatives have become damagingly out of tune with the attitudes and values of parts of British society. Although they accepted Labour's spending targets on health and education in 2001, the Conservative position was still well to the right of the median voter. Though closer to public opinion on Europe, this had limited issue saliency and did not convert sufficient numbers of voters to the Tory cause. Instead, the Conservatives' free market, social authoritarian message saw them competing in an electoral space which contained few target voters. For Norris and Lovenduski, the gulf between the Conservative position and the prevailing 'policy mood' resulted in part from the 'selective perception' of Tory politicians.[18] The Conservative parliamentary party sits to the right of the median voter, favouring tax cuts over increased public spending and holding strong Euro-sceptic views, leaving it adrift of the electoral centre ground. By relying on gut instincts and anecdotal evidence from canvassing in Tory strongholds, rather than opinion polls, Conservative MPs wrongly assumed that their message accorded with the views of target voters.

The Conservatives also appeared to be out of tune with some prevailing cultural attitudes and attributes of contemporary British society. Hague's warning that Britain would become a 'foreign land' under a Labour second term reinforced the caricature of an intolerant party – ironically the Conservatives already appeared 'strangers in their own land', trapped in the past.[19] Hague's uneasy reaction to the death of Diana, Princess of Wales early in his leadership contrasted with both the public mood and Blair's adept response. More significantly, his prioritising of the 'nuclear' family above other lifestyle choices did not fit comfortably with a society that has seen growing numbers of people who live alone, cohabit rather than marry, raise children as single parents or remain childless.[20] John Townend's comments on immigration showed that sections of the party have still to come to terms with, and learn to benefit politically from, the development of a multicultural society.

Thatcherism extolled the virtues of individual liberty, choice and consumerism in a market economy, but many Conservatives were less inclined to accept an extension of choice and diversity in the social and cultural arenas.

Hague's early flirtation with social liberalism crumbled when he met resistance from Tory authoritarians, but Michael Portillo's cultural critique gained further prominence.[21] He urged the party to become more inclusive and socially tolerant, citing the unattractiveness of the social authoritarian message to young, professional and metropolitan voters as a key factor in the 2001 defeat. The ageing of the Conservative Party membership and its core vote adds to (and helps explain) the perception that the party is 'out of touch'. A refashioning of both the public face of the Conservative Party (notably its parliamentary candidates) and the Conservative message in the light of economic, social and cultural change are essential steps to political recovery.

WHITHER CONSERVATISM?

During the previous period of opposition for the Conservative Party, it was seriously hampered by ideological disputes at every level. Under Hague it was much more fortunate, in this respect at least. The battle between paternalistic 'wets' and economic liberal 'dries' had been won long ago by the latter. Garnett argued in Chapter Six that traditional 'conservatism' is irrelevant to an understanding of the contemporary Conservative Party, however counter-intuitive this might seem at first sight. The party of 1997 was dominated by economic liberals: the only sceptical voice, that of Lilley in his Butler lecture, was quickly silenced.

But this did not save the party from principled disagreement. While Thatcher's speeches suggested that One Nation Tories were inevitably pro-European (and thus traitors both to herself and to their country) she had better reason than most to question this sweeping assessment. Geoffrey Howe, the most effective critic of her European policy in 1990, had also been her chief ally in the Cabinet battles against the 'wets'. But the fact that the conflict over Europe was not in itself ideological did not make it less dangerous to the Conservative Party, and Hague was well advised to defuse the issue early in his period as leader.

Despite the prevailing ideological consensus in their ranks, Europe did not exhaust the potential for division among Conservatives. The clash between 'mods' and 'rockers' proved much more serious, insofar as it prevented the party under Hague from developing a clear (let alone persuasive) narrative.[22] Broadly speaking, the clash was between convinced Thatcherites who nevertheless disliked many of the practical results of their own creed – particularly the upsurge of rootless individualism which had cut a swathe through social institutions and traditional modes of behaviour – and equally faithful Thatcherites who regarded recent developments as either laudable or inevitable, and urged their party to embrace them. It can be argued that the latter 'mod' faction was seeking to iron out important contradictions in Thatcherism, while the 'rockers' were exhibiting a species of denial that could almost be described as 'false consciousness'. Despite the eloquence of Portillo and his allies, the 'rockers' were bound to win because the majority of the party could not bring itself to accept that the internal contradictions of Thatcherism had played a significant role in the 1997 result. Apart from strong residual loyalty to the martyred leader, the age-profile of the party and its hostility to 'experimental' lifestyles also ensured that the dominant message presented by the 2001 manifesto featured the unpopular social authoritarianism which so many commentators still confuse with conservative ideology.

Ultimately Hague sided with the 'rockers', despite his own sympathy for a more 'inclusive' approach. His populist speeches jarred with the early photo-calls which had been a more reliable indicator of his personal views; thus, rather than symbolising a breach with the past, he came to embody it. His tactical switch may have been an electoral mistake, but it accurately reflected the balance of forces within a party that later elected Iain Duncan Smith, who was generally depicted as a 'head-banger', let alone a mere 'rocker', on social matters.

THE END OF THE CONSERVATIVE STATE?

For much of the twentieth century, the Conservative Party was a staunch defender of the British constitution and Union, preferring incremental changes that maintained the essential elements of the 'Westminster model' to fundamental reform. But Thatcherism, the Blair governments' constitutional reform programme and EU membership have weakened key tenets of the Conservative state. In particular, the development of a multi-level polity challenges parliamentary sovereignty and executive autonomy.

Thatcherism's uneasy mix of support for key elements of the constitution and a neo-liberal view of the state ultimately undermined the legitimacy of the constitution and Union, and thus the Conservative view of the state.[23] They sought on the one hand to 'roll back the state' by reasserting the free market and reforming the welfare state but, on the other, to restore the authority of a strong state and promote social order and traditional values.[24] The centralisation of power weakened Parliament, local government, the Union and a range of intermediate institutions. The Conservatives paid insufficient attention to the constitutional questions this provoked. Major's proposals to bolster the Union, for example, came too late to turn the pro-devolution tide in Scotland. This failure to develop a pragmatic programme of reform allowed New Labour to develop a liberal constitutional reform agenda that includes devolution, the incorporation of the European Convention on Human Rights into British law, reform of the House of Lords and the introduction of proportional representation for 'second-order' elections.

The Thatcher and Major governments brought about radical changes in the British state. Privatisation and the creation of new regulatory bodies; the Next Steps reforms of the civil service; marketisation and the New Public

Management, and the creation of a plethora of quangos transformed a hierarchical system of government into a looser one of governance.[25] This fits with the neo-liberal vision of an 'enabling state' that steers rather than directs policy activity – though the reforms were introduced in an *ad hoc* manner – but challenges the Tory vision of a strong state capable of exercising control over the policy process.

EU membership has also changed the British polity and challenged the Conservative vision of the state.[26] The primacy of Community law, the increased provision for qualified majority voting and the extension of Community competence into many core policy areas have eroded state autonomy. Together with the increased role of local government, regional actors and pressure groups in EU policy networks, this has produced a system of multi-level governance in which the state does not enjoy monopoly power in EU decision making and the executive faces a range of domestic pressures when developing its European policy. The nation state remains the most important actor, but the experience of the 1990s showed that a Conservative government in a minority in the EU and under pressure from domestic actors found its autonomy constrained significantly.

The Conservative Party has historically proved adept at pragmatically shaping or adapting to change in the British state. Now it must adapt to the end of the Westminster Model, the development of a multi-level polity and the erosion of parliamentary sovereignty. The Conservatives have accepted Scottish and Welsh devolution – though a future Conservative government would almost certainly face the awkward task of working with non-Conservative administrations in Scotland and Wales – and have a more positive attitude towards local decision making than in the Thatcher era. Although the first-past-the-post system has penalised the Conservatives in recent general elections, the party remains adamant in its opposition to electoral reform, fearing that proportional representation would consistently put anti-Tory coalitions into power.

THE END OF THE CONSERVATIVE NATION?

The advantages accruing to the Conservative Party from its identification with the nation state, national identity and the national interest have declined. Hague found that identifying the Conservatives as defenders of the 'British way' brought neither issue hegemony nor electoral rewards. A Thatcherite state patriotism based on the defence of the constitutional status quo, a Unionism that presents legislative devolution as a stepping-stone to independence, and an ethnic view of the nation at odds with the development of a plural society does not offer a viable politics of nationhood. The Conservative view of the nation has to be reworked in the light of new challenges.

Since 1997, the Conservative Party has been caught between two visions of nationhood: a pluralist vision that embraces devolution and Britain's multi-ethnic society, and an authoritarian individualist one associated with Euro-scepticism and English nationalism. The Conservatives should develop an integrative patriotism that fosters a sense of Britishness and presents a positive case for the Union while embracing diversity and devolution. A clearer view of the relationship between Britishness and English identity is required. This might see the Conservatives become a more explicitly English nationalist party, or one that advocates a quasi-federal arrangement that looks to rework Britishness in the context of the revival of English and Scottish identities.

The Conservatives after Hague

Iain Duncan Smith's 2001 leadership election victory did not, at the time, appear conducive to a reorientation of Conservative politics or to a recovery in the party's electoral fortunes. A confirmed Thatcherite and Euro-sceptic, Duncan Smith had been critical of Portillo's message of cultural renewal, and of Clarke's calls for a move to the electoral centre ground. He won 60.7 per cent of the ballot of Conservative Party members, but secured only thirty-nine votes on the first ballot of MPs and fifty-three votes on the second ballot.[27] Less than a third of the parliamentary party had supported him. The Euro-sceptic character of the new Shadow Cabinet reflected Duncan Smith's core support, but significantly some of its most prominent members were 'modernisers'. However, a year into Duncan Smith's leadership, the Conservatives appeared to have learned some of the lessons of the 1997–2001 period and were taking steps (albeit tentatively) to address them. They had, though, made little impact in the opinion polls.

COMING TO TERMS WITH DEFEAT

There were similarities between the Conservative reactions to the 2001 and 1997 election defeats. In both instances, a new leadership spoke of a clean break with the recent past but found itself entangled in disputes about the appropriate route to recovery. After 2001, senior Conservatives again engaged in public acts of contrition in an attempt to show that the party recognised its failings and was addressing them. David Willetts, for example, declared an end to the 'Tory war on single mothers' while Oliver Letwin dispensed with the tough rhetoric on asylum. At the 2002 party conference, the new Chairman (her chosen title) Theresa May denounced those who had let the party down and told delegates that the Conservatives must ditch their reputation as a 'nasty party'. Earlier, Duncan Smith had suspended the Monday Club's links with the Conservative Party and sacked Shadow Rural Affairs Minister Ann Winterton after she told a racist joke at a constituency function. He also refused membership of the Carlton Club in protest at its refusal to accept women members. At a practical level, the leadership pledged to increase the number of women and ethnic minority candidates, but only six women had been selected in the twenty-eight constituencies that had chosen their prospective parliamentary candidates by September 2002.[28] Attempts by Central Office to impose candidates on local associations were likely to meet stern resistance.

In an echo of the Hague period, modernisers and traditionalists differed in their diagnoses of the party's ills and their prescriptions for recovery. Duncan Smith had criticised Portillo's analysis during the leadership contest, but the modernisers appeared to gain the upper hand thereafter. Their verdict was that the focus on Europe, asylum and tax cuts, plus the absence of a positive message on public service reform, had made the Conservatives unelectable. If they were to turn their fortunes around, the Conservatives had to neutralise the negative aspects of their public persona and foster an outlook that resonated with those sections of British society where they had lost support, particularly women and the young. Getting the symbolism right was the first task; the policy substance would follow.

The right of the party were unconvinced, bemoaning the lack of a clear low tax, anti-euro message and the high profile given to 'minority' issues. Duncan Smith, like his predecessor, finds himself with a foot in both camps. He has taken the modernisers' message on board but is a traditionalist by instinct. The tone had changed, but on issues such as marriage and the family, the traditional position remained. The Shadow Cabinet thus imposed a three-line whip against legislation allowing unmarried and gay couples to adopt children.

A DISTINCTIVE NARRATIVE

The most obvious difference between the post-2001 Conservative Party and that led by Hague was the emphasis on public services and the near silence on Europe, asylum and tax. This marked a concerted effort to concentrate on the issues that mattered most to voters, to restore the party's credibility and earn the trust of the electorate on health and education. A co-ordinated policy review process and the emergence of new Conservative think tanks (such as Policy Exchange) suggested a heightened interest in ideas.

Two themes came to the fore in Conservative discourse: first, an emphasis on society and helping the vulnerable, and, second, a critique of centralised provision of services and support for decentralisation. The Conservative vision of society once again looked to US 'compassionate conservatism' and marked a deliberate shift in emphasis from Thatcher's much-quoted (but frequently misinterpreted) comment that 'there is no such thing as society'.[29] The party emphasised localism and decentralisation, highlighting the role of local associations and voluntary organisations, and pledging to 'trust the people' with a greater role in welfare provision. Letwin highlighted the social roots of crime and looked to a 'neighbourly society' to tackle them.[30]

But the family and marriage were still viewed as key social institutions.[31] Decentralisation underpinned the Conservative approach to improved public service provision. The centralised, top–down method of welfare provision that had characterised the NHS had largely failed; the spending increases announced in Gordon Brown's 2002 budget would not produce the desired improvements. Efficient health provision required the break-up of monopoly state provision. The state would continue to provide most of the funding, but control over budgets and operational decisions would be 'devolved' to hospitals and schools, health care providers and parents.

The 2002 document 'Leadership with a Purpose: A Better Society' fleshed out these themes and linked them to new policy initiatives. Conservative strategists compared it with Margaret Thatcher's 1975 'The Right Approach' policy which provided an early statement of the Thatcherite critique of the post-war consensus and its free market alternative. But the comparison was overstated: though it provided some themes, it did deliver a particularly distinctive or compelling narrative.[32]

HEADLINE POLICIES

Policy announcements were in short supply in Duncan Smith's first year as the Shadow Cabinet explored policy options at home and abroad. In March 2002, Duncan Smith said that the mission of the Conservative Party would be to 'champion the vulnerable' in British society. Six months later, he identified 'five giants' that the Conservatives would seek to topple: failing schools, crime, sub-standard healthcare, child poverty and insecurity in old age.[33] Twenty-five policy initiatives were then unveiled at the 2002 party conference. These included greater independence for schools and foundation hospitals, state contributions towards the cost of private operations, extending the right to buy to housing association tenants, and rehabilitation for persistent young offenders and drug addicts. Whether these met the goal of helping the vulnerable was open to doubt; middle-class voters appeared the most likely beneficiaries.[34]

The focus on public services meant taking on Labour on their own ground: something of a gamble even when Labour's record in the area had been disappointing. The government's failure to deliver reform may make the electorate more willing to consider radical solutions, but opinion polls suggested that the 2002 budget increase in national insurance to pay for further NHS spending (which was opposed by the Tories) was popular with both Labour and Conservative voters. Both main parties support further decentralisation, but the government is likely to depict the choice on health as one between Labour support for a reformed NHS and tacit Conservative support for a social insurance system.

Two key areas were largely absent in the 2002 pronouncements on policy: tax and Europe. On the former, Duncan Smith and Shadow Chancellor

Michael Howard asserted that improvements in health and education now took priority over tax cuts. But the Conservatives were still likely to fight the next general election with a commitment (and specific pledges) to lower taxes. The single currency issue was avoided but Conservative Euro-scepticism hardened. Shadow Foreign Secretary Michael Ancram ruled out withdrawal from the EU but called for significant revision of the treaties.[35] Duncan Smith stated that the Conservatives would never support euro membership under his leadership. He abandoned Hague's Keep the Pound campaign, preferring to keep the party's powder dry for a future referendum. 'Europe' will remain centre stage in British politics given the prospect of a referendum on the euro and the reform of the EU ahead of its eastward enlargement. Nor can Conservative divisions on Europe be expected to disappear – on both sides of the fault-line, Europe is an issue that defines the political identity of many Conservatives, some of whom will put principle before party.

A euro referendum will prove an important moment for the Conservatives. A clear 'Yes' vote would force the party to rethink its strategy, perhaps by reaching an accommodation with EMU membership – which may strengthen the hand of pro-Europeans – or moving to a 'harder' scepticism that demands fundamental renegotiation or even withdrawal from the EU. A 'No' vote would destabilise the Blair government but Euro-sceptic success in a single-issue referendum will not necessarily produce a significant upturn in Conservative electoral fortunes, particularly if the 'No' campaign distances itself from the Tory leadership.

Credibility and leadership

The Conservatives struggled to provide effective opposition to the Blair Government in 2001–2. In part, this was beyond their control as the September 2001 terrorist attacks on New York and Washington brought bipartisan support for the 'war on terror' and a US–UK assault on Iraq. Even here, Duncan Smith's firm backing for Blair on Iraq was criticised by former Tory ministers Sir Malcom Rifkind and Douglas Hogg. On domestic policy issues such as the placing of Railtrack into administration and the A-level marking fiasco, the Conservatives failed to expose and exploit the government's failings.

Less than a year after becoming leader, Iain Duncan Smith was already facing criticism from within his own party and speculation about a leadership challenge.[36] Modernisers complained about the slow pace of change, traditionalists about the direction in which the party appeared to be moving. Unlike Hague, he was unable to detract attention from his and the party's poor opinion poll ratings by getting the better of the Prime Minister in the House of Commons. The botched Shadow Cabinet reshuffle of summer 2002 (which saw David Davis dismissed as Party Chairman while on holiday) and the resignation of Dominic Cummings, the party's director of strategy, further weakened the leader's position.

The Conservatives made limited inroads into Labour's opinion poll lead in 2002, nudging up towards the 35 per cent mark before falling away again in the face of negative publicity ahead of the party conference in October. In the May 2002 local elections they scored 33 per cent of the vote and made a modest net gain of seats. Opinion polls and focus groups suggested that the Conservatives still had much work to do to overcome the negative perceptions of the party.[37]

Conclusion

The 1997–2001 period confirmed that the journey back to power would be a long and gruelling one for the Conservative Party. The Conservatives made little headway in this period, Hague bequeathing Duncan Smith many of the problems he had faced in 1997. These are so serious that a restoration of Conservative fortunes cannot be taken for granted: a lengthy period in opposition seems likely, though the size of the (albeit shrinking) Conservative core vote should be sufficient to stave off the Liberal Democrat challenge in the party's heartlands and keep the Tories in second place.[38]

In the short-term, a restoration of Conservative fortunes appears most likely to come about through a combination of difficulties for the government and greater public confidence in the Tories. In 1997 and 2001, the Conservatives suffered from the decline of strong partisan allegiances as former Conservative voters deserted them. Yet dealignment may also provide some salvation – a series of elections since 1997 showed that Labour's electoral coalition of traditional working-class support and voters in 'middle England' is a loose one.[39] The Blair government established (somewhat fortuitously) a reputation for governing and economic competence in its first term but in the second term this could be undermined by the war on terror, economic problems, the single currency issue, sleaze or a failure to deliver improvements in public services. Should Labour move further to the left, as the tax increases announced in the 2002 budget suggested, the Conservatives might also be able to recoup support in the electoral centre ground. The Boundary Commissions should also alleviate some of the anti-Conservative bias in the electoral system, though changes will probably not occur before the next general election.

To recover, the Conservatives must develop a clearer political strategy and sense of direction than they managed under Hague. A number of options may present themselves.[40] In a party where Thatcherite values are now more deeply rooted than in the 1980s, support remains for a strategy that puts 'clear blue water' between New Labour and a Conservative Party positioned to the right of the median voter. In this scenario, the Conservatives could embrace radical neo-liberalism (supporting privatisation of the welfare state) a 'harder' Euro-scepticism (advocating a fundamental renegotiation of Britain's membership of the EU) and English nationalism (more explicitly defending English interests). The Thatcherites are divided on social issues, with views ranging from libertarianism to social authoritarianism. Though the social liberal agenda is unlikely to prove electorally decisive and will repel some traditional conservatives, the cultural conservative agenda pursued by Hague after 1999 is an alien one to large numbers of voters under the age of forty.

Right-wing populist parties with charismatic leaders enjoyed some electoral success under the proportional representation systems of continental Europe in 2002. But the experience of the Conservatives under Hague strongly suggests that the Tories will not regain power by appealing primarily to their own core vote. A move further towards the electoral centre ground offers the best prospect of a sustained success. Here, Conservative values such as personal freedom, choice and community would be reworked in the light of social and political change, while the party establishes a credible commitment to fair, efficient, effective and affordable welfare provision. Such themes would have to be forged into an attractive narrative, delivered in a sustained fashion by an effective leadership. This is not an easy option, nor does it guarantee success. But, after the failings of the Hague period, the shock of a second successive Labour landslide may prompt the new Conservative leadership to embark a political transformation of the scale the party underwent when it recovered from previous heavy defeats. If not, a party viewed as the 'natural party of government' less than a generation ago seems set to endure a lengthy period in opposition.

Notes

1 A. Gamble, 'The crisis of Conservatism', *New Left Review*, 214 (1995) 3–25.

2 W. Hague, *A Fresh Future for the Conservative Party* (London, Conservative Party, 1997).

3 See also D. Denver, G. Hands, J. Fisher and I. MacAllister, 'Constituency campaigning in Britain, 1992–2001: centralisation and modernisation', paper presented at the Political Studies Association annual conference, University of Aberdeen, 5–7 April 2002.

4 D. Butler and D. Kavanagh, *The British General Election of 2001* (London, Palgrave, 2002), pp. 37–40; T. Hames and N. Sparrow, *Left Home: The Myth of Tory Abstentions* (London, Centre for Policy Studies, 1997).

5 D. Willetts with R. Forsdyke, *After the Landslide: Learning the Lessons from 1906 and 1945* (London, Centre for Policy Studies, 1999), p. 106, argued that after a heavy defeat 'the party needs to exaggerate the extent to which it has changed'.

6 A. Seldon and P. Snowdon, *A New Conservative Century?* (London, Centre for Policy

Studies, 2001), pp. 43–6; Butler and Kavanagh, *The British General Election of 2001*, pp. 48–50.

7 See also R. Kelly, 'Conservatism under Hague: the fatal dilemma', *Political Quarterly*, 72:2 (2001) 197–203, and P. Cowley and S. Quayle, 'The Conservatives: running on the spot', in A. Geddes and J. Tonge (eds), *Labour's Second Landslide* (Manchester, Manchester University Press, 2002), pp. 47–64.

8 Butler and Kavanagh, *The British General Election of 2001*, p. 43.

9 S. Walters, *Tory Wars. Conservatives in Crisis* (London, Politico's, 2001), pp. 63–71.

10 P. Lilley, 'Butler Memorial Lecture', the Carlton Club, London, 20 April 1999. www. peterlilley.co.uk/speeches.phtml?action=show&id=16.

11 J. Bara and I. Budge, 'Party policy and ideology: still New Labour?', in P. Norris (ed.), *Britain Votes 2001* (Oxford, Oxford University Press, 2001), pp. 26–42.

12 See *Lessons from the 2001 General Election: Winning Back the Missing Conservatives* (London, Tory Reform Group, 2001).

13 D. Kavanagh, 'A leader in need of a story to tell', *Financial Times*, 16 September 2001, argues that 'voting is an expressive act in which support for a party or candidate is a form of self-characterisation'.

14 See A. Tyrie, *Back from the Brink* (London, Parliamentary Mainstream, 2001); Seldon and Snowdon, *A New Conservative Century?*, Ch. 1.

15 J. Bulpitt, 'The discipline of the new democracy: Mrs Thatcher's domestic statecraft', *Political Studies*, 34:1 (1986) 19–39.

16 See J. Buller, 'Understanding contemporary Conservative Euro-scepticism: statecraft and the problem of governing autonomy', *Political Quarterly*, 71:3 (2000) 319–27.

17 D. Baker, A. Gamble and D. Seawright, 'The European exceptionalism of the British political elite', paper presented to the ECPR Joint Sessions, Mannheim, March 1999.

18 P. Norris and J. Lovenduski, 'The iceberg and the Titanic: electoral defeat, policy moods and party change', paper presented at the EPOP annual conference, University of Sussex, 15 September 2001.

19 W. Hague, 'The last chance election for Britain', speech to the Conservative Spring Forum, Harrogate, 4 March 2001; W. Hague, 'Identity and the British way', speech to the Centre for Policy Studies, London, 19 January 1999.

20 A. Cooper, 'A party in a foreign land', in E. Vaizey, N. Boles and M. Gove (eds), *A Blue Tomorrow. New Visions for Modern Conservatives* (London, Politico's, 2001), pp. 9–29; M. Durham, 'The Conservative Party, New Labour and the politics of the family', *Parliamentary Affairs*, 54:3 (2001) 459–74.

21 See T. Hames, 'Portillo', *Prospect*, June 2001.

22 In the 1960s, scooter-riding 'mods' regularly clashed with 'rockers' on motor bikes in English seaside resorts. *The Times* leader column, 'Mods and rockers: the real division in the Tory Party', 6 July 1998, used the terms to distinguish between social liberals and social conservatives in the Shadow Cabinet.

23 See D. Marquand, 'The twilight of the British State? Henry Dubb versus sceptred awe', *Political Quarterly*, 64 (1993) 210–21.

24 See A. Gamble, *The Free Economy and the Strong State*. 2nd edition (London, Macmillan, 1994).

25 See D. Richards and M. Smith, *Governance and Public Policy in the United Kingdom* (Oxford, Oxford University Press, 2002), Ch. 5.

26 See for example, N. Nugent, 'Sovereignty and Britain's membership of the European Union', *Public Policy and Administration*, 11:3 (1996) 3–18.

27 See P. Lynch and M. Garnett, 'Conservatives' convictions: 2001 Tory leadership election', *Politics Review*, February 2002; K. Alderman and N. Carter, 'The Conservative Party leadership election of 2001', *Parliamentary Affairs*, 55 (2002) 569–85.

28 N. Watt, 'Here is the new look Tory Party ... same as the old one', *Guardian*, 16 September 2002.

29 See G. Streeter (ed.), *There Is Such a Thing as Society* (London, Politico's, 2002).

30 O. Letwin, *Beyond the Causes of Crime* (London, Centre for Policy Studies, 2002).

31 D. Willetts, 'Making sense of society, speech to Policy Exchange, London, 17 September 2002.

32 See D. Finkelstein, 'Time for Tories to move beyond the T-word', *The Times*, 9 October 2002.

33 I. Duncan Smith, 'Defeating the five giants', speech at Toynbee Hall, London, 13 September 2002.

34 See P. Riddell, 'Policies will help middle classes more than poor', *The Times*, 9 October 2002.

35 M. Ancram, 'Building true partnerships of nations in Europe', speech to the EPP-ED group, 9 May 2002.

36 Critiques of Duncan Smith's leadership include R. Darwall, *Paralysis or power? The centre right in the 21st century* (London, Centre for Policy Studies, 2002) and K. Mac-Kenzie, 'Duncan Smith ate my party', *The Spectator*, 11 May 2002.

37 See A. King, 'Rusty model, no longer trustworthy', *Daily Telegraph*, 7 October 2002.

38 Francis Maude warned that the Liberal Democrats could overtake the Conservatives. See A. Sparrow, 'Maude warns of Tories as third party', *Daily Telegraph*, 20 August 2001. A special unit to tackle the Liberal Democrat challenge was established at Central Office.

39 P. Dunleavy, 'Elections and Party Politics', in P. Dunleavy *et al.* (eds), *Developments in British Politics 6*. Revised edition (London, Palgrave, 2002), pp. 127–50.

40 See I. Crewe, 'A new political hegemony', in A. King (ed.), *Britain at the Polls, 2001* (New York, Chatham House/Seven Bridges Press, 2002), pp. 220–4.

INDEX